Authenticating Culture in Imperial Japan

Twentieth-Century Japan: The Emergence of a World Power
Irwin Scheiner, Editor

Authenticating Culture in Imperial Japan

Kuki Shūzō and the Rise of National Aesthetics

Leslie Pincus

UNIVERSITY OF CALIFORNIA PRESS

Berkeley   Los Angeles   London

University of California Press
Berkeley and Los Angeles, California

University of California Press, Ltd.
London, England

© 1996 by
The Regents of the University of California

Pincus, Leslie, 1950–
    Authenticating culture in imperial Japan: Kuki Shūzō and the rise
of national aesthetics / Leslie Pincus.
        p. cm. — (Twentieth-century Japan ; 5)
    Includes bibliographical references and index.
    ISBN 0-520-20134-5 (alk. paper)
    1. Kuki, Shūzō, 1888–1941. I. Title. II. Series.
B5244.K844P56 1995
181'.12 — dc20   95–12978
                                                                 CIP

Printed in the United States of America
9 8 7 6 5 4 3 2

The paper used in this publication meets the minimum requirements
of the American National Standard for Information Sciences — Perma-
nence of Paper for Printed Library Materials, ANSI Z39.48–1984.

*For my mother Sylvia, who never saw this book
reach print but always knew it would. And for
my father Leonard, who taught me by example
the virtue of intellectual integrity.*

Contents

Figures

Acknowledgments

This book has evolved, along with my own intellectual development, through various stages of research, dialogue, and reflection, from Ph.D. thesis to manuscript. At each stage in the process, I received the support — moral, intellectual, and financial — of a great many friends, colleagues, and institutions. I would like to express my deepest gratitude to my teachers at the University of Chicago, who, each in his or her own inimitable style, contributed not only to the completion of this book but also to my education in the broadest sense of the word. To Norma Field, with whom I experienced the pleasures of thinking in dialogue, and who showed me the virtues of building bridges between the abstract and the concrete. To Harry Harootunian, who helped me discover the meaning of critical thinking. His insights served as signposts leading me through what often seemed an unchartable intellectual terrain. And to Bill Sibley, who taught me to attend closely to language, and whose inspiring example provided the occasion for my own discovery of the possibilities of translation. Their continued friendship and support has sustained me in my work. Thanks also go to Jan Bardsley and Aki Hirota, who welcomed me into their dissertation writing group when I arrived at UCLA, overwhelmed by the tasks that lay ahead. Without their moral and intellectual support, I never would have finished the thesis during my first year of teaching at UCLA.

Further, I would like to express my appreciation to those in Japan who made my research possible: To Satō Akio, who generously gave me access to Kuki Shūzō's private library at Kōnan University in Kobe;

and to Asukai Masamichi at the Humanities Research Institute of Kyoto University, who sponsored me during a year of Ph.D. research. During my various trips to Tokyo, Igarashi Akio of Rikkyō University extended limitless reserves of hospitality and assistance, as well as keys to the reading room in the Faculty of Law and Politics. Sakabe Megumi at the University of Tokyo and Tada Michitarō in Kyoto shared ideas and sources unstintingly.

I am deeply indebted to all the friends and colleagues who generously read the manuscript in its evolution from dissertation to book for suggestions that led me beyond the limits of my own thinking: Chungmoo Choi, Ted Fowler, Jim Fujii, Tom LaMarre, Herman Ooms, Robert Scharf, Shu-mei Shih, Miriam Silverberg, Mariko Tamanoi, and Stefan Tanaka. Thanks also go to Kerry Ross, my research assistant at UCLA, who performed the laborious task of proofreading the entire manuscript, to Zennō Yasushi, who untangled linguistic knots for me, and to all the graduate students at UCLA who, in discussions and seminars, helped me to refine the logic invested in this project. My heartfelt gratitude to Jim Fujii and Ellen Radovic, steadfast friends who renewed my courage at each barrier standing in my way. And to Norma Field, Masao Miyoshi, Emily Ooms, and Anne Walthall, whose moral support and practical advice helped me to negotiate the perils of the profession.

For financial assistance at the dissertation stage, I would like to express my appreciation to the Humanities Division and to the Center for East Asian Studies of the University of Chicago, as well as to the Japan Foundation and the Social Science Research Council for dissertation research grants during 1986 and 1987. My thanks also to UCLA for research support over the past several years.

An earlier version of the prologue appeared under the title "In a Labyrinth of Western Desire: Kuki Shūzō and the Discovery of Japanese Being," in the fall 1991 issue of *boundary 2,* reprinted in 1993 by Duke University Press in *Japan in the World,* edited by Masao Miyoshi and Harry D. Harootunian. Parts of chapter 1 were published in *Contacts Between Cultures: Eastern Asia: Literature and Humanities,* edited by Bernard Hung-Kay Luk; selected papers from the 33d Congress of Asian and North African Studies (Lewiston, New York: Edwin Mellen Press, 1992) as "Kuki Shūzō and the Lure of Biography."

Introduction

Contemporary Japan has come face to face with a crisis. Every aspect of our life is tainted by the West, a condition commonly believed to be "modern." But this is a dangerous delusion, one which must be dispelled.

Kuki Shūzō, "Nihon bunka"

The sensibility of an era is not only its most decisive but also its most perishable aspect.

Susan Sontag, "Notes on Camp"

In 1921, Kuki Shūzō (1888–1941) retraced a well-traveled route aboard the Japanese mail steamer *Kamomaru*, bound for Marseille via Singapore, Colombo, and Suez. The journey by sea, inaugurated with the opening of Japanese ports in the mid-nineteenth century, offered ample time for geopolitical meditation as ships traversed oceans, circumvented continents, and docked at ports attesting to the reach of European colonial power. Like the travelers of the Meiji era (1868–1912), Kuki duly noted the inequities of global power and proprietorship along the way, and like his predecessors, he, too, directed his gaze in awed expectation toward a Western horizon. However, for Kuki, a student of Western philosophy from Tokyo Imperial University, what lay beyond that horizon was no longer as unfamiliar or unanticipated as it had been for his Meiji predecessors.

Kuki spent the better part of a decade in Europe familiarizing himself with current philosophical and literary developments, from poetic modernism to German phenomenology. During his long sojourn, he also commenced his career as a writer, publishing poetry as well as essays on aesthetics and philosophy. In the intervals between scholarly and literary pursuits, Kuki availed himself of metropolitan pleasures in European cities, now the site of modernist experimentation and a burgeoning jazz age. Soon after his return to Japan in 1929, he joined the philosophy faculty at Kyoto Imperial University, and in late 1930, Kuki published the work for which he became best known, *"Iki" no kōzō* (The Structure of Edo Aesthetic Style).[1] He would remain at his post at Kyoto Imperial University through the 1930's, a decade that witnessed intensifying repression within Japan and aggressive imperialism abroad.

Toward the end of 1939, in a telling variation on his first journey to Europe, Kuki undertook another passage across a narrower stretch of sea—the prerequisite tour of Manchuria and China for scholars and writers in recognition of Japanese empire. Not only chronologically but also symbolically, *"Iki" no kōzō* is located between these two voyages, the first to the West via its extensive imperial possessions, the second to the Asian continent, now claimed by Japanese imperial expansion.

A brief but demanding text, *"Iki" no kōzō* addresses an elusive sense of style, *iki,* which circulated in the erotically charged atmosphere of the Edo pleasure quarters, the Kabuki theaters, and the popular arts of the late Tokugawa period (1600–1867).[2] The adepts of this style included the female geisha, who provided pleasure and entertainment, and the male *tsū* (connoisseur, dandy) who patronized the quarters and the arts. Whether in attire or deportment, they cultivated a rarefied blend of sobriety and audacity. The qualities they prized—restrained wantonness, playful bravado, and an expertise in the practices of the quarters—became the celebrated motifs of the literature and lyrics, librettos, and woodblock prints that flourished in the cultural life of Edo. *"Iki" no kōzō,* in four central chapters, undertakes an analysis of *iki,* first as a form of consciousness authenticated by language and literature, then in its concrete manifestations in art and nature. This extended inventory of cultural artifacts, verbal and material, gathered from the archives of Edo history is framed by introductory and concluding chapters devoted to issues of method and theory. The idiom of these framing chapters is heavily indebted to more recent developments in modern philosophy,

---

1. Throughout this study, I refer to the version of *"Iki" no kōzō* included in *Kuki Shūzō zenshū,* 1:1–83; hereafter referred to as *KSZ.*

2. Though the term *iki* is translated in Japanese-English dictionaries as "chic" or "stylishness," I have chosen to use the Japanese in deference to Kuki's central claim that the phenomenon of *iki* is culturally incommensurable and consequently untranslatable.

most notably, a Heideggerian hermeneutics of Being. Under what historical conditions did this unlikely encounter between the archival remains of Edo and an increasingly international discourse on existential hermeneutics take place? This question serves as a point of departure for my own inquiry into *"Iki" no kōzō* and into the wider reflection on culture to which it contributed.

Since its appearance in 1930, *"Iki" no kōzō* has been neglected, admired, and reviled in turn. Some hail it as a text that successfully captures the essence of Japanese culture. Others condemn it as a pernicious example of *Nihonjinron*, that ubiquitous discourse on Japanese uniqueness. Most recently, *"Iki" no kōzō* has reemerged, however equivocally, in discussions of postmodernism and Japan. The aesthetic style commemorated in the text has incurred drastically disparate translations, from "bordello chic" at the sordid depths to "a breath of luminous delight" at the metaphysical heights. Why has a study of an early-nineteenth-century aesthetic style become the occasion for such disparity of opinion, and why does it figure in debates on culture, whether in the 1930's, the 1970's, or the present?

On the occasion of its first publication in 1930, *"Iki" no kōzō* shared space in the intellectual journal *Shisō* (Thought) with Nakai Masakazu's exploration of the structure of "machine aesthetics," Iwasaki Akira's discussion of "talkies" and the proletariat, and Noro Eitarō's treatise on contemporary contradictions of Japanese capitalism.[3] The table of contents alone suggests the dimensions of a new divide between divergent historical and ideological dispositions. While other contributors to *Shisō* fixed their sights on contemporary transformations of culture and social structure, Kuki gazed back toward what he called Japan's "spiritual culture," an enduring and authentic cultural endowment. Though *"Iki" no kōzō* received little critical acclaim when it first appeared, the retrospective and inward disposition it invoked would become widely disseminated in critical reflection on culture and modernity during the 1930's.

In a dialogue on *"Iki" no kōzō* published in 1979, Tada Michitarō and Yasuda Takeshi—both cultural historians who shared Kuki's connoisseurship of the pleasure quarters—observed that the tenth printing of the text in 1966 marked the threshold of its "second life," bringing a degree of popularity that had eluded *"Iki" no kōzō* in the prewar and immediate postwar years.[4] To be sure, *"Iki" no kōzō* fell between disci-

3. See issues 29 and 30 of *Shisō* (January and February 1930).

4. Beginning with Tada and Yasuda, *"Iki' no kōzō" o yomu*, *"Iki" no kōzō* and its author became the centerpieces of a number of articles and special issues of major intellectual journals. See for example *Gendai esupuri* 144 (1979), *Shisō* (March 1980), and the series

plinary and generic cracks in the period directly following its publication. While the scholarship on Kuki rarely addresses the issue in print, those interested in Kuki's career suggest in low tones that, very likely, he was isolated within early Shōwa academe, that his scholarly credentials were the subject of some question, and that his personal propriety was always in doubt.[5] *"Iki" no kōzō*, suggests one interested scholar, was not considered a scholarly work in its own time;[6] on the other hand, the erudition of its vocabulary, whether philosophical jargon or Edo lyrics, never lent itself to a mass audience. Nevertheless, Tada and Yasuda marvel at the longevity of this book on the arts and register their amazement at the interest it has finally elicited from a post-*Anpo* generation of students.[7] They find it an intriguing paradox that *"Iki" no kōzō* has secured its widest readership when the style it celebrates has so completely vanished from everyday life.[8]

This chronocultural fault line dividing the textual thematics of *"Iki" no kōzō* from the everyday experience of its postwar readers (a disparity that, incidentally, already existed in the interwar years) was not an uncommon textual occurrence in the late 1960's and 1970's. These were the years when the publishing phenomenon of *Nihonjinron*, discussions of Japanese uniqueness, reached unprecedented heights. As if to both mark the final disenchantment of postwar aspirations toward a genuine political democracy and savor the dubious rewards of massive economic growth, these reflections on Japaneseness, suggest its critics, use myths of collective belonging and unique cultural endowments to divert attention from contemporary contradictions.[9] In the belated celebrity of this

---

"Kuki Shūzō no sekai" by Sakabe Megumi in *Kikan asuteion*, nos. 8, 10–15 (April 1988/January 1990).

5. Tada Michitarō was one of those who suggested this explanation for the prewar neglect of *"Iki" no kōzō* in our discussion during the spring of 1994. Surprisingly, Kuki never served on the board of editors for the in-house Kyoto Imperial University journal of philosophy, *Tetsugaku kenkyū*, nor did he contribute to its pages, a fact that set him apart from his colleagues. This absence, whether by choice or necessity, would seem to confirm Kuki's academic isolation.

6. This was the hypothesis of Sakabe Megumi, author of a number of articles on Kuki Shūzō, offered in correspondence with the author.

7. "Anpo" is the Japanese abbreviation for the United States–Japan Security Treaty signed in 1951, but it is used to indicate the era of protest that surrounded the renewal of the treaty in 1960.

8. Tada and Yasuda, *"Iki' no kōzō" o yomu*, 5–6.

9. I am indebted to Harry Harootunian for this insight into the context for the postwar upsurge of *Nihonjinron*. See his discussion in *Things Seen and Unseen*, 437–38. Intellectual historian Kanō Masanaō speculates that *Nihonjinron* makes its appearance when mass social movements are in recession: a "philosophy of resignation sanctioned by an over-

"second life," *"Iki" no kōzō* appeared to have found a new place among a multitude of books offering disaffected readers shelter within the embrace of an imaginary community—comfortingly homogeneous and triumphantly exceptional, fundamentally unchanging and yet supremely adaptable to the harsh demands of modernity.[10] Not surprisingly, *"Iki" no kōzō* has been cited as an exemplar of *Nihonjinron*.

The critical history of this text, then, is a belated one coming "after the fact," a history in a retrospective mode with a mission to recover a neglected national monument. Indeed, *"Iki" no kōzō* presented an attractive prospect for those assembling a canon of Japaneseness in the postwar era. First of all, the text was largely untainted by the strident rhetoric of *kokusuishugi* (national essentialism) or other variations of the ultranationalistic rhetoric so prevalent in the 1930's. For those of a more liberal leaning, the setting for the text, the enterprising culture of an incipient middle class in the latter days of Edo, presented the possibility of native, and non-Western, antecedents for a civil society. Moreover, the understated eroticism of a style prized by prostitutes and their clients in a site devoted to sensual pleasures may have been just risqué enough to appeal to an academic generation less austere and less censored than their prewar predecessors. *"Iki" no kōzō* offered not only the outlines of a repressed history of sensuality, but more crucially, a meditation on a sensibility uniquely Japanese. That sensibility was constructed of apparent opposites—a penchant for play and a requirement for discipline and sacrifice—an improbable combination not unfamiliar to postwar citizens enjoying the pleasures of consumerism while paying the price for high-growth economics. All of these factors contributed to the renewed currency of *"Iki" no kōzō* among producers and consumers of *Nihonjinron*.

As a convergence of state, corporate, and academic interests, the highly profitable media enterprise of *Nihonjinron* is peculiar to the postwar era. Yet critics and apologists alike frequently chart a much longer history for *Nihonjinron* extending back to the interwar era of *"Iki" no kōzō* and beyond.[11] In *The Myth of Japanese Uniqueness*, Peter Dale situ-

---

bearing state . . . it conceals internal contradictions beneath a representation of the Japanese as cohesive and transhistorical." "Nihon bunkaron no rekishi," 35.

10. Marilyn Ivy critically addresses an even more recent "postmodern" recycling of *Nihonjinron* in "Critical Texts, Mass Artifacts." For a recent sample of current criticism of *Nihonjinron* by Japanese scholars, see the anthology edited by Shisō-Bunka Kenkyū Iinkai and Nihon Kagakusha Kaigi entitled *"Bunka" o yosō kiken shisō*.

11. The origins of *Nihonjinron* are not infrequently located in *kokugaku*, the nativism of the late eighteenth and nineteenth centuries. One principal objective of nativist scholar-

ates the origins of *Nihonjinron* in the cultural nationalist reaction of the latter half of the Meiji era, the "intellectualization of Japanese conservatism." Charging its advocates with a "defection from the modern" into the refuge of older, often authoritarian, forms of social life, Dale traces similar patterns of reactionary thought through the interwar and postwar eras. For Dale, *"Iki" no kōzō* counts as one of a trove of "prewar texts of an ultra-nationalist cast of thought." These prewar texts would later be plundered by more facilely conformist postwar contributors to *Nihonjinron* who neglected to note that they were "heir to the ideological patrimony of Japanese fascism."[12]

On the opposite side of the debate, sympathetic readers claim that *"Iki" no kōzō* accomplishes precisely what *Nihonjinron* professes to do — confer knowledge about *Nihonteki na mono*, things irreducibly and essentially Japanese. In a 1979 issue of *Gendai esupuri* (Contemporary Spirit) devoted to the Edo sources of contemporary Japanese aesthetic consciousness, cultural historian Minami Hiroshi begins his essay with this homage to Kuki's work: "If I had to choose one book about Japanese aesthetic consciousness, there is no question it would be Kuki Shūzō's *"Iki" no kōzō*."[13] Omodaka Hisayuki, co-editor of Kuki's collected works, contends that Kuki's credentials as a philosopher are singularly Japanese, and not simply because he displayed an enduring interest in Japanese culture. Distinguishing Kuki from the largely German-schooled academic orthodoxy of the interwar years, Omodaka claims that Kuki's philosophy extends its roots deep in the native soil of an aesthetic sensibility and Shintō myth.[14]

Clearly, these differing assessments of *Nihonjinron* are closely linked to vested interests, progressive or conservative, in the social prospects of our own era. Not without a share in those interests, I find myself in agreement with the judgment, if not always with the methods, of those who seek to disclose the ideological disposition of the postwar discourse on Japaneseness. Yet however significant an episode *"Iki" no kōzō* may be in the history (or prehistory) of *Nihonjinron*, I have chosen not to

---

ship was to define what was essentially Japanese in contrast to a perceived foreignness that had penetrated the grain of social life. While China occupied the place of the other in the nativist scheme, the rhetoric of its scholars was redeployed in the 1930's and 1940's as part of the project to overcome a Westernized modernity.

12. Dale, *The Myth of Japanese Uniqueness*, 38–42, 17.

13. Minami, *"Iki" no kōzō o megutte*," 32.

14. Omodaka, "Kuki sensei o keibo shite," in *Kuki Shūzō bunko mokuroku*, unnumbered preliminary page.

reduce my own reading of the prewar discourse on culture to the dimensions of a reactionary repository for contemporary conservatism. This kind of reduction — premised as it is on the assumption that *Nihonjinron* has enjoyed a continuous, unilinear history over the span of a century, if not longer — risks obscuring the historical specificity of widely divergent historical conjunctures. Nor do I wish to suggest, as critics of *Nihonjinron* occasionally do, that the discourse on Japaneseness poses critical problems absolutely unique to Japan.

At least provisionally, then, I will reserve those historical judgments that *Nihonjinron* seems to demand of critical observers of Japan's present circumstances. Instead, I propose to excavate — and by "excavate" I mean a process of exposing and reconstructing selected textual remains — a discursive site in Japan's intellectual history before the Pacific War, attending as closely as I can to both its intricacy and its historical specificity. Beginning with Kuki's intellectual itinerary, I will explore the genealogies of a newly inflected discourse on Japanese culture and chart its course through the 1920's and 1930's. This discourse addressed itself critically to both the epistemological and social presumptions of an increasingly expansive modernity, a modernity perceived as inimical to Japanese cultural distinctiveness and authenticity. *"Iki" no kōzō* — both a destination and a beginning in Kuki's itinerary — offers a promising point of departure for this inquiry because it demonstrates with unusual clarity and complexity the philosophical derivations, the modernist affiliations, and the ideological orientations of the interwar discourse on culture.

I have granted this exemplary status to *"Iki" no kōzō* despite the fact that its recorded history of reception begins, to a large degree, not in the 1930's but several decades after the Pacific War.[15] From all accounts, *"Iki" no kōzō*, however neglected as an object of scholarly discourse, was widely read by a generation of scholars and university students. At a time when Marxism had begun to show signs of collapse under official pressure, Kuki was among a growing number of intellectuals who appeared to offer an alternative solution to the predicament of modernity

---

15. Clearly, the editors of Iwanami Shoten in 1930 considered Kuki's study of Edo style significant enough to warrant publication both in the most prestigious of Iwanami's intellectual periodicals, *Shisō*, and as a book in its own right. Cultural historian Tada Michitarō and Aeba Jun, the present executive editor at Iwanami Shoten as well as editor of *Shisō*, have both speculated in conversation that the philosopher Hayashi Tatsuō, a member of Iwanami's board of editors when *"Iki" no kōzō* was under consideration, was perhaps the most influential voice in the choice to publish Kuki's manuscript.

in Japan.[16] In the last analysis, however, I have singled out Kuki's study of Edo style not for its empirically ascertainable influence of one author on another (assuming such an undertaking is even possible) but for its capacity to reveal the shape of a discursive formation and to illuminate the interpretive battles from which history is generated. *"Iki" no kōzō* spoke eloquently for a discursive orientation extending across disciplinary boundaries, from literature and cultural history to ethnology and social theory. This representative status of a presumably marginal text attests to the ubiquity of a disposition toward culture that would prove to have fateful historical consequences.

This said, I would like to present an initial perspective on the interwar reflection on culture through the lens of its most recent "postmodern" reading in the late 1980s. In "One Spirit, Two Nineteenth Centuries" and its Japanese-language predecessor, "Edo no seishin" (The Spirit of Edo), Karatani Kōjin offers an ironically ambivalent interpretation of *"Iki" no kōzō*. The article also provides the occasion for a sweeping critique of a prevailing "modernization theory" that persists in viewing a Western-generated model of material and intellectual development as both necessary and universal. Karatani begins by entertaining the possibility of plural and heterogeneous historical temporalities prior to their absorption into the systematic unity and self-appointed universality of a "Western narrative/history" — (the slash presumably punctuating the written, and therefore fabricated, nature of a linear history). Freed from its historical confinement in the "pre-modern," Japan's nineteenth century, he ventures, might better be represented as the "culmination of a maturation process," a process that ushered a Japan not yet subject to modernization into epistemological terrain anticipating the more liberating prospects of postmodernity.[17]

"Kuki was without doubt the only philosopher," proposes Karatani, "to seek the philosophical meaning of the [Japanese] nineteenth century in the 'modernization' of Japan." He recognized in *iki* "a world of pure surface devoid of all meaning and interiority"; that is to say, a world delivered from the metaphysics of depth (the ranking piety of the West, if we are to believe Roland Barthes).[18] Karatani grants Kuki the rare distinction of discovering a utopian moment of "exteriority" — an ex-

---

16. Terada, "Kuki tetsugaku no shūhen," 2–3.
17. Karatani, "One Spirit," 616–17.
18. Ibid., 622, 627. Interestingly, Barthes discovered an antidote to Western metaphysics in a "Japan" that, after a brief visit, he imaginatively recreated in *Empire of Signs*. See 55, 74–75.

emption from self-regulating and self-enclosed systems of modern discourse—in the cultural production of late Edo. That distinction, however, is far from an unqualified one. As will become clear in the course
of this chapter, Karatani positions *"Iki" no kōzō* in a precarious disequi-
librium between a "mode which in some senses had already transcended
the modern" and an oppressive imperialist regime spawned by a modern
epistemology.[19]

Why has *"Iki" no kōzō* drawn renewed interest in a discussion on postmodernism and Japan? Karatani would appear to be suggesting that its
author, Kuki Shūzō, caught an anticipatory glimpse of a postmodern
disposition in the cultural style of nineteenth-century Edo. And it is
perhaps in this anticipation that Karatani discovers a strategy for side-
stepping the modern and lifting its imposition of unilinear historical
necessity and universal rationality—an imposition that worked to the
detriment of (Japanese) difference. For my own part, even at the risk of
reinvoking the historical narrative Karatani aims to suspend, I hesitate
to disengage a postmodern "sensibility" from the material history of the
late capitalist era in which it was first detected. Critics point out that, at
its worst, postmodernism represents an accommodation of the transnational entrepreneurial culture and "fragmenting social landscape"
emerging in the 1970's. At its best, the postmodern message of emancipation, one that seeks to give voice to others and yet denies them access
to more universal sources of power, is ambiguous.[20] There is, it seems
to me, too much at stake to revel (transhistorically or ahistorically) in a
disposition so closely associated with the pervasive, if varied, systems
of control and with the gross inequities of wealth and well-being that
proliferate in our own historical present. Further, Karatani's implication
that Edo, if not Japan, was postmodern ahead of its time (and before
the West) may in fact bear witness to the repetition, if not continuity,
of history despite its alleged postmodern interruption. Very possibly,
the current discovery of the "postmodern" in the Japanese past pays
silent homage to the interwar discourse on culture by borrowing its
tactics of reversal—extending to Japan the same world-historical priority that the West has long claimed for itself.[21]

One might perhaps more productively seek a resemblance to the

<hr>

19. Karatani, "One Spirit," 627.
20. Harvey, *The Condition of Postmodernity,* 113–18.
21. For a similar cautionary note, see Ivy's comments on a discussion between Karatani Kōjin, Asada Akira, and Jacques Derrida on the issue of a "Japanese native decons-
truction" before the movement itself in "Critical Texts, Mass Artifacts," 438–39.

postmodern not in the mirror of Edo but rather in the early Shōwa discourse on culture. There one discovers a voice anticipating the ambiguities and ironies of the postmodern critique of modernity. The postmodern is marked by its incredulity toward the grand narratives that have reigned over modern history, those broad interpretive schemas that determine the subject of history, its truth, and its end.[22] Issuing from a desire to suspend the hierarchical distinctions put in force by the Enlightenment, the postmodern project has devoted itself to the articulation of difference and the identification of marginal sites that escape the control of a ruling center. Yet by the admission of its own advocates, the postmodern is regularly revisited by the very unities it hopes to exile. Roland Barthes noted that the attempt to imagine a symbolic system outside the limits of Western metaphysics is "like trying to destroy the wolf by lodging comfortably in his gullet": the values we drive out return in the language we speak.[23] Does difference itself risk becoming a hegemonic concept? Does its celebration once again serve to suppress the voices of those others for whom the postmodern supposedly speaks?

Half a century before the first sightings of the postmodern, a similar set of contradictions undermined the critical reflection on modernity in interwar Japan. There was, however, one exceptional circumstance: the Japanese reflection was colored by more passion and more pathos than its European postmodernist successor because the metanarratives opposed by the Japanese had so recently been (self-)imposed under the impending threat of colonization. The most dominant of the grand narratives that came into force along with Japan's coerced entry into the world market might be summed up in the slogan *bunmei kaika* (civilization and enlightenment). Circulating widely in the years following the Meiji *ishin*,[24] this powerful ideological notion simultaneously authorized Japan's accelerated modernization and consigned Japan to a universal schema of historical development in which a modernized West inevitably prevailed.[25] As something of an afterthought to Japan's successful if belated modernization, a number of writers and theorists during the

22. Lyotard, *The Postmodern Condition*, xxiii–xxiv.
23. Barthes, *Empire of Signs*, 8.
24. This term is conventionally translated as the Meiji "Restoration." However, a close look at the character compound and its Japanese definition suggests rather the idea of changing into something completely new, a renovation.
25. See Karatani's analysis of the self-alienating effects of linear history in "Fūkei no hakken," 5–43, translated by Brett de Bary as "The Discovery of Landscape" in *The Origins of Modern Japanese Literature* (Durham, N.C.: Duke University Press, 1993), 11–44.

1920's and 1930's attempted to restore to Japan its difference from reigning "Western" values — values already deeply entrenched in the specialized languages of a European-derived discourse and the everyday life of
these same intellectuals. The philosopher Watsuji Tetsurō (1889–1960),
well versed in the vocabulary of Nietzsche, Kierkegaard, and Heidegger,
deciphered that difference hermeneutically in the epiphanies of what he
called Japan's spiritual history. Novelist Tanizaki Junichirō (1886–1965), in
his most experimentally modernist narratives, plotted a return to distinctively Japanese sites and sensibilities. The disciples of philosopher Nishida Kitarō (1870–1945), who called themselves the *Kyōtogakuha* (Kyoto school), defined Japan's uniquely appointed world-historical mission
according to a Hegelian logic of history.[26] After several generations of successful assimilation to the West, Japanese intellectuals had little choice but
to delineate Japaneseness against, and within, dominant discursive
modes derived from the West. To put it in the form of a question: How
was one to disavow the modern when historical modernity had, in a very
strong sense, already become "Japanese"? As if in anticipation of the postmodern critique of modernity half a century later, this reapprehension of
Japan wavered ambiguously between critical protest and reaction.

To a large degree, this inquiry into Japaneseness was conducted
within the confines of culture — "culture" not in the broad, anthropological sense of the material and symbolic production of a way of life
but in the narrow and normative sense of moral and aesthetic value.[27]
This conjuncture of aesthetics and the nation was not without precedent
in Japan. In the mid-Meiji era, following a period of radical social and
cultural experimentation, public officials and publicly oriented intellectuals began to seek ways to domesticate the newly installed nation-state
and to insulate the populace from traumatic social transformation.[28]
Taking the name Seikyōsha (Society for Political Education), a group of
scholar-publicists who shared common misgivings over the excesses of
"Westernism" and the threat of Western imperialism inaugurated a jour-

---

26. As a self-conscious faction, Kyoto-school philosophy refers to a group of younger
disciples of Nishida Kitarō—Nishitani Keiji, Kōyama Iwao, and Kōsaka Masaaki are
among the most prominent—active in Kyoto Imperial University's philosophy department from the mid-1930's through World War II. The beginnings of a more loosely organized Kyoto school go back to the joint tenure at Kyoto Imperial University of Nishida
and Tanabe Hajime, beginning just after the end of the World War I.

27. The distinction was suggested to me by a reading of Bourdieu's *Distinction*, 1–2.

28. Stefan Tanaka explains that this unsettling social transformation that followed on
the heels of Japan's entry into the world market "became (and still is) synonymous with
foreignness." "Beauty," 2.

nalistic project to define the nation and construct a cultural foundation for its autonomy.[29]

The principal contributors to this undertaking—Shiga Shigetaka (1863–1927), Kuga Katsunan (1857–1907), and Miyake Setsurei (1860–1945)—were concerned with the issue of knowledge. Convinced that cultural and intellectual acquiescence to the West, no less than military vulnerability, invited the decline and perhaps even the loss of national sovereignty, they urged that Japan selectively resist the assault of new knowledge—knowledge ostensibly universal but in actuality particular to the West and its various nations. They argued that a viable nation-state requires national subjects in possession of a "sense of nation": that is to say, a certain kind of impassioned collective knowledge. Yet the question of just what to designate as the content of this knowledge and how to go about nationalizing the populace remained unresolved. In answer to the question Shiga first posed in the title of his article, "How Can Japan Be Made Japan?" he tentatively proposed that Japan be distinguished by its "aesthetic sense."[30]

While Seikyōsha members anticipated Kuki's generation in their inclination toward aesthetics as the privileged idiom of the nation, the mode in which they expressed that inclination belonged to an earlier era. Unlike the Shōwa cultural theorists, who endeavored to distance themselves from Enlightenment norms, the Meiji nationalists tempered their resistance to the West with a healthy respect for the benefits of "civilization," whether instrumental reason, enlightened progress, or scientific technology. Intellectual historian Fujita Shōzō captures another trait of the Meiji era with the celebrated statement of Fukuzawa Yukichi: "The founding of the nation-state is the cause not of public officialdom but of each private individual."[31] As yet, no breach had sun-

---

29. Shiga Shigetaka, returning from a trip to the South Seas in 1886, wrote, "If the colored races do not now exert themselves, then ultimately the world will become the private possession of the white race." Japan, he suggested, should exert itself by expanding its economic interests in the South Pacific. This "state-of-siege" mentality persisted despite Japan's rapid gains in industrial wealth and military strength. See Pyle, *The New Generation*, 55–57.

30. The suggestion was made in one of Shiga's pieces for *Nihonjin* (July 3, 1888), quoted in Pyle, *The New Generation*, 68. In a slightly earlier article, Shiga had naturalized the issue in organic terms: Must we, he asked, "uproot the whole of Western civilization and transplant it in Japanese soil?" See "Ikani shite Nihonkoku o Nihonkoku tarashimubeki ya," *Kokumin no tomo* (October 21, 1887), also quoted in Pyle, 56. Several years later, in an attempt to locate the populace in a newly nationalized landscape, Shiga would endow the natural features of the archipelago with unique national value in a language sanctioned by scientific authority in his *Nihon fūkei-ron* (1894).

31. Fujita, *Seishinshiteki kōsatsu: Ikutsuka no danmen ni sokushite*, 136–39.

dered private feeling from public purpose, cultural expressivity from political aspiration. Nor had new modes of social and economic relations isolated the individual as an atomized unit of exchange. By the end of the Meiji era, however, novelists of *shishōsetsu* (personal fiction) and philosophers of the "inner life" and "personality" had begun to develop technologies of the self—a new site of socially unmediated, interiorized subjectivity. These technologies, first elaborated at the level of the individual, were swiftly redeployed at a collective level, where they enabled Shōwa cultural theorists to mystify the state as collective subjectivity and to extend its authority into the hearts and minds of individuals.

The Meiji nationalists had experienced their own historical dislocation with great concreteness and immediacy; they had embarked on a mission to engender the nation with an acute awareness of the artfulness and artifice of their project.[32] By the time the Shōwa cultural theorists appeared on the scene, the immediacy of the Meiji transformation had vanished, and history could be either reimagined as undisrupted continuity or suppressed in favor of an eternal and unchanging present. The assimilation of the European cultural sciences during the first decades of the twentieth century enabled scholars to modify and complete the task first identified by Meiji nationalists—that of regathering what had been dispersed and restoring it into reconstituted unities and continuous histories of the spirit.[33]

Kuki Shūzō, one of those who took up the task with a passion, identified *iki*—a provocative style esteemed by plebeians rather than gentry—as a privileged sign of the distinctiveness of Japanese culture. Kuki's preferred cultural style, dating from a period closely preceding Japan's epoch-making encounter with Commodore Perry's Black Ships, invokes the final moments of what he presumed to be a self-possessed culture not yet wrenched away from its native habitat, a culture not yet anticipating a modern future. Nevertheless, the foe from whom Kuki had to wrest this stylistic artifact was not so much the West as it was

32. As was so common among Meiji intellectuals and artists, the principal figures in this undertaking had negotiated two distinct worlds in the course of their education—a childhood spent in provincial samurai households committed to traditional intellectual pursuits and a higher education in thoroughly Westernized institutions down to the very language of instruction. This particular conjuncture gave them an appreciation for the chasm between a pre-Meiji past and the transformed present to which they belonged: "We members were largely brought up on Western literature and science; it is easier for us to read the novels of Scott than to read the *Genji monogatari.*" Quoted from the Seikyōsha manifesto in Pyle, *The New Generation,* 70.
33. This phrasing is inspired by Michel Foucault's critique of the subdiscipline of the history of ideas in *The Archaeology of Knowledge,* 12.

Japan's own Enlightenment, under whose reign Tokugawa culture had become the object of some disrepute. With the publication of *"Iki" no kōzō*, Kuki aspired to resituate a marginalized historical moment in the center of Japan's self-understanding. Kuki may well have thought that the very eccentricity of his preference would serve to heighten the degree of difference he hoped to interpose between Japan and the West. Yet ironically, the terms by which he articulated Japan's difference from the West were clearly marked by a long and productive apprenticeship to European letters. It should not be surprising, then, if *"Iki" no kōzō* is haunted by the specter of occidentality it sought to banish. The question Fredric Jameson first addressed to postmodernism—does it transcend, or does it reproduce, the logic of what it opposes?—has disturbing (if retrospective) relevance for the endeavor to recover Japan's cultural authenticity during the interwar years.[34]

In his exploration of the ambiguities posed by *"Iki" no kōzō*, Karatani Kōjin observes that Kuki's attempt to define a sensibility outside of Europe's modernity took the form of "a citation of the anti-Western elements of Western thought."[35] Kuki endorsed the German neo-idealist defense of culture, applauded Bergson's sanctification of subjective experience, and followed Heidegger in pursuit of authentic (and decentered) Being. He embraced the European cultural hermeneutic for its methodological capacity to reclaim a selectively cherished past. In the most general terms, this extended episode in the history of European philosophy represented an attempt to stave off the imperious claims of instrumental reason and restore to human experience, individual and collective, the integrity and profundity it had presumably lost to a modernity of mechanized means and mass dimensions. It was precisely because Kuki shared both the experience and the critical perception of what had proven to be a transnational historical moment that he felt such a strong affinity with the voices of discontent raised by these German and French philosophers. The theoretical idiom of *"Iki" no kōzō* itself bore witness, however unwittingly, to the interval of a heterogeneous modernity that irrevocably severed early Shōwa Japan from its pre-Meiji past.

It should be recalled, however, that these defensive postures in Europe's philosophical modernity were not without Eurocentric resonances—resonances that routinely excluded or diminished the non-

34. Jameson, "Postmodernism and Consumer Society," 111–25.
35. Karatani, "One Spirit," 627.

West under the guise of a universalizing vocabulary. The world-historical ambitions of Wilhelm Dilthey's cultural hermeneutic and the universalist cast of Heidegger's existential phenomenology did not exempt these projects from interests more narrowly circumscribed—to the West, or, in Heidegger's case, to Germany. Moreover, the possibility of this expansive gesture in European theoretical discourse reflected, however faintly, a continuing imperialist project on the part of the West to extend its control, material and ideological, to the far reaches of the globe. Many of the Japanese writers and theorists who traveled to Europe discovered that these covert principles of imperialist ambition and cultural exclusion operated more overtly in the racial perceptions that shaped European images of its cultural others. Since the beginning of the Meiji era (1868), Japanese travelers had documented virulent strains of racism in Europe and America, whether directed toward themselves or toward other races and ethnicities.

Confronted with a reception by the West that was at best ambivalent, Kuki tempered his commitment to European philosophical discourse with a measure of cultural self-defense. Drawing on the discursive resources he had gleaned from Europe, Kuki discovered in *iki* an existential disposition that was free, he claimed, from Western obsessions with identity and certainty, untainted by a rationality of ends. An implausible synthesis of apparently contradictory attributes, *iki* offered the prospect of a logic emptied of instrumentality, replacing purposeful, belabored love with disinterested free play. This was a logic, claimed Kuki, unknown in the West.

On first glance, it would seem ironic that the same modern discursive resources that had enabled Kuki to discover an aesthetic "way of being" beyond the horizon of Western metaphysics also encouraged him to subordinate that same "way of being" to an absolute logic of racial identity and cultural closure. Emptied of its historical and social specificity, subjected to the logic of organicism, *iki* became the chosen signifier for Japan, gathering into its interpretive folds those moments Kuki deemed most representative of Japanese culture. In this manner, a single word was assigned the task of representing the identity of an inimitable collective subject against the claims of Western universalism. Kuki reenlisted the purposeful passion disavowed by the stylistic requirements of *iki,* this time in the service of national culture. Further, in what may be the most disturbing irony of all, this national passion, initially articulated as a resistance against the hegemonic thrust of Western civilization, would be recruited in defense of Japan's own escalating imperialism in Asia.

The exceptionality of spirit that Kuki claimed for Japan in *"Iki" no kōzō* would soon serve as a rationale for Japan's domination of Asia and the spilling of Asian blood. These ironies were not, however, exclusive to Japan; rather, they were inscribed in aesthetic modernism—an increasingly international disposition to which Kuki subscribed—as one distinct ideological possibility. Aesthetic modernism discovered emancipatory potential in the modern but also condoned its most oppressive possibilities: imperialism, racialized nationalism, and mechanized warfare, to name a few. Whether in East Asia or Europe, modernism provided a means to "restructure domination as an aesthetic object."[36]

At this point, one might ask what was sacrificed in Kuki's theoretical transaction, conducted as it was within discursive contours shaped by imperialism. At the very least, Kuki forfeited the historicity of the popular culture of Bunka-Bunsei (a period roughly equivalent to the first half of the nineteenth century), when the aesthetic style of *iki* came into its own. This historical interval came during the latter half of a long and eventful Tokugawa reign (1600–1867), a reign that created the conditions, however inadvertently, for social and cultural forms far exceeding the limits of official imagination. As the era progressed, an official hierarchy anchored in Confucian ethics, with samurai or warriors on the top and merchants and artisans on the bottom, lost its moorings. During the eighteenth century, economic and cultural dominance already had begun to drift east from Kamigata (the Osaka-Kyoto region), an older mercantile center and site of the ancient court, to the Tokugawa administrative center in Edo, the locus of new forms of productivity and wealth among *chōnin* (townspeople). In officially designated *akusho*—literally, "places of odium"—where an official Confucian version of order and propriety no longer held sway, Edo townspeople celebrated an efflorescence of real wealth and unrealized aspiration in new and widely disseminating cultural forms. Within this historical setting, the exacting stylistic requirements of *iki* represented the newly emerging cultural productivity and autonomy of a rising mercantile class in defiance of a nearly bankrupt samurai bureaucracy.

In his choice of late Edo as the native place of Japanese cultural authenticity, Kuki would seem to set himself apart from other contributors to the interwar discourse on culture—whether cultural historians, novelists, or ethnologists—who overwhelmingly identified archaic, nonurban, and noncapitalist forms of cultural creation as testimony to an authentic Japanese spirit. Edo, on the other hand, was separated from

36. Berman, "Foreword: The Wandering Z," xix.

Kuki's own moment by hardly more than a century, and the cultural artifacts Kuki so meticulously catalogued were clearly the creation of urban commoners in a historical setting foreshadowing, if not actively anticipating, the economic and social contours of a modern capitalist order to come.

Yet despite the eccentricity of Kuki's historical preferences, the inspiration for his project and the strategies he employed were not unlike those of other contributors to the discourse on Japanese culture. Kuki's interpretive study of *iki* summons up not so such much the urban topography of Edo's low-lying plebeian quarters as an unchanging landscape of the Japanese spirit. If the substance of Edo popular culture was recovered as a metaphor for the eternal present of Japanese being, that recovery was accomplished at the expense of the local resonances — especially, new relations of social and cultural power — of a particular cultural moment that closely preceded the relentless centralizing processes invoked by the Meiji state.

The costs of Kuki's transaction, however, were exacted not only from the accounts of a past history. *"Iki" no kōzō* and the discourse on culture of which it was part also wrought its effects on the historical contemporaneity occupied by its author and readers. Against the backdrop of this more recent history, Kuki's recourse to European discursive strategies reflected other convergences between Japan and the West — convergences that went well beyond merely a generic apprehension of modernity. At the end of the nineteenth century, Europe faced the prospect of disintegrating traditions and a process of social leveling that threatened, or promised, a society of drastically different proportions. The humanistic endeavors inaugurated during that era — the *Kulturwissenschaften* (cultural sciences), *Lebensphilosophie* (philosophy of life), and cultural hermeneutics — offered refuge in a conception of culture as truth and guaranteed a restoration of cultural continuity with a carefully crafted past. For the intellectual guardians of that past, these endeavors conferred symbolic capital and promises of social privilege no longer inherited by birth. Invented under the impending eclipse not only of cultural but also of traditional class differences, these new cultural disciplines sought to restore those differences in the guise of new ethnic and national identities. To a large extent, this was the elitist enterprise of a self-styled cultural aristocracy, and as Marxist critic Tosaka Jun (1900–1945) pointed out in the 1930's, one that encouraged its practitioners to withdraw from the scene of contemporary social processes into aestheticized reminiscence and subjective interiority.

In Japan, the strategies derived from this European enterprise were first enlisted in a defense of culture during the 1920's, often referred to as Japan's decade of modernism. This was the era when the effects of modernization, initiated by the Meiji *ishin* and Japan's realignment with the West, penetrated deep into the grain of everyday life. In a transfigured cityscape of streetcars and high buildings, cafés and dance halls, new social constituencies rose up from below to become active participants in what was dubbed in transliterated English *modan raifu* (modern life). As if to lure these urban masses into visibility, culture invoked mechanized technologies to accelerate and multiply its representations — in motion pictures, phonograph records, one-yen books, and the rhythms of jazz. Yet these conspicuous representations of modern urban culture would slip into concealment between the lines of *"Iki" no kōzō*.

When Kuki returned to Japan at the end of the decade in 1929, the city of Tokyo was preparing to celebrate (with full imperial fanfare) the completion of its modern reconstruction from the ruins of the 1923 great Kantō earthquake. No doubt the scene that greeted his homecoming resembled the capitals of Europe more than he might have imagined from his distant vantage point in Paris. Among contemporary observers, there were those who welcomed this modern transformation as a cultural revolution with the potential to empower new social classes. Kuki, however, saw it not as a liberating transcultural modernity, or as acceptable cultural borrowing, but rather as a sign of the invasive presence of the West. In an essay from the mid-thirties, Kuki recalled his first impressions upon returning to Japan in 1929: "When I walked around the city, wherever I looked, English words were everywhere, on all the billboards. One had the impression that this was a colony, like Singapore or Colombo. Even the newspapers were full of foreign words, and somehow it made me feel ashamed."[37]

In this new cityscape, Kuki read the signs of cultural colonization, signs that threatened a leveling of all cultural differences at the expense of the indigenous past. At the conclusion of *"Iki" no kōzō* he would make a plea to his readers to overcome a temporary lapse in collective memory and recall Japan's spiritual culture. Kuki purported to speak in the voice of Japan. His was a polemic against the trespassing of the West into a domain of authentic Japanese culture. This cultural populism notwithstanding, Kuki's defense of culture, like the cultural criticism of his European counterparts, masked a resistance of the few against the rising tide of mass culture. Hence his sympathy for Baudelaire's dandy, that

37. Kuki, "Gairaigo shokan," *KSZ*, 5:91.

purveyor of aristocratic style who pitted himself against the undistinguished crowds of mid-nineteenth-century Paris (even as he reveled in them). Revealing, too, is Kuki's choice of *iki* as a privileged signifier for Japan, a tribute paid to those select individuals who successfully distinguished themselves through mastery of a demanding code of etiquette, style, and discernment. Is it possible, then, that the anxiety of contamination pervading *"Iki" no kōzō* is as much an anxiety over the internal emergence of mass culture — and the specter of mass politics — as it is an anxiety over the external presence of the West?

The contradictions that shadow *"Iki" no kōzō* become palpable in a linguistic fissure running through the text. The title itself already suggests an unlikely alliance between two disparate languages. *Iki*, a word with its roots in the popular culture of late Edo, expresses an appreciation of style in a colloquial, even performative mode. *Kōzō*, a weighty analytic term of more recent origin, suggests the continuing dialogue of Japanese intellectuals with forms of Western knowledge.[38] One insightful commentator describes the text as a "magnetic field of language" where a thoroughly mastered philosophical terminology is charged with "capturing alive the language of everyday life."[39] But this "language of everyday life" is also an aestheticized language, and one that had lost much of its contemporary resonance by the time *"Iki" no kōzō* was written. Kuki himself attributed this linguistic fissure to an "unbridgeable chasm" between conceptual language and experiential reality, an attribution to which subsequent chapters in this book will attend closely.[40]

Most critical assessments of *"Iki" no kōzō* view the text as a resourceful synthesis of Western methods and Japanese subject matter. In the common parlance, a certain unique Japanese thing (often conjured up in images of density and opacity) is submitted to the bright illumination of rigorous (Western) analytic thought. Depending on the perspective of the critic, this so-called synthesis is deemed either a positive accom-

38. Tada Michitarō suggests that this combination of "pure Japanese" with a "difficult, Western-style analytic term" became a fashionable choice for book titles in the late 1960's, as in Doi Takeo's well-known *Amae no kōzō* (Tokyo: Kobundo, 1971), translated by John Bester as *The Anatomy of Dependence* (Tokyo and New York: Kodansha International, 1977). From the perspective of *Nihonjinron* critics, this publishing vogue would reflect the scientific-empirical pretensions of postwar *Nihonjinron*. Tada speculates that Kuki's prescience in this matter accounts in part for the belated popularity of *"Iki" no kōzō*. See Tada and Yasuda, *"Iki" no kōzō" o yomu*, 6.

39. Sugimotō, "Tetsugakuteki zuan," 1–3.

40. Kuki, *"Iki" no kōzō, KSZ*, 1:73–74.

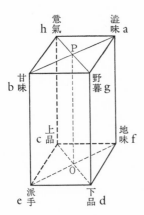

Figure 1. Kuki's geometrical representations of a Japanese system of taste

a *shibumi* (astringent, sober, severe)
b *amami* (sweet)
c *johin* (elegant, high class)
d *gehin* (vulgar, low class)
e *hade* (flashy)
f *jimi* (somber)
g *yabo* (boorish)
h *iki*

plishment or a violation. In the preface to *Nihon no shisō* (Japanese Thought), Maruyama Masao, postwar historian and ardent believer in the efficacy of rational fictions, commended *"Iki" no kōzō* for its structural clarity: *"'Iki' no kōzō* is undoubtedly the most successful example of a three-dimensional elucidation of the internal structure of a concept integral to the way of life of a particular era."[41] Maruyama's reference to three-dimensionality is no doubt a literal reference to the geometric figure appearing in the text of *"Iki" no kōzō*, a figure in which Kuki schematically represented a Japanese system of taste (Figure 1). On the other hand, connoisseurs of Edo culture, as well as those less sanguine about the unconditional benefits of rationality, have expressed doubts about the merits of Kuki's "geometry of taste" and more generally about the validity of a methodological approach derived from the West. What such doubts often imply is that Western methods, far from being innocent, violate the "Japaneseness" of the object in question.

41. Maruyama, *Nihon no shisō*, 4. In this introduction to a series of critical essays on modern Japanese culture and thought, Maruyama deplores the poverty of intellectual history in Japan. I should mention that his praise for Kuki is conditional. Though he credits Kuki with clarity of exposition, *"Iki" no kōzō* does not meet his expectations for a more comprehensive historical analysis that would situate a concept diachronically as well as synchronically. In other words, Kuki's analysis fails to account adequately for historical temporality.

Heidegger raised very similar questions concerning the "cultural ethics" of *"Iki" no kōzō* in "A Dialogue on Language." Modeled on a conversation between Heidegger and the scholar of German literature Tezuka
Tomio, these retrospective reflections came long after Heidegger's extended dialogue with Kuki in the late 1920's. In the "Dialogue," Heidegger insinuated that Kuki's attempt to "say the essential nature of Eastasian art" was already endangered by the philosophical idiom in which
he spoke.[42]

More recently, Karatani, an attentive reader of both Kuki and Heidegger, has pointed out another and more disturbing side to this encounter between German and Japanese philosophers. Not without sympathy for Kuki's (and Heidegger's) reminiscence of something beyond
the expansive and imperious reach of modern knowledge, Karatani suggests in characteristically ambiguous fashion that Kuki pursued "the forgotten 'being' of the modern world in the aesthetic way of life of the
nineteenth century."[43] And yet, even as Kuki discovered the distinctiveness of Edo, he had already buried it beneath modern epistemological categories. Up to this point, Karatani would appear to be merely
adding a degree of specificity to Heidegger's vague apprehension that
the methodological language of Kuki's inquiry fatefully compromised
its content. But here Karatani parts company with Heidegger to impli-
cate German and Japanese philosopher alike in what he deems a peculiarly modern conspiracy: Heidegger's return to the question of Being
was never far from his faith in the historical mission of a German *Volk*.
Kuki replicated this potent proximity between intellectual culture and
reactionary politics when he deployed what he called a "hermeneutics
of national being" to identify the eccentricities of Edo as the dwelling
place of the Japanese spirit. Both philosophers, charges Karatani, imposed a despotic system on the cultural-existential disposition they
hoped to rescue from the ravages of modernity. And in both cases, that
despotic system harbored ideological potential for imperialism and nationalistic fanaticism.[44]

At the level of formal analysis, what Karatani's critique suggests is
that the notion of synthesis between matter and method—a Japanese
substance cast in a Western form—does not adequately describe the
transaction conducted in *"Iki" no kōzō*. Rather, the concept of an essential

42. Heidegger, "A Dialogue on Language," 1–4, 13–15.
43. Karatani, "One Spirit," 623.
44. Karatani, "Edo no seishin," 8–10; "One Spirit," 621–23.

Japaneseness proves to be the discursive effect of a method with a content all its own. In other words, the form of Kuki's inquiry — a form of which western Europe could no longer claim sole possession — conferred a meaning that was in no way ideologically neutral. The Japan that Kuki and fellow travelers discovered occupied a new discursive space defended on all sides against the modern, yet this aesthetically rarefied space was articulated in terms that were distinctly modernist. Raymond Williams has identified two senses of the term "modern," the first progressive in its orientation, the second reactionary: "'modern' as a historical time, with its specific and then changing features; but 'modern' also as what Medvedev and Bakhtin, criticizing it, called 'eternal contemporaneity,' that apprehension of the 'moment' which overrides and excludes, practically and theoretically, the material realities of change, until all consciousness and practice are 'now'." The modern in this second and more reactionary sense is a set of conditions in which the "true nature of life" is confronted with a threatening modernity demanding cultural and social transformation. Ultimately, this paradoxical configuration of a "modernism against modernity"[45] drew Kuki's aesthetics of national being into collaboration with the more disturbing ideological developments of the 1930's.

Japanese scholarship has largely depicted Kuki as a lone figure against the backdrop of the interwar years, situating him at the margins of reigning academic orthodoxies and scholarly propriety. Unlike most of his fellow philosophers who spent a requisite year or two in Germany, Kuki traveled extensively in western Europe, dividing the better part of an eight-year stay between Germany and France. During his tenure on the faculty of philosophy at Kyoto Imperial University, Kuki's personal eccentricities and an unorthodox interest in French philosophy kept him at a distance from Kyoto-school philosophy, with its focus upon German idealism. As an interpreter of existential phenomenology, Kuki called attention to the significance of *gūzensei* (contingence), the neglected remainder, he believed, of a Western philosophical obsession with certainty. As an aesthetician, he defended the value of poetry against the contemporary literary hegemony of prose. And as the author of *"Iki" no kōzō*, he elevated a vulgarized historical moment to the status of cultural icon.

Though none of these observations is without foundation, the focus on Kuki's exceptional status has obscured the outlines of a larger dis-

45. Williams, *The Politics of Modernism*, 76.

course on the crisis in modern culture in which *"Iki" no kōzō* takes part. The presumption that "a man and his work" form an inviolable unity has diverted attention away from less organic congruences that transect biographies and texts. I have instead attempted to distance myself from the self-evidence of the work and the truths that form inside it in order to reveal a field of discourse. In his introduction to *The Archaeology of Knowledge,* Michel Foucault radically resituates the borders of the book beyond "the title, the first lines, and the last full stop." Rather, he suggests, a book is caught up "in a system of references to other books, other texts, other sentences: it is a node within a network."[46] I begin from the assumption that the meanings of this text, *"Iki" no kōzō,* will stand out only within networks of relations to other texts and events. Rather than ferreting out meaning from between the lines of a single work, I have looked for significance in the spaces between texts, as well as in the breaches between textual production and social practices. Within these coordinates, *"Iki" no kōzō* becomes one promising locus from which to explore the textual and historical complexities attending the reflection on modernity and culture during the interwar years in Japan.

Suspending the unities already formed by a work, an oeuvre, a discipline, and perhaps most crucially, a national tradition frees the problems those unities pose, as well as the problems they exclude. Instead of identifying what is unique about *"Iki" no kōzō,* I examine the historical disposition that links it to other contemporary theoretical and literary projects. Rather than enshrining Kuki in a national canon of modern Japanese philosophy, I trace the circuit by which traveling theories are domesticated in order to rearticulate the nation-state as an exceptional space of authentic culture. In place of reiterating what is Japanese about *iki,* I ask why and in what form cultural authenticity became an issue for a discourse extending across national boundaries. And, rather than preserving the aesthetic autonomy and transcendence of spirit exalted by the work, I attempt to coerce the sanctified sphere of art and culture back into confrontation with the conditions of its social formation.

I have read the text as a discursive site from a number of convergences, intellectual and material. These convergences have led my own inquiry across disciplinary and cultural borders, from Paris in the 1920's to Edo a century earlier, from the cloistered circles of German phenomenology to the neon lights of Ginza, from the inception of the cultural

---

46. Foucault, *The Archaeology of Knowledge,* 23.

sciences in Europe of the late nineteenth century to the Japanese critique of modernity in the early twentieth century. What has guided me has been a concern for history, or more precisely, for the historicity of an intellectual enterprise that sought its own place beyond history. In the chapters that follow, I have ventured a number of readings against the grain in my endeavor to reveal the connections — so assiduously denied by the practitioners of what Theodor Adorno has called *Kulturkritik* — linking aesthetics and culture with social processes.

CHAPTER I

Exotic Seductions
and the Return to Japan

*Furusato no "iki" ni niru kō o haru no yoru no René ga sugata ni
kagu kokoro kana*
*Breathing in the aura of René on a spring evening, in my soul, like
the fragrance of "iki" from my native place*

Kuki Shūzō, "Nocturne," from *Pari shinkei*
(Paris Mindscapes)

Je ne me souviens point de toi, car je ne t'oublie jamais
*Wasureneba koso omoidasazu sōrō (What need to remember when I
have never forgotten you)*

Poem attributed to the Edo courtesan Takaō,
translated into French by Kuki Shūzō, in
"Geisha"

*At the very moment when the native intellectual is anxiously trying
to create a cultural work he fails to realize that he is utilizing techniques and language which are borrowed from the stranger in his
country. He contents himself with stamping these instruments with a
hallmark which he wishes to be national, but which is strangely reminiscent of exoticism.*

Frantz Fanon, *The Wretched of the Earth*

Kuki's relationship with the West was an enduring one.
His personal tastes drew him toward an urbane cosmopolitanism, his
academic interests toward European arts and letters. Until an untimely
death at the age of fifty-three, Kuki remained a dedicated, though not
uncritical, student of Western philosophy. This chapter and the next are

devoted to tracing Kuki's itinerary between Japan and the West, exploring those moments along the way that served to prepare the ground for
"Iki" no kōzō. Rather than attempting a biography in the sense of an
imaginative reconstruction of a life — which might then become explanatory of an oeuvre — I have chosen to read biographical traces as allegory
for a broader social and discursive history, a history that has been largely
excised from Kuki's aesthetic enterprise. In this first chapter, I address
the less theoretical aspects of Kuki's transcultural itinerary — his complicated genealogy, both personal and historical, his Taishō education, his
European encounters. This background sketch raises the perplexing
questions that ultimately give shape to my reading of *"Iki" no kōzō:* Under what conditions did Kuki's cosmopolitan disposition lend itself to
an insular culturalism? By what logic did his modernist aesthetic tastes
become tempered by a resistance to social and historical modernity? In
what manner did his defense against Western racism become infiltrated
by Europe's exoticizing images of Japan, among (cultural) others? These
paradoxical problems set the scene for what I refer to as Kuki's "rhetorical return to Japan."

Steeped in the cultural cosmopolitanism of Taishō, Kuki left Japan in
search of the best Europe had to offer. During an extended eight-year
stay, to a degree rare among his Japanese colleagues, Kuki successfully
negotiated the peculiarities of European intellectual and social life. Not
one to confine himself to the study or seminar room, he ventured out
into the streets of Paris, visiting its urban scenery by day, its bistros and
brothels by night. In a 1936 essay titled "Shosai manpitsu" (Jottings in
My Study), Kuki defended the unconventional diversity of his interests — interests ranging from film and burlesque to pleasure outings and
carousing — which he feared some might find lacking in scholarly deco-
rum. In response to gestures of disapproval, imagined or real, Kuki
maintained that experience of any sort might become the occasion for
philosophical reflection: "It is my deepest felt conviction that a wide
experience is indispensable to the philosopher. For that reason, I have
expended great efforts not to be cast in the mold of 'university professor.'
I want to first experience all variety of things and then think through
those experiences from a different perspective. This is why I have not
spent all my time hunched over a desk."[1] The more personal of the
documents from his years in Europe suggest that Kuki moved with
grace and ease in European social circles, taking his pleasures in varied

1. Kuki, "Shosai manpitsu," *KSZ*, 5:42.

company. Yet it was during those same years in Europe that he began to turn his gaze back toward Japan with a desire to recover a cultural disposition that he believed to be threatened by the West. Sakabe Megumi, author of a recent study of Kuki, notes perceptively that the text of *"Iki" no kōzō* germinated in the highly charged space between Kuki's seduction by a Paris he considered his second home and his longing for a first home in Japan.[2] What were the conditions that precipitated Kuki's rhetorical return to Japan? And by what route did he make that return? Before addressing these questions directly, however, a brief account of what some consider to be Kuki's earliest encounter with the West is in order.

The Problem of Origins: Biography and History

It seems fitting to initiate this discussion of occidental beginnings with an episode concerning origins—the origins both of a life and of an intellectual project. The appearance of Kuki's collected works in 1981, some forty years after his death, provided an occasion less for the reassessment of an intellectual figure of the interwar years than for provocative exposés of the scandal surrounding his conception (an event that, in all likelihood, took place in the West). This scandal has insinuated itself into much of the scholarship addressing Kuki's writings. All too often, readers decipher in *"Iki" no kōzō* the traces of an ill-fated Oedipus complex, shifting the burden of explanation to questions of personal psychology. What is at stake in this Oedipalization of discourse? To answer that question, let us first consider the story that has provided so much grist for the Oedipal mill.

The story begins shortly before Kuki Shūzō's appearance in the world and soon after Japan's borders with the world had become largely permeable. It concerns a scandal implicating Meiji figures of nearly mythic proportions, one of whom was Kuki's father. Kuki Ryūichi (1852–1931), a provincial samurai with a pragmatic view toward the future, began his career in the early years of Meiji as a student of Fukuzawa Yukichi, Japan's foremost advocate of *bunmei kaika* (civilization and enlighten-

---

2. Sakabe, "Kuki Shūzō no sekai," (2) "Pari shinkei," 207. This is the second of a series of articles titled "Kuki Shūzō no sekai" by Sakabe in *Kikan asuteion*.

ment). At thirty-three, when he had already made his mark on the Ministry of Education as an architect of national culture for the new state, he was appointed to the post of Japanese ambassador to the United States. In the mid-1880's, Ryūichi arrived in Washington, D.C., with his wife Hatsu. As if to contrast with Ryūichi's brilliant career, the biography of Kuki's mother begins and ends in shadows. Renowned for her elegance and beauty, Hatsu was rumored to have a past in the Kyoto geisha district of Gion. She had come to the Kuki household as a second wife and bore three children to the successful bureaucrat before the family left on its diplomatic mission.

The biographical complications begin in America, with the appearance of Okakura Kakuzō (1862–1913), a person soon to make a name for himself both in Japan and the West as a preeminent interpreter of Japanese culture. On his return by way of America from an official survey of art in Europe, Okakura stopped off in Washington, D.C., to pay his respects to his senior colleague from the Ministry of Education, Kuki Ryūichi. It seems that just at the time of his visit, Hatsu was suffering from an unnamed ailment, the nature of which has remained unclear: a difficult pregnancy, some say, or the emotional anguish of an oppressive marriage. Both conjectures are telling in light of what was to transpire. Whatever the cause of Hatsu's condition, it was decided that she would return to Japan under the protection of Okakura. During the month-long journey, Okakura and Hatsu became involved in a love affair that had fateful consequences for their own lives and those of their families. Ultimately, the affair destroyed both households and precipitated the end of Okakura's bureaucratic career. Hatsu, overcome in the end by the miseries of a devastated marriage and an illicit liaison, withdrew into an increasingly impenetrable seclusion.[3]

Despite the fact that much labor has been expended on providing calendrical proof that Shūzō, the fourth child, was in fact the legitimate son of Ryūichi, the events that preceded his birth continue to cast a shadow of doubt on his paternity. That shadow lengthens even further in light of narrative details attending Shūzō's early years. A child divided between two estranged homes, Kuki came to know "Uncle Okakura" in

3. According to biographers, Hatsu's pleas for divorce after her return to Japan were refused by Ryūichi. He finally divorced her when she showed signs of insanity. Though the dates are unclear, Hatsu may well have spent the last thirty years of her life confined to a solitary corner in a hospital until her death in 1931. A devastated Okakura left for India in 1901, a trip that opened a new chapter in his life and work. See Ōka, "Hatsuko, Tenshin, Shūzō," 8–15.

his mother's house in the Negishi district of Tokyo.[4] Many years later, in a rare autobiographical revelation, Kuki would call Okakura his "spiritual father" and reminisce about the time when the mistress of a tea-shop mistook him for Okakura's son. An Okakura biographer writes that Kuki told close relatives, only half in jest, that Okakura could well be his real father.[5]

As might be imagined, this story has inspired a number of biographical essayists to explore the psychoanalytic possibilities of Kuki's entangled origins. It is not uncommon for writers of such essays to find the imprint of Oedipus on even the most philosophical of Kuki's texts. The most recent and the most compelling of these essays is the first article in Sakabe's series "The World of Kuki Shūzō." The title and subtitle of this first installment, closely translated, reads "The Shadow of Tenshin: On the Tracks of Longing for 'the Father' Locked in the Heart of the Philosopher Who Submitted Japan's Unique Spiritual Landscape to Analysis."[6] The article merits a close examination because it offers insight into the politics of a psychoanalytic approach.

In Sakabe's version, the dramatic circumstances surrounding Kuki's origins are decisive not only for a personality but also for an oeuvre: "Already from before birth in his mother's womb and extending through his childhood, Shūzō was pulled into the vortex of this drama. The atmosphere that enveloped him put a stamp so indelible on the mind of the young Shūzō that it determined the fundamental attributes not only of his character but also of his thought." This "indelible stamp" took the shape of an irrevocable and unresolvable Oedipus complex—a triangle with an added angle to accommodate two fathers: one father, real but forbidding; the other, unreal and the object of an Oedipal ambivalence wavering between love and rivalry. In sum, what Sakabe identifies in Kuki's psyche is a complicated Oedipal rectangle. Surrounded by discord, Kuki's unconscious solution, explains Sakabe, was to pose as the son of Okakura. As a self-styled illegitimate son, his existence was itself evidence of adulterous sin, a doubling of the guilt of the illicit couple.[7]

In the Oedipus complex as it was explicated by Freud, the boy—threatened (if only symbolically) with castration in reprisal for his fanta-

4. Kuki, "Negishi," *KSZ*, 5:227.
5. Sakabe, "Kuki Shūzō no sekai," (1) "Tenshin no kage," 196.
6. Ibid., 190.
7. Ibid., 194–95, 196–97.

sies of killing the father and possessing the mother — gives up the fantasy of murder and seduction in exchange for the lesser privilege of identifying with the father. The successful resolution of the complex allows for the restoration of a threatened cosmic order and the integration of the boy-child's personality. Such a resolution, suggests Sakabe, was not possible in Kuki's case. The father, split in two, has no clear identity for the child, the cosmos lies in ruins, and the cause of its destruction is lodged in the depths of the son's being. Marked by the sign of "anti-Oedipus," Kuki was left, says Sakabe, to shoulder a fate he would be compelled to think and act out until the end of his life.[8]

At this point, one might wish to supplement Sakabe's rendering of the Oedipus complex with a less narrowly personal revision. Certainly, the Lacanian rereading of Freud has forced Oedipus out of the closeted nuclear family into a larger linguistic and social nexus. Or, following the lead of Deleuze and Guattari, one might consider rejecting Oedipus wholesale as a parochially modern Western affair, a form of internal imperialism that has enabled Western societies to colonize interior subjectivity. However, if one delves further into Sakabe's analysis, one finds that Oedipus does in fact have social and political resonances, however muted. In fact, it is psychoanalysis that exonerates Kuki and his works from historical responsibility. Having first dramatized the childhood Oedipal upheaval, Sakabe traces the anti-Oedipal or "schizoid" contours of Kuki's thought, contours most clearly visible in Kuki's predilection for trilogies without dialectical resolution, a thesis and antithesis that never resolve into a synthetic unity. Kuki's intellectual project is eternally torn between eroticism and religious spirituality, between an admiration of Stoicism and a taste for Epicurianism. This, says Sakabe, is the discursive incarnation of the child's ruined cosmos without hope of reconciliation.

Here Sakabe's argument drifts into an explicitly political register. Deprived of a family model of integration and harmony, Kuki had no choice but to do without the security offered by fixed collectivities and assume the difficult burden of a thoroughgoing individualism rare in prewar Japan. Banished from the family circle into the lonely exile of a harsh individualism, how could Kuki have acceded to a "family-state," in other words, to an emperor-system ideology representing Japan as a family under the paternal authority of the emperor? Following up with another rhetorical question, Sakabe asks, "How could Kuki have had

8. Ibid., 197–99.

any commerce with the notion of the traditional community that thinkers like Watsuji and Nishida incorporated into their thinking?"[9] With
eloquent simplicity, Sakabe has enmeshed the child in a family scandal
only to rescue the intellectual from embroilment in what is considered
by a number of postwar Japanese thinkers to be a historical scandal—
the complicity of prewar intellectuals with a family-state ideology that
underwrote the repression and militarism of the 1930's and 1940's.

Clearly, at stake in Sakabe's Oedipalization of discourse are the ideological credentials of a single intellectual, an issue I will both rephrase
and rethink in the concluding chapter. But the wider and more fundamental question here is whether the historical and social dimensions of
discourse should be sacrificed at the altar of individual psychology.
What enables Sakabe to vindicate Kuki's thought politically is a tacit
disregard for the historical settings and textual networks in which *"Iki"
no kōzō* is interpolated. Rather than Oedipalize Kuki's writing, I have
chosen to historicize it. In a tactical reversal, I prefer to read the fragments of Kuki's biography as a metaphor for the more encompassing
ambiguities that marked the relations of early Shōwa cultural theory to
its historical antecedents. A reading such as this places Kuki at the troubled crossroads of Japan's modernity; it foreshadows the tensions tran-
secting his intellectual project—tensions between Japan and the West,
state and culture, past and present.

For the moment, then, let us consider the complexities of Kuki's parentage as symbolically suggestive of the intellectual genealogy of an era.
Obviously, the confusion surrounding Kuki's paternity evokes the problem of filiation in an intellectual project that argued for Japanese exceptionality in a language rooted in modern theoretical discourse. Furthermore, this personal drama metaphorically situates Kuki at the threshold
of a powerful reassessment of Enlightenment values. Kuki's antipathy
toward a father who had aligned his ambitions with those of the Meiji
state might signify the son's refusal to inherit the materialist and pragmatic ethos of *bunmei kaika*. He would then choose not to devote his
career to state-building and political power, at least not in the unambiguously official and public role of his father. Ultimately, Kuki suppressed
the disturbing memories not just of a personal past but also of a recent
collective history of modernization. The seductive but shadowed figure
of Kuki's mother, Hatsu, suggests the receding allure of the Edo geisha,
and along with her, of a more distant cultural past prior to Japan's West-

9. Ibid., 198.

ernized modernity. We might also speculate along with the biographers that something resembling Hatsu's image served as a beacon for Kuki's return to Japan following his cosmopolitan dalliance with European women.

Okakura, the third figure in this trilogy, played the role of pathfinder in the territory of cultural theory. To his "spiritual son" he bequeathed a plan showing how to transform the pre-Meiji past into a repository of cultural value. In an essay called "Okakura Kakuzō-shi no omoide" (Memories of Mr. Okakura Kakuzō), Kuki recalled that he was deeply impressed by Okakura's *Book of Tea* and *Ideals of the East,* adding that he read them in the original (English) during his stay in Europe.[10] Okakura, a onetime cultural administrator for the Ministry of Education who, through force of circumstance and personality, ended his life as an outsider, was one of the first major figures in modern Japan to discover in cultural theory an adequate substitute for politics. Okakura's endeavor, in *Ideals of the East,* to relocate the Hegelian dialectic from Europe to Asia anticipated Kuki's own adaptation of European theoretical strategies to the task of identifying Japan's difference from—and, ultimately, its superiority to—the West.

Many of Kuki's intellectual generation shared Okakura's perception that "the word 'modernization' means the occidentalization of the world."[11] But by the 1920's, what Okakura registered as a threat largely had become a reality. Okakura maintained that Japan's long period of relative isolation, *sakoku,* had transformed his country into the "living museum" of Asia. This conception of Japan's aesthetic mission had enduring impact on subsequent considerations of Japanese culture. Whether the haiku revival of Masaoka Shiki, the ethnography of Yanagita Kunio, or the cultural hermeneutics of Kuki and Watsuji, the cultural artifacts attesting to Japanese authenticity had become largely archival. At the turn of the century, Okakura was optimistic in his conviction that Japan's cultural credentials would remain intact in the Meiji atmosphere of internationalism and cultural exchange. A generation later, Kuki saw a need to call for a renewed *sakoku* in hopes of forestalling the obliteration of the Japanese spirit. Ironically, it was his long exposure to the West that brought him to this realization.

10. Kuki, "Okakura Kakuzō-shi no omoide," *KSZ,* 5:238.
11. Okakura, "Modern Problems in Painting," 76–86.

Migrant Mentors and the Cosmopolitan Disposition

In one of his more personal essays, Kuki recalls that during his middle-school years he had considered becoming a botanist. While the natural science of botany became an avocation rather than a career, his passion for collecting found an equally if not more efficacious application in the discipline of culture science. When Kuki entered the First Higher School in Tokyo in 1905, he initially chose to study German law with thoughts of a career in foreign diplomacy. He began his studies of the German language with Iwamoto Tei, an eccentric character much revered by his students despite a reputation for failing entire German language classes.[12] In his study of the elite higher schools in Meiji Japan, Donald Roden explains that Iwamoto was among those less-renowned philosophy graduates from Tokyo Imperial University who joined the higher school faculties at the turn of the century. Viewed by their students as "teachers of life" rather than as academic specialists, they "stressed the importance of cultivation from within, of self-examination, and of seeking new meaning in life in a realm of philosophy and art."[13] According to the memoirs of Watsuji and others, Iwamoto's punishments were strict, his favoritism blatant, his teaching methods unconventional.[14] In the liberal environment exclusive to this most elite of academic institutions, Iwamoto prepared his German-language students with only the briefest of grammatical training before immersing them in original texts. Kuki claims that it was Iwamoto who inspired him to change specializations from law to philosophy: "I learned my love of philosophy from *Sensei*. Although I might have made the deci-

12. Iwamoto is thought to be the model for Hirota-*sensei* in Natsume Sōseki's novel *Sanjurō*. This fictional teacher—given to didactic pronouncements on art, ethics, and the perils facing contemporary Japan—was referred to as the "Great Darkness" by his students. Nakano, "Kuki Shūzō," 136.

13. Roden, *Schooldays in Imperial Japan*, 161–62.

14. One can surmise from biographical fragments and memoirs of former Taishō-era students that the environment of the First Higher School was intensely homosocial, if not homoerotic, a circumstance that might be linked to the gender bias in the literary and philosophical discourse produced by its published graduates. I mention this in part because it provides a needed counterpoint to the claims of biographers who credit Kuki with a sympathy not only for the feminine but also for feminism. As we shall see, when woman becomes central to the discourse on culture, she becomes a sign manipulated in a discursive trade among men.

sion to leave law for the humanities on my own, if it hadn't been for *Sensei*, I cannot imagine that I would have ever majored in philosophy."[15] Whether one credits Iwamoto's idiosyncratic methods or his idealist inspiration, Kuki acquired a rare dedication to philosophy and multilingual credentials of the highest degree.

In 1909, Kuki began his studies in philosophy at Tokyo Imperial University under the guidance of Raphael Köber (1848–1923), a Russian of German extraction who played a major role in training a generation of Japanese philosophers and humanists.[16] A devoted adherent of German idealism and thoroughly schooled in the hermeneutic strategies of nineteenth-century humanism, Köber came to the university as a foreign specialist in 1909 on the recommendation of the philosopher Edmond von Hartman, who was hailed as the last of the great speculative idealists. Köber remained at his post until the outbreak of World War I.

One of Köber's more exceptional students, Watsuji, credits his expatriate mentor with raising the standard of philosophical studies in Japan and preparing the intellectual ground for *kyōyōshugi*. *Kyōyōshugi*, from the German *Bildung*, refers to a Taishō philosophical movement that extolled the virtues of self-cultivation, particularly in what concerned aesthetic, ethical, and spiritual accomplishments. Köber trained his students in the methods of philology, the key, in his view, to the riches contained in the sources of Western tradition. He instilled in them a profound reverence for *Geist*, a word that translates as "spirit" but that refers specifically to a tradition of inwardness, spirituality, and cultural refinement characteristic of nineteenth-century German neo-idealist thought. He encouraged the mastery of classical languages so that his Japanese students might discover for themselves the sources of this spiritual tradition in ancient Greece. Finally, he taught his students that beauty and art are the essence of culture. In the words of Sakabe, Köber "sowed the seeds of humanism in Japan."[17] For future reference, let us simply note Marx's observation that this humanist disposition was accompanied by a durable inclination to substitute an abstract "man" for people in specific social circumstances.

For those like Kuki and Watsuji who later would become prac-

15. Kuki, "Ikkō jidai no koyū," *KSZ*, 5:107.
16. Sakabe notes that Nishida Kitarō audited Köber's first year of lectures at Tokyo Imperial University. Among his students who became most widely known were Watsuji Tetsurō, Kuki Shūzō, and Iwashita Sōichi (a scholar of European medieval philosophy). Sakabe, "Kuki Shūzō no sekai," (1) "Tenshin no kage," 191–92.
17. Ibid., 193.

titioners of hermeneutics under the sway of Dilthey and Heidegger, Köber provided an early initiation into the art of interpreting cherished texts. As Sakabe astutely notes, the rediscovery of the Japanese past in early Shōwa was heavily indebted to the nineteenth-century European hermeneutic enterprise:

> The tradition of spirituality in Japan and the Orient was, in a manner of speaking, discovered anew through the mediation of Europe. More specifically, it was only after the Japanese had acquired the experience of the profound spirituality lodged within the tradition of the liberal arts and *humanismus* — a tradition creatively transmitted in the form of nineteenth-century hermeneutics and philology — that they rediscovered a tradition of similar proportions in Japan.[18]

Formulated in the context of nineteenth-century humanist scholarship, hermeneutics offered these Japanese theorists a mode for collective self-understanding through the selective appropriation of documents from the past.

The prevalence of German mentors and models in Taishō Japan was not without precedent. For the early Meiji travelers who went to Europe in pursuit of statecraft, the newly unified Germany — a Germany that had just emerged as the leading continental power in the 1870's under the strong arm of the Wilhelmian monarchy — was a fitting exemplar for Japanese national ambitions. The wavering (and eventually comatose) hero of Mori Ōgai's "Maihime" (The Dancing Girl), himself an aspirant to Japan's new bureaucratic elite, arrives in Berlin only to be overawed by "this most modern of European capitals."[19] The monumental space of Berlin's magnificent thoroughfare, Unter den Linden, stretching from the Brandenburg Gate to the Hapsburg Palace, reflects (and belittles) the hero's ambitions for himself and his country. Equally ambitious but more pragmatic than Ōgai's hero, the real architects of the Meiji state found their preferred model for state institutions in the conservative Prussian constitutional monarchy rather than in the more liberal Anglo-American or French traditions.

Like Germany, a relatively late-developing Japan underwent an accelerated transformation from an agrarian economy to urban, industrial capitalism. Perhaps because of that historical common ground, both societies sustained an intense intellectual reaction to the socially dislocat-

18. Ibid., 193.
19. Mori, "The Dancing Girl," 151–56.

ing—and for some, disenfranchising—forces unleashed by industrialization and modernization. In "A Sense of an Ending and the Problem of Taishō," Harry Harootunian discerns a growing tension in imperial Japan between progressive *embourgeoisement* and statist claims at the end of the Meiji era, a tension that gave way to a rupture between politics (in the narrow sense of the word) and culture.[20] Through strategic institutional arrangements, explains Harootunian, the new Meiji state effectively identified the public sphere with the emperor, prohibiting access to all but an elite core of official experts. A newly installed educational system functioned to transform the populace at large into loyal imperial subjects rather than a participatory citizenry. Yet even as the dynamic and open-ended era of *rikkoku* (establishment of the state) receded into history,[21] the massive social and economic reforms enacted by the new state had created the conditions for the emergence of private interest and individual ambition as a social force. With the end of Meiji came a sharp rise in demands from new constituencies for a greater share of national wealth and a larger role in the disbursement of social power. In turn, the state attempted to counter perceived excesses of self-interest by raising the stakes on political activity and further restricting the private sphere to ever more unpolitical forms of expression.

Within and against this disposition of power, an emerging middle class attempted to defend the autonomy of its own values from both a corporatist state and a materializing mass society. By the beginning of the Taishō era, intellectuals hailing from the highest echelons of the imperial educational system had come to express their aspirations in the neo-idealist idiom of culture. More than a few concluded that a rejection of politics was the best way to defend culture, choosing the ideality of subjective interiority over politics.[22] Kitamura Tōkoku (1864–1894), who came of age when the concept of *rikkoku* was fading into the historical archives, narrated not so much his disillusionment with politics but the displacement of his political aims from one medium to another:

I now aspired to become a great statesman, to make possible the revival of the Orient which was in a pitiable state of decline. . . . Oh, what madness it was to hold such thoughts for such a long time. . . . In 1885 I lost hope

20. Harootunian, "Introduction: A Sense of an Ending," 12–18. For the summary that follows, I am deeply indebted to this essay, as well as another essay by Harootunian in *Japan in Crisis:* "Between Politics and Culture," 110–55.

21. Fujita, *Nihon seishinshiteki kōsatsu,* 151.

22. Harootunian, "Between Politics and Culture," 128–30.

and was plunged into such despair that to some extent, I realized the wrongness of the thoughts I had hitherto maintained. At this point I aspired to become a novelist. But I did not think of becoming a creative artist, rather I wanted to be like Victor Hugo. Like Hugo I wanted to dominate a political movement with the brilliant power of my writing. It was at that time that I traveled and came to appreciate a change of scene and as a result of my association with all kinds of people I became a student of human sentiments.

Turning away from the corruption and crass materialism of practical politics, Tōkoku transformed himself into an architect of the self, an "engineer of the inner life."[23]

This elevation of the private sphere was not necessarily at odds with what is commonly referred to as "Taishō democracy," the liberalizing trends beginning after the Russo-Japanese War and extending through the 1920's. Sponsored largely by a new, urban middle class, Taishō democracy represented a sustained endeavor to extend political and civil rights more widely to newly nationalized masses.[24] The relative liberalism of the era is associated with the names of Minobe Tatsukichi (1873–1948), a constitutional legal theorist who transformed a deified emperor into an organ (albeit the supreme organ) of the state, and Hara Kei (1856–1921), prime minister from 1918 until his assassination, who presided over the uneasy expansion of party politics. But the figure who most tellingly represents the liberal position of the middle-class intelligentsia is Yoshino Sakuzō (1878–1933), a political historian and publicist who strove to give direction to the popular movements emerging in the first decades of the twentieth century. From the outset, Yoshino exhibited a reticence toward the enactment of mass sovereignty — a reticence revealed in his preference for the term *minponshugi* (government based on the people) over *minshushugi* (democracy) — and little "inclination to question fundamentally the raison d'être of the state."[25] Tetsuo Najita argues persuasively that Yoshino's critique of existing political institutions was based less on pragmatic political concerns than on a philosophy fed by the twin sources of Christian humanism and German neo-

---

23. Kōsaka, *Japanese Thought in the Meiji Era*, 271, 286.

24. These first decades of the twentieth century did, in fact, witness a decline in the dominance of traditional political elites — the *genrō*, or "elder statesmen," and the Privy Council — and a relative increase in power for the Diet and political parties.

25. Matsumoto, "The Roots of Political Disillusionment," 40–41. See also Kuno, "The Meiji State, Minponshugi, and Ultranationalism," 70–71.

idealist philosophy.[26] Troubled by the rise of factional strife and special-interest politics and apprehensive over the radically leftist turn in political criticism, Yoshino finally rejected practical political organization and parliamentary institutions in favor of democracy as a "pure metaphysical ideal." In Najita's words, "[Yoshino] now hypothesized that individuals could disengage themselves completely from external institutional constructs. Men, he argued, were totally autonomous spiritual entities, separated from any external organization and its will. . . . Men, he concluded, were by nature spiritual, and as such they created their own personalities from within, and, in turn, fashioned culture around them."[27] Along with other middle-class theorists of Taishō democracy, Yoshino had inherited the disposition toward interiority and the privatized expression of ideals first formulated by Kitamura Tōkoku.

Neither pragmatic nor revolutionary, Yoshino justified his reservations toward participatory democracy through recourse to German theories of cultural distinctiveness and "national spirit." And despite his leanings toward a Christian cosmopolitanism, Yoshino relied on a Hegelian dialectic to uphold the sovereign nation as the site of *Geist,* a spirit that insured historical continuity and national identity. In his endeavor to reconcile the universal ideals of enlightenment thought with the nationalist faith in the distinctiveness of cultures—the dual legacy of the Meiji era, according to Najita—Yoshino gave voice to the popular spirit of Taishō democracy that embraced, at least in its early stages, belief in "constitutionalism at home and imperialism abroad."[28]

This precarious balance between universal ideals and national spirit was also implicit in the philosophical cosmopolitanism circulating in the Taishō institutions of higher learning where Kuki received his education. As an intellectual movement, cosmopolitanism was closely associated with the literary and artistic *Shirakabaha* (White Birch Society), but also with the Japanese dissemination of German idealist thought, particularly neo-Kantianism. Marked by a penchant for universal ideals and a desire to cultivate a (generalized) "humanity" in accordance with

26. Najita, "Idealism in Yoshino's Political Thought," 61–62.
27. Ibid., 57.
28. Ibid., 31–32; Matsuo, *Taishō demokurashī no gunzō,* 2–4. Matsuo makes the point that the era of Taishō democracy overlapped with the precipitous consolidation and expansion of Japanese imperialism. He locates the beginnings of the movement in popular opposition to the Portsmouth Treaty (1905), the settlement mediated by the United States at the end of the Russo-Japanese War. Newly nationalized masses who had shouldered the burdens of war and took pride in victory perceived the treaty as overly conciliatory toward a defeated Russia.

ethical and aesthetic norms, the cosmopolitan disposition is perhaps most vividly captured in the self-portrait of *Santarō no nikki* (The Diary of Santarō) by philosopher Abe Jirō (1883–1959). Standing as a discursive monument to Taishō cosmopolitanism, *Santarō no nikki* was received with great enthusiasm in 1914 by a youthful audience. Santarō, a fictional diarist, records the migrations of his interior life in a confessional mode. It is deep within the self, maintains Santarō, rather than in external necessity, that the universal values of Goodness, Truth, and Beauty lie. "The only conversations that interest me now," he claims solipsistically, "are with myself." Turning his back on the futility of the present, he feels sympathy with the poet-philosophers of old and "walks the great road of life." Why does the diarist commit his personal quest to print? "The cry of one individual in the dark seeking the light" will, he claims, "serve as a reference for others and benefit the world of thought."[29] A "truth seeker" priding himself on his superiority to "the child of society," Santarō styles himself a "missionary" for spiritual enlightenment.[30] His creator, incidentally, would soon seek Japanese roots for that enlightenment in the Tokugawa era.

This Taishō version of cosmopolitanism necessarily implied an elitist disposition. The humanist virtues it extolled were acquired by means of an education — education in the sense of the formation of character through exposure to art and philosophy — that required a considerable degree of leisure and wealth. The cosmopolitan concentration on values of an intangible and universal nature encouraged adherents to withdraw into an expanded and enriched realm of interiority while distancing themselves from more immediate and more material social realities. Beyond an abstract relation between individual character and a generalized (and cultivated) humanity, there were no half measures for engaging with a compromised outer world.

In the Japanese intellectual context, cosmopolitanism also meant that thinkers and writers continued the practice, initiated during the Meiji era, of turning to the West, primarily western Europe, in search of master texts. Inspired to inquire at the source, many traveled to the West in search of knowledge and experience. Like their Meiji predecessors, these intellectual travelers were interpreters rather than rote imitators of Western modes of knowledge. The immense and continuing labor of transla-

29. Abe, *Santarō no nikki*, 13–17. *Santarō no nikki* was published in two parts, appearing respectively in 1914 and 1929.
30. Roden, *Schooldays in Imperial Japan*, 213.

tion, beginning in the mid-nineteenth century, from European languages to Japanese demanded interpretation and elicited ongoing
critique. But unlike the previous Meiji generation, the Taishō students
who set their sights on the West were no longer primarily in search of
pragmatic and utilitarian knowledge oriented toward the public goals
of modernization and state building. The accomplishment of those practical goals had produced a new appreciation for private interest in Japanese society. By late Meiji, the consolidation of an overbearing state that
narrowly limited entry to the political sphere compelled private interest
to seek expression in an autonomous and interiorized realm of subjectivity. From the perspective of the new Taishō intellectual, often disaffected
from politics and the state, the Meiji ideal of *bunmei,* or civilization, had
taken on the pejorative sense of crass materialism and dubious pragmatism. In its place, Taishō thinkers raised the banner of *bunka,* a translation of the German *Kultur.*[31] Soon after World War I, Thomas Mann
articulated the distinction between the two terms with the utmost economy: "Culture equals true spirituality, while civilization means mechanization."[32] With the expansion of technology and rationalization, the
term "civilization," once the worldly (and European) ideal of human
progress, now suggested a threatening process of dehumanization. In
contrast, the term *Kultur* restored with its semantic resonances a humanity at risk — not, however, without adding its own burden of ideological weight. Thomas E. Willey, in his study of the nineteenth-century
neo-Kantians, remarks that the notion of *Kultur* was "steeped in nostalgia for preindustrial times and immersed in a reverence for its own classical heritage."[33]

Though in later years Kuki's lectures included lengthy discussions of
British utilitarianism, he was all but silent on the noteworthy history of
its dissemination in Meiji Japan.[34] In an essay published in the 1928 edi-
tion of *Nouvelles littéraires,* Kuki rewrote Meiji intellectual history for his
French readers, suggesting that Japan had never been captivated by the

31. Harootunian, "Introduction: A Sense of an Ending," 15–17.

32. Braudel, *On History,* 182, citing Thomas Mann from *Manuel de sociologie* by Ar-
mand Cuvillier, (Paris, 1954), 2:670.

33. Willey, *Back to Kant,* 14. Willey adds that the development of the notion of *Kultur*
signified the awakening of bourgeois talent in late-nineteenth-century Germany. The same
may be said about a Japanese intellectual bourgeoisie in the early decades of this century.

34. According to Thomas R. H. Havens, positivism and, to an even greater degree,
utilitarianism circulated widely in Japan during the better part of the Meiji era. A number
of John Stuart Mill's works were translated and reissued through the turn of the century.
"Comte, Mill," 221.

instrumental virtues of civilization celebrated by Spencer and Mill: "Fortunately, the Japanese spirit was not receptive to [utilitarianism]. We turned away from it without having found any satisfaction. More recently, when this same utilitarianism, in the guise of 'pragmatism,' tried to gain entry in our home, we knew how to politely close our doors."[35] When Kuki arrived in Europe in 1922, he sought entry at the gates of those European thinkers who were critically reassessing their own inheritance of secular rationalism and instrumental reason. But before expanding on Kuki's intellectual encounters in Europe, let me first explore some of the less scholarly outlets for his cosmopolitan tastes.

Parisian Predilections

Paris in the mid-1920's held a special attraction for Kuki, inspiring collections of poetry with titles such as *Pari shinkei* (Paris Mindscapes), *Pari no negoto* (Paris Sleep Talk), and *Pari no mado* (Windows of Paris).[36] What is perhaps most striking about these otherwise unremarkable poems is the obsessive frequency with which the names of Parisian women, Parisian landmarks, and Parisian styles are reiterated, as if the aura created by the foreign names alone guaranteed success in Japan's literary marketplace. Like an eroticized *Guide bleu*, Kuki's poetry suggests an affinity with the Japanese *sharebon* of the late Edo period, highly literate guides to the Edo pleasure quarters for discerning readers. In fact, Kuki had his own reputation for being adept at *asobi* — "play," in the sense of erotic commerce and stylized consumption. Paradoxically, in *"Iki" no kōzō*, the notion of play takes on serious tones, invoking as it does both an idealized ethos of the Edo pleasure quarters and the domain of post-Kantian aesthetics. It was between those dual addresses that Kuki sought cultural authenticity and the structure of Japanese being.

Among the notebooks dating from Europe is a single unlabeled one, its pages filled with names — "Madame Reine," "Maria Nosegay," "Mlle. Suzy" — each followed by an establishment, an address, and, not infre-

---

35. Kuki, "Bergson au Japon," *KSZ*, 1:261.

36. Much of this poetry was published in 1926 and 1927 editions of *Myōjō*, the poetry journal of Yosano Tekka and Yosano Akiko, under the penname Omori Keizō. It has been reprinted as *Pari shinkei* in *KSZ*, 1:107–218.

quently, a ranking. A stray page lists names alone, here more for phonetic resonance than for practical reference. Even before Kuki's departure for Europe, there had been stories of evening pleasures in
Shinbashi, an entertainment district in Tokyo, and after his return, there
were rumors of early-morning commutes to the university from the teahouses in the Gion geisha district. For his library shelves, along with
scholarly works on Edo culture and art, Kuki collected illustrated guides
to Japan's most celebrated geisha. One might even say that prostitutes
and demimondaines marked the crucial sites in the imaginary mapping
Kuki superimposed on the cities he inhabited—Tokyo, Paris, Kyoto.

What lesson is to be drawn from Kuki's overlapping interests, both
theoretical and practical, in the boulevards and bistros of 1920's Paris,
the teahouses and cafes of 1930's Gion, and the pleasure quarters of Kaseiki Edo? First, whatever the chosen context—Europe or Japan, past
or present—Kuki presents the image of a latter-day *tsū,* a dandy-
connoisseur of the pleasure quarters. Reminiscences of Kuki rarely leave
out his impeccable taste and sense of style. In the 1930's, on the campus
of Kyoto Imperial University, when most of his colleagues dressed in
kimono, Kuki had a reputation for the fine tailoring of his European
suits. The dandylike persona that Kuki cultivated both in his personal
life and in his writing was perhaps less at home in the intimacy of the
close-knit *machi* (neighborhoods) of Edo than in the isolation and anonymity of the modern metropolis.

Not only did Kuki have the air of an urban exile about him, but his
long sojourn in Europe, coming as it did between a permanent move
from Tokyo to Kyoto, seems to have confused the issue of his provenance: "In Tokyo, people treat me as if I were from Kyoto," Kuki wrote,
"while in Kyoto, they treat me as though I were a Tokyoite."[37] What is
clear, however, is his thoroughly cosmopolitan and urbane sensibility.
As a quasi-expatriate, Kuki resembled the European modernists who
gathered, whether by choice or necessity, in the cultural capitals of Europe. In the unpublished essay "Tokyo and Kyoto," Kuki begins by taking issue with his former mentor, Köber *Sensei.* To Köber's claim that
one could practice philosophy anywhere, Kuki argues that "the place
one lives will naturally be reflected in his philosophy." In Kuki's view,
Kyoto was a city suffused with nature and history; Tokyo, on the other
hand, was virtually without either. But for the flavor of contemporary
life, along with its most desirable commodities, Kyoto was no match

37. Kuki, "Tōkyō to Kyōto," *KSZ,* 5:190.

for Tokyo. Referring to at least one section of his own itinerary, Kuki expresses the hope that the "content of his thought would reflect the richness of Tokyo while the form would mirror the tranquility of Kyoto."[38] Arguably, the form of Kuki's philosophy reflected less the local ambiance of Kyoto than the transnational range of his intellectual migrations.

As for Kuki's more remote destinations, the new metropolitan cities of Europe, most notably Paris, presented themselves as transnational capitals of an art without frontiers. In reality, as Raymond Williams points out, these were also centers of a new imperialism, where "the old hegemony of capital over its provinces was extended over a new range of disparate, often totally alien and exotic, cultures and languages."[39] It was this geopolitical reality that tempted Europeans to pursue their aesthetic and philosophical interests in the East. Conversely, the accompanying representation of the West as "the moment of the universal under which particulars are subsumed" lured Kuki into Western geographical and discursive domains and cast its shadow over his inquiry into the particularity he called Japan.[40] In such circumstances, Kuki could hardly avoid equivocation; subject to the expansive gestures of aesthetic and philosophical modernism, he was also suspicious of, even rebellious toward, its claim to universality.

Kuki's affinity for modernism extended beyond the realm of everyday taste to his literary and philosophical interests as well. This was especially evident in the existentialist treatises on *gūzensei* (contingence) that he published during his years of tenure at Kyoto Imperial University. Here, Kuki developed the notion of *kaikō*, the fortuitous encounter, and assigned to it an initiatory significance in the domains of philosophy, aesthetics, and sociality. Premised on the absence of any causal or necessary relation, the fortuitous encounter occurs with utter unpredictability, placing the self in a dynamic relation to an other. Confronted with the sudden and problematic manifestation of difference, the astonished self posits the possibility of the other in its own future. This accidental encounter with the other marks the inception of desire. Rarely speculating on what might follow a single encounter, Kuki preferred instead to imagine an infinite repetition of fortuitous encounters never pursued to the end. Read alongside the poems and biographical fragments, the notion of *kaikō* suggests not the "knowable community" belonging to a

38. Ibid., 5:191–92, 5:194.
39. Williams, *The Politics of Modernism,* 77–78.
40. Sakai, "Modernity and Its Critique," 477.

bucolic or precapitalist past but Baudelaire's "love at last sight," the
fleeting glance exchanged by strangers, guarded from familiarity by the
density and anonymity of the modern city.[41]

Kuki's stylistic discernment, his taste for urban pleasures, and his predilection for prostitutes and games of chance, recall the modernist portraits of the French poet he most admired, Charles Baudelaire. The poet
of *Les fleurs du mal* figures prominently in *"Iki" no kōzō*, more prominently, in fact, than Kuki's culturally particularist thesis should have allowed. Peering out from the structural foundations of *"Iki" no kōzō* is
the portrait of the dandy so distinctively drawn by Baudelaire. What
were the qualities attracting Kuki to that protomodernist figure? One
was the dandy's "aristocratic superiority of mind," his "love of distinction in all things." The dandy was a man with "no other calling but to
cultivate the idea of beauty in [his] person, to satisfy [his] passions, to
feel and to think." In addition to the attribute of good taste, the dandy
possessed a disposition of mind that set him apart from the ordinary.
The possessor of an implacable will and extraordinary pride, he rebelled
(in spirit) against the status quo and maintained an imperturbable posture of cool detachment.[42]

Though Kuki retraced the features of Baudelaire's dandy for his own
portrait of *iki*, he did not demonstrate Baudelaire's trenchant insight
into the social context that gave rise to this particular social type. Baudelaire astutely located his narcissistic rebel in a period of transition when
"democracy is not yet all powerful and aristocracy is only just beginning
to totter and fall." A figure displaced in an era when social distinctions
were crumbling, the dandy established a new version of aristocracy
based on style. Protesting against the division of labor and the industri-
ousness of a society yielding to bourgeois domination, the dandy pa-
raded his leisure on the streets of modernizing cities. His basic requirements consisted of time and money, both in unlimited supply.[43]

The quest of Baudelaire's dandy for distinction in the face of cultural
leveling and social rationalization has powerful implications for Kuki's
project. The Japanese dandy-philosopher shared with Baudelaire a perception that modernity threatened to replace the particularity of experience and a meaningful past with mediocrity and a dull uniformity. But

41. See Benjamin's exposition of Baudelaire's poem "À une passante" (To a Passerby)
in *Charles Baudelaire*, 44–46.
42. Baudelaire, *The Painter of Victorian Life*, 127–32.
43. Ibid.

unlike Baudelaire, Kuki maintained virtual silence concerning the social conditions that generated his own discourse on *iki*, whether those belonging to his own moment in history or to Edo a century earlier. In his reading of Edo, the pleasure quarters appear as a landscape of the spirit, abstracted from the nexus of money and class in which they once had been embedded. In his reading of the contemporary cultural map, he concealed an apprehension of a proliferating mass culture behind the veneer of a common cultural endowment.

But before Kuki retraced his steps back to a homogeneous Japan in *"Iki" no kōzō*, the seductive elegance of *iki* was sufficiently cosmopolitan to be susceptible to cross-cultural grafting. In the mid-1920's, the aesthetic style of *iki* was assimilated, if only provisionally, to the Parisian scene. In a poem titled "Sakana ryōriya" (Seafood Restaurant), the poet imagines escorting his Parisian companion to Prunier, taking the opportunity to display his culinary and aesthetic tastes. Assuming the coquettish voice of his feminine companion, the poet inventories her attire in free verse:

Dressed in black silk
My figure will shimmer
   against silvery walls,
A chaste white rose at my breast
A strand of pearls at my throat
Around my wrist, a platinum watch
And on my finger, a white diamond ring.
A hat, the color of sea grass,
   Set low at a seductive slant.
Allow me a touch of red on my lips,
And tell me once more I'm your princess of the sea.[44]

Here, the Parisienne, her hat cocked rakishly over one eye (*iki ni kaburu*), partakes of the subtle allure of *iki*. Other poems discover *iki* in the sultry voice of a chanteuse or in a young boy's discernment in matters of the heart. Nevertheless, at the same time that Kuki was lyricizing the allure of *iki* in Paris, he already had begun to store lists of "things Japanese" in a file folder labeled "'Iki' ni tsuite" (Concerning "Iki").[45] Con-

44. Kuki, *Pari shinkei*, KSZ, 1:119–20.
45. Though the dates during which Kuki compiled this file are unclear, one biographer suggests that he started collecting notes on the subject of *iki* even before he left for Europe. Publication dates of texts cited in these lists and notes indicate that he continued to file data even after the completion of an early draft in 1926.

sensus has it that Kuki began to devote serious attention to the aesthetics of *iki* during the latter half of his stay in Europe.

Race, Woman, and the Return to Japan

The poems produced during Kuki's years abroad bear
witness not only to a fascination with Paris, but also to a troubling sense
of difference and exclusion. In one titled "Kiiroi kao" (Yellow Face),
Kuki constructs a series of Europe-centered discourses on Asians, each
in the voice of a different European persona. The "common man" won-
ders whether the Oriental suffers from jaundice. The Positivist suggests
that perhaps his ancestors overindulged in pumpkins and water from
the Yellow River; the metaphysician claims that the yellow races were
stigmatized for insulting the gods in a prior world. Finally, the episte-
mologist posits a category for the concept of a yellow race, but only as
an afterthought.[46] Since the tone betrays no trace of irony, one might
speculate that Kuki endeavored to reproduce fragments of actual discourse. Much later, when he wrote his philosophical treatises on contingence, Kuki noted with obsessive frequency the contingent character
of race. To illustrate the notions of "exteriority" and "exceptionality,"
principal attributes of contingence, Kuki invoked the image of a single
Japanese in Europe, perceived as yellow—and hence "contingent"—
because white skin was perceived by Europeans as both the rule and an
essential human attribute.[47]

Certainly there is no lack of evidence for virulent strains of racism in
Europe during the 1920's and 1930's. Since Meiji, Japanese travelers to
the West had documented varieties of racism in Europe and America,
whether directed at themselves or others. Among writers, this awareness
often took the form of denigrating self-portraits painted through the
imagined eye of the racist viewer. Mori Ōgai, one of the more self-
assured Japanese sojourners in Europe, imagined the protagonist of
"Maihime" (The Dancing Girl) as sallow and strange among the German crowds. Natsume Sōseki, observing the "tall and good-looking"

46. Kuki, *Pari shinkei, KSZ,* 1:143–44.
47. See for example *Gūzensei no mondai, KSZ,* 2:24; "Gūzensei ni kansuru ronkō,"
KSZ, 2:277–78; "Gūzensei" (lecture delivered at Ōtani University in 1929), *KSZ,* 2:325–26.

English who passed him in the streets, suddenly came across a different figure, a distorted image of self-estrangement and degradation:

Then I see a dwarf coming, a man with an unpleasant complexion — and he happens to be my own reflection in the shop window. I don't know how many times I have laughed at my own ugly appearance right in front of myself. Sometimes I even watched my reflection that laughed as I laughed. And every time that happened, I was impressed by the appropriateness of the term "yellow race."

Sōseki was more than half convinced that he and his fellow Japanese were despicable, and even if they had deserved the respect of Europeans, he mused, the Europeans would "have no time to know us and no eyes to see us."[48] In this last observation Sōseki was describing what has more recently been referred to as racial seeing — a form of (mis)vision rooted in an unequal distribution of geopolitical power — a vision that blots out the existence of an individual and replaces it with the generic features of race.

Though Kuki himself left no diaries or memoirs from his European years, we have one description of him from that time in Herman Glockner's *Heidelberger Bilderbuch,* a description as favorable as it is racially telling. Here Glockner reproduces the words of his mentor, Heinrich Rickert, who is fresh from his first encounter with Kuki:

Today I made arrangements to give a private tutorial to a Japanese. He is a rich samurai from the Land of Enchantment and he has asked me to read Kant's *Critique of Pure Reason* with him. A gentleman of exceptional aristocratic bearing, he gives a completely different impression from other Japanese. He is tall and slender with an oval face. The nose is almost European; the hands, extraordinarily delicate and graceful. His name is Baron Kuki; he tells me it means "nine devils."[49]

Perhaps it is an exaggeration to claim that Kuki encouraged the exoticization of his person and place of origin by reviving the dead metaphor, "nine devils," buried in his own name. Be that as it may, Kuki's exceptional status in Rickert's eyes as an honorary European only proves the rule of racial seeing.

Following his last stay in Paris, on the journey by sea back to Japan

48. Natsume Sōseki, "A Letter from London," quoted and translated in Miyoshi, *Accomplices of Silence,* 57. Cited from *Natsume Sōseki zenshū,* 12:36, 13:87.

49. Ishimatsu, "Haiderubāgu no Kuki Shūzō," 4.

in 1929, Kuki wrote several essays, among them a defense of Japanese culture. In "Nihon no bunka" (Japanese culture), Kuki touched on the subject of Lafcadio Hearn, an American writer of mixed European parentage who spent the latter half of his life in Japan with his wife, who happened to be Japanese. Not infrequently, Kuki reported, Europeans would ask him what could possibly have possessed Lafcadio Hearn to return to Japan; how, they wondered, could a Westerner "in his right mind" have married a Japanese woman? As if to blunt the edge of a brutally racist and obviously rhetorical question, Kuki offered the overly generous explanation that such suspicions arose from Europe's lack of understanding of Japanese culture. But the exchange is significant, too, for its linkage of the feminine image to questions of race and nationality. In *"Iki" no kōzō*, the nationally — and by implication, racially — inscribed feminine figure serves as the principal sign of Japanese cultural authenticity. In that text, Kuki rediscovered, for himself and for readers, the allure of the Japanese woman, and along with her, the "beauty of Japanese culture."[50] It was not, however, the contemporary "modern girl" who Kuki recognized but rather the rarefied and exoticized image of the Edo geisha.

This redirection of connoisseurship in exotic images of femininity from the French demimonde to the Edo geisha quarters brings to mind a contemporary but fictional example from Tanizaki's *Tade kuu mushi* (Some Prefer Nettles). The protagonist, Kaname (a name signifying pivot or turning point), seeking escape from a passionless marriage with an aspiring modern woman, succumbs to the charms of Louise, a prostitute of dubious racial origins. Kaname, by virtue of some credentials never specified, has managed to pay his visits to Louise in Mrs. Brent's exclusive, quasi-colonialist brothel in Kobe's international enclave. Louise's hybrid body is irresistibly seductive, her genius for racial disguise suggestively sinister. Painstakingly powdered from head to toe, her body combines the white radiance of European power and the dark (flawed) traces of oriental mystery: "He found something of his longing for Europe satisfied in his relations with Louise," yet it was "the dark glow of her skin, with its faint suggestion of impurity, that had attracted Kaname." This duskiness of Louise's skin, tainted by the exotic, is the first marker in the hero's uneasy awakening to the "intolerable dislocation" caused by his cosmopolitan tastes.[51] From this awakening begins

50. Kuki, "Nihon no bunka," *KSZ*, 1:233–36.
51. Tanizaki, *Some Prefer Nettles*, 160–62, 171.

his self-imposed seduction by the traditional beauty of Kansai (the Kyoto-Osaka region in western Japan, less quick to modernize than Tokyo in the east). Although Kuki preferred the medium of theoretical discourse rather than novelistic narrative, like Tanizaki, he also would return to an exoticized Japan via a seduction by racialized femininity.

A Collector of Japanese Taste

Kuki's first undated writing on *iki,* reproduced in his collected works as "'Iki' ni tsuite," favored the form of lists arranged by category: those things that evoked *iki* and those that did not; natural objects, sensory objects, and art objects; relations between *iki* and other terms of taste. Under the heading "Sounds," for example, Kuki listed skylarks, bushwarblers, wild geese, ducks, frogs, water, rain, and falling leaves. Under "Design," he meticulously documented the kimono designs that dominated various periods during the Tokugawa era. Once determining that vertical stripes, so typical of *iki,* gained popularity as a kimono design during the early nineteenth century, he proceeded to enumerate the multiple varieties of vertical stripes: *sensuji* (a thousand lines), *mijinjima* (line-thin stripes), *komochijima* (alternating thick and thin stripes), *yatarajima* (a striped medley), and more.[52]

In these innumerable lists, Kuki often invoked his objects through the intermediary of poetry, song, and fiction — an early sign of his faith, later to be reinforced by hermeneutics, that art could guide one to the heart of meaning and value. At this stage, Kuki gathered his literary allusions with a relative lack of discrimination, ranging widely through history, from the tenth-century *Kokinshū*[53] and Bashō's seventeenth-century haiku to contemporary poetry. Later, he would narrow his focus to the popular culture of late Edo: *gesaku* (playful and parodic fiction), *nagauta* (long narrative songs, often an accompaniment in the Kabuki theater), Kabuki dialogue, and *ukiyoe* (woodblock prints). This process of historical sifting represents the labor of scholarship, a labor that had already commenced in the notes of "'Iki' ni tsuite." In the final version

---

52. Kuki, "'Iki' ni tsuite," in *KSZ,* special volume, 22–26.

53. The *Kokinshū* was the first of many collections of poetry compiled under imperial order. Completed in 905, the *Kokinshū* contains 1,111 poems, almost all *waka,* a traditional thirty-one-syllable poem that has dominated the Japanese poetic tradition. See Keene, ed., *Anthology of Japanese Literature,* 1:76.

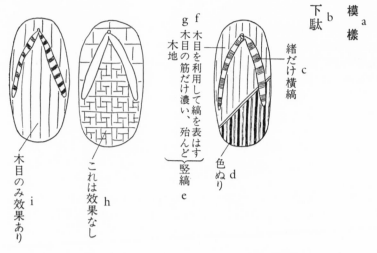

a design
b wooden sandals
c horizontal stripes only on thong
d stained color
e vertical stripes
f stripes expressed using the grain of the wood
g only the grain of the wood is dark, the rest is plain, unstained wood
h this is without effect
i only the grain of the wood has the proper effect

j architecture
k window
l bamboo
m wall
n wood (simple)
o stone wall
p the entire effect is realized in the bamboo on the windows

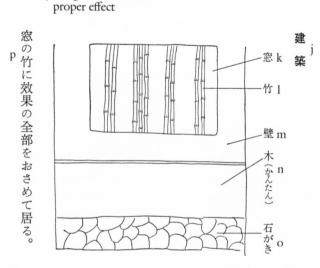

Figure 2. Kuki's sketches of *geta* (wooden sandals) and teahouse architecture from "'Iki' ni tsuite"

of *"Iki" no kōzō,* the carefully cited and copious references to encyclopedias of Edo custom, Kabuki, haiku, and *gesaku* would largely disappear. Kuki chose to present his archival scholarship as if it were a second nature shared by all Japanese.

Kuki supplemented the notes with sketches of the objects that expressed the taste he endeavored to define (Figure 2), whether teahouse facades, kimono patterns, or designs for Japanese *geta* (wooden sandals; Figure 2). In the drafts that followed, however, these visual representations disappeared from the text, leaving language to bear the full burden of representation. In the interval between his first notes and the final draft, Kuki shifted his focus from the tangible objects of taste to the interiority of its subjects. As we shall see, *iki* was to become a disposition of the soul, inward and metaphysical rather than manifest and material.

Nevertheless, Kuki began with a world of things accessible to the senses, his interpretive comments directly linked to the objects he invoked. For a vocabulary of taste and visual images of style he relied on recently published compendia of Edo *fūzokushi* (histories of customs and mores): *Reflections on the Customs of the Tokugawa Era, A History of Japanese Society in the Premodern Era, An Edo Miscellany.* For the most part, these were reference works that described in the most concrete terms the material culture and colloquial language of the Tokugawa era, documenting the changes in fashion and custom from generation to generation. Under a typical entry for *iki,* Kuki would have found descriptions dwelling almost exclusively on appearances. Based on his readings from one of these works, Kuki jotted down the following characteristics for *iki:* contrast, asymmetry, delicate subtlety, simplicity; under each, he appended appropriate fashions and styles.

One can almost imagine him sitting in the study of his Paris apartment, turning the pages of *An Edo Miscellany,* his gaze lingering on an illustration of a Yoshiwara prostitute, her hairdo alluringly casual, or a Fukagawa geisha, her elongated figure enhanced by a kimono of slender stripes, her sash tied at a suggestive slant. The working women, "flappers," and chorus girls who occupied the Paris streets just outside Kuki's window could hardly have provided a more striking contrast.

Kuki prefaced a short piece from the Paris years titled "À la manière d'Hérodote" with the following words: "Just as their sky is different and their rivers have a different nature from those in other countries, the Japanese are the complete opposite of the Europeans in their customs and habits." He then made two lists, briefly contrasting Japanese and European customs. Under *onna* (woman), Kuki wrote in French that Japanese women are "more feminine and polite than men." In France, on the other hand, it was the men who were said to be more feminine and polite; the women, wrote Kuki, "act like army commanders." Japanese women wear an *obi* (sash) to protect themselves from attack by men; French men button themselves up in defense against assault by women.[54] Behind Kuki's redirected taste for a distinctively Japanese allure we begin to discern an acute discomfort with the increasingly active presence, socially and sexually, of a modern woman seeking emancipation.[55]

What Kuki neglected to acknowledge in his short pieces from the Paris years was the fact that the 1920's had brought striking change to Japan as well as to Europe. Within a drastically modernized Japanese cityscape, the "modern girl" was out in force, strolling the Ginza and laboring in new jobs on streetcars, in factories, in offices, and in cafés. Separated from the Edo artifacts he described by a distance both spatial and temporal, Kuki was moved by a nostalgic longing for an imaginary past and beset by an anxiety over a transfigured present. With the clarity of his representations he hoped to recall the fading image of a past he himself projected.

One of his sketches depicts the alignment of flagstones on a Kyoto street. As one approaches the corner, Kuki explains, the eye momentarily perceives the stones in vertical parallels rather than diagonal lines. At that moment, *iki* comes into play, awakening desire in the perceiver.[56] Beyond the dry precision of Kuki's language, the reader detects the note taker's investment in a habitat already destined to disappear or to be preserved as a historical relic. The most faithful and the most lyrical chronicler of that vanishing habitat was Nagai Kafū (1879–1959), renowned novelist and diarist. In his discursive ramblings through a rapidly reconstructing Tokyo, Kafū lamented the loss of sentimental sites and deplored the wreckage caused by careless "progress": "As I amble

54. Kuki, "À la manière d'Hérodote," *KSZ*, 1:246–47. This is one of a series of short essays collected under the title "Choses japonaises," inspired perhaps by Chamberlain's "Things Japanese," a compendium of Japanese exotica. Though the editors of the *zenshū* surmise that all of these essays were written during Kuki's stay in Paris, it is unclear whether any were actually published or presented publicly there, other than the first essay, "Bergson au Japon."

55. In later philosophical writings, Kuki would find women ill-equipped for an existential adventure reserved exclusively for a male-gendered humanity; women were assigned to a different and lesser category of their own. "Ningen to wa nani ka," *KSZ*, 3:40–41.

56. Kuki, "'Iki' ni tsuite," 30.

down the new concrete highways . . . I see . . . that I must shed my old notions of beauty as a cicada sheds its shell." The city no longer offered "a delicate balance between the moods of the writer and the facts of his life."[57] Between jabs at the purveyors of thoughtless modernization, Kafū did in fact manage to recreate that delicate balance between mood and fact through elegiac renderings of encounters between memory, traces of a vanishing past, and jarring interruptions of novelty.

Compared with Kafū, Kuki was a less lyrical but more methodical collector of Edo relics.[58] And unlike Kafū, Kuki spent little time bemoaning the losses suffered to modernization. Rather, he believed the spirit that had created Edo artifacts was still very much intact, even in the midst of Japan's modernity. Ultimately, Kuki would immortalize this Japanese spirit by recessing it beyond time and beyond the reach of the material and social processes of contemporary society. His verbal collection of tasteful objects, accumulated in notes during the years abroad, was linked early on to the contemporary issue of national cultural identity. But it was only after the encounter with hermeneutics, particularly in its Heideggerian form, that Kuki was able to pull this diverse assortment of lists and notes into the tight symbolic weave of collective meaning and value.

57. Translated from Kafū's diaries in Edward Seidensticker's *Kafū the Scribbler*, 143–44.
58. It is interesting to note that Kuki borrowed many of his architectural and design examples from Nagai Kafū's *Edo geijutsuron*, first published in 1920.

CHAPTER 2

Encounters Across Borders

The Philosophical Quest for Experience

An individual self without a world is unimaginable. It would be impossible for an individual in possession of a world and a community to lapse into the similitude of universality.

Kuki Shūzō, "Existential Philosophy"

The advent of modernity increasingly tears space away from place by fostering relations between "absent" others, locationally distant from any given situation of face-to-face interaction. In conditions of modernity, place becomes increasingly phantasmagoric.

Anthony Giddens, *The Consequences of Modernity*

The years Kuki spent in Europe were intellectually rich and productive ones. From the scientific rigor of an established neo-Kantianism to the more intuitive approaches of *Lebensphilosophie,* phenomenology, and existentialism, Kuki multiplied his encounters with leading intellectual figures and doctrines in the Europe that followed World War I. For the most part, he divided his scholarly attention between German and French intellectual worlds. Deeply instilled with the cosmopolitan values of Taishō academe, Kuki arrived on the continent with a reverence for *Kultur* as it had been elaborated by the German neo-idealists — an interiorized humanist haven from the dislocations of social modernity. During the next seven years in Europe, he further expanded and elaborated that haven by drawing upon the more inward and antirationalist moments of contemporary European theoretical discourse.

Along with his European colleagues, Kuki closely followed developments at the forefront of philosophical endeavor, particularly recent challenges to naturalist and neo-Kantian orthodoxies. Andrew Feenberg points out that in the first decades of the twentieth century, those challenges increasingly took the form of new theories of life and experience, theories that had already begun to take root in Japan by way of William James (1842–1910), Henri Bergson (1859–1941), and Nishida Kitarō (1870–1945).[1] Kuki applauded the endeavor to reassess critically a legacy of instrumental reason, and he shared the desire of European philosophers to salvage a domain of authentic experience from what was seen as an increasingly defiled everyday life.

If this discourse on experience originated in Europe and North America, by the 1920's its range had become widely transnational, both in the cultural complexion of its practitioners and in the material conditions of modernity that provided its occasion. In Japan, notably, the mid-1920's saw a certain fulfillment of liberal political aspirations in an expansion of (male) suffrage and civil rights. During those same post-earthquake years, a new value system of commodities took shape, transforming the lifestyles of a growing urban populace. Increasingly, this populace was reimagined in newly disseminating media as "the masses," modeled on Soviet realities and Marxist ideology.[2] In fact, Marxism and monopoly capital both came into their own toward the end of the decade, while advocates of proletarian literature and aesthetic modernists carved up the world of letters. In Japan as elsewhere, the appearance of a new, mass society, the construction of a rootless urban space, and the eclipse of the individual by large industry and big capital all provided the adverse conditions for a rise of interest in subjective experience. Yet despite, or perhaps precisely because of, the international dimensions of these new realities, Kuki gradually narrowed the focus of experience to the dimensions of what he called the Japanese *minzoku*, revising its terms to favor an ethical and spiritual endowment exclusive to Japan. The word *minzoku*, as Kuki used it, means variously or even simultaneously "race," "people," "nation," and "ethnic group." Kuki drew, no doubt, on the semantic resources of the German *Volk* — "folk" in English — and as a translation, "folk" would have the advantage of invoking the German fascist politics associated with the term. Its agrarian resonances, however, make it less desirable as an equivalent for the urban and urbane character in Kuki's usage of what I will continue to call simply *minzoku*.[3]

---

1. Feenberg and Arisaka, "Experiential Ontology," 173.
2. Takazawa, *Shōwa seishin no pāsupekutibu*, 11–13.
3. For the adjective *minzokuteki*, I use the term "national."

While *"Iki" no kōzō* may indeed document Kuki's attempt to resist the hegemonic thrust of a discourse constructed by and for the West, his own project to enclose Japan within a hermeneutic horizon became entrapped within the narrow byways of that same European-derived discourse.[4] The present chapter pursues Kuki's tracks through the varied terrain of European philosophical discourse as he made his way toward the cultural closure of Japan.

The Itinerary: An Overview

In his article, "Bunkateki nashonarizumu no mondai" (The Problem of Cultural Nationalism), Kunō Osamu remarks that during the years following World War I, more than a thousand government-sponsored scholars studied in Germany.[5] In 1922, soon after his arrival in Europe, Kuki joined a number of other Japanese scholars who gathered in Heidelberg to study philosophy. Heidelberg had become the center of a major branch of neo-Kantian philosophy known as the Southwestern school. While the adherents of the Southwestern school subscribed to a common neo-Kantian agenda to determine the prior (transcendental) conditions of knowledge, they applied those epistemological concerns primarily to the human rather than the natural sciences.[6] Their principal objective was to provide a systematic philosophical foundation for historical and cultural studies. The list of

4. As I will demonstrate in chapter 4, interpretation itself—the hermeneutic enterprise engendered during the rise of Europe's new imperialism—was a distinctively European construction of the world.

5. Kunō, "Bunkateki nashonarizumu no mondai," 55–58. Kunō suggests that this interval in Europe was crucial in determining the conciliatory position the vast majority of intellectuals, including former Marxists, took toward emperor-system fascism in Japan. Witness to the failures of internationalist socialist movements and the cosmopolitan avant-garde to make inroads with the masses of "late-developing" European societies, the Japanese intellectual travelers, argues Kuno, were disposed to reappraise these political and cultural movements as an "enemy from without."

6. Willey, *Back to Kant,* 132. The other major branch, known as the Marburg school, focused primarily on the logic of the natural sciences. Interestingly, it was the representative practitioners of this school—Herman Cohen, Paul Natorp, Rudolf Stammler, and Ernst Cassirer—who remained committed to a politically progressive vision (102–8, 171–73). This school, which addressed its theoretical concerns largely to the logic of mathematics and science, attracted far fewer Japanese students during the 1920's than the Southwestern school.

Japanese intellectuals drawn to this neo-Kantian enterprise is an impressive one, one that anticipates the range of views that would figure in the intellectual politics of Japan's interwar years. Hani Gorō, later a member of the Kōzaha, or orthodox faction of Japanese Marxism, returned from Weimar Germany advocating a "critical Marxism" infused with neo-Hegelian, neo-Kantian, and Heideggerian motifs.[7] Ouchi Hyōe, another noted Marxist historian, would join ranks with the revisionist Marxist faction, the Rōnōha. Miki Kiyoshi, a student of Nishida Kitarō and perhaps the best known of the Heidelberg group, would assimilate neo-Kantianism and Heideggerian existentialism to his early interest in Marxism.[8] Abe Jirō already had made his mark as a spokesman for *Kyō-yōshugi*, a Japanese-styled *Bildungsphilosophie*.[9] Amano Teiyū, Kuki's life-long friend and heir to his private library, would become a preeminent Kantian scholar.

Along with his Japanese compatriots, Kuki attended the lectures of Heinrich Rickert (1863–1936) on the history of philosophy, epistemology, and aesthetics.[10] In private tutorial with Rickert, Kuki read Kant's *Critique of Pure Reason;* with Eugen Herrigel (1884–1955), later known for his *Zen in the Art of Archery,* he studied Kant's transcendental philosophy. In autumn 1924, after a brief tour of Switzerland and the Alps, Kuki left for Paris, where he remained for the next three years. During those years, he attended courses in philosophy at the University of Paris and visited the acclaimed French philosopher Henri Bergson, now aged and infirm. He also produced a number of manuscripts, including several collections of poetry, *tanka* (a traditional Japanese poetic form of thirty-one syllables) and free verse, some of which were published in 1925 and 1926, a study in Japanese poetics titled *Ōin ni tsuite* (On Rhythm and Rhyme) (1927), and a preparatory draft of *"Iki" no kōzō,* "'Iki' no honshitsu,"(1926).

In 1927, Kuki returned to Germany, not to Heidelberg this time but to Freiburg, to study phenomenology under Oscar Becker and Edmund

---

7. Duus and Scheiner, "Socialism, Liberalism, and Marxism," 709.

8. Even before the appearance of *Being and Time,* Miki had integrated early versions of Heidegger's philosophy into his 1926 *Pasukaru ni okeru ningen no kenkyū.*

9. In lieu of a translation of the term *Bildung,* Willey describes it as "moral and aesthetic cultivation through classical education." *Back to Kant,* 15. For the sake of brevity, I will translate *Bildungsphilosophie* as a philosophy of self-cultivation.

10. Rickert's 1922 and 1923 lectures included "From Kant to Nietzsche: A Historical Introduction to the Problem of the Present," "Introduction to Epistemology and Metaphysics," and "The Philosophy of Art." "Kuki Shūzō nenpu," *KSZ,* supplementary volume, 291–92.

Husserl. It was in the home of Husserl that Kuki first made the acquaintance of Martin Heidegger. No doubt this most charismatic of Husserl's students made a strong impression on Kuki, as he did on more than a few Japanese thinkers. Heidegger, for his part, seems also to have been favorably impressed by Kuki. In "A Dialogue on Language" (1959), the German philosopher eulogized his Japanese colleague, reminiscing over leisurely visits with Kuki at the Heidegger home.[11] At the end of the year, when Heidegger took his leave to teach at the University of Marburg, Kuki followed to attend the German philosopher's lectures on Kant's *Critique of Pure Reason* and Leibniz's logic, as well as his seminars on Schelling's *Treatise on the Essence of Human Freedom* and Aristotle's *Physics*.[12]

In 1928, Kuki returned to Paris where, according to Stephen Light, he engaged Jean-Paul Sartre, still a student at the École Normale, presumably for weekly language tutorials. The timing, as Light demonstrates, was crucial, since Kuki, fresh from his encounter with Heidegger, would have been the first to introduce Sartre to this new turn in German philosophy. Judging from Kuki's notes, his discussions with Sartre, hardly language lessons in the conventional sense, ranged widely over contemporary intellectual developments in France. Light surmises that these notes later became an invaluable resource for Kuki's lectures on French philosophy at Kyoto University, lectures that served to introduce a German-leaning Japanese philosophical establishment to French philosophy.[13]

Toward the end of this second sojourn in Paris, Kuki accepted an invitation from French writer and scholar Paul Desjardins to attend the August 1928 philosophical *décade* on "Man and Time, Repetition in Time, Immortality or Eternity." Beginning in 1911, three *décades* — devoted respectively to literature, philosophy, and politics — were held yearly at Desjardins's medieval abbey in Pointigny, a rustic village in the Bourgogne.[14] These *décades* had become the occasion for a gathering of

11. In his carefully researched monograph, *Shūzō Kuki and Jean-Paul Sartre,* Stephen Light suggests that Kuki enjoyed a special rapport with Heidegger during his stay in Freiburg. Light quotes a line from an October 1927 letter addressed to Husserl in which Heidegger enumerates his pressing concerns: "with lectures and the two studies and the talks in Köln and Bonn and in addition Kuki" (30 n. 15).

12. Several years earlier, Tanabe Hajime had evinced a similar preference for Heidegger, and in the years following, the vogue for Heideggerian philosophy swept through the Japanese philosophical establishment.

13. Ibid., 3–4, 15. Light includes a reproduction of the notebook Kuki kept during his meetings with Sartre. Kuki's lectures, *Gendai Furansu tetsugaku kōgi,* were first published in 1957 and constitute volume 8 of *KSZ*.

14. Ibid., 6–7, 31 n. 19. "Décade" refers, no doubt, to the ten-day period devoted to each of the three fields.

celebrated writers, scholars, and public figures from France as well as from other parts of Europe, the United States, and, with the appearance of Kuki, Japan. After a forced hiatus during World War I, the *décades* resumed in 1922 in a spirit of peaceful reconciliation and cross-cultural understanding. Sakabe notes that the 1928 *décades* proved to be one of the last glimmers of postwar pacifism. The end of the 1920's brought with it in quick succession a series of fateful if not disastrous events — a worldwide depression, the acceleration of Japanese militarism, and the rise of Nazi power.[15]

The summer of 1928 was, however, reletively serene; the guest list for the *décades* included French writers André Gide and Roger Martin du Gard, the Russian philosopher Nikolai Berdyayev, and the English critic Lytton Strachey.[16] Sharing the podium with figures like Alexandre Koyré and Raymond Aron among others, Kuki delivered two lectures (in flawless French, rumor has it) on "The Notion of Time and Repetition in Oriental Time" and "The Expression of the Infinite in Japanese Art."[17] Under the aegis of the generous cosmopolitanism of the *décades,* Kuki gave his first public presentation of a highly stylized, carefully selective, and deliberately different representation of Japan and the Orient.

Through the auspices of Kuki's friend and benefactor Amano Teiyū, the written version of these lectures came to the attention of Nishida, then nearing retirement from the philosophy department at Kyoto Imperial University, shortly before Kuki's return to Japan. In a letter addressed to his junior colleague Tanabe, Nishida recorded a slightly qualified but generally positive impression of Kuki: "In any case, he appears to be a highly cultivated person. [For "cultivated," Nishida used the German word *Bildung.*] It would be desirable to have someone like that come as a lecturer."[18] Presumably, Nishida's assessment, facilitated by Amano's orchestration, paved Kuki's way for a post at the university directly after his return to Japan in 1929.[19]

During nearly a decade in Europe, Kuki's continuing engagement with a selection of salient issues in contemporary European philosophy

15. Sakabe, "Kuki Shūzō no sekai," (4) "Pontinī kōen," 106–7.
16. Light, *Shūzō Kuki and Jean-Paul Sartre,* 6–7.
17. These two lectures were published in France as *Propos sur le temps* in 1928 by Philipe Renouard and later in Japanese as *Jikanron.* The French version has been reprinted with Japanese translation in the first volume of *KSZ,* 263–96. In *Shūzō Kuki and Jean-Paul Sartre,* Light provides an English translation of both lectures under the title "Considerations on Time": "The Notion of Time and Repetition in Oriental Time" and "The Expression of the Infinite in Japanese Art," 41, 42, 51.
18. "Kuki Shūzō nenpu," *KSZ,* supplementary volume, 293–94.
19. Nakano, "Kuki Shūzō, " 143.

found expression in the successive stages of his project on Edo aesthetic style. In addition to the undated notes and sketches collected in a file labeled "'Iki' ni tsuite," Kuki completed an unpublished draft in 1926 titled "'Iki' no honshitsu" (The Essence of "Iki").[20] With strategic revisions and substantial additions, this draft would become the template for two published versions of *"Iki" no kōzō*. The first of those versions appeared in the January and February 1930 issues of the intellectual journal *Shisō* within a year of Kuki's return to Japan. The final version, only slightly revised, came out as a monograph from Iwanami publishers at the end of the same year. This incremental process of drafting *"Iki" no kōzō* is inseparable from Kuki's intellectual formation in Europe. With the theoretical resources he had amassed from the repositories of French and German philosophy, Kuki successfully assembled the random notes and sketches of "'Iki' ni tsuite" into a discursive form adequate to a representation of Japanese cultural authenticity.

An Ambivalent Neo-Kantian

In the notes collected under the title "'Iki' ni tsuite," Kuki's recourse to theory of any kind was still rare. One finds little sign of a productive encounter with hermeneutics, or for that matter, with any of the theoretical strategies that would be crucial to the later drafts. His rare ventures into theoretical territory were confined almost exclusively to the province of neo-Kantian philosophy, less in its guise of a rigorous critical method than as a mission to define and expand the domain of culture.

In Germany, the rise of neo-Kantianism represented a revival of idealism in the face of both the expansive ambitions of the natural sciences and the development of mass industrial society during the final decades of the nineteenth century. The philosophers who identified themselves as neo-Kantians invoked the name of their forebear in the hopes of recovering a Kantian faith in the primacy of consciousness and moral autonomy based on a universal rational order. To accomplish this increasingly untimely task, the sphere of consciousness had to be placed outside the deterministic nexus of causal processes; hence the distinction between two separate epistemological spheres—the *Naturwis-*

---

20. "'Iki' no honshitsu" has been reproduced in *KSZ*, 1:87–108.

senschaften, the natural sciences, and the *Kulturwissenschaften,* the cultural sciences.

Wilhelm Windelband (1848–1914), having issued a declaration of war on positivism in 1894, was the first to suggest a distinction between the natural and cultural sciences based on methodological differences. Adding further refinements, Rickert drew the limits of concept formation in natural science at the point where individual events could no longer be subsumed under general laws. And Wilhelm Dilthey (1833–1911), German historian and philosopher, choosing to distinguish the two areas of knowledge as much by matter as by method, argued that history and the other cultural sciences pertain to internal processes, in other words, to those processes that were supposed to partake of the lofty and inward dimensions of *Geist.* He would rename this branch of studies *Geisteswissenschaften.*[21]

To all appearances, the battle to reclaim a distinctive domain of human activity from positivist ambitions was fought on textual terrain. But as Edward Said's now familiar pronouncement cautions, "texts have ways of existing that even in their most rarefied form are always enmeshed in circumstance, time, place, and society — in short, they are in the world, and hence worldly."[22] Willey suggests that there were, in fact, more worldly, if less readily apparent, conditions for the development of the *Kulturwissenschaften.* In his view, the discourse on culture and *Bildung* represents "the moral and aesthetic defense of a privileged but increasingly beleaguered caste" in flight from the failures of bourgeois liberal politics in the late nineteenth century. Having largely abandoned the contemporary field of social practice to others, neo-Kantians, in particular those of the Southwestern school, presumed to represent the range of meaningful human activity in the rarefied and retrospective idiom of *Kultur.* The conditions for appreciating and participating in a shared humanist tradition consisted of a classical education and a moral and aesthetic cultivation inaccessible to any but the most educated social classes. As Willey demonstrates, neo-Kantianism was clearly an elitist enterprise marking its own distance from a new industrial working class as well as from the commercial and industrial bourgeoisie.[23]

In chapter 1, I noted correspondences between the German and Japa-

---

21. Makkreel translates *Geisteswissenschaften* as "Human Studies," in part to distinguish it from the *Kulturwissenschaften* (Cultural Sciences). *Dilthey,* 35–37.

22. Said, *The World, the Text, and the Critic,* 35.

23. Willey, *Back to Kant,* 16.

nese accessions to modernity — correspondences that prepared the Japanese intellectual ground for a positive reception of German neo-idealist thought. It should come as no surprise that an emergent Japanese middle-class intelligentsia, already persuaded of the importance of self-cultivation and the "inner life," discovered a worthy model in this philosophical creation of the late-nineteenth-century German bourgeoisie. While this vast inward expansion of subjectivity tested the narrow boundaries of private life drawn by an overbearing state, it promptly became an elitist bulwark against the rising prospects of a mass constituency. In Japan as in Germany, this philosophy that identified human consciousness as guarantor and arbiter of value expressed the ideology of a new middle class in the aristocratic idiom of cultural value.

The textual sources of neo-Kantianism had already begun to circulate through the Japanese higher schools and universities in the latter part of the Meiji era. In a 1928 essay written in France, Kuki alluded to the encouraging response to Kantian philosophy in Japan as early as the 1890's, when enthusiasts initiated "Kantian evenings" devoted to discussions of transcendental philosophy.[24] Soon after the turn of the century, translations and commentaries began to appear in increasing numbers.[25] During the Taishō years, neo-Kantianism rose to a dominant position in academic philosophical discourse, where it offered a disciplinary apparatus and scientific legitimacy to a widespread predilection for the spiritual goods of culture.

Neo-Kantianism makes its appearance in the notes of "'Iki' ni tsuite" in the form of three of its central premises: universalism, rationalism, and a faith in the primacy of culture. The *Kulturwissenschaften* philosophers of the Southwestern school claimed that the objects belonging to the distinctively human domain of culture are defined by their nonrecurring individuality; yet at the same time, they sought universal criteria for knowing and judging those singular objects. In the flux of history (then haunted by the nihilistic specter of relativism), they discerned universal and abiding values and affirmed a "common core of cultural val-

24. Kuki, "Bergson au Japon," *KSZ*, 1:261.
25. For an extended discussion of neo-Kantianism in Japan, see Adams, "The Feasibility of the Philosophical in Early Taishō Japan." According to Adams, translations of and commentaries on Kant's writings began with the translation of the *Prolegomena* in 1913 and continued through the midtwenties. The bicentennial celebration of Kant's birth in 1924 provided the occasion for commemorative issues of major philosophical journals (121–26).

ues upon which all or at least most civilized men could agree."[26] They presumed that all of humanity shares values related to common norms of "the good," "the true," and "the beautiful." Nevertheless, the search for universal values (*Güter*) inevitably led them back to the place where they supposed these become manifest: in the particular products or "goods" (also *Güter* in German) of a historically specific culture. Paradoxical though it may seem, the universalist premise of the *Kulturwissenschaften* could potentially function to both conceal and legitimize the privilege accorded to one particular culture. In other words, the cosmopolitan rhetoric of the *Kulturwissenschaften* harbored possibilities for a return to cultural particularism. The possibilities for such creative ironies had already been broached in mid-Meiji with the geographical vagaries of Okakura's Hegelian "Spirit" and the drift toward the particular of Miyake Setsurei's title for his 1891 essay, "Shinzenbi Nihonjin" (The Good, True, and Beautiful Japanese).[27]

In "'Iki' ni tsuite," Kuki briefly entertained the universalist premise of neo-Kantianism. Next to a series of schematic representations of a Japanese system of taste, he proposed that the system of a particular *minzoku* — Japan in this case — might be understood as a single modification in a universal system of taste. In other words, Japan might potentially be subsumed under norms that apply to all cultures. It is, however, of some significance that Kuki prefaced this remark with a conditional clause: "If one were able to construct a schema of taste with universal features."[28] Perhaps this rhetoric of hypothesis already betrays Kuki's doubts, soon to deepen, that a universal norm was possible or even desirable. But according to the (only apparently) contradictory logic of cosmopolitanism, Kuki's retreat to an insular form of culturalism may well have been prefigured in a cosmopolitan discourse that had migrated from its European center toward a non-Western periphery.

Kuki's passion for analytic classification, already apparent in "'Iki' ni tsuite," testified to his belief in the efficacy of rational structures. In this, he was closely allied to the conceptualism and rationalism of neo-Kantian thought. In those rare moments devoted to theoretical concern in the notes, Kuki introduces analytic distinctions derived from neo-Kantian aesthetics — between mathematical and nonmathematical art, for example, or between natural and artistic form. According to neo-

26. Willey, *Back to Kant*, 147.
27. Miyake Setsurei's essay is cited and discussed in Pyle, *The New Generation*, 150–56.
28. Kuki, "'Iki' ni tsuite," *KSZ*, supplementary volume, 13.

Kantians anxious to recertify philosophy as modern knowledge, synthetic reason rather than intuition is the source of knowledge. The real, not something simply there for the taking, has to be constructed by the categories of pure intellect. Ultimately, Kuki would find this intellectualist formulation inadequate, advocating instead the epistemological efficacy of immediate experience. And yet, despite a growing distrust for the powers of pure intellect, Kuki never abandoned the trappings of reason. Even at those junctures where he endeavored to articulate the irrational, as he would in the philosophical treatises on contingence, he subjected his efforts to a categorical logic inherited from Kant.[29]

Kuki's conviction that philosophical understanding is inherently rational reappeared with regular frequency in his writings. In "Tetsugaku no shiken" (My Own View of Philosophy), he concluded that "logical judgment as a mediatory agency in the understanding of being constitutes the distinctive character of philosophy. That is why philosophy is fated in its essence to be a form of rationalism."[30] How, then, was philosophical understanding to be reconciled with the nonrational nature of experience? That was a problem Kuki broached in *"Iki" no kōzō* and explored further in his philosophical writings of the 1930's. "'Iki' ni tsuite," does, however, offer a glimpse into the particular kind of power he invested in logical categories and conceptualist methods. Even at this early stage, he had already begun to schematize his thoughts on Japanese taste in the shape of geometrical figures, irregular hexahedrons of varied proportions, each angle occupied by a particular term of taste (See Figure 1). Alongside these figures he appended the following explanation: "The schematic value of this six-sided figure lies in the possibility . . . for all the varieties of taste that belong to our nation to be situated at fixed points, whether on the surface or in the depths of the figure."[31] The abstract precision, whether of tone or of the schema itself, belied the very essence of *iki,* a style that, as Kuki himself claimed, refused all but the merest hints of the erotic and deferred any commitment, whether to love or to meaning. Why then the rational abstrac-

---

29. See especially *Gūzensei no mondai, KSZ,* 2:1–264. This philosophical tract on contingence was originally a monograph published by Iwanami Shoten in 1935. The editor of Kuki's collected works, Omodaka Hisayuki, has published a French translation, *Kuki Shūzō: Le problème de la contingence* (Tokyo: University of Tokyo Press, 1963).

30. Kuki, "Tetsugaku no shiken," *KSZ,* 3:108–9. This article first appeared in the June 1936 issue of *Risō.*

31. Kuki, "'Iki' ni tsuite," *KSZ,* supplementary volume, 12.

tions, the geometric elaborations? Was it not these feats of intellect that transformed *iki*, along with an indigenous repertoire of taste, into a determinate category, precisely situated and contained by the rigid shape of the schema? Firmly fixed in place, *iki* might then be claimed as a permanent and exclusive possession of the nation. Kuki deployed the rational resources of neo-Kantian aesthetics not only to stake out the distinctive terrain of Japanese culture but also to impose, by means of a consensus of taste, identity upon a collective subjectivity soon to be constructed in *"Iki" no kōzō*.

In later writings, Kuki would critically reassess both the universalist and rationalist premises of neo-Kantian aesthetics. But even after his defection from the neo-Kantian camp, he remained steadfastly faithful to the third premise of *Kulturwissenschaften* — that culture constitutes a privileged domain of human activity with its own distinct logic. In "'Iki' ni tsuite," Kuki gave a brief indication that his thoughts were moving in this direction. On a final page labeled "Conclusion," he transcribed two quotes in the original German from *Asthetik und allgemeinene Kunstwissenschaft* (Aesthetics and a Comprehensive Study of Art) by Max Dessoire, a leading neo-Kantian aesthetician.[32] The first quote, under the German heading *Sprache* (language), suggests that an investigation of aesthetic value has much to gain from the "wisdom contained in the categories of language constructed over time, and, in particular, from adjectives of praise and blame."[33] Dessoire thus makes a decisive connection between impalpable aesthetic value and its material manifestation in a shared language that bears witness to that value. This observation must have struck a responsive chord in Kuki, who was then entertaining the possibility that *iki* might serve as the verbal key to the treasury of Japanese cultural meaning and value.

The second quote, under the Japanese heading *Zentai to bubun, bunseki sayō* (The Whole and the Parts, the Function of Analysis), makes the following claim: "Despite the fact that the aesthetic object represents a whole greater than the sum or collection of its parts, it can be represented 'scientifically' (*wissenschaftlich*) only through analysis."[34] Aesthetics, considered by many to lie at the heart of culture, obeys a logic separate from that of the natural sciences — the logic of organicism. As Dessoire's statement indicates, the concrete particulars of any aesthetic

32. Dessoire's *Asthetik* was published in 1906 in Stuttgart.
33. Kuki, "'Iki' ni tsuite," *KSZ*, supplementary volume, 45.
34. Ibid.

object were supposed to add up to an incalculable whole. German cultural theory customarily identified this ineffable whole with *Geist*, a mysterious cultural totality, inimitable, incommensurable, and exceeding the reach of conceptual language. The dimensions of *Geist* had been designated at the end of the eighteenth century by Herder, who defined *Geist* as the impress of a collective attribute shared by everyone in a particular collective group, whether national or regional, but shared in special concentration by its most creative members. With the advent of the nineteenth century, Hegel's *Phenomenology of Spirit* confirmed the collective dimensions of *Geist* in its *wirhaftige* or "we-like" character and firmly located its truth in "inwardness."[35] This notion of *Geist*, as I mentioned in chapter 1, was absorbed into Japan through neo-idealist texts and teachers. Though Kuki eventually replaced *Geist* with the more Heideggerian formulation of Being, the organicist logic remained the same: a given cultural artifact shares in the ineffable, inward, and incalculable value of a larger whole. In the last analysis, as Kuki would later make abundantly clear, that whole was less apt to be a generalized humanity than a particular national group.

From *Lebensferne* to *Lebensphilosophie*

The neo-Kantian reflection on culture had a powerful impact on a generation of Japanese thinkers, an impact that Kuki absorbed not only directly but also indirectly through its assimilation into other but related strains of European philosophical discourse. Nevertheless, as a movement, neo-Kantianism had lost its currency in European intellectual circles by the beginning of World War I. Kuki was in good company when he abandoned Rickert's Southwestern school for more promising theoretical possibilities. In fact, most of the Japanese students in Heidelberg during the immediate postwar years left neo-Kantian high ground for less orthodox and more experiential philosophical terrain. Kuki's most candid and most timely statements of disaffection appear in the more "academic" of his Paris *tanka*. In one, he notes that the works of Kant are gathering dust on his shelves. In another, he expresses his growing skepticism toward the crucial terms of Kantian epistemology:

---

35. Marcuse, *Hegel's Ontology*, xxiv.

The words "objective" and "universal"
These days, I take them with a grain of salt.

With regret, perhaps, for what now seemed a misguided allegiance to Kant, he notes the discrepancy between subjective experience and conceptual norms:

I grieve for myself, so hard to capture
in categories, for so many years.[36]

In a 1928 essay titled "Bergson au Japon," the same essay in which Kuki documented the early predominance of neo-Kantianism on the Japanese intellectual scene, he dated the end of the neo-Kantian monopoly with the first translations of Bergson's works in 1910: "It was precisely at this moment, when occidental philosophy was represented in Japan almost exclusively by critique and logic, that the name of M. Henri Bergson suddenly made its appearance. . . . Bergson served principally to revive our desire for metaphysics. Our spirits, starved by the critical formalism of German neo-Kantianism, received 'heavenly nourishment' from Bergsonian metaphysical intuition."[37] What Kuki and others found most objectionable in the neo-Kantian enterprise was the notion of *Lebensferne,* a programmatic injunction that philosophy keep its distance from the raw material of life. The neo-Kantians preferred a dispassionate perspective, concentrating on issues of a methodological and formal nature. Nishida and Tanabe Hajime (1885–1962) earlier had begun to question the intimate relationship between philosophy and science that so deeply marked their chosen discipline throughout the Meiji era and much of Taishō. And as Robert Adams explains, even in their endeavor to assimilate a neo-Kantian logic of scientific knowledge, they shared a common critical objective—to pose the question of the "limits of the hegemony of the scientific perspective. Nishida had looked to Bergson early on to validate his own suspicions of a philosophical enterprise dominated by the claims of neo-Kantianism. Later, in his university lectures, Kuki would invoke Dilthey for his critical assessment of neo-Kantian epistemology: "There is no real blood running in its veins, only the watered-down sap of reason."[38]

To the cerebral approach of the neo-Kantians Bergson offered a com-

---

36. Kuki, *Pari shinkei, KSZ,* 1:189, 1:190.
37. Kuki, "Bergson au Japon," *KSZ,* 1:261–62.
38. Adams, "The Feasibility of the Philosophical in Early Taishō Japan," 105, 60–61, 67. Kuki, "Gendai tetsugaku no dōkō," *KSZ,* 9:372.

pelling alternative. In his essay on Bergson in Japan, Kuki reiterated
Bergson's philosophical mandate: "To philosophize means to place oneself, through an effort of intuition, right in the center of concrete reality."[39] For Kuki as well as for Bergson, the appeal to "concrete reality"
referred to the inner, affective experience of the subject, to the disposition of the soul. Anything else—whether images, representations, or
signs—could only be derivative, and as such, unworthy of philosophy.[40]
Bergson confirmed Kuki's suspicion of theory, recommending instead
an unmediated leap into the immediacy of the real.

Bergson had succeeded to a tradition in French thought that, since
the seventeenth century, had opposed the dominant current of Cartesian
rationalism. The nature of that opposition was perhaps best expressed
by an early-nineteenth-century philosopher whom Bergson claimed as
his forebear, Maine de Birain. An ardent advocate of inward experience,
Maine de Birain (1766–1824) had revised the Cartesian formula for the
subject's certainty of existence from "I think" to "I feel." In Japan, as in
Europe, Bergson was received as a defender of the values of spirit and
feeling against the successive claims of positivism and neo-Kantianism.
For Kuki, profoundly dissatisfied with the disembodied (and disaffected) subject of neo-Kantian epistemology, Bergson offered the possibility of bringing feeling and desire into philosophical focus.

In "'Iki' ni tsuite," Kuki appealed briefly to Bergson's authority when
he overturned the realist tenet that art imitates nature. Rather, insisted
Kuki, we are able to understand nature only through the mediation
of art, or as his example demonstrates, through the mediation of an
aestheticized feminine body: "Why the expression 'a willow-waisted
woman'? It is not because a willow waist resembles the willow tree, but
rather because the willow tree resembles a willow waist. Before we make
the judgment in each individual case that a woman's waist is like a willow, we have already made the more universal judgment that the willow
is like a woman's waist."[41] Kuki based this reversal of naturalist priorities
on a Bergsonian epistemology that situated an affective and creative
subject at the origin of knowledge. In this view, art enjoyed greater intimacy with the subject than did a more external nature; art, as Oscar
Wilde's mimetic modification would have it, supplanted life as the origi-

39. Kuki, "Bergson au Japon," *KSZ*, 1:260.

40. See, for example, Bergson's "Introduction à la métaphysique," 230–33, which originally appeared in *Revue de métaphysique et de morale* in 1903.

41. Kuki, "'Iki' ni tsuite," *KSZ*, supplementary volume, 14–15.

nal. Sōseki had first experimented with this modernist conceit in his most "theoretical" of novels, *Kusa makura* (Pillow of Grass).[42] The unnamed narrator of that fiction, hamstrung between an invasive bureaucratic apparatus and the reproductions of banality in mass entertainment, seeks refuge in rarefied — and fetishized — aesthetic categories. In strict modernist fashion, art becomes a means to concentrate on a substance that is absolutely one's own. But as Adorno suggests in the case of another modernist, Paul Valéry, the absolute separation from the real world necessary for this exclusive intimacy between subject and art presages the impoverishment of both the subjective essence and its aesthetic production.[43] True to form, the modernist project of Sōseki's narrator remains ironically unrealized, thus casting doubt on the validity of his aesthetic aims. Lacking Sōseki's powers of irony and critical self-reflection, Kuki took the apotheosis of the subject at face value. In any case, Bergson's appearance in the notes is a significant one, preparing the way for what I will call the inward migration of *iki*. In other words, Bergsonian subjectivism signals a shift from the objects of taste to its subjects, from the autonomy of the aesthetic function to its supremacy.

In "Bergson au Japon," Kuki went on to explain that it was through the mediation of Bergson that Japanese intellectuals had first come to appreciate German phenomenology:

Husserl first . . . not as "pure logician," but as "phenomenologist." Then Max Scheler, philosopher of life (*Lebensphilosophe*), and, most recently, Martin Heidegger, author of *Being and Time*. Among the points in common between Bergsonian philosophy and German phenomenology, those that seem most salient to us are precisely those that distinguish both from neo-Kantian philosophy: on the one hand, the Bergsonian demand to abandon overly precise distinctions between the content of knowledge and its form; on the other hand, Husserl's notion of "intentionality" or Heidegger's "Being-in-the-world." Perhaps this correspondence is simply a result of a common method of intuition. In any case, we in Japan have been led from neo-Kantianism to "phenomenology" by way of Bergsonian philosophy.[44]

In sum, what Bergson and the phenomenologists shared was a refusal of the neo-Kantian agenda of *Lebensferne*. From Kuki's perspective, all of these thinkers were "philosophers of life," no longer willing to hold themselves aloof from experience.

---

42. Natsume Sōseki, *Kusa makura*, translated as *The Three Cornered World* by Alan Turney (Washington, D.C.: Regnery Gateway, 1988).

43. Adorno, *Prisms*, 23.

44. Kuki, "Bergson au Japon," *KSZ*, 1:259–60.

The Philosophical Pursuit of Experience

Kuki completed "'Iki' no honshitsu," the preliminary draft of *"Iki" no kōzō*, in 1926, at the end of his first stay in Paris. And though he had not yet met Husserl or Heidegger, phenomenology already had begun to insinuate itself into the structure of *iki*. In the introductory remarks of this 1926 draft, Kuki cited Tanabe Hajime's 1924 article "Genshōgaku ni okeru atarashiki tenkō—Haidegā no sei no genshōgaku" (A New Turn in Phenomenology—Heidegger's Phenomenology of Life). During his trip to Europe as a government-sponsored scholar, Tanabe studiously avoided the neo-Kantians, choosing instead to explore new phenomenological territory in Freiberg. On his return to Japan in 1924, he introduced a Japanese academic audience to the earliest Heideggerian revisions of Husserlian phenomenology. Tanabe paid special attention to the phenomenological concept of intentionality, which found a receptive audience among Japanese thinkers. Husserl used this term to demonstrate that consciousness fundamentally refers beyond itself. Heidegger took his teacher's insight one step further, replacing intentional consciousness with "Being-in-the-world," a term indicating the radical immanence of human existence in its surroundings. With these crucial concepts, phenomenology proposed to situate the subject irrevocably and inextricably in a world. Kuki's early encounter with phenomenology by way of Tanabe's article proved to be an extremely productive one for his project on Edo style. It is perhaps not an exaggeration to say that the concept of intentionality facilitated the initial transformation of the annotated lists of "'Iki' ni tsuite" into the theoretical narrative of "'Iki' no honshitsu." In that narrative, *minzoku* played the role of a collective existential subject, culture served as the intended content of consciousness, and Japan became a world of its own. To understand how phenomenology sanctioned this narrative, we need to return to Tanabe's earliest appraisal of the phenomenological project.

Tanabe prefaced his remarks with the conviction that phenomenology would overcome the limitations of neo-Kantian philosophy. Like Kuki, Tanabe was critical of neo-Kantianism for its self-imposed distance from life and for its commitment to formal norms and abstract truths. He recognized the need for a union between "philosophy as science" and "philosophy as life" and called for a philosophy that would provide a worldview. Though he welcomed Husserl's call for a philosophy that would return to "the things themselves," he charged that Husserl had strayed from his own objective.[45] Husserl had proposed to return philosophy to everyday life in the world, but the methods he chose were too abstract and intellectualist for many of his early adherents. The inquirer arrived at an adequate description of phenomena only after a laborious "process of purification and elevation to the *eidos*," a purely formal essence.[46] In Tanabe's eyes, this abstract intervention into the analysis of everyday life was highly suspect. Further, Tanabe objected to the extraterritorial status Husserl granted himself as knowing subject.[47] For the fulfillment of the phenomenological promise, Tanabe looked instead to Husserl's most remarkable student, Heidegger. Basing his comments on Heidegger's 1922 lectures at Freiberg, Tanabe confessed at the outset that Heidegger's revisionist phenomenology interested him more for its methods than its results.[48]

For the most part, Tanabe's call for a concrete philosophy remains at the level of generalities. There is, however, a single word that, if only by dint of repetition, calls attention to itself—the word "experience." Tanabe expressed his view that philosophy should both speak from and address itself to experience, and phenomenology, he believed, could fulfill that double mandate.[49] Phenomenologists had defined the fundamental structure of consciousness as meaningful experience and proposed to make that experience the object of their analysis. Tanabe's report to his colleagues provided just one signal of a major shift in philosophy during the first decades of the twentieth century, from empiricist and idealist paradigms to new doctrines of life and experience. Certainly, there were other envoys of this shift—William James in the United States, for example, and Nishida in Japan, both of whom assigned a new ontological role to experience: experience was no longer to be a category of knowledge or perception but rather their precondition. In *Zen no kenkyū* (A Study of Good), published in 1910, Nishida first presented his notion of "pure experience," an originary and unobjectifiable field anterior to reflection, judgment, and the subject/object split.[50] Through subsequent encounters with neo-Kantianism, Hegel,

45. Tanabe, "Genshōgaku ni okeru atarashiki tenkō," 1–2, 1, 4, 5–6.
46. Bubner, *Modern German Philosophy*, 17.
47. Tanabe, "Genshōgaku ni okeru atarashiki tenkō," 7–8.
48. Despite the fact that Tanabe's reservations regarding the content of Heidegger's new project are largely unspecified, his 1924 article gives a rare glimpse into the philosophical formulations anticipating *Being and Time*. I can only speculate that the still unambiguously theological tenor of Heidegger's early versions dampened Tanabe's enthusiasm.
49. Tanabe, "Genshōgaku ni okeru atarashiki tenkō," 1–2.
50. Translated as Nishida, *An Inquiry into the Good*, xvii–xviii, 3–10.

Fichte, and phenomenology, Nishida continued to revise and refine this notion of pure experience in an ongoing philosophical exploration.[51] In addition, Japanese writers, notably Sōseki, Shimazaki Tōson, and other authors of the *shishōsetsu* form (personal fiction) had worked out the concrete particulars of this realm of experience in explorations of the subjective interiority of their largely middle-class male protagonists.[52] By the mid-1920's, Kuki clearly had taken notice of the new phenomenological engagement with experience, whether through Tanabe's article or through other channels. But before exploring the nuances of experience in Kuki's study of Edo aesthetic style, I would like to consider the notion itself in broad historical terms.

Long since naturalized as part of our everyday vocabulary, the word "experience" would seem to warrant no special attention. Nevertheless, the concern for experience emerged in the center of philosophical discourse at a particular moment in history and was attended by its own social formation and ideological features. For the moment, let us suspend the self-evidence of this most ordinary of words and question the conditions of its ubiquity in theoretical discourse during the first decades of this century. In "A Dialogue on Language," Heidegger recalled the prevailing atmosphere during the early 1920's at the time of a particular lecture attended by a number of Japanese scholars at the University in Freiberg, one of whom, no doubt, was Tanabe: "Everyone," he tells his quasi-fictionalized Japanese discussant, "was talking about experience (*Erlebnis*), even within phenomenology."[53] Heidegger's discussant immediately links the doctrine of experience with the figure of Wilhelm Dilthey. Though the discussant never specifies the nature of that link, we should observe that Dilthey's first step in his endeavor to provide an experiential grounding for historical understanding had been to distinguish *Erfahrung,* merely "a phenomenal construct," from *Erlebnis,* or real experience. While Dilthey argued that *Erlebnis* brings inner and outer realities into relation, his description of *Erlebnis* had a decidedly inward bent: "*Erlebnis* is in possession of its givens, but external experi-

---

51. Feenberg and Arisaka, "Experiential Ontology," 173–86. The authors point out that James and Nishida anticipated the directions to be taken by phenomenology and existentialism.

52. See, for example, the stream-of-consciousness techniques used in Natsume Sōseki's *Kusa makura,* or the nearly psychoanalytic association of ideas in Shimazaki Tōson's *Anya kōrō,* translated as *A Dark Night's Passing* by Edwin McClellan (Tokyo: Kodansha, 1976).

53. Heidegger, " A Dialogue on Language," 35.

ence (*äussere Erfahrung*) confronts its givens."[54] Deriving its authority from "life" (*Leben*), *Erlebnis* might better be translated as "lived experience," that is, experience deeply felt and, literally, lived through (*er-leben*).

In Dilthey's view, the fundamental constituent of experience is time, not the quantitative, empty time of the positivists but an unmeasurable, qualitative time: "Concrete time is comprised . . . of the uninterrupted progress of the present, what was present constantly becoming the past and the future becoming the present. The present is the filling of a moment of time with reality; this is experience. . . . Only in the present is there fullness of time, and therefore, fullness of life." Experience is not only temporal but also necessarily meaningful: "The smallest unit which we can describe as an experience is whatever forms a meaningful unit in the course of a life."[55] We will have further opportunity to explore Dilthey's terminology in the context of hermeneutics, but for the moment, simply note that his theory of experience implied inwardness, self-possession, and value.

An even greater champion of experience, Henri Bergson, introduced the notion of the *durée* (duration), an inner, subjective reality bearing the structure of time. Simply put, the *durée* means time as experience, an interior duration that "is the continuous life of a memory that perpetuates the past in the present." In this interior duration, where the present is ceaselessly enriched by the past, the subject can lay hold of its true self: "There is one reality, at least, which we all seize from within, by intuition and not by simple analysis. It is our own person in its flowing through time — our own self, which endures."[56] The analysis of time as experience, then, disclosed a concern for the subject, but a subject freed from a reified world impoverished by quantification and mechanistic analysis. Bergson distinguished the domain of the *durée* as an interior site where questions of practical interest and personal profit have no pertinence. In this sense, his notion of experience shared common ground with the aesthetic faculty as it had first been elaborated by Kant — a disinterested appreciation of form.[57]

As a way to put this philosophical interest in experience in critical perspective, it might be useful to return once again to "A Dialogue on

---

54. Makkreel, *Dilthey*, 147.

55. Dilthey, *Pattern and Meaning in History*, 98–99.

56. Bergson, "Introduction à la métaphysique," 277, 206.

57. Interestingly, Benjamin observes that Bergson "defines the nature of experience in the *durée* in such a way that the reader is bound to conclude that only a poet can be the adequate subject of such an experience." *Charles Baudelaire*, 111.

Language" and consider the textual provocation for Heidegger's comment on the ubiquity of experience. Heidegger had just finished issuing cautionary counsel against expressive views of language when his discussant burst forth with a reverential tribute to all that is inward and "pertains to the soul" in language. This is the moment when Heidegger reminds his discussant of the philosophical preoccupation with experience. He appears to be calling attention to a misrecognition on the part of his discussant, a misrecognition obscuring his earliest attempts to overcome the limitations of metaphysics. He explains to his discussant: "To experience in this sense always means to refer back — to refer life and lived experience back to the 'I.' Experience is the name for the referral of the objective back to the subject. The much-discussed I/Thou experience, too, belongs within the metaphysical sphere of subjectivity."[58] Heidegger earlier had argued in *Being and Time* that there must be a "who" that "maintains itself as something identical throughout changes in its Experiences . . . and which relates itself to this changing multiplicity in so doing." Much of his effort in that unfinished work was directed toward deconstructing the "soul substance" or the reification of consciousness common, in his view, to *Lebensphilosophie* and all "personalitic" movements.[59]

If, as Heidegger claimed, the philosophical exploration of experience unfailingly leads back to the territory of the subject, we might next ask what kind of a subject Dilthey, Bergson, and even Heidegger (despite his disclaimers) had in mind. *Being and Time* offers some provocative clues, particularly in those passages where we are told not what this subject is but rather what it strives not to be. In a rarefied language of his own making, Heidegger describes the conditions in which Dasein or "being there" — the name he gave to the specifically human mode of Being — ordinarily finds itself. In its everyday existence, Heidegger maintained, Dasein has fallen into compliance and alienation: "Dasein, as everyday Being-with-one-another, stands in *subjection* to Others. It itself *is* not; its Being has been taken away by the Others. . . . Everyone is other, and no one is himself." This inconspicuous domination by anonymous others in a world of prefabricated meanings finds its concrete referent in the mass society that had taken hold in the early decades of this century. In such a society, said Heidegger, all genuine, exceptional, and awe-inspiring possibilities of Being are suppressed. He called

58. Heidegger, "A Dialogue on Language," 35–36.
59. Heidegger, *Being and Time*, 150. See in particular 71–77 and 149–53.

this collective condition "publicness:" "By publicness everything gets obscured, and what has thus been covered up gets passed off as something familiar and accessible to everyone."[60] In the words of George Steiner, a sympathetic Heidegger interpreter, "Heidegger's diagnosis relates, to be sure, to Engels' perception of the dehumanization of the individual in a mass society and to Durkheim's analyses of *anomie.* . . . But what Heidegger has to say possesses a particular moral-psychological bite and a prophetic shrewdness. Distance from being, averageness, the leveling downward of sentiment and expression in a consumer society 'constitute what we know as "publicness."'"[61] To this state of radical estrangement from oneself in publicness Heidegger gave the name "inauthenticity."[62] *Being and Time,* however, offers Dasein the opportunity to (re)attain authenticity, but only by means of a "call to conscience," a call (necessarily nondiscursive in nature) signaling the recognition of one's own finitude.

The "Dialogue" reiterates Heidegger's view, first articulated in *Being and Time,* that the notion of experience came to a philosophical dead end in an essentialized subject.[63] Yet at the same time, he implies that the social and political conditions of modern existence — its publicness — are thoroughly mired in inauthenticity. In the earlier work, Heidegger resolved the dilemma with the recommendation that Dasein extricate itself from inauthenticity by means of a retreat from publicness into an interior site of conscience. One critic of *Being and Time* has charged that "total secession was commended as the possibility of self-assertion. Publicness, politics, society were held here not only as beside the point, but also as corrupting."[64] On his own terms, then, Heidegger fell back

60. Ibid., 164, 165.

61. Steiner, *Martin Heidegger,* 92.

62. One might pose the question here of why an "interpreter" like Steiner is required to spell out the practical, social-historical references of what Pierre Bourdieu has called Heidegger's "euphemized discourse." In other words, why did Heidegger disguise his assessment of everyday life in urban, industrial society as a revelation of the truth of human existence? The role of this kind of expression, in Bourdieu's words, "is to mask the primitive experiences of the social world and the social phantasms which are its source, as much as to disclose them; to allow them to speak, while using a mode of expression which suggests that they are not being said." As Bourdieu points out, Heidegger's opposition between "authenticity" and "inauthenticity" in *Being and Time* is suspiciously similar to the division between "masses" and "elite"; his censure of "publicness" suggests a distrust, if not a wholesale rejection, of the modern civil society with which that term (in German, *öffentlichkeit*) is closely associated. Bourdieu, *The Political Ontology of Martin Heidegger,* 78–85.

63. Heidegger, "A Dialogue on Language," 36.

64. Zimmerman, *Heidegger's Confrontation with Modernity,* 25, quoted from Winfried Franzen, *Von der Existenzialontologie zur Seinsgeschichte: Eine Untersuchen über die En-*

into the metaphysical trap he professed to have eluded. Despite his efforts to circumvent any recourse to experience, he retraced its inevitable return to the subject. Ultimately, Heidegger's "call to conscience" as a remedy for the alienation endemic to modern mass society recuperated the status of a self-possessed and inward subject.

Another critic of the philosophical obsession with experience, but one with a Marxist receptivity to its class resonances, was Walter Benjamin. In his essays on Charles Baudelaire, Benjamin supplied a more material context for the pursuit of experience: "Since the end of the last century, philosophy has made a series of attempts to lay hold of the 'true' experience as opposed to the kind that manifests itself in the standardized denatured life of the civilized masses." As the context for this "denatured life," Benjamin pointed to the hallmarks of modernity: large-scale industrialization, anonymous crowds, and commodity culture. Under such conditions, he argued, experience could not but wither, having lost its vital connections with a rich past both personal and collective. Labor in an industrial age had come to resemble the deathlike operations of the machine itself — discrete, repetitive, and manipulative.[65] Mechanical modes of production had fostered a commodity culture in which the proliferation of identical objects, particularly cultural artifacts, insured their loss of "authenticity," severing them from time, memory, and authoritative tradition. "The authenticity of a thing," wrote Benjamin, "is the essence of all that is transmissible from its beginning, ranging from its substantive duration to its testimony to the history which it has experienced. Since the historical testimony rests on the authenticity, the former, too, is jeopardized by reproduction when substantive duration ceases to matter. And what is really jeopardized when the historical testimony is affected is the authority of the aura." The Benjaminian aura is a "unique manifestation of a distance," the authority of origins in a cherished past.[66] The aura infuses objects, as well as the experience of those who encounter them, with a rich and layered time — this in contrast to the empty and homogeneous time of the commodity. Not given to simple nostalgia, Benjamin endowed the destruction of the aura with two distinct faces: one gazed back inconsolably, lamenting the death of experience and the disintegration of memory

twicklung der Philosophie Martin Heideggers (Meisenheim am Glan: Verlag Anton Hain, 1975), 71.

65. Benjamin, *Charles Baudelaire,* 110, 110–12, 132–33.

66. Benjamin, *Illuminations,* 221, 222.

along with the human soul; the other looked forward to the promise of liberation from the authority of a past enshrined in canonical tradition.

In Benjamin's view, the philosophers who directed their efforts toward resurrecting experience had little choice but to blind themselves to the contemporary cultural and social processes that had dictated its disintegration. Benjamin classified these efforts under the heading of "philosophy of life." The point of departure for this philosophy of life, he argued, was not man's life in society. It was against the requirements of an outer social world of practical interests and invasive control that, as we have seen, Bergson and others had sounded anxious warnings.[67] Thoughts of this outer world inspired in them amorphous fears of unnatural and mechanical incursions into the domain of life, incursions that threatened to abridge or abort the substance of inner experience. The appeal to experience, then, can be read both as a protest against and an imaginary refuge from an unacceptable social reality. To put it slightly differently, philosophy countered the increasingly rationalized, mechanized, and "mass" quality of everyday life by constructing a world of creativity and freedom for a newly authenticated subject. This was a world, however, that existed only on the condition that the subject (presumably one sufficiently endowed materially and spiritually) retreat within. When this sort of subject was collectivized, as it almost inevitably was, the name given to the inward site of experience that embraced memory, meaning, and creativity was "culture."[68]

All of these ideological echoes resonate powerfully in Kuki's appeal to experience in "'Iki' no honshitsu." Here he defined experience with the Greek *ousia,* a word Heidegger used to mean "something present to us."[69] In this sense, experience refers to a presence in which the past continues to dwell. Further, as if to bear witness to Heidegger's critical insight, the cultural experience that Kuki invoked with the word *iki* pointed directly back to the collective subject, in this case the Japanese *minzoku.* In fact this was the ultimate significance of *iki.* As a tentative conclusion to "'Iki' no honshitsu," Kuki wrote, "Only when we have

---

67. Benjamin, *Charles Baudelaire,* 109–11.

68. More than a few Japanese philosophers, including Kuki, Watsuji, and Miki, agreed that the bias toward the individual of Heidegger and of European philosophy in general left crucial questions concerning collectivity and sociality unanswered. Chapter 4 will demonstrate that a concern for collectivity was in fact crucial to the narrative meaning of Heidegger's *Being and Time,* as well as to the hermeneutic enterprise in general. But these social dimensions were overlooked by Japanese theorists.

69. Heidegger, *Being and Time,* 46–49.

grasped the essential meaning of *iki* as the self-expression of the being of our *minzoku* have we reached a complete understanding."[70] This term, "the being of our *minzoku*" (*minzoku sonzai*), operated as a collective equivalent for the pristine subject of experience — philosophy's object of desire, according to Benjamin, since the end of the last century. When Kuki invoked this new collective subject, he was not referring to the atomized, alienated, urban masses of the 1920's, those who went by the name of *ne nashi gusa* ("grass with no roots," or the *déraciné*) in the popular lyrics of the time, nor was he alluding to a cultural vanguard, conscious purveyors of a heterogeneous modernism, nor did he have a disenfranchised peasantry in mind. Rather, this nationally determined "being" designated a homogeneous cultural community imaginary in its essence, a community preserving the spiritual legacy of the past in the interiority of a shared consciousness.

Japanese philosophers generally chose to render the concept of *Erlebnis* (lived experience) in *Lebensphilosophie* and phenomenology with the word *taiken*. A character compound that brings the body into play, *taiken* generated its own set of effects in the Japanese philosophical discussion of experience. Specifically, it facilitated the tendency of Japanese theorists to embed experience in nature and thus remove it from the reach of critical thought. In *"Iki" no kōzō*, Kuki assigned the notion of *taiken* a double role, both ontological and epistemological: *taiken* both insured the continuing presence of the past to consciousness and tapped an enriched and fundamental mode of apprehending the world far superior to the limited scope of reason.

In *Keywords,* a critical compendium of social and cultural vocabulary, Raymond Williams shows that both of these meanings — a knowledge gathered from the past and a rich and dynamic consciousness — have been active in modern European uses of the term "experience" as well. Further, he suggests that the two meanings have moved increasingly closer together within a "common historical situation," presumably the rise of positivism. Williams points out that experience as an appeal to the whole consciousness, to an individual's entire being, is part of a general movement that underlies the development of "culture," particularly, I would add, as it was defined in the context of the nineteenth-century cultural sciences.[71] The historical affinity that Williams notes between notions of experience and culture is especially noteworthy in

---

70. Kuki, "'Iki' no honshitsu," *KSZ,* 1:106.
71. Williams, *Keywords,* 126–29.

light of developments in Japanese cultural theory. In *"Iki" no kōzō,* the experience in question, decidedly collective, also goes by the name of "spiritual culture."

Japan as the Haven of Experience

For a number of Japanese thinkers, the philosophical mission to defend experience acquired a specificity of locale only implied in European discourse. For these thinkers, the threat to the autonomy and integrity of experience originated not in a vague apprehension of a machinelike outer world but rather in the West and its insidious incursions across Japan's cultural borders. The experience they sought to defend was the collective experience of the Japanese *minzoku,* or "indigenous culture," as they defined it. Increasingly, Japanese cultural theorists identified the West with the negative attributes that had infiltrated the notion of "civilization": the vulgarity of materialism, the callousness of rationality, the cunning of reason. Kuki had become selectively forgetful of his own historical antecedents—in particular, the massive industrialization and rationalization of society proceeding apace since the Meiji era. That forgetfulness allowed him to reimagine Japan as a haven for experience and a refuge for culture.

In the essays collected under the title "Choses japonaises," Kuki offered a French-speaking audience a brief glimpse of the vast gulf separating Japan and Europe: on one side, a materialistic West blinded by the dim light of reason, on the other, Japan, a nation imbued with a spirit of ethical idealism. In one of those essays, "L'Âme japonaise" (The Japanese Spirit), Kuki begins with his own rendition of a verse by Motoori Norinaga, the most renowned of the eighteenth-century nativist scholars:

> You ask
> What is the Japanese spirit?
> The blossom of a mountain cherry
> Exhaling its perfume in the morning light.

The fleeting beauty of the blossoms, Kuki explains, does not express the sadness of life; rather, "it signifies a spirit always ready to offer itself up and die for its ideals. The morning light is the moral ideal, the same light that Plato spoke of in his allegory of the cave. This verse gives expression to an absolute contempt for all that is material. In one word, idealism."

Europeans, continues Kuki, have condemned the Japanese tradition of self-sacrifice for one's lord, or *harakiri,* as either naive or barbaric. But it is the Europeans who are themselves naive and ignorant, blinded by the prejudices of Christianity. The "tragic heroism" of *harakiri,* Kuki argues, is a quintessential expression of Japanese idealism. From Ōtomo no Yakamochi in the eighth century to General Nogi (whose suicide following the death of the Meiji Emperor in 1912 became the subject of heated controversy in the press) in the twentieth, the Japanese have drawn on a moral force that transcends the mediocrity of reason. Inverting the metaphor of enlightenment, he writes: "The faint light of reason fades to nothing in the presence of that greater radiance born of darkness." [72] Kuki's reading of Motoori's poem might well have scandalized its author, who had nothing but contempt for the Confucianized customs of a Tokugawa warrior class. Motoori's "Japanese spirit" aspired rather to the recovery of an archaic accord between words and things expressed in the earliest Japanese classics — an accord essentially Japanese, according to Motoori, despite its mediation by Chinese letters. Kuki's interpretation ignored the troubled legacy of *junshi* — the custom of following one's lord in death — bequeathed by the Tokugawa era.[73] His tribute to ritual suicide also sidestepped the reactions of stunned ambivalence to the suicide of General Nogi and his wife as they were registered in the contemporary press. Carol Gluck underscores the anachronistic tenor of that event at the close of the Meiji era: "In a nation in the midst of a solemn celebration of its modernity, its foremost soldier and hero of the Russo-Japanese War had followed a custom that had been outlawed by the Tokugawa shogunate as antiquated in 1663." [74]

The ambiguities surrounding Nogi's suicide were captured in fiction as well, perhaps most poignantly by Natsume Sōseki. In *Sore kara* (And Then), published in 1909 before Nogi's death, Soseki measures the estrangement of his modern protagonist, Daisuke, from the feudal code and martial virtue still inhabiting the now distant past of his father's generation of new capitalist entrepreneurs. Daisuke, not yet confronted

---

72. Kuki, "L'Âme japonaise," *KSZ,* 1:252, 1:250–51.

73. Soon after the establishment of the Tokugawa shogunate, *junshi* was not only prohibited by law but was subjected to a number of legalistic critiques.

74. Gluck, *Japan's Modern Myths,* 221.

with his own fallibility and finitude, recalls the story of his father's close escape from obligatory ritual suicide with distrust and aversion: "How could he have thought of going through with such a gruesome affair! Every time his father recounted the past, Daisuke found him more distasteful than admirable. Or else he thought of him as a liar."[75] Irrevocably cut off from his father's history, Daisuke is nevertheless soon to discover himself inescapably trapped in the more cerebral but equally tragic paradoxes of his own contemporaneity. In the later novel, *Kokoro,* an older and now reclusive *Sensei,* upon hearing of the successive deaths of the Meiji emperor and General and Mrs. Nogi, memorializes the passing of an imperial era, pays tribute to a new state ideology, and atones for distinctively modern sins with a highly privatized suicide.

In the years following this ambiguous ending of the Meiji era, Nogi's life (and death) was heroized and solemnized in official commemoration, in textbooks, and in the popular press, his persona transformed into a "symbol for loyalty and self-sacrificing service to the state." Gluck observes that Nogi's suicide roughly coincided with a renewed interest in *bushidō* (the way of the warrior), codified during the Tokugawa era. *Bushidō* had begun to gain common currency in the years immediately following the Russo-Japanese War (1904–1905). The resources of this warrior ethos were deployed by bureaucrats and opinion leaders as moral exhortation for corrupt statesmen, as a model for entrepreneurial businessmen, as a utopian invocation of a rural past, and, most crucially, as an ethos for a newly constructed middle-class and imperial subject.[76] No doubt Kuki's praise of ritual suicide drew some of its inspiration from this reconsecration of samurai ideals in the service of an enterprising and expanding nation-state.

In "L'Âme japonaise," the complexities of this recent history, along with reason itself, were banished from the realm of the Japanese spirit. Kuki was by no means alone in his penchant for cloaking a critique of instrumental reason in the garb of absolute cultural difference. This mirror-image opposition between an intuitive, idealistic East and a rationalist, materialistic West had been drawn early on in the cultural theories of Okakura Tenshin. Watsuji Tetsurō expanded and refined these cultural antitheses in his studies of Japanese spiritual history and climate. The protagonist of Tanizaki's *Tade kuu mushi* (Some Prefer Nettles) (1928), finding the contradictions of a (Westernized) Japanese mo-

---

75. Natsume Sōseki, *And Then,* 38.
76. Gluck, *Japan's Modern Myths,* 226, 180, 222–25.

dernity distasteful, assumes the fictional task of reimagining Japanese culture in a highly aestheticized and unspecified past. The oppositions discovered in that novel then became the organizing axes of the seductive imagery of Tanizaki's eulogy of Japanese culture in *Inei raisan* (In Praise of Shadows). In the mid-1930's, the Marxist philosopher Tosaka Jun chronicled the shrill ubiquity of these diametrical oppositions in the glut of Japanist discourse following the 1931 Manchurian Incident. Yet Tosaka's scathing critique of the absurdity of the bland generalities, foreign derivations, and patent falsehoods of this discourse on the "Japanese spirit" did little to stem the intellectual tide. After the outbreak of the Pacific War, a similar set of oppositions determined the tone of the debates on "Overcoming the modern" in which "the blood of the Japanese" was pitted against "Western knowledge."[77]

During his Paris years, Kuki began to work out these cultural oppositions in anecdotal form. In another of the essays collected under the title "Choses japonaises," Kuki describes a disagreeable encounter with an American woman in the salon of one of the finer hotels of Deauville: "The musicians had just finished playing a meditation by Thaïs, and the melody was still resonating delightfully in my ear when a woman dressed in a gown of gold silk, her charm and distinction in perfect harmony, turned and addressed me. Among other things, she spoke of her brother in Chicago who counted several Japanese diplomats among his friends. She told me he was an engineer, adding, 'You know, that vocation is very prosperous!'" The essay continues in the same vein with another tale of the crass intrusion of dollars and cents in a conversation overheard amid the elegance and beauty of the Côte d'Azur. These incongruous encounters among the privileged society of a cosmopolitan and cultured elite provide a new occasion for Kuki to draw the line between Japan and the West:

In all good will, we cannot fathom the kind of mentality that acts and speaks by the law of the dollar weight alone, that mental necessity to level everything to the horizon of money. To our taste, there could be no uglier proverb imaginable than "time is money." And yet, at the moment I write, this

---

77. Tosaka, *Nihon ideorogīron*, 287–92; Tanizaki, *In Praise of Shadows*, 8–42, especially 8–12, 14–15, 17–22, 24–26, 30–35; Takeuchi, *Kindai no chōkoku*, 68. Ironically, this critique, in its broadest outlines, was hardly unique to Japan. In Europe, too, following the end of World War I, conservative intellectuals in the Weimar republic began to mount a series of defenses of the German *Geist* against the "dark force" of industrial technology, Enlightenment rationalism, and the political ideals of the French Revolution. See Zimmerman, *Heidegger's Confrontation with Modernity*, xvii–xviii.

proverb is being adopted and adored all over the world. Born in the new world, it has successfully invaded the old world as well. Under such compelling circumstances, shall we also join in and announce our intention to take the same path? No, our logic is different. *We,* at least, shall take a different path.[78]

Kuki was clearly disturbed by the *embourgeoisement* of culture and the downward leveling of sensibility. While his misgivings about a capitalist ethos may have been shared widely across ideological lines, his response betrays the more reactionary interests of class. At ease in privileged society, well-equipped with leisure, wealth, and status, he had no trouble affecting aristocratic disdain for money and disparaging those unable to do the same. Even more significantly, what begins as a predictable class reaction ends in a dichotomy of essence between Japan and the West. Kuki reimagined Japan as a cultural aristocracy, a superior people endowed with sufficient symbolic capital to adopt a posture of disinterest toward material concerns. As he put it, the values of the samurai class — nobility of spirit, valor, and generosity — had survived the dismantling of Japan's feudal caste system to become lodged in the spirit of the nation.[79]

History as the Intentionality of the Collective Subject

Kuki's claim that Japan represented a privileged site of culture was closely allied to his reassessment of the meaning and function of history. Here, too, his reading of phenomenology, particularly in its hermeneutic inflection, was decisive. Of late, hermeneutics has been hailed for the radicality of its historical consciousness, its recognition that no reflection, however esoteric or reflexive, is free from the entanglements of history. This assessment will be subjected to serious question in chapter 4, but for the moment, let us return once again to Tanabe's 1924 introduction to the Heideggerian turn in phenomenology and speculate on what kind of historical consciousness Kuki discovered there.

Tanabe explained that the phenomenological approach to history re-

---

78. Kuki, "Time is Money," *KSZ,* 1:248–49.
79. Ibid.

lies centrally on the notion of intentionality. By historical intentionality Tanabe meant that the orientation or perspective of the subject is crucial in determining meaning and that objects might "mean" differently depending on one how one engages them. "What we call meaning," he wrote, "is something that is realized by the subject, and accordingly, it is meaningful only in relation to the subject."[80] Tanabe's reading of intentionality conformed to Husserl's equation of "things themselves" with the pure contents of human consciousness. In other words, the consciousness of a subject was to be the guarantor of the authenticity of the totality of what is real. Heidegger, on the other hand, already had begun to revise intentionality in a more deconstructive direction. In *Being and Time,* he strove to decenter a subject entrapped in inauthenticity, demonstrating the degree to which Dasein in its everyday existence is subjected to meanings that are not of its own making. Perhaps the outlines of that project were not yet apparent in those earliest of Heidegger's lectures attended by Tanabe, or perhaps Heidegger already had begun to deliver the mixed messages that became his chosen style. At any rate, Tanabe saw the subject primarily in terms of mastery over meaning rather than subjection to it.[81] In his later philosophical writings on contingence, Kuki would, in fact, directly challenge the subject's presumption to mastery—a challenge, however, that he extended only to an individual subject seeking to renew its own existence through unanticipated encounters with difference.[82] Kuki appeared singularly disinclined to submit collective subjectivity to that same risk. In his reflections on Japanese culture, he invariably situated the collectivity firmly

80. Tanabe, "Genshōgaku ni okeru atarashiki tenkō," 7.

81. In the view of literary theorist Terry Eagleton, the central desire of the phenomenological project is precisely this reassertion of subjective mastery over the world: "The crass positivism of nineteenth-century science had threatened to rob the world of subjectivity altogether, and neo-Kantian philosophy had tamely followed suit: the course of European history from the later nineteenth century onwards appeared to cast grave doubt on the traditional presumption that 'man' was in control of his destiny, that he was any longer the creative centre of his world. Phenomenology, in reaction, restored the transcendental subject to its rightful throne." *Literary Theory,* 58. In this regard, it should be noted that long before Heidegger's turn toward art, and even before *Being and Time,* he bestowed upon the poet the role of shaper within a genuine experiential world. Presumably it was only within a "fallen," public world that the subject was seen as deprived of creative control over his own works.

82. Kuki produced a body of work on *gūzensei* after his return to Japan in 1929, much of which is included in *Gūzensei no mondai.* In addition, a series of essays and lectures (including his 1932 doctoral thesis at Kyoto Imperial University) is collected under the title "Gūzensei ni kansuru ronkō, *KSZ,* 2:265–384.

and securely at the creative origin of a predictably meaningful world. In this more conservative vision, he concurred with Tanabe's reading of historical intentionality.

This particular understanding of the notion of intentionality had decisive effects for the role history would play in Japanese cultural theory. In Tanabe's words, "History is not an imitation of the facts of the past. Rather, history manifests the way in which the present envisages the past, how it acknowledges the past, and in what manner it preserves or annuls the past. Thus, history is actually a sign of the way in which the present itself exists." This articulation might have lent itself to a Nietzschean insight into history as an embattled arena for competing interpretations. In this view, the historical record is envisaged as a palimpsest on which each successful bid for historiographical hegemony superimposes itself on other, less victorious histories. Tanabe chose rather to tame the Nietzschean "will to power" lurking in history with an appeal to Dilthey's concept of a unified cultural style: "The cultural style of the past is an expression of the existence of that past. In the cultural forms of any given era, there is a common and unified style that runs through all the various cultural domains — art, literature, religion, morality, scholarship, economics — what Dilthey has called a cultural system."[83] For Dilthey, the source and guarantor of that unity of cultural style was nothing less than *Geist,* the collective spirit and life force of an era. The style of an era and its indwelling *Geist* passes on like a legacy to those able sympathetically to recognize its fundamental affinity with the present. Dilthey's popularizers later extended his formulations to make explicit and atavistic equations between the collective spirit of an era and a "historical *Volk* as a unique expression of the life force."[84]

Although Kuki devoted little attention to history in "'Iki' no honshitsu," a few brief allusions indicate that he had chosen to follow Tanabe's lead in the direction of Dilthey. In the opening lines, Kuki explained that history is "the embodiment of a unique cultural form" and cited Tanabe to support his own claim that the "conscious being of the *minzoku*" creatively and organically generates its own unique language and meaning: "the concrete language and meaning of a given *minzoku* as an expression of its very being," he wrote, "are deeply dyed in the unique experience of that *minzoku.*"[85] With this, Kuki had virtually trans-

83. Tanabe, "Genshōgaku ni okeru atarashiki tenkō," 17–18.
84. Zimmerman, *Heidegger's Confrontation with Modernity,* 12.
85. Kuki, "'Iki' no honshitsu," *KSZ,* 1:89.

formed history into experience, that is to say, into an interiorized duration where the collective subject finds testimony to its identity and continuity. An abode for the "collective spirit," this inward history provided a refuge from the cultural and social disruptions that had so deeply marked the engagement with modernity in Japan.

The historical understanding that Kuki acquired through his early encounters with *Lebensphilosophie* and phenomenology stood in sharp contrast with theories of developmental history that had prevailed through the ideological reign of "civilization and enlightenment." One of Japan's earliest and most articulate advocates of "civilization," Fukuzawa Yukichi, envisaged history as a movement through predictable stages of civilization toward a future of ever greater material and intellectual wealth. The movement of history was presumed to be both progressive and universal. In the early stages of Meiji modernization, this view implied that the "civilized" present of the West represented the inevitable and desirable future of a still "semicivilized" Japan.

In his 1928 essay "Bergson au Japon," Kuki began to revise notions of progress to account for the singularity of a separate Japanese reality: "When one speaks of progress, one simultaneously speaks of tradition. Our oriental thinking, insofar as it is prepared to study occidental thinking, will never attain true progress unless it is abundantly nourished by its own tradition. Thus, we must pursue our own tradition in order to project beyond it."[86] Ultimately, this new attentiveness to tradition required a secession from dominant modes of Enlightenment historiography.

During the same year, in his *Propos sur le temps* (Considerations on Time), Kuki issued a more direct challenge to an already thoroughly assimilated concept of linear and progressive time. In its stead, Kuki entertained the notion of a cyclical and repetitive "oriental time." In keeping with his cosmopolitan predilections, he discovered models for "an identical time repeating itself in perpetuity" not only in Buddhist karmic causality and Hindu notions of kalpa (cosmic periods) but also in Pythagorean and Stoic conceptions of the "Great Year."[87] In Buddhist thought, this is the time of transmigration, "indefinite rebirth, the perpetual repetition of the will, the endless return of time." Quoting from *Milanda-panha,* Kuki offers a demonstration of Buddhist skepticism to-

86. Kuki, "Bergson au Japon," *KSZ,* 1:257.

87. Kuki, "Bergson au Japon," as translated in Light, *Shūzō Kuki and Jean-Paul Sartre,* 45.

ward historical time: "Of past, present, and future duration, the root is ignorance; from ignorance come the dispositions of the will."[88] Buddhism, he explains, discerns in this will the root of all evil and the cause of all suffering. For the one who would be liberated from this time of transmigration, there are, Kuki explains, two methods—transcendent, intellectualist liberation and immanent, voluntarist liberation:

> Transcendent, intellectualist liberation is the *nirvāna* of the religion of Indian inspiration. Immanent, voluntarist liberation is *Bushidō,* the way of the *bushi,* the moral ideal of Japan. The first consists in denying time by means of the intellect in order to live, or rather to die, in nontemporal "deliverance," in "eternal repose." The second consists in an unconcern with time, in order to live, truly live in the indefinite repetition of the arduous search for the true, the good, and the beautiful.[89]

Inserting a note of modern secular skepticism, Kuki grants that the time of transmigration is no less imaginary than the notion of an afterlife in Christianity. What is not in question, however, is the philosophy of *bushidō,* a uniquely Japanese ethical idealism, according to Kuki, that created its own culturally specific response to Buddhist truths.[90] In this essay, Kuki uses the props of "oriental time" to set the stage for the appearance of an intangible cultural property. Japan, he suggested to his European audience, should be valued not for its hard-won material resemblance to the West but rather for its spiritual distinctiveness from the West.

While Kuki's Japanized version of "eternal repetition" represented a gesture of defiance against the normative force of a unilinear history imposed by the recent geopolitical (im)balance of power, it simultaneously aligned itself with the conservative revolution in interwar Germany. A number of thinkers of the Weimar period (1918–1933), in particular Oswald Spengler and Ernst Jünger, issued their own refutations of a forward-moving, progressive time, offering in its place a reactionary return to preindustrial notions of community in the name of the German *Geist.*[91] Not far in the offing, German fascism would invoke a "mys-

---

88. Ibid., 44.
89. Ibid., 50.
90. Kuki, "La notion du temps et la reprise sur le temps en orient," *KSZ,* 1:284 n. 8.
91. Bourdieu, *The Political Ontology of Martin Heidegger,* 20. In recent critical literature, Heidegger has been increasingly linked to "reactionary modernist" Ernst Jünger—an explicit advocate of National Socialism—particularly in what concerns fascistic theories of labor. For a detailed discussion, see Zimmerman, *Heidegger's Confrontation with Modernity,* xxiii–xix, and chapters 4 and 5.

tical and millenarian dynamic" powered by an urge to "overcome"—a dynamic that allowed the folk to stand within yet soar above tradition.[92] In similar fashion, but under the auspices of the Japanese spirit, Kuki turned to an indigenous tradition in order to reclaim cultural authenticity from the clutches of Enlightenment history. On this common ground, Kuki's project contributed to a larger enterprise aimed at replacing the rootlessness of modern urban-industrial society with an organic community grounded in national soil.

Heidegger began to make his own contribution to this antiprogressive enterprise early in his career. In his lectures immediately after World War I, the German philosopher sought precedents for a critique of Enlightenment history in the German Romantics. He praised Herder, who "saw historical reality in its manifold and irrational fullness and above all the independent self-worth of every nation, every age, every historical manifestation in general. . . . Historical reality was no longer seen exclusively in a schematic-rulebound, rationalistic-linear direction of progress." In the same lecture, Heidegger went on to identify a new awakening of "the view for individual, qualitatively original centers of reality and contexts of reality." In such a view, the "categories of 'ownness' (*Eigenheit*) become meaningful and related to all shapes of life, i.e. *this* [life] first becomes visible as such." Significantly, Heidegger's category of *Eigenheit*—an existential possibility extended to individual Dasein in *Being and Time*—clearly had early affinities with the nation. "The objectifying experience (*Erfahrung*) of science," an experience promoted by though not original to the Enlightenment, according to Heidegger, "de-vivifies (*ent-lebt*) the lived experience (*Erlebnis*) of the people."[93] He praised the project of German idealist thinkers to rescue myths, folklore, and the primitive community from the Enlightenment stigma of barbarism. In Japan, cultural critics of the 1930's, most notably Kobayashi Hideo, took up this clarion call against the modern historiographical predilection for objectification. According to Kobayashi, any rational historiographical intervention amounted to the wholesale impoverishment of all that was meaningful in history. Instead, he proposed an engagement with history in the form of epiphany—an immediate, affective intuition of the heroic moments dwelling in an intimate collective past.[94] But before Kobayashi could articulate this notion of immac-

92. Mosse, "Introduction," 8–9.
93. Originally from Heidegger's 1919 lectures. Translated in Zimmerman, *Heidegger's Confrontation with Modernity*, 20.
94. Kobayashi, "Rekishi to bungaku," 295–300.

ulate history, Kuki staged an exemplary epiphany on the cultural-historical site of late Edo.

Husserl and the Dangers of Sameness

If sanctioned historical methods had become suspect, how was one to go about capturing the content of culturally authentic experience? Beginning in the mid-1920's, Kuki began to leave signs of his search for such a method in the preliminary drafts of *"Iki" no kōzō*. In *"'Iki' no honshitsu,"* he already had begun to turn away from Husserlian phenomenology in favor of the Heideggerian revision as a method appropriate to the understanding of culture. In the first chapter of that draft, "Bunka genshō no minzokuteki tokushūsei" (The National Particularity of Cultural Phenomena), Kuki offered the beginnings of an explanation for his preference. In his critique of the concept of "ideation through variation," Kuki's reference to Husserl was abbreviated and oblique but nevertheless unmistakable. The concept, as the scholar of German philosophy Rüdiger Bubner explains, was central to Husserl's new science of phenomena. Husserl had proposed a science of phenomena that promised an absolute knowledge of what is universally and essentially true about things. One gains access to these universal essences by an act of intellectual imagination. Starting from a contingent and subjectively present view of a thing, the investigator freely invents alternatives until "what is intended stands before his gaze in full 'self-givenness.'"[95] Such an intellectual distillation of the world, argued Kuki, threatens to reduce what is unique and different in culture to universal abstractions: "To take a phenomenon imbued with national nuance and submit it freely to variation, to carry out what is called an intuition of essence in the domain of possibility—this will lead to nothing more than the generic concept implied by the phenomenon in question."[96] These alternatives, freely varied in the mind of the observer, "suggest the pallor of shadows," Kuki wrote in "Jitsuzon tetsugaku" (Existential Philosophy): "The reality of the real," Kuki insisted, "cannot be embraced by universals."[97] In its Husserlian form, the phenomenological

---

95. Bubner, *Modern German Philosophy*, 17–18.
96. Kuki, "'Iki' no honshitsu," *KSZ*, 1:92.
97. Kuki, "Jitsuzon tetsugaku" in *Ningen to Jitsuzon*, *KSZ*, 3:78.

method was ill suited to guarantee the integrity, particularity, and continuity of culture.

In the same philosophical meditation, Kuki added a further dimension to his critique of Husserl, one that casts a revealing light on the
material realities and ideological anxieties that shaped the cultural theory of *"Iki" no kōzō:*

> If we rely exclusively on intuition of essences, "this particular thing" (*kore*)
> will never have a chance. Consider for a moment something like a phono-
> graph needle. Its number and model constitute one *idea,* a formal unit.
> From the point of view of use, as long as we have the number and model
> of the needle, we can freely substitute one individual for another . . . each
> is equivalent to all the others. . . . Everything produced mechanically ac-
> cording to the principle of mass production possesses this quality.[98]

Here Kuki drew an unflattering comparison between the phenomenological method and new forms of production. This critical comparison
reveals that Kuki's apprehensions of the impoverishment of experience
and the threat to Japanese distinctiveness originated not simply in the
universalist ambitions of Western knowledge but also in technologies
of mass production already deeply embedded in the Japanese socioeco-
nomic terrain. We should bear in mind that "equivalence"—whether
mechanical or political (universal equality)—represents a sensibility that
Walter Benjamin located firmly on the side of the twentieth-century
masses.[99]

Interestingly, Kuki's spiritual forebear, Okakura, had concluded his
Ideals of the East on a nostalgic note, with visions of a utopian pastoral.
Faced with the encroachment of the West and Japan's nearly completed
industrial revolution, he argued that Asia must preserve the beauty, individuality, and humanity of simple life and simple labor—"For to
clothe oneself in the web of one's own weaving is to house oneself in
one's own house, to create for the spirit its own sphere."[100] A generation
after Okakura, a second industrial revolution integrated mechanized
technologies into the everyday life of an increasingly urbanized Japanese
populace. As we shall see in later chapters, high culture and academe
were by no means exempt from the transformations wrought by mecha-

98. Ibid., 3:72.
99. Benjamin, "The Work of Art in an Age of Mechanical Reproduction," in *Illuminations,* 222–23. I will address the social implications of Kuki's aesthetics at greater length
in chapter 5.
100. Okakura, *Ideals of the East,* 237.

nization, or from its attendant systems of mass production and consumption. These transformations not only brought Japan into closer cultural proximity with the West but also extended access to cultural representation to newly enfranchised masses within Japan. Faced with impending shifts in the balance of cultural and social power, Kuki assumed a task of nearly impossible proportions—the defense of culture from the leveling effects of the masses and the machine. He carried out that struggle on the imaginary terrain already claimed by German cultural theory, the inner life of the spirit.

Heidegger and the Temptation of Difference

While Husserlian phenomenology threatened to reduce culture to indistinguishable units of standardized and universalized proportions, Heidegger's version, along with its hermeneutic heritage, enabled Kuki to stake out the exclusive territory of the Japanese spirit. Because the subject of Heideggerian philosophy and hermeneutics is so central to an analysis of *"Iki" no kōzō,* I will reserve that discussion for a chapter of its own and explore here just one particular aspect of Kuki's encounter with Heidegger. This encounter reveals yet another stage on Kuki's journey toward the theorization of cultural difference, one that took him through the exotic byways of the European imagination. Chapter 1 offered an initial glimpse of the cross-cultural itineraries of racism and exoticism, particularly as they traversed the seductive female body inscribed in the discourse of national being. Those same itineraries made their way through more abstract discourse as well, in particular, cross-cultural assessments of aesthetic and philosophical endowments.

Since the nineteenth century, Europeans had begun to fathom a way out of the impasse of their own reason in the remote civilizations of the Orient. From the oppressive confines of the European salon, one French artist articulated the emancipatory hopes raised by encounters with Japanese art: "Look at the Japanese . . . and you will see life outdoors in the sun, without shadows."[101] From expeditions of purloin, plunder, and investigation, Europeans returned home with tangible artifacts and invented images of different worlds. One destination among others for these exoticizing exploits, Japan nevertheless left a deep im-

---

101. Paul Gauguin, quoted by James A. Michener in *Floating World,* 238.

pression on the European imagination, perhaps most graphically in the
visual arts during the latter part of the nineteenth century.

Oddly enough, it was often in Europe that Japanese artists, writers,
and thinkers first surrendered to the spell of their own faraway island
country. In one of a series of short essays drafted during his stay in Paris,
Kuki measured the distance that separated Europe from Japan in revealing terms:

Since coming to live in Europe, I have realized again and again that Europeans have absolutely no understanding of my country. I am not surprised; it
is so far away, beyond Persia, beyond India, beyond China. Out there, far
away, amid the eternal waves of the Pacific Ocean, lies the island of the Rising
Sun. The difference between the customs of the inhabitants of that island and
those of the Europeans is as immense as the distance between them.[102]

Here, Kuki had already begun not only to widen the cultural breach
between Japan and Europe but also to exoticize it in a language reminiscent of the other. In the boldest possible formulation, one might say
that Japanese travelers reappropriated Japan from Europe as an exoticized object. Just as *ukiyoe* were first reimported back into Japan from
Paris museums and private European collections after World War I,[103]
less tangible aspects of the cultural past were newly rediscovered by Japanese visitors in Europe. But whether material or ethereal, the artifacts
of Japanese culture had become indelibly inflected by Europe's fascination with, or depreciation of, one of its cultural others.

The discursive dimensions of this highly mediated cultural self-
discovery stand out most clearly in the encounter between Kuki and
Heidegger during the 1920's as Heidegger recalled it in "A Dialogue on
Language." Judging from the clarity of his recollections, Heidegger
must have been greatly impressed by Kuki's efforts to explain Japanese
art and communicate the meaning of *iki*. Some thirty years after the
fact, he was still able to paraphrase the explanation of his Japanese
friend: "[Kuki] spoke of sensuous radiance through whose lively delight
there breaks the radiance of something suprasensuous." A pleasing turn
of phrase perhaps, but the distinction Kuki drew between the sensuous
and the nonsensuous is the very distinction on which Western metaphysics turns, claimed Heidegger. Kuki's attempt to "say the essential
nature of Eastasian art" was already betrayed by the language of the

102. Kuki, "C'est le paysan," *KSZ*, 1:254. For a translation of the entire essay under
the title "A Peasant He Is," see Light, *Shūzō Kuki and Jean-Paul Sartre*, 77–78.
103. Michener, *Floating World*, 243–45.

dialogue. In hindsight, Heidegger concluded that Kuki had been unable to resist the temptation of the West—a temptation enticing him to submit the nature of Japanese art to the discriminating language of European aesthetics.[104] But interestingly, the "Dialogue" suggests one further temptation never explicitly acknowledged in the text—the temptation compelling Kuki to invest his description of *iki* with Heidegger's desire for the unutterable beyond of Western metaphysics.[105] Heidegger, for his part, was seduced by the "enchantment" and "mystery" that suffused their cooperative conjuring of the "Eastasian world." If Heidegger's total ignorance of Japanese encouraged him to find an absolute other in the Japanese language, it was perhaps, conversely, Kuki's intimate familiarity with the West that led him to promote Heidegger's project.

As an afterthought, the Inquirer of "A Dialogue on Language" adds that the presence of Kuki's wife, dressed in "festive Japanese garments," made "the Eastasian world more luminously present," an understandable response, but an intriguing one as well, in light of the fact that the feminine image was to become emblematic of cultural difference in *"Iki" no kōzō*. Though *iki* had originally been an epithet applied to both genders, Kuki's interpretation weighed heavily toward its feminine manifestations—a gender preference suggesting that Kuki himself was implicated in an exoticizing discourse on the Orient that consistently feminized its object.

In an unsparing critique of this encounter, Peter Dale accuses both Kuki and Heidegger of cloaking themselves in an obscure and hermetic language for the purpose of self-aggrandizement. It is ironic, Dale says, that the two rivaled one another in deliberate mystification: "Kuki steals his mentor's rhetorical thunder by interpreting *iki* in such an impalpably vague manner that it leaves Heidegger pleasantly bewildered, by confirming his original assumptions about the untranslatability of Japanese." For Dale, who holds this deliberate mystification liable for an ill-fated political reaction, the irony is a bitter one. Drawing from Adorno's *The Jargon of Authenticity*, Dale elaborates on the tactics common to the

---

104. Heidegger, "A Dialogue on Language," 14, 4, 2–5.

105. The "Japanese"—or "J," as Heidegger's discussant is identified—now well advised of the reifying trap of metaphysics, amends Kuki's definition of *iki* in a direction that follows Heidegger beyond oppositions between subject and object into the mysteries of being: *"Iki* is the breath of stillness of luminous delight . . . the pure delight of the beckoning stillness. The breath of stillness that makes this beckoning delight come into its own is the reign under which that delight is made to come." Ibid., 44–45. See also the introduction, 21, on Tezuka Tomio as the model for the Japanese discussant.

German and Japanese philosophers: "The rhetorical mode of vaporous yet plausible profundity, of 'dressing up empirical words with aura,' is the polemical tool favored by the reactionary in his battle to preserve the mystique of a tradition from the logic of a mature modernity."[106] Dale's insistence on the reactionary character of this discourse, whether German or Japanese, is not unfounded.[107] Karatani Kōjin has drawn an even more direct ideological line between the related projects of Kuki and Heidegger and the fascist developments in their respective societies.[108] Nevertheless, Karatani acknowledges a certain degree of ambiguity in Kuki's project. There was, he suggests, an impulse toward historical critique that prompted Kuki to pit a moment in Japan's nineteenth century against the totalizing project of modernity. Dale, on the other hand, is unequivocal in his condemnation of all forms of Japanese cultural exceptionalism, citing atavistic pathologies of personal and collective psychology as the principal cause of reaction. In so doing, he risks losing sight of the complex network of historical relations in which this discourse on culture took shape. To identify just one of those ambiguities, we might explore for a moment the darker side of exoticizing impulses circulating in European salons.

Asiaticism and the Transference of Culture

Heidegger offered Kuki an affirmative though ultimately negligible reflection of Japan as an imaginary and desirable site of difference. Exoticizing discourse may endow its object with unfathomable mystery as a distancing mechanism, a way depriving the object of historical content. Exoticism also can produce that same dehistoricizing distance by demeaning its object and depriving it of value. In the Europe that emerged profoundly shaken from World War I, old anxieties

---

106. Dale, *The Myth of Japanese Uniqueness,* 69, 73. In his remarks on the Heidegger-Kuki exchange, Karatani Kōjin supports Dale's view, explicitly attributing their mutual mystifications to an exoticizing impulse: "The fact that Heidegger found something profoundly unfathomable in the concept of *iki* was not a matter of his own exoticism alone. Kuki himself had explained *iki* to him in just such a manner." See "Edo no seishin," 9.

107. Dale, however, attributes Japanese cultural reaction to the unfortunate triumph of puerile traditional beliefs over a mature modernity, a premise with which I do take issue. What I propose is rather that the potential for reaction resided within the formal and thematic possibilities of modernism itself.

108. Karatani, "Edo no seishin," 9.

of contamination and corruption resurfaced, fears of vulnerability to a dreaded otherness, gained representation in a discourse on what critics of this invasive foreign corruption chose to call "Asiaticism."[109] In attempts at symbolic exorcism, guardians of European purity and privilege called on an array of nineteenth-century intellectual resources, in particular the vestiges of developmental history, to reimagine Asia as Europe's depreciated other. No doubt, Kuki had such defensive gestures in mind when he lamented Europe's tenacious misperceptions of Japan.

Kuki offered a striking sample of such misunderstanding in the conclusion of his lecture for the 1928 Pontigny *décade*, "L'Expression de l'infini dans l'art japonais" (Expression of the Infinite in Japanese Art). This particular sample came from the pen of the French writer and connoisseur of Japanese poetry André Suarès. Kuki quoted at length from the preface of *Hai Kai d'Occident* in which Suarès's faint praise for the brevity of Japan's poetic forms quickly yields to allegations of racial inferiority. In a combination of paraphrase and citation from Suarès's introduction, Kuki provides this lengthy commentary for his almost exclusively European audience:

As for the heart of such poetry, as for the content of "the entire art of Nippon," [Suarès] professes that Japan contents itself with mere objects, with the fleeting instant, that the Japanese are unaware of any aspiration to the infinite, to eternity. [Suarès] says: "Here, we live only to live forever. Virtually our sole desire is to endure forever. The need to be eternal is inseparable from our perishable condition. . . . Over there, to the contrary, in the empire of the Rising Sun, such a desire is unheard of. . . . The spirit of man is the locus of all space and all time, but only on one condition: that the spirit of man create a metaphysics capable of leading to mathematics. The Far East has remained a total stranger to such developments. Their art and poetry are founded on a principle opposite to our own. All is spatial in their spirits. . . . To all appearances, their art never turns inward, or scorns to do so. The geometrical point must resolve itself in an instance of thought, and knows itself as such. These words have no meaning for the yellow race.[110]

---

109. For documents of European "Asiaticism" during the interwar years, see Massis, *Defense of the West,* and Guénon, *East and West*. A not so distant relative of Asiaticism is the "yellow peril," a specter first raised as the underside of European imperialism in the latter part of the nineteenth century. The "yellow peril" was resurrected at regular intervals by events that suggested a stronger Asian presence in global geopolitics: Japan's victory over Russia in 1905, for example, and a decade later, the Bolshevik revolution in Russia. See Dower, *War Without Mercy,* 155–63, and Irokawa, *The Culture of the Meiji Period,* 214–16.

110. Kuki, "L'Expression de l'infini dans l'art japonais," *KSZ,* 1:267.

To demonstrate the degree of misapprehension in Suarès's introduction, Kuki begins his lecture with an emblematic quote from Okakura's *Ideals of the East:* "The history of Japanese art is the history of Asian ideals."[111] And in the style of Okakura, Kuki invokes Chinese Taoism, Indian Buddhism, and native *bushidō* as testimony to Japan's aspiration to the infinite, to the interiority of its art, and to the depth of its thought.[112]

No doubt the passage Kuki quotes from *Hai Kai d'Occident* was only a small sampling of what could only have been widespread attempts to reaffirm a threatened European monopoly on cultural value and spiritual depth. In response to such devastating dismissals of the Japanese aesthetic and philosophical legacy, Kuki assumed a precariously equivocal position. He attempted to defend Japan's difference from the West and, simultaneously, to argue for its worth in terms of a European hierarchy of value. In *"Iki" no kōzō,* Kuki took further steps to safeguard Japan's identity within a secure horizon of culture. Yet the identity he so jealously guarded had long since been infiltrated by "the desire of the West" — an equivocal expression meant to imply both Europe's exoticizing desire for (Japanese) difference as a form of self-authentication and Japan's desire to acquire Western knowledge/power and, thereby, recognition from the West.

Before Kuki put his stamp on the final version of *"Iki" no kōzō,* he had in fact acknowledged something of this complex play of desire across cultural boundaries. Both in "'Iki' no honshitsu" and in the first published draft of *"Iki" no kōzō,*[113] Kuki concluded with a passage that testified to the circuitous path of cultural self-discovery. Following a litany of Japanese artifacts already imported by the West — *ukiyoe,* haiku, screens, lacquerware, kimono — Kuki remarked: "It may be that Western culture, in a manner so gradual that it has gone unnoticed by us, is in the process of transplanting *iki* as well. . . . No one would deny that some form of *iki* has been introduced into the music of Debussy and Ravel." Kuki puts this instance of cultural graft in the context of a larger European debate on Asiaticism: "Western scholars are now arguing the issue of

111.   The original is found in Okakura, *Ideals of the East,* 8.

112.   It is ironic that, in the interest of convincing a European audience of Japan's worth, Kuki dismissed popular art forms crucial to the aesthetic of *iki*: "For most Europeans, Japanese art consists only of woodblock prints of women and landscapes or of tea service in multicolored porcelain. Often such things are worth little more than nothing. The truly great works of art remain virtually unknown." Kuki, "L'Expression de l'infini dans l'art japonais," *KSZ,* 1:281.

113.   The first draft appeared in two installments of the journal *Shisō,* January and February 1930, approximately nine months after Kuki's return to Japan.

oriental taste, whether it is 'fashion or influence.' The 'Asian invasion' has become the basis of their fears in all its cultural ramifications." Kuki was well aware of the vogue for the Orient among European intelligentsia, as well as of the anxieties inspired by the specter of Asiaticism. What he seems to have overlooked was that the debate on Asiaticism represented, at best, forms of exoticism, and at worst, racial hysteria. In Kuki's eyes, European interest in Asia attested to Japan's cultural ascendancy over the West. The aesthetic style of *iki* could not fail to captivate Europe: "The special cultural value of *iki* cannot but elicit interest and awed astonishment [from Westerners]. And if it is the case that *iki* has not already sent its roots into Western soil, the future will surely bring opportunities for its transplantation." It is in the following line that Kuki acknowledged not only the circular trajectory by which Japan would recover its own culture but also the moment of alienation that had insinuated itself into Japan's recognition of its own image: "Chances are that *iki* will once again be imported back into Japan. When that happens, we cannot but recollect *iki* as *something that belongs to us* and recognize it anew."[114] In the final version of *"Iki" no kōzō*, Kuki excised this passage from the text. Only a reference to the act of recollection survived the revision, a barely decipherable trace of the heterogeneous origins of culture. The faintly familiar strain in the melodies of Ravel or in the paintings of Degas had nothing to do with *iki* or with the "essence" of Japanese culture. In the disposition of national cultures, resemblances, Kuki was soon to caution, are always deceptive.

114. *"Iki" no kōzō*, *Shisō* version, in *KSZ*, supplementary volume, 102–3. The organic image of transplanting is particularly telling in view of the fact that Kuki deployed a logic of organicism to foreclose on cultural borrowing.

CHAPTER 3

History or Value

The Vicissitudes of Edo Culture

Verweile doch, du bist so schön. (Stay awhile, you are so beautiful.)
Johann Wolfgang von Goethe, *Faust*

To articulate the past historically does not mean to recognize it "the way it really was." It means to seize hold of a memory as it flashes up at a moment of danger.
Walter Benjamin, "Theses on the Philosophy of History"

Once culture itself has been debased to "cultural goods," with its hideous philosophical rationalization, "cultural value," it has already defamed its raison d'être.
Theodor Adorno, *Prisms*

Kuki's itinerary thus far suggests that the "structure" of *iki* began with a certain affinity for modernist images—the women of fashion in Europe's most cosmopolitan of cities, the ambiance of Paris bistros, Baudelaire's dandy, the impressionist melodies of Debussy. In Marburg, Kuki had offered *iki* to Heidegger as an exotic metaphysics that both reproduced the gestures of and beckoned from beyond modern aesthetics. Like so many intellectuals and artists in the first decades of the twentieth century, Kuki joined the migration into and between metropolitan centers that formed the social base of modernism. He found his pleasure and his inspiration in the "miscellaneity of the metropolis," in accidental encounters in cities of strangers.[1] In intellectual

---

1. Williams, *The Politics of Modernism*, 14–15.

terms, he profited from the cosmopolitan gatherings in the cultural capitals of Germany and France.

Against this backdrop of European modernism, the discursive contours for *"Iki" no kōzō* begin to emerge, but only partially; the settings for Kuki's project are plural, complex, and overlapping. In an endeavor to bring some of these other settings into view, we need to turn back to Japan — both to Kuki's own historical present and to Japan's varied and variable pasts. Any text that addresses the past offers, at the very least, a double exposure of history, representing both its selected historical period and the contemporary moment in which the text is produced. This effect of double exposure is especially striking in *"Iki" no kōzō*, a text passionately invested both in an episode of Tokugawa cultural history and in the urgency of its own early Shōwa present. Between these two moments, Kuki performed a kind of discursive alchemy, transmuting traces of absence into signifiers of valued presence. As if to further complicate this double-layered discursive operation, a web of texts interposes itself between *"Iki" no kōzō* and its historical object, a genealogy of reflection on Tokugawa history both preceding and succeeding Kuki's project. The cultural setting of Edo, evoked in *"Iki" no kōzō* by a rich intertextual network assembled from the archives of the late Tokugawa era, was by no means a permanent installation; rather, it was constructed and reconstructed at different moments and from different perspectives throughout Japan's modern history. These multiple perspectives provide both the sources and the thematics for the present chapter, a meditation on what Nietzsche called "the uses and disadvantages of history."[2] As one particular perspective on Edo culture within this genealogy, *"Iki" no kōzō* begins to assume its own particular historicity and ideological significance.

Reinhabiting a Japanese Past

The first years of Shōwa witnessed a powerful revival of interest in the past, the most conspicuous sign of which was a significant expansion of the readership for serialized historical novels. This was an era of massive tomes of historical fiction for mass consumption — *Daibosatsu tōge* (The Daibosatsu Pass) by Nakazato Kaizan, *Naruto Hichō* and

2. Nietzsche, "On the Uses and Disadvantages of History for Life," 57.

Miyamoto Musashi by Yoshikawa Eiji.[3] But it was not only mass audiences who had developed a taste for (national) history. Increasingly, writers of more elite literature as well as intellectuals turned their attention to an indigenous past. In 1929, Shimazaki Tōson began to trace out the monumental dimensions of *Yoake mae* (Before the Dawn), his reassessment in fictional form of a personal and collective history framing the Meiji transformation. With the advent of the 1930's, Tanizaki Junichirō, already known for his "diabolical modernism," virtually abandoned contemporary contexts for his fiction in favor of exoticized historical settings. In 1935, he began a translation of the eleventh-century classic *Genji monogatari* into modern Japanese, a task that occupied him for the next five years. Scholars of the fledgling discipline of *minzoku-gaku* (ethnology), Yanagita Kunio and Origuchi Shinobu, turned respectively to ancient rural traditions and the literary antiquity of the Heian period. And, beginning in the 1920's, Watsuji Tetsurō, having first made his academic mark with studies of Nietzsche and Kierkegaard, devoted himself to research on ancient Japan, early Buddhism, and a two-volume study of the "spiritual history" of Japan.[4]

This renewed attention to the past came at the end of the 1920's, Japan's decade of modernism — the period in which the culture gap between Japan and the West closed considerably. Massive reconstruction after the great Kantō earthquake in 1923 had visibly reinforced a sense of discontinuity with the past. The new and imposing skyline of a rebuilt Tokyo served as a condensed and centralized symbol of Japanese empire — an empire built in the image of an imperialist West with its own Japanese "mission" to bring progress to Asia.[5] In the course of the 1930's, Kuki numbered among those who became earnest accomplices of empire. Yet, in a peculiarly modern paradox, this recognition of Japan's colonial mission with its promises of modernization was not incompatible with a nostagic yearning for a vanishing past. In the 1920's, Kuki and others registered Japan's distance from a nonmodern past with a profound sense of loss and longing. Increasingly, the historical past was imagined as an abode of the Japanese spirit, an abode from which contemporary Japan had been forcibly exiled.

For many of these writers and thinkers, the issue became one of re-

3. Keene, *Dawn to the West*, 760–61.
4. Watsuji, *Nihon kodai bunka, Genshi bukkyō no jissen tetsugaku, Nihon seishinshi kenkyū,* and *Zoku Nihon seishinshi kenkyū.*
5. Peattie, "Introduction," 9.

turn. In 1933, Tanizaki wrote in his lyrical essay *Inei raisan* (In Praise of Shadows): "I know that I am only grumbling to myself and demanding the impossible. If my complaints are taken for what they are, however, there can be no harm in considering how unlucky we have been, what losses we have suffered, in comparison with the Westerner. The Westerner has been able to move forward in ordered steps, while we have met superior civilization and have had to surrender to it, and we have had to leave a road we have followed for thousands of years."[6] While Tanizaki acknowledged that neither Japan nor he himself would ever relinquish the material gains of modernization, he did believe it possible to recapture in the imaginary domain of literature a vision of what had been lost.

In response to Tanizaki's call for a native place of the soul in literature, literary critic Kobayashi Hideo argued that the possibility for return had long since been foreclosed.[7] Alluding to his origins in the anonymity of metropolitan Tokyo, Kobayashi wrote:

Looking back at my life, from the time I was little, my spirit was beset by an endless and varied succession of changes coming all too quickly. That is why I never had the leisure to nourish powerful memories rooted in solid realities, memories to last a lifetime. . . . Tanizaki spoke of "a literature that might discover the native place of the soul," yet it is not even clear whether I possess a real-life native place, not to mention a literary one.[8]

In Kobayashi's view, the dislocations of modernity had inflicted an irredeemable loss of memory, both personal and collective. But for cultural critics with more positive ambitions (and less appreciation of tragic irony), the historical disruptions and personal losses cited by Kobayashi represented merely a temporary lapse of memory—a kind of cultural amnesia—remediable through new forms of archival intervention and interpretation. Kuki and Watsuji, both convinced that Tanizaki's "home for the spirit" was still very much intact, sought its recovery in a carefully selected legacy of the cultural past. Both philosophers, whose formation had been heavily mediated by the European cultural sciences, had mastered the art of transforming the relics of history into a value-laden pres-

---

6. Tanizaki, *In Praise of Shadows*, 8.
7. Kobayashi quoted Tanizaki in "Kokyō o ushinatta bungaku," 211–12.
8. Ibid., 214–15. The Marxist historian Hani Goro underscored the same ironies in the title of his 1931 critique of contemporary ethnological endeavor: "Kyōdo naki no kyōdo kagaku" (A Science of the Native Place without a Native Place).

ence; both had perfected the technique of ransacking the historical archives while annulling historical time.

The apprehensions that propelled this project were, however, not limited to merely a vague sense of cultural homelessness. Taishō had been an era of popular protest and social ferment. New social constituencies rising from below demanded a larger share not only of the benefits of modernization but also of political power. Democratizing tendencies, however, met with formidable obstacles in the way of institutional arrangements, repressive state controls, and elitist political parties. "Taishō democracy" left in its wake disappointment on the Left and political reaction on the Right. Those with progressive leanings, discouraged by the unfulfilled promise of democracy, turned to the historical record for explanations of the failures and inadequacies of the present. Those who were threatened by the inroads of mass culture and the possibilities of mass politics argued that the dangers facing Japanese culture came from without, that Japan had fallen sway to the West. As self-appointed guardians of cultural authenticity, Kuki and others focused their efforts on constructing a hegemonic unity in the shape of a collective cultural past. A safe haven from the upheavals of history, this newly constructed past might then recontain an indeterminate present.

The Modern Imagines Edo

While some turned to far-distant pasts, Kuki focused his attention on that last flowering of culture in the Tokugawa era, shortly before *kaikoku*, the opening of the country to the West. It was during this period, often referred to as Kaseiki,[9] that the style of *iki* circulated most widely among the cultural sophisticates of Edo. Kuki may well have been drawn to this particular cultural episode precisely because of its proximity to the modern, both in time and in style. The aesthetics of *iki* along with its cultural setting represented for Kuki less a Japanese premodernity—which, in a universal order determined by developmental history, would inevitably yield to a Westernized modernity—than a worthy rival to the modern in native guise. In an early-

9. "Kaseiki" literally refers to two eras, Bunka (1804–1817) and Bunsei (1818–1829). As a distinctive period culture, however, Kaseiki extends roughly from the Kansei reforms of 1790 through the Tempō era (1830–1844).

nineteenth-century urban landscape invested with diverse possibilities for pleasure, Kuki attended with painstaking care to the cultural style of Edo — its volatility, playfulness, parody, and pastiche — a disposition that lent itself to modernist (some would even say postmodernist) possibilities.

Nevertheless, Kuki's preference for late Edo culture has impressed many a reader as eccentric, if not perverse. In the annals of modern Japanese historical reflection, the Tokugawa era has been much maligned and marginalized — first, under the auspices of a Meiji enlightenment historiography, which sought to propel Japan upward on the ladder of civilization, and once again by a postwar modernization historiography aiming to rehabilitate a "feudalistic" Japan along the lines of an exemplary American model. Orthodox Marxists cited the Tokugawa era as a moment of aborted development and the source of twentieth-century absolutism. With some notable exceptions, the Tokugawa period, as Asao Naojiro demonstrates in the introduction to the series *Nihon no kinsei* (Japan's Early Modern Era), has consistently suffered the negative attributes of "dark" and "constricted."[10] The latter half of the Tokugawa era, the period in which Edo style came into its own, has received an even greater share of slander as the declining stages of a decadent and benighted era.

In marked contrast to the largely negative tenor of these previous appraisals of the Tokugawa era, a recent series of "Edo booms" extending through the 1970's and 1980's has shed a more positive light on Tokugawa history. Perhaps in the aftermath of "high-growth economics," Japanese living in relative affluence amid proliferating networks of information and goods recognize a more appealing image of themselves in the social and cultural consumer life of Edo.[11] In a different vein, a

10. Asao, ed., *Sekaishi no naka no "kinsei,"* 10–11. Asao compares this negative image of the early modern period with a more affirmative view of *chūsei*, the Japanese medieval period. While post-Meiji historiographers found the seeds of a "world-historical universality" in medieval Japan, they stressed the particularity of the Tokugawa era.

11. In a 1986 issue of *Gendai shisō* devoted to "An Encouragement of Edo Studies," a centerfold by artist Sugiura Hinako features quick sketches of Edo characters under the title "A Mirror of the Edo Tsū." Next to the *tsū's* imposing portrait, she compares the results of a contemporary survey with popular Edo ambitions: "Until the 1970's, when Tokyo youth were asked what they would do with a million yen, the answers were 'travel,' 'a motorcycle,' 'a stereo system.' Now, in 1986, it seems that 'clothing' ranks as number one. In this preference, Tokyo young people share something with the mentality of the *tsū* who whiled away his time in Yoshiwara and staked his life on fashion." Consumption, not only as high fashion but as a way of life, has drawn Edo closer to contemporary Japan, suggests Sugiura. In contrast to this affinity, however, Sugiura gauges the depth of the

part of the renewed attention to Edo has taken the form of a critical reflection on the relentlessly modern urban renewal of the 1960's, when Tokyo seemed bent on obliterating its past altogether.[12] More recently, in a postmodern updating of *Nihonjinron*, the artful play of Edo textuality and consumption has become one of the chosen forms in which Japan presumably exhibits its cultural incommensurability.[13] On a more positive note, this extended period of reassessment of Edo history has also provided the occasion for new and fruitful endeavors in Tokugawa historiography, both in Japan and abroad.

Drawing from this fund of historiographical resources, I offer here a quick sketch of the historical period that so intrigued Kuki and that has provoked such varied assessments in scholarly retrospection.[14] When Tokugawa Ieyasu, the most successful of the strongmen to emerge from an extended period of civil anarchy, first marched into Edo in 1590, he found little more than a fishing village, a receptive harbor, and a castle built by Muromachi warlord Ōta Dōkan in 1457, nearly in ruins. For its strategic location on the Kantō plain, for its heights, rivers, and bay, a victorious Ieyasu chose this village as the center of a reign that would persist for 270 years. In the hopes of preventing further challenges and strengthening their hegemony, Ieyasu and his immediate successors instituted a number of strategic administrative arrangements that transformed both the political and physical topography of the realm. Their imposition of control over space would have the most far-reaching, if unintended, effects. Ambitious plans for a castle town — nearly a century in the making — emulated and rivaled the imperial capital of Kyoto. The residences of some 230 *daimyō*, or feudal lords, were laid out in the spacious higher land of western Edo surrounding the shogunal castle, while a service sector of tradesmen and artisans was relegated to the cramped low-lying land to the east.[15] In time, this social hierarchy mirrored in a topography of high and low would be seriously destabilized, if not overturned.

---

cultural rupture between Edo and the present when she writes next to a typically stylized Bunsei-era portrait of an *iro musume* (a seductive young girl), 'This is indeed a strange and wondrous face.'" Sugiura, "Edo tsū kagami," 46.

12. Tamai, *Edo,* 7–9.

13. Miyoshi and Harootunian, "Introduction," 396.

14. In the following sketch, I have found the following texts especially useful: Nishiyama, *Edo seikatsu bunka;* Nishiyama, *Edokko;* Nishiyama et al., eds., *Edogaku jiten;* Hayashiya, ed., *Kasei bunka no kenkyū;* Miyoshi, "Beyond the End of the Open Road"; and Harootunian, "Late Tokugawa Culture and Thought."

15. Nishiyama et al., eds., *Edogaku jiten,* 2–4.

The Tokugawa bid to master space extended far beyond Edo, beginning with a tactical reshuffling of fiefs for a politically advantageous ar-
rangement of historical allies and foes. Of even more far-reaching significance, the rulers set in motion a system called *sankin kōtai,* which
required *daimyō* from the domains to spend alternate years in Edo.
These periodic processions to and from Edo with full entourage ex-
hausted *daimyō* coffers and insured the continued hegemony of the military government in Edo. But the constant flow of traffic along roads
lined with station towns led finally to what Masao Miyoshi has described as "dedomainalizing the samurai, and creating an absolute cir-
cumference within which extended one common space for all."[16] While
daimyō movements were kept under close surveillance, the routes that
now traversed the realm facilitated forms of travel, commerce, and communication that either exceeded official control or escaped bureaucratic
notice. The primary destinations of many travelers, most notably the
cities in the west—Osaka, Kyoto, and Kobe (historically referred to as
Kamigata)—and Edo in the east, became centers of commerce, consumption, and culture. The flow of people and goods along the roads
and through the cities was none too favorably countenanced by a reigning neo-Confucian ethos of natural economy, social hierarchy, and spartan lives.

Whether in Osaka, "the merchant of the realm," Kyoto, "the courtly
lady," or Edo, "the errand boy" and administrative center, people's
lives—particularly those of the artisans, merchants, and "outcast" enter-
tainers and prostitutes relegated to the bottom of the social hierarchy—
came to differ vastly from official expectation.[17] As cities swelled with
the influx of people from the countryside, fixed class lines and roles began to blur. With the end of the Genroku era (1688–1703), an agrarian
economy already had begun to give way to a mercantile one, and economic power had fallen into the hands of merchants. Expanded production and diversification of goods made wealth and extravagant consumption a sustained reality for some and a recurrent fantasy for others.
Samurai on fixed rice stipends grew increasingly impoverished as they
subsidized a new taste for luxury, placing themselves in precarious debt.
Merchants, on the other hand, accumulated wealth as warehouse man-
agers, exchange brokers, dealers, and money lenders (some of whom

16. Miyoshi, "Beyond the End of the Open Road," 7.
17. These common epithets for the three cities are cited in an early manuscript of
Harootunian, "Late Tokugawa Culture and Thought," 5 n. 14.

held samurai purse strings). In the words of Hayashiya, the new merchants of the Tokugawa era "created a world that overwhelmed the warrior class with the power of money."[18]

Within this burgeoning and semi-illicit town economy, if one wished to indulge in conspicuous consumption and demonstrate cultural connoisseurship, the place to do so was in the pleasure quarters. As part of the official disposition of space, the Tokugawa rulers initially had established brothel districts, confined by walls and moats and banished to the margins of the city, with the intention of containing moral laxity and its potential license for private interest. Ironically, it was precisely the separation of these *akusho* or evil places—defiantly named such by the Edo townsfolk—from the normal order of life that transformed them into centers of a vibrant though illegitimate plebeian culture.[19] In these enclaves of pleasure, where the necessary condition for success was money rather than class, townspeople gave expression to their expansive productive power in intricate patterns of play and diverse cultural forms. In the opulent times of Genroku, the townspeople of Osaka and Kyoto first recognized their own realities and desires in the new genre of *ukiyo zōshi* (stories of the floating world) devised by Saikaku, and their tragic possibilities in the lyric-realist *jōruri* (librettos for puppet plays and Kabuki) of Chikamatsu.

During the course of the eighteenth century, Kamigata, traditionally more commercially advanced because of its proximity to the Inland Sea, yielded economic predominance to Edo. The center of culture also drifted eastward to Edo, along with the coveted title of Miyako, the capital. By the late eighteenth century, Edo hosted an urban population of over one million, a conservative estimate excluding all those travelers, tourists, vagabonds, and vendors who wandered in from the provinces. The late-eighteenth-century writer of popular fiction Shikitei Samba attested to Edo's exemplarity as a city of consumption and style with the comic epithet: "Edo is the land of splendor. Without it there would be no place to sell things."[20] In some of its features, this latter-day Edo prefigured the modern, with a mobile and unstable population, a highly developed cash economy, a wide circulation of goods and services, and the beginnings of a mass culture. This incipient mass culture was per-

---

18. Hayashiya, "Kasei bunka no rekishiteki ichi," in *Kasei bunka no kenkyū*, 13.

19. In addition to the pleasure quarters, the other noted place of ill repute was the Kabuki theater.

20. Quoted from Shikitei Sanba's *Ryūhatsu shinwa ukidoko* in an unpublished manuscript version of Harootunian's "Late Tokugawa Culture and Thought," 6.

haps nowhere so evident as in a burgeoning publishing industry, with scores of booksellers, hundreds of lending libraries, and copies of popular editions averaging over ten thousand.[21] Edo had become a center for the dissemination of new forms of knowledge, art, and entertainment. In its pleasure quarters, private homes, and publishers' shops, diverse groups of people might gather to discuss anything from botany and "Dutch medicine" to *haikai* (comic linked verse) and *rakugo* (a form of comic storytelling).

The predominance of Kamigata town culture had been associated with the upper stratum of merchants, primarily the *tonya,* officially commissioned wholesale agents whose interests were tied to those of the rulers and whose territory extended to commercial towns throughout the realm. In contrast, Edo culture, while linked more broadly to lower strata in the merchant class, was deeply dyed by the local color of this one particular city, especially the pride and mettle for which its native populace became renowned. Whereas the aesthetic preferences of Genroku culture in the west had inclined toward an opulent and flamboyant aesthetic inspired by court ideals and Chinese tastes, Edo sensibilities — particularly after the Kansei reforms (1790) imposed self-restraint on a prodigal merchant class — favored more subdued forms of display. The Kamigata ideal of *sui* referred to a mental disposition cultivated by patrons of the pleasure quarters, a disposition that required from its aspirants both a thorough familiarity with the customs of the quarter and an intimate knowledge of the subtleties of the human heart. Once *sui* migrated to Edo, however, the Chinese ideograph with which it was written acquired the new reading of *iki* as well as the stylistic stamp of this newer, insurgent city in the east.[22] By Kaseiki, the period that provided Kuki with most of his illustrative examples, the stylistic attribute of *iki* had diffused widely through the everyday life of Edo townfolk and lodged itself in an assortment of concrete objects. In the subgenres of popular verbal fiction that multiplied in late-eighteenth-century and early-nineteenth-century Edo, *iki* became highly conceptualized and codified: *sharebon* (books of dandyism) illuminated the secrets of style and etiquette in the quarters; *kokkeibon* (humorous books) offered comic sketches of familiar locales and characters conspicuously lacking in style;

21. Nishiyama et al., eds., *Edogaku jiten,* 330–38.
22. The reading *"iki"* attached itself to a large number of different ideographs, varying with context and rhetorical purpose. This "slippage" between signifier and signified was a common characteristic in the popular literature of late Edo.

ninjōbon (books of human feeling) narrated melodramatic intrigue among geisha, their patrons, and their lovers. The visual art of the *ukiyoe* kept pace with literary endeavor, its subjects ranging widely from portraits of the most celebrated Yoshiwara courtesans and Kabuki actors to scenes of erotic encounter, everyday custom, familiar places, and distant views. In these new forms of cultural expression recent scholarship has recognized a demonstration of autonomy from, even disdain for, the ruling ideology on the part of those at the bottom of the official hierarchy.

This last claim already brings us beyond the brink of an interpretive controversy in Tokugawa historiography—the question of what this emergent popular culture signified: an escape for the oppressed classes of Tokugawa society? A regrettable cultural interlude of trivial and perverse propensities? An ornately decorated veil concealing the slow disintegration of feudalism? The birth of humanism, or the new ethos of a rising merchant class? In his anthology on Kaseiki culture, Hayashiya takes issue with those historians who would depict the latter years of the Tokugawa era as a time of unremitting degeneration. Such a history, he argues, is told from the point of view of the ruling class, whose power and control did indeed deteriorate as the era drew on. Hayashiya and the other contributers to *Kaseiki bunka no kenkyū* narrate a different kind of history, one that charts the rise of the popular classes along with a newly created social and cultural world.[23] They depict the "culture of play" with all its eroticism and earthy satire as a sign not of escapism or decadence but rather of vigor and resistance.

Though the historiographical controversy addressed by the Hayashiya volume came after Kuki's time, one might ask whether *"Iki" no kōzō* anticipated this affirmative postwar reassessment of late Edo culture. After all, Kuki also sought to invest a marginalized historical moment with renewed significance. And like the contributers to the Hayashiya anthology, Kuki read the carnal text of Edo culture as something other than a sign of moral decay. In the aesthetic style of *iki*, he identified—and celebrated—a playful wantonness, a spirit of resistance, and a new form of knowledge acquired in the quarters.

Within the limited critical literature on *"Iki" no kōzō*, some scholars attribute popular and progressive sympathies to Kuki's interpretation of Edo culture. Yasuda Takeshi and Tada Michitarō, in their dialogue on *"Iki" no kōzō*, note Kuki's choice of an aesthetic that was popular and

---

23. Hayashiya, "Kasei bunka no rekishiteki ichi," in *Kasei bunka no kenkyū*, 18–19.

profane (*zoku*) rather than aristocratic and sacred (*sei*), and they commend his interest in *seikatsu bunka* (the culture of everyday life). Tada and Yasuda themselves identify a historical context for *iki* in the popular culture of high consumption that flourished in the pleasure quarters, the theater districts, and the riverside fish markets of late Edo, marked by a ceaseless flow of goods, people, and information.[24] They credit Kuki with an attentiveness to a new social constituency and to the common everyday life of an urbanized Edo.[25] Though Tada and Yasuda may themselves contribute to recent historiographical recognition of the linkage between material production and mental life in a protocommodity culture, Kuki's own contribution is far more questionable. As will soon become evident, Kuki expended much interpretive energy to conceal precisely those material conditions that attended the aesthetic style he celebrated. In fact, it is the act of concealment that begins to suggest the ideological resonances of *"Iki" no kōzō*.

Edo: The Genealogy of a Metaphor

These ideological resonances will sound more clearly if we reverse historical direction for a moment and situate Kuki's text toward the end of a genealogy of successive reflections on the culture, particularly the popular culture, of the Tokugawa era. Another of the multiple settings for *"Iki" no kōzō*, this genealogy of cultural-historical interpretation reveals both the continuities and discontinuities of Kuki's reflection with those that preceded it. Two things become evident. First, the history of controversy cited in the Hayashiya volume over critical

24. Tada and Yasuda, *"Iki" no kōzō" o yomu*, 22. Though the authors briefly inventory some of the material aspects of Kaseiki culture, they fail to mention the development of a cash economy and the centrality of money in the verbal fictions of the day.

25. Given the perspective of Tada and Yasuda, *"Iki" no kōzō* seems a progressive alternative to the negative appraisal of merchant culture in Watsuji Tetsurō's *Zoku Nihon seishinshi kenkyū*. For Watsuji, merchant culture represented an unfortunate but anomalous episode in Japan's history, the single example of a western *Gesellschaft* society based on an ethos of calculated self-interest and opportunism. He argued that this historical episode was at odds with the fundamental altruism of the Japanese spirit and the dominant mode of a *Gemeinschaft* community. See Bellah, "Japan's Cultural Identity," 583–85. In fact, Kuki and Watsuji had much more in common than this line of reasoning would suggest. Though their choices of cultural moments and actors differed, both sought in the relics of the past proof of an enduring cultural community, unique by virtue of a special spiritual and ethical endowment.

assessment of the late Tokugawa period begins not in postwar debates but long before, in the earliest stages of Japan's engagement with modernity. Japanese enlightenment thought was crucial in determining the metaphoric language in which that cultural-historical battle was waged. Second, while Kuki may have been the first thinker in Japan's modern history to reclaim Edo as the native place of the Japanese spirit, his preoccupation with Tokugawa history was by no means unprecedented.

By the 1920's, that historical episode already had acquired a highly charged if equivocal significance among scholars and writers. Separated from Japan's precipitous modernization and engagement with the West by the Meiji *ishin,* the Tokugawa period was distant enough to represent a radical difference from the present, yet at the same time it was close enough to the present to have left visible traces. For intellectuals committed to progressive social visions, those traces often represented obstacles to be overcome in the interests of enlightenment and modernization. For neo-idealists aspiring to universal ethical value, the same traces served as reminders of Japan's untoward detour in the journey of the Spirit. Participants in the early Shōwa Marxist debates, increasingly pessimistic about Japan's revolutionary prospects, searched the archives of Tokugawa history for explanations of the peculiarities of power and capital in contemporary Japan. The more orthodox among them focused on "feudal remnants" from the Tokugawa past to account for absolutist tendencies in contemporary Japan.[26] For Kuki, on the other hand, the cultural remnants of the Tokugawa era attested to the continued presence of Japanese cultural authenticity.

The genealogy of reflection on the Tokugawa era begins almost as soon as the Meiji *ishin* marked it as history. The transformations inaugurated in the last decades of the nineteenth century forced Japan into a dramatic confrontation with its immediate historical antecedents. While the Meiji *ishin* may have first been fueled with restorationist rhetoric, once securely installed, its new leaders ruthlessly suppressed the past, initiating massive reform and restructuring according to models provided by the modern European nation-state. No doubt the new rulers hoped to erase the memory of the disorder that led to their own seizure of power, but many also believed that if Japan was to become a viable modern state, they would have to make a clean break with the past. Fukuzawa Yukichi, perhaps the most eloquent advocate of modernization, depicted the pre-Meiji past as an era of unrelieved stagnation and benighted darkness. As if to confirm nineteenth-century Western no-

26. Dower, "E. H. Norman, Japan and the Uses of History," 35.

tions of an "oriental mode of production," Fukuzawa claimed that Japan's history had begun with Meiji when the country adopted Western civilization as its own. Later, Fukuzawa would advocate that Japan dissociate itself from Asia and join the ranks of a "civilized" West.[27]

The term that Fukuzawa and others used to refer to intellectual and material forms of modernization was *bunmei kaika* (civilization and enlightenment). It implied not only that enlightenment lay on the side of what was modern and Western but also that Japan's immediate past was to be cast into the obscurity of shadows. This stigma of darkness and deviance would adhere to Tokugawa culture through its various reinterpretations. Interestingly, when that past was later retrieved by cultural theorists of Japaneseness, it was often represented in the very terms suggested by the modernizers, but with the values inverted: benighted darkness became the mystery of shadows, irrational bias became fertile indeterminacy, and perverse particularity became exceptional uniqueness. It is not without historical significance that Tanizaki Junichirō called his elegy to the traditional aesthetic *In Praise of Shadows*. "The quality that we call beauty," he wrote, "must always grow from the realities of life, and our ancestors, forced to live in dark rooms, presently came to discover beauty in shadows, ultimately to guide shadows towards beauty's ends."[28] For Tanizaki and others seeking cultural authenticity, shadows came to represent not merely a historical necessity but a cultural choice against enlightenment.

Though beyond the scope of this genealogy, two types of more orthodox historiographical inquiry bear mention, if only to provide a broader backdrop for these more culturally oriented reflections. At the turn of the century, historians inaugurated the subdiscipline of *kinseishi* (early modern history) in newly instituted departments of *kokushi* (national history) at the major Imperial Universities. Relying on European historiographical methods, the founders and early representatives of this new historiographical endeavor were inclined to see progress where their early Meiji predecessors saw only stagnation; in a teleological schema in which development was assumed to pass through fixed stages, the Tokugawa era was envisioned as a way station on the way to *kindai*, a universal modernity.[29] Contemporary with the rise of this

27. Jansen, "Japanese Imperialism," 71.
28. Tanizaki, *In Praise of Shadows*, 18.
29. Asaō, ed., *Sekaishi no naka no "kinsei,"* 22–23. According to Asaō, Uchida Ginzo, founder of the history department at Kyoto Imperial University, was the first to elucidate the concept of *kinsei* (the early modern era) in Japanese history. Unlike those before him whose notion of history was limited to the feats of principal political figures, Uchida

evolutionary historiography, a more conservative cast of scholars drew on traditional intellectual resources to generate a "national morality" in hopes of nationalizing, or more accurately, domesticating a restive populace. Under the rubric of *kokumin dōtokuron* (theories of national morality), Inoue Tetsujirō, the most notable figure in this group, produced studies of Tokugawa-era Confucianism and nativism.[30]

One of the first thinkers to approach the national question from an aesthetic perspective, Okakura Tenshin undertook the reconstruction of a Japanese cultural tradition in a theoretical idiom derived from the West. In his defense of native culture against the onslaught of Westernization, Okakura assumed that aesthetics is the key to cultural autonomy and collective identity—an assumption prescient of the next generation of cultural theory. In *Ideals of the East* (1903), he claimed that Japanese art, a repository of Asian ideals, represented the culminating moment in a pan-Asian Hegelian dialectic.[31] It was Okakura who taught Kuki that one might grasp the entirety of Japanese culture under the heading of several all-encompassing idealist categories.[32] Yet despite these affinities with Kuki's project, Okakura still shared many of the ideological premises of *bunmei kaika*. His evolutionary orientation toward history, his nationalist zeal, and his sympathy for values of a public rather than a private nature place him among the company of such exemplary Meiji thinkers as Fukuzawa Yukichi and Katō Hiroyuki. He praised the attainments of Japanese art in terms of light, strength, and vitality—the metaphors of a modernizer.

Convinced that the contest between modern nations would be fought on the battlefield of culture, Okakura dedicated himself to the construction of an exportable canon of Japanese art. In marked contrast with Kuki, however, his canon had no place for the popular art of the Tokugawa era. The rigid constraints of the Tokugawa regime, he wrote, "crushed the vital spark of art and life" and deprived works of ideality. He found, for example, in the woodblock prints of late Edo "no embodiment of national fervor in which all true art exists."[33] (Ironically,

---

redirected the focus to "deeper levels" of Tokugawa society. Anticipating French annals historians, he discerned progress in the less dramatic "minutiae" of daily life, production and exchange, and cultural activity—progress that would enable Japan to "make a giant leap into an era of global intercourse."

30. Maruyama, *Studies in the Intellectual History of Tokugawa Japan*, xviii–xx.

31. Okakura, *Ideals of the East;* see especially the first chapter, "The Range of Ideals," 1–13.

32. See "'Iki' no honshitsu" (1926), the unpublished preparatory draft for *"Iki" no kōzō*, in which Kuki acknowledges his debt to Okakura, *KSZ*, 1:94.

33. Okakura, *Ideals of the East*, 199.

Kuki would discover in these same prints proof of the ideality of Japanese culture.) In Okakura's view, if the Tokugawa era made any contribution at all to the grand sweep of Japan's cultural development, it consisted in the popularization of ideals, rather dubious praise from the pen of a cultural elitist.

In the latter half of Meiji, poet and essayist Kitamura Tōkoku, deeply disillusioned with the dominant ethos of the Meiji state, discovered a suffering comrade-in-arms in the oppressed commoner of the Tokugawa era.[34] But Tōkoku's relation to the Tokugawa commoner was an ambivalent one, just as it would be in the case of Abe Jirō a generation later. Tōkoku compared the disappointment of Meiji middle-class ambitions to the plight of the Tokugawa commoner. Both groups, he argued, suffered abuses of power and limitations on individual freedoms under an oppressive system of political control. Having already abandoned his political ambitions, Tōkoku believed that the impetus toward new ideals in his own era could emerge only from among men of letters. Not surprisingly, then, it was in the popular art and literature of the Tokugawa era that he sought the origins of an anticipatory cry for freedom. And though he believed he could in fact discern in Tokugawa art the emergence of a popular voice, the voice he heard was muffled and distorted, barred from the expression of noble sentiments or elegant taste.

One of the few early writers who shared Kuki's unqualified enthusiasm for the popular arts of Edo was the writer Nagai Kafū. In fact, excerpts from Kafū's 1920 *Edo geijutsuron* (A Study of Edo Art) appear in the pages of *"Iki" no kōzō*. The tone of *Edo geijutsuron,* however, like so much of Kafū's fiction, is elegiac: "As I observe the imitation of Western civilization in contemporary Japan, from the reconstruction of the city to houses, gardens, utensils, and clothing, all signs of the general trend in the tastes of our era, more and more do I grieve for the passing of Japanese culture." All too aware that Edo existed only in relics and traces, Kafū paid tribute to a world he saw disappearing before his eyes. Often, his fictional characters wander the margins of the city in a melancholy mood, seeking remnants of both a personal and a cultural past. Without the same ideological investment as Kuki, Kafū clearly recognized the impossibility of resurrecting Edo culture. Rather, his appeal to the traditions and tastes of that era often served as a tactical foray against current abuses of a bureaucratic state and a self-righteous bourgeoisie. In the last lines of his preface to *Edo geijutsuron,* Kafū wrote that

34. The following paragraph summarizes Kitamura Tōkoku's argument in "Tokugawa shi jidai no heiminteki risō," 139–56.

his aim was both to lampoon contemporary life and to find solace in his reveries of a life gone by, a life that could be reimagined only in the ruins it had left behind.[35]

Tsuda Sōkichi (1873–1961), a liberal historian who, much like Kuki, was educated under the reign of the cultural sciences in the first decades of the century, gave particular attention to the Tokugawa era, although his interests extended across centuries and continents. According to his English-language translator, Tsuda's multivolume study of Japanese thought began with the desire to liberate the recent history of the Meiji *ishin* from a monopoly of sectarian interpretation.[36] To prepare the ground for this inquiry, Tsuda turned his attention to the more distant history of Japan's earliest historical chronicles, progressively making his way toward his own immediate prehistory. In the view of Maruyama Masao, Tsuda's historiographical undertaking began as a reaction to the "national morality" school: "Essentially he sought to grasp not just the 'doctrines' or the 'schools' of Japanese thought, but what he called the *jisseikatsu* — the texture of life as it was lived; he tried, in other words, to elucidate the main ideological currents of each period in relation to the everyday life attitudes of the classes that played a dominant role in the development of Japanese culture."[37] Accordingly, Tsuda gave much greater evidential weight to the marginalized productions of popular culture and minor genres than to an established and elitist canon. Of the four volumes in his *Bungaku ni arawaretaru kokumin shisō no kenkyū* (An Inquiry into National Thought as Revealed in Literature), two were devoted to situating the literary production of the Tokugawa era in a carefully elaborated social and political context.[38] Anticipating Maruyama's own study of Tokugawa intellectual history, Tsuda discerned a fundamental and ultimately fatal contradiction between the social ethos and political structure of a military aristocracy and the vigor and aspirations of the common people. While an artificially prolonged official system oppressed the people from above, the natural economic and cultural activity of the people "corroded that same oppressive system from within." Unlike many of his predecessors, Tsuda recognized signs of a thriving economic life and cultural energy among the Tokugawa towns-

35. Nagai Kafū, *Edo geijutsuron*, 185.

36. Tsuda, *An Inquiry into the Japanese Mind*, 4–5.

37. Maruyama, *Studies in the Intellectual History of Tokugawa Japan*, xxi–xxii.

38. Though Tsuda kept his distance from the Marxist scholarship that was soon to come to the fore in historical research, Marxists would later claim him as "a pioneer of studies rooted in the theory of 'ideology.'" Ibid.

folk, especially during the Genroku period in the late seventeenth century, the culmination, in his view, of Tokugawa popular culture. However, with the end of the Genroku, Tsuda claimed, culture declined and languished during the long period extending through the eighteenth century and the first half of the nineteenth.[39] He subtitled the second part of his Tokugawa study "The Era of Stagnation of Plebeian Literature" — an inevitable cultural affliction given the profound contradictions underlying Tokugawa society. Despite a restrained admiration for the intellectual and artistic activity of Tokugawa commoners, Tsuda represented the entire period as an "eventless history" in which there was "less fluctuation than might appear on the surface," when "both system and custom, somehow or other, persisted without change."[40]

Nearly a decade later, Abe Jirō published *Tokugawa jidai no geijutsu to shakai* (Art and Society in the Tokugawa Era), a study nearly as ambitious as Tsuda's. Abe's text presented Tokugawa culture from a perspective contrasting sharply with its near contemporary, *"Iki" no kōzō*, particularly in the relation it proposed between culture and collectivity. Also steeped in European cosmopolitanism, Abe had already recorded his quest for *Bildung* in his semifictional *Santarō no nikki* (The Diary of Santarō; 1914) and elaborated a theory of universal ethics in his *Jinkakushugi* (Personalism; 1917). *Tokugawa jidai no geijutsu to shakai* begins with several revealing reminiscences about his trip to Europe in 1922. It seems he brought with him a sizable collection of Utamaro prints as anticipated souvenirs for new acquaintances in Europe. After offering several of the prints to his Heidelberg landlady, a lover of things Japanese, Abe chose for his own wall a print by Utamaro, *Two Women at a Mirror Stand*. Next to a reproduction of that same print, Abe describes the image and the effect it had on him:

The one woman wearing a pale yellow *yukata* with vertical stripes, facing forward toward the mirror as she parts her hair with a red comb . . . within no time at all, the gentle grace of her posture and face began to soften my heart. But as more time passed, the wantonly loosened undersash, her knee slipping out from the red underskirt — all this began to throw my mind into confusion. Unable to bear it any longer, I finally pulled the print down from the wall. One day when the landlady came into my room and noticed it missing, she asked me what I had done with the Utamaro. I explained to her that because the image was not uplifting (*erhebend*), I had developed a

<hr/>

39. Tsuda, *Bungaku ni arawaretaru kokumin shisō no kenkyū: Heimin bungaku no jidai*, 2–5.

40. Ibid., 3, 92.

certain aversion for it and taken it down. In her straightforward German way, she asked, "Well, then why did you give the same print to me?" "True, it isn't uplifting, but it is pleasing (*anmutend*); isn't that enough?" Such was my answer, and even now I cannot accuse myself of being untruthful.[41]

Some time after that first confession of vacillation between pleasure and propriety, Abe finds himself lost in thought in a room filled with *ukiyoe* at the Louvre in Paris. Once again he hesitates between attraction and repulsion. Filled with warm affection and nostalgia at the sight of these works of "delicate sensuality" and "playful beauty," Abe is nevertheless struck by a quality in them that he describes as dark and twisted. Why, he asks, did this art find it necessary to express itself in a "form so unaccountably strange?" Drawn to "a culture that claimed a blood connection" with him, Abe is, nevertheless uncomfortably aware of a barrier that separates him from the cultural artifacts of the Japanese past.[42] In *Tokugawa jidai no geijutsu to shakai*, Abe attempted to account for what he perceived as the moral inadequacy of the era that preceded his own, but at the same time, he hoped to identify its spiritual contribution to the realization of human values.

Across the hall from the *ukiyoe* exhibit, a gallery devoted to European Impressionist painting leads Abe toward thoughts of a more comparative nature. Though the popular art of the Tokugawa period was in no way technically inferior to contemporary European art, Abe muses, it was an art crossed by shadows, stigmatized by its origins in a web of social contradictions and moral deficiencies. Tokugawa commoners, seeking refuge from the binding restrictions of official Confucian morality, escaped into the *akusho* (evil places), areas of the city specially designated for prostitution and Kabuki theater. The *akusho* represented safe islands of freedom and beauty for the popular classes in a society that otherwise blocked all avenues for creative expression. Hence, the popular culture of the Tokugawa era, Abe argues, evolved under the sign of a peculiar aberration: "In principle, beauty and goodness are in accord, moving together along parallel paths. In this case, however, goodness did not have the impetuosity to invade and conquer the beauty of the *akusho,* while beauty did not have the boorishness (*yabo*) necessary to resist the good and declare its independence." According to Abe's dialectical schema, the intensification of this schism between morality and

41. Abe, *Tokugawa jidai no geijutsu to shakai*, 23–24. Abe uses the German adjectives in his own text.

42. Ibid., 17–18.

beauty eventually led to the downfall of the pleasure quarters, but at the same time, the process of disintegration itself became the "path by which the spirit of man, which had been unnaturally abducted, returned to its original nature."[43] Filtered through the universalizing lens of Hegelian and neo-Kantian theory, Tokugawa society became a dialectical breeding ground for transcendent ethical value. That value, however, was to be fully realized only in a radically altered future. In this manner, Abe gave theoretical shape to his own ambivalence. He managed to re-appropriate a questionable cultural past and yet maintain a "proper" ethical distance from it. In good cosmopolitan style, Abe detailed Japan's unique contribution to the stock of universal values. But clearly, *Tokugawa jidai no geijutsu to shakai* resolves the tension between the particular Japanese experience and universal values on the side of the universal. In so doing, the text submits Japan's history to the demands of a universalizing discourse constructed by and for the West.

There is another ambivalent note in *Tokugawa jidai no geijutsu to shakai,* but one that is sounded very softly. In his preface, Abe makes the observation in a surprisingly dispassionate manner that the collections in the national museums of Europe memorialize the plunder accumulated from centuries of global expansion. Without further explanation, Abe shifts the terms of discussion from plunder to tribute, saluting Europeans for their dedication to preserving art in a spirit of nationalism.[44] In other words, Abe's passing glance at European imperialism never leads to a sustained reflection on the cultural hegemony of the West that marked his generation so deeply. Nor does it lead him, as it would Kuki, to reimagine indigenous culture through newly nativized eyes.

This, however, is not to suggest that the rupture between Abe's history of Tokugawa art and society and Kuki's inquiry into Edo style was by any means total. Clearly, both philosophers relied on European discursive strategies to transmute the cultural relics of the past into present value. They shared alike in the gains made by the nineteenth-century German philosophical construction of the cultural sciences, in particular the liberation of an autonomous, interiorized subject from the exigencies of a "disenchanted" external world. Armed with the compensatory power of *Geist,* Abe and Kuki both sought to redress mundane life in urban, industrial society with conceptions of culture as an interiorized ethical and aesthetic endowment. Like their German counterparts, they

43. Ibid., 18–19, 42–43, 99.
44. Ibid., 15.

substituted an understanding of culture for the practice of politics, attempting in the process to construct what I would like to call a "hegemony of the spirit," a cultural unity over which they might prevail.

This common ground notwithstanding, *"Iki" no kōzō* does, in fact, mark a significant break with the cosmopolitanism it both manifested and displaced. While Abe's hegemony of the spirit transcended national borders, Kuki endeavored to contain that hegemony within more narrowly defined ethno-cultural boundaries. The universal whole to which Japan made its special contribution had yielded its centrality to an endowment exclusive to Japan. Nevertheless, we should not forget that Kuki charted his rhetorical return to Japan — a motif that would become central to the Japanese Romantic school poets of the 1930's — along the routes of a disavowed cosmopolitanism.[45] This disavowal of universal norms signaled another crucial discontinuity dividing *"Iki" no kōzō* from *Tokugawa jidai no geijutsu to shakai.* Abe had projected Tokugawa cultural history forward by means of a Hegelian dialectic. Contradictions at a "lower stage" of thought and world (with the emphasis on the former) were to be surpassed in a higher, and qualitatively different, truth. As we saw in chapter 2, Kuki already had defected from any such grand historical narrative. In *"Iki" no kōzō,* he attempted to deliver Edo culture from universalizing modes of history, whether positivist or dialectical. Unsurpassed by modern historical development, the aesthetic style of *iki* had a "heroic affinity"[46] with the present, in defiance of normative conceptions of progress.

While Abe had hoped to transcend disturbing differences through the realization of a universalized ethical subject, Kuki sought to reveal beneath a veil of universalizing pretension the true particularity of the Japanese subject. Rather than transcend differences, Kuki celebrated them. In his eyes, the woodblock prints of Utamaro, Torii Kiyonaga, and other late-Edo *ukiyoe* artists were the graphic signs of a worldview uniquely Japanese. The delicate sensuality and erotic overtones of these works became the privileged motifs in a theory of cultural exceptionalism. In short, the culture of the late Edo period, far from a distorted refraction, was a highly polished mirror in which Japan might recognize the true image of its collective "lived experience" (*Erlebnis*). Jürgen Habermas describes this posthistoricist engagement with the past, its rebel-

---

45. For a pioneering study in English of the Romantic school, see Doak, *Dreams of Difference.*

46. I have borrowed this expression from Jürgen Habermas, "Modernity," 5.

lion against "the false normativity in history," as the disposition of a distinctively modernist mentality.[47] Yet, as should become clear in subsequent discussions, the inspiration for Kuki's withdrawal from a universal historical schema was antimodern, a reaction to the social and cultural forms of industrialized mass society. Here again we confront Kuki's paradoxical position as a "modernist against modernity."

According to Kuki's scenario of a Japanese secession from normative history, Edo of the late eighteenth and early nineteenth centuries became the chosen historical moment for a newly reimagined present. Kuki was perhaps the first thinker in modern Japan to rescue this moment from the universalist impulse of Meiji assimilation and Taishō neo-idealist cosmopolitanism; he may also have been the first to resituate Edo in the center of a Japanese discourse on collective self-understanding. But the production of this discourse required not only that Kuki forget nearly half a century of material and intellectual modernization but also that he transform Edo into a manifestation of timeless spirit. To a greater extent than many of those whose reflections on the Tokugawa era preceded *"Iki" no kōzō*, Kuki weaves the verbal artifacts of Edo into the fabric of his text, and yet despite this rich verbal collection, the material texture of the popular culture of late Edo is effaced by a dominant interpretive mode that seeks to divest culture of its historicity.

From Historical Archive to Abiding Presence

The first thick description of the Edo historical milieu in *"Iki" no kōzō* comes after the theoretical pronouncements of the introductory chapter, in a second chapter entitled "'Iki' no naihōteki kōzō," (The Intensive Structure of *"Iki"*). Here, the text becomes a dense weave of performative language borrowed from *gesaku*, *nagauta*,[48] Kabuki, and the colloquialisms of the Edo dialect as Kuki explores the meaning of *iki*. Consider, for example, the following passage, in which the reader is introduced in quick succession to an array of heroic types celebrated in the low-lying, plebeian districts of early-nineteenth-century Edo:

47. Ibid., 5–6.
48. *Nagauta* are the long narrative songs often performed on the Kabuki stage.

In the fires that flared up so frequently in Edo, called by the populace *Edo no hana* (blossoms of Edo), fearless firefighters and scaffold men boasted that even in the cold of winter they wore a single cotton *happi* (livery coat) and nothing on their feet save white *tabi* (socks). They prized these signs of *otokodate* (plebeian gallantry). *Edo no ikibari* (Edo pluck) and *Tatsumi kyō-kotsu* (Tatsumi chivalry) are indispensable to *iki*. *Inase, isami, denpō* all possess an unassailable style and grace.[49]

In passages such as this, Kuki excised the notes and annotations of the archival sources that, in earlier drafts, had recorded the tracks of his own scholarship. Yet in a world already separated from Kaseiki Edo by a century of accelerated change, the idiom of Edo commoners was no longer self-evident. In the modern metropolis that stood in the place of what had once been Edo, an urban populace spoke a standardized language that, by Kuki's day, was more receptive to Western neologisms than to Edo dialect. And yet Kuki's narrative dispenses with explanation and notation on the premise, or in the hope, that the language of the Tokugawa era need not be deciphered. Rather, *"Iki" no kōzō* offers that language as if it were a second nature, if not for its Shōwa readers, at least for its author. Behind the scenes, Kuki conducted a discursive exchange of historicity for value: the specificity of Edo culture, nowhere more contingent and ephemeral than in its sensibility, was sacrificed to enduring ethical and spiritual values. The concrete place of cultural production in a latter-day Edo gives way in *"Iki" no kōzō* to the abstracted space of the Japanese spirit.

A self-styled heretic, Kuki defied a historical narrative that had irrevocably separated his own present from its antecedents. Out of a desire that a (reimagined) past not be lost to a modern history of successive dislocations, he represented a moment in the past as if it were both the historical origin and the timeless expression of authentic Japanese subjectivity. During the same early Shōwa years, Watsuji gave theoretical shape to this recovery of historical presence with his theory of "cultural layeredness" (*bunka no jūsōsei*). Watsuji posited a historical dialectic peculiar to Japan, one that would conserve rather than surpass what had come before. The result, he suggested, was history in the form of an archaeological "tell"—an accumulation of the remains from successive eras, its layers or strata transforming historical time into cultural space.

<hr>

49. Kuki, *"Iki" no kōzō*, KSZ, 1:18. These three words—*inase, isami*, and *denpō*—circulated within the plebeian neighborhoods and popular fiction of Edo and referred to the valued attributes of *otokodate*: style, courage, and tenacity.

In Japan, he claimed, it was possible to "see history before one's eyes," in peasant artifacts, for example, or the trappings of traditional theater. And yet in the last analysis, what was most essential, he argued, remained invisible (and thus indisputable): in the deepest layers of culture, the life and experience of the folk subsisted independent of institutions and material appearances.[50]

Though Kuki abandoned the Hegelian dialectic that Watsuji deployed in altered form, both philosophers staged interpretive encounters with a carefully selected past in an attempt to reapprehend contemporary Japan. The methods they used, whether Watsuji's *jūsōsei* or Kuki's cultural hermeneutic, insured that their reapprehension would have a retrospective cast and that it would be limited to culture narrowly defined as interiorized ethical and aesthetic value. For many contemporary Japanese thinkers nourished on nineteenth-century German neo-idealism, culture in this narrow sense became a more than adequate replacement for social or political practice. In this sense, the cultural histories Kuki, Watsuji, and others produced during the early Shōwa years encouraged forms of collective self-recognition severed from the material specificity of both the past and the present. Ultimately, such histories would contribute to the aestheticization of the political sphere.

Historical Specificities: Time, Space, Class

While Kuki's aim was to transform the aesthetics of *iki* into a national ontology, history makes its entrance in *"Iki" no kōzō* in the form of illustrative examples (albeit of a mode of being meant to transcend history). Kuki tracks down the essence of *iki* by narrowing the historical focus to a defining moment bounded by time and space — the distinctive period culture of Kaseiki. For the most part, the compendia of Edo customs and mores to which Kuki had recourse depicted the material culture and colloquial language of the Tokugawa era in the most concrete terms, documenting the changes in fashion and custom

50. The above is a summary of Watsuji, "Nihon bunka no jūsōsei" in *Zoku Nihon seishinshi kenkyū*, 59–70. See also 65, 69–70. Watsuji's theory of culture is a remarkable illustration of Derrida's definition of the dialectic as the discursive means of transforming expenditure into presence.

from generation to generation. Under a typical entry for *iki*, Kuki would have found descriptions dwelling almost exclusively on appearances. In the preliminary stages of his inquiry, Kuki jotted down the following characteristics for *iki*: contrast, asymmetry, delicate subtlety, and simplicity. Under each characteristic, he catalogued appropriate fashions and styles.[51] Much of this data found its way into *"Iki" no kōzō*, but only as external signs of a deeply interiorized subjectivity.

These concrete descriptions, as well as fragments of popular lyrics and literature, attest with lively detail to a style that reached the height of its popularity during the first part of the nineteenth century among certain segments of the Edo population. Under Kuki's interpretive lens, *iki* became a timeless expression of taste, symbolic of the spiritual and ethical disposition of the Japanese *minzoku* as a whole, but Kuki's own sources suggest possibilities for a very different reading—a reading in which social and historical division rather than cultural unity is the central motif.

The Edo sources cited in *"Iki" no kōzō* and its preliminary drafts define *iki* in terms of differences and exclusions, whether in space, time, or social strata. Kuki begins with a saying popular among the commoners of Edo: "'Neither rustic boors (*yabo*) nor goblins (*bakemono*) live east of Hakone'; such was the pride of the 'pure' child of Edo (*kissui no Edokko*)." The visual and homophonic resonances of *sui*—the ideograph for *sui* is frequently read as *iki*—suggest that those born and bred in Edo possessed an unparalleled sense of style and refinement. Within Edo, that stylistic flair was best displayed in the pleasure quarters, those specially designated districts devoted to elaborate forms of play, erotic encounters, and cultural display. A real knowledge of *iki* demanded a long apprenticeship in the pleasure quarters, whether as a prostitute (*yūjo*) or a dandy-connoisseur (*tsū*). The lines that Kuki quotes from Tamenaga Shunsui's *Harutsugedori* (The Feathered Herald of Spring; 1836) clearly establish the criterion used to distinguish *iki* from its opposite, *yabo*: "A *yabo* (rustic boor) doesn't know a thing about the world. Why, even in his wildest dreams, he's never so much as seen a brothel! That's why the *tsūkunshi* (dandy-connoisseurs of the quarters) heap slander on him."[52] Even earlier, the *sharebon* of the late eighteenth century had underlined the importance of expertise in the quarters to the attain-

51. Kuki, "'Iki' ni tsuite," *KSZ*, supplementary volume, 18. As his source for this catalogue, Kuki cites Saitō Ryūzō's *Kinsei Nihon sezōshi*, 804–17.

52. Kuki, *"Iki" no kōzō*, *KSZ*, 1:18, 1:31.

ment of taste, using humorous parallels to Buddhist enlightenment tales: "Unless one sits on a triple-thick mattress for nine years, he will not penetrate the secret of how to buy a courtesan."[53] Those without the means to learn the customs and etiquette of the quarters were endlessly chided for their ignorance. In a language that both mirrored and parodied Confucian definitions of sagehood, Kyōden explained that only a genuine *tsū* knows the difference between *tsū* and *yabo;* those who are incapable of differentiating are *yabo.*[54] In this manner, those "in the know" cloaked themselves in the hermetic tautologies of taste and displayed their superiority to all that was common and ordinary. Though one might learn, in time, to become a *tsū* with the proper credentials of style and deportment, a person of rural origins (suggested by the ideograph for "field" in the character compound for *yabo*) was definitely at a disadvantage. During the era of *sharebon,* the indignities of *yabo* might be suffered equally by an uncouth Edoite, a rural farmer, or a samurai hailing from the provinces.

As the urban population of Edo expanded and townspeople became increasingly affluent, the officially authorized district for licensed prostitution, Yoshiwara, gave way to the Okabashō. Made up of five districts in the low-lying section of the city (*shitamachi*), Okabashō literally meant "the hill places," but speculation has it that the name played off the similar sounding *hoka bashō,* or the "other" — that is, unauthorized — places.[55] Among these unlicensed pleasure districts, Fukagawa, the most frequented of all in the latter years of Edo, provided the settings for Tamenaga Shunsui's *ninjōbon,* theatrically staged and illustrated fictions about the sentimental entanglements among geisha, their clients, and their lovers. Bounded by rivers and crossed by canals, Fukagawa was inhabited primarily by lumber dealers, boatmen, shipping agents, and fishmongers. For the most part, the women who entertained in the teahouses and on the pleasure boats that plied the canals were the daughters of boatmen and fishermen, raised amid the clamor and commotion of the district. *Edokko* themselves, they were known for their pluck and determination, as in this line from a popular ditty in which the place name Fukagawa is transformed into *Futagawa,* literally, "many-women river": "*Futagawa,* known for its mettle and stubborn pride."[56] As an

53. Quoted from Santō Kyōden's *sharebon* entitled *Yoshiwara yōji,* in Jo Nobuko Martin, "Santō Kyōden and His Sharebon," 122.
54. Nishiyama, *Edokko,* 139–42.
55. Nishiyama et al., eds., *Edogaku jiten,* 558.
56. Nakaō, *Sui — tsū — iki,* 168–69.

enclave of play, Fukagawa was less ceremonious than the Yoshiwara, more apt to resist the pressures of orthodoxy. The Fukagawa geisha, increasingly the exemplar of Edo style and talent, was easily recognizable, as in this line that Kuki quotes from *Sendō shinwa* (The Confidences of a Boatman): "Even when she goes out of the neighborhood, one look at her hairdo will tell you she's a girl from Fukagawa."[57] She wore her hair dressed with water instead of oil, done up in the most casual manner. By the early nineteenth century, consensus had it that she, above all others, was in possession of that elusive sense of style called *iki*.

Kuki's Edo sources situate *iki* not only in a circumscribed space but also during a specific historical interval. *"Iki" no kōzō* documents changing tastes in the feminine face, figure, and fashion over the years. As for the face: "Saikaku expressed the ideal of voluptuous beauty during the Genroku period [1686–1703] when he said, 'The face in fashion today is slightly rounded.' In contrast, Kaseiki favored the refined elegance of an oval-shaped face." Next, the body: "A slender figure, long and willow-waisted, is thought to be one of the objective expressions of *iki*. The one who proclaimed this with the faith of a fanatic was Utamaro."[58] After the restrained and subtle aesthetic of Utamaro (1753–1806), Kuki notes a degeneration into the "cloyingly sweet" (*amattarui*) women of Kunisada (1786–1864). The sober colors and linear designs that typified *iki* reached the peak of their popularity during Kaseiki.

The popular fiction of that same era, roughly the first decades of the nineteenth century, is filled with meticulously detailed descriptions of the attire of its heroes and heroines, a sign no doubt of the importance accorded to style in the everyday life in an incipient consumer society. Though Kuki himself assigned a different significance to these descriptions, the literary fragments he culled from Edo sources often read like the captions in a fashion magazine. In fact, the *gesaku* fiction of late Edo was preoccupied with consumption of all kinds, a preoccupation that ran directly counter to Kuki's deciphering of *iki*. In these lines, Kuki quotes Tamenaga Shunsui's description of the geisha Yonehachi — for many, the epitome of *iki* — as she slips out of the quarter for a secret tryst with her lover Tanjirō: "To go with her kimono made from *uedafutori*, a fabric of wide grey vertical stripes, she wears a *kujiraobi*, a wide sash with *koyanagi* black satin on one side and a crepe of purple stripe on the

57. Kuki, *"Iki" no kōzō, KSZ*, 1:46–47.
58. Ibid., 1:44.

other."[59] A kimono with a vertically striped pattern was an unmistakable sign of *iki*. Until Hōreki (1751–1763), Kuki noted, the only striped designs on kimonos were horizontal; not until Kaseiki did vertical stripes become the dominant fashion. The temperate taste of Kaseiki is often attributed to the severity of the sumptuary laws issuing from the Kansei reforms (1787–1793). These restrictions on luxury brought the downfall of the *fudazashi*, the rich rice brokers of Edo, who had long enjoyed a virtual monopoly over the finance of shogunal retainers. In the pleasure quarters, the *daitsū* — the wealthiest and most renowned dandy-connoisseurs, recruited largely from the ranks of the Edo *fudazashi* — gave way to smaller merchants, while the *taiyu*, or highest class of courtesans, yielded to town geisha. The aesthetic style of *iki* also underwent subtle change, from ostentation and a glossy sheen to moderation and a muted glow. In short, Kaseiki was an era of "cotton kimono with silk linings."[60]

Just as Kuki located the aesthetic style of *iki* in a particular time and place, he also attributed it, however provisionally, to certain social strata in Edo society. To illustrate the disposition associated with *iki*, Kuki invoked the rakish and reckless hero of the Kabuki stage Sukeroku. The epitome of *otokodate* (plebeian gallantry), Sukeroku demonstrates his uncommon flair for picking women and quarrels. Swaggering through the quarters, a band of Edo *murasaki* (purple) tied around his head, Sukeroku provokes all who cross his path: "Hey you young'uns, step right up and pay your respects!"[61] Most significantly, he picks his quarrels across class lines, in particular, with his archrival, the uncouth Ikyu, a bearded samurai who publicly suffers the sting first of Sukeroku's wit and finally of his sword. Under the dramatic talents of the actor Ichikawa Danjurō II, Sukeroku evolved into his classic form in the middle of the eighteenth century as the mirror image of the "real-life" *fudazashi* and great *tsū*, Oguchiya Jiegyō. It is said that Oguchiya would saunter into the quarter dressed exactly the same as his stage replica.[62] This symbiotic relation between stage character and historical person underscored both the capacity of the *chōnin* to materialize his fantasies with theatrical gesture and the potential of the theater to represent real custom in its contemporaneity.

59. Ibid., 1:64.
60. A popular saying from the era, quoted in Hosoi and Pigeot, "La structure d'iki," 43. This review article offers one of the more useful discussions of *"Iki" no kōzō*.
61. Kuki, *"Iki" no kōzō, KSZ*, 1: 18.
62. Nishiyama, *Edokko*, 136.

In company with Sukeroku, the prostitutes, geisha, merchants, artisans, and laborers conjured up on the pages of *"Iki" no kōzō* bear witness to the class affiliations of *iki* and the popular culture from which it emerged. Nevertheless, as the subsequent discussion will bear out, class was not an issue Kuki chose to address. For Kuki, Kaseiki culture occupied a site that was far less historical than symbolic. Despite the "local color," *"Iki" no kōzō* summons not the urban topography of Edo but rather the eternal landscape of the Japanese spirit. In other words, *iki* is removed from its historical coordinates of time and space and relocated in the timeless reaches of national subjectivity.

The Structure of Iki: Nationalizing Desire

Relying on the specialized language of systematic philosophy, Kuki explains how he will go about elucidating the structure of *iki:* "As our first task in understanding the meaning revealed by *iki* as a phenomenon of consciousness, we must identify the attributes that comprise the meaning of *iki* and elucidate that meaning *intensively.* As our second task, we must distinguish this meaning from other similar meanings and clarify it *extensively.*"[63] It is the first of these tasks, the identification of the internal attributes of *iki,* that brings the problem of history most clearly into focus. Kuki distinguished three attributes in the semantic structure of *iki: bitai,* a word that Kuki himself translated with the French *coquetterie; ikuji,* which might be translated as "fearless pride," or more colloquially, "pluck"; and *akirame,* "resignation." Drawing on Aristotelian ontology, Kuki rendered the structure of *iki* as a synthesis of "causes." *Bitai,* he explained, which has its biological basis in human sexuality, is the "material cause" of *iki. Ikuji* and *akirame* together constitute the "formal cause," for Kuki the source of the national character of *iki.* As we shall see, Kuki associated these last two attributes with the traditions he deemed central to the Japanese cultural experience.[64] Paradoxically, Kuki may have found his inspiration for this tripartite schema in European sources, a subject I will return to presently,

---

63. Kuki, *"Iki" no kōzō,* 21.

64. According to Aristotelian ontology, the formal cause is "that which makes a thing all the more that thing." See *Tetsugaku jiten,* s.v. *keisōin.* Kuki did in fact suggest that a unique ethnic disposition gives the Japanese privileged access to the secrets of desire.

but in any case, what he aspired to in his definition of *iki* was a synthetic concept in which seemingly contradictory attributes were reconciled in a comprehensive totality—a totality ultimately signifying Japan.

Kuki turned first to *bitai*, a word that might be best rendered in English by "seductiveness" or "erotic allure." The allure of *iki*, he explained, always implies "relations with the other sex outside of the norm." Despite this ordinary beginning, Kuki's language quickly assumes a double edge, moving from illicit liaisons on the order of "keeping a mistress" to a phenomenology of desire reminiscent of Heidegger's existential ontology. *Bitai*, he wrote, "is a dualistic attitude in which a monistic self posits the other sex in relation to itself and constructs a possible relation between itself and the other. The eroticism and captivating allure of *iki* is nothing other than the tension produced from this dualistic potential." But this allure lasts only as long as it remains in the realm of possibility. Once the conquest is made, allure is destined to disappear: "The secret of erotic allure is to continuously decrease the distance [between oneself and the other] while never allowing that distance to be completely annihilated."[65] To illustrate that relation, Kuki proposed an unusual interpretation for Zeno's "Achilles paradox," an exposition of the logical contradictions of motion. According to that paradox, the fleet-footed Achilles is fated never to overtake his slow-paced rival, the tortoise. In Kuki's view,

Achilles does well to press on eternally in his pursuit of the tortoise. We must not forget what lies at the foundation of Zeno's paradox. In the perfected form of erotic allure, the dualistic and dynamic possibility between the sexes must be made absolute as possibility. The vagabond who renews a "lasting finitude," the debaucher who revels in a perverse infinity, Achilles who "pursues eternally" without falling—these are the only kind of human beings who know true allure.[66]

For Kuki, the logic or illogic of Zeno's paradox was not at issue. Rather, what interested him was the image of an infinite approach between self and other, the ceaseless pursuit without final attainment. This relation between self and other was to become the core of a broader existential vision of intersubjectivity.[67]

While this analysis of *bitai* offers an interesting insight into the struc-

65. Kuki, *"Iki" no kōzō, KSZ,* 1:16, 1:17.
66. Ibid., 1:18.
67. Kuki treats philosophical notions of intersubjectivity in *Gūzensei no mondai, KSZ,* 2:5–264; and *Ningen no jitsuzon, KSZ,* 3:1–292.

ture of desire, it is not necessarily consistent with literary representations of erotic liaisons in the Edo pleasure quarters. One need only refer
to the frank sexuality of Tamenaga Shunsui's *ninjōbon*. We have no
doubts about what transpires between the heroine Yonehachi (perhaps
the most often cited female exemplar of *iki*) and her lover Tanjirō, despite a discreet interruption by the temple bell:

> Snuggling up closer, Yonehachi wrapped herself around his knees and
> looked up at him guilelessly: "I'm so happy and . . ." [Tan] "And . . . what?"
> [Yone] "I want to stay just like this forever." All eyes, he gazed back at her,
> completely taken with her beauty. [Tan] "Oh, I can't wait any longer." So
> saying, he snuggled up even closer. [Yone] "Hey, that tickles!" With a quick
> apology, Tanjirō pulled her down to the floor and . . . just at that moment,
> the evening bells at the Asakusa Kannon temple rang out.[68]

Most immediately apparent is the discrepancy between the playful in-
dulgence of Shunsui's prose and the humorless austerity of Kuki's theoretical reflections. Though the style of *iki* is associated with a certain
degree of discrimination, even moderation, in matters of love, it hardly
required the denial of sexual fulfillment. Yet, as we shall soon see, Kuki
was determined to transform *iki* into a philosophical challenge to a
Western rationality of ends. Nevertheless, the style and sensibility associated with *iki* was not quite as ascetic as Kuki might have imagined.

In his study of late-Tokugawa culture, Harry Harootunian notes that
a central motif in Edo art and culture was the concentration on the body
and the often "gargantuan indulgences coming from the joys of the
flesh." The body, as "the maker of custom," gave voice to a new social
world that no longer conformed to the requirements of the traditional
ruling class.[69] The warrior class had legitimized its exemption from production with Confucian theories of a hierarchical separation between
those who rule with the mind and those who labor with the body. To
reverse that hierarchy in cultural representations amounted to an act of
subversion. Whether the earthy satire of *kibyōshi*, the erotic and aesthetic
connoisseurship of *sharebon*, or the sentimental dalliances of *ninjōbon* —
these popular cultural forms violated the official version of order and
propriety. Not surprisingly, *gesaku* writers and *ukiyoe* artists often chose
the pleasure quarters as their preferred setting, places where the unrivaled economic power of merchants gave that class the status they were
denied in the official hierarchy.

68. Tamenaga, *Shunshoku umegoyomi*, 55.
69. Harootunian, "Late Tokugawa Culture and Thought," 173–76.

As for the aesthetic style of *iki,* it represented the ultimate refinement and highest validation of the customs and styles that reigned in a world devoted to pleasure. *Iki* demanded a form of second-degree asceticism, a mastery of excess that only the most experienced devotees and inhabitants of the pleasure quarters could attain. For the *tsū,* this meant avoiding the emotional entanglements of love: "To know where to stop when one wishes is called *tsū,*" explained the writer of one *sharebon.*[70] For the courtesan or geisha, it meant not having to take the first comer.

In an essay on Kaseiki *ukiyoe,* Akai Tatsurō suggests that the erotic realism of Eisen Keisai (1790–1848) and Utagawa Kunisada (1786–1864) attests to the value accorded to the everyday life of the urban populace. The Kaseiki woodblock print artist typically represented the Fukagawa geisha engaged in her quotidian round of activities: kneeling at her mirror stand, returning home from the bathhouse, taking a music lesson, visiting a shrine.[71] In a similar vein, Hayashiya argues that the popularity of *ninjōbon* in the first decades of the nineteenth century was a sign not of decadence but rather of an intense interest in the human individual. The representation of *ninjō,* a wide array of human feelings from despair and bewilderment to desire and affection, signified, he claims, a human liberation in the domain of literature.[72]

All of these readings of Edo culture suggest that the pervasiveness of feeling and flesh in late-Edo cultural production signified the ascendancy of a new kind of human subject deemed worthy of representation. The urban commoners of late Edo had come into possession of social and economic resources that enabled them to represent the life they actually lived rather than the life they were instructed to live. But how could Kuki have noted the social and political implications of the carnal cast of Edo culture when he was in flight from realities of the same order in his own time? For this early Shōwa thinker, culture had come to mean the denial of the social sphere, not its expression. Kuki disembodied the aesthetic style of *iki,* both literally, by demanding abstinence from its possessors, and figuratively, by severing it from its own material history. While he acknowledged that the pleasure quarters had fostered the aesthetic style of *iki,* Kuki was persuaded that it had transcended its material context to become the expression of an abiding Japanese spirit.

70. From Kubo Shunman, *Kokon seirō hanashi no yōda,* quoted in Martin, "Santō Kyōden and His Sharebon," 101.

71. Akai Tatsurō, "Ukiyo ni okeru kasei," in Hayashiya, ed., *Kasei bunka no kenkyū,* 264–68.

72. Hayashiya, "Kasei bunka no rekishiteki ichi," in *Kasei bunka no kenkyū,* 34–35.

The Japanese spirit comes into clearer focus when Kuki turns his attention to the next of the three attributes of *iki* as form of consciousness. "*Iki*," he explains, "is a vivid reflection of the moral ideals of Edo culture. As one of its moments, '*iki*' includes *ikuji*, the fearless pride of the *Edokko*."[73] Kuki uses the word *ikuji* to convey the sense of self-esteem, strength of will, and daring valued by the urban commoners of Edo. Borrowing from Kabuki and *nagauta* lyrics, Kuki once again invokes a cast of Edo characters — laborers, firemen, fishmongers, and prostitutes. It is the women of the quarters, however, who elicit Kuki's boundless admiration. Popular songs had it that the Edo prostitute was sought after for her pride as well as her beauty. The following lines from a *nagauta* summon up the mood that prevailed inside the walls of Yoshiwara: "Boors can hold fort outside the walls; inside, three thousand houses rival in beauty, matching their pride and testing their mettle." Paradoxically, the seductiveness of *iki* implied a spirit of resistance to the other sex: "If he's wealthy but boorish, send him packing, this time and next!"[74] Such, says Kuki, was the moral imperative of the Yoshiwara prostitute, who valued her name far more than money. He credited her with an aristocratic asceticism that led her to reject material values in favor of honor and pride. To the man of her choice, she pledged undying loyalty (*shinjūdate*): "Once you've taken the plunge, your name is mud; that's what the god of love knows, the one who ties the knot in a whore's undersash."[75]

No doubt the lyrics of *nagauta* idealized the lives of women whose livelihood depended on marketing their bodies. But what is perhaps most remarkable in Kuki's interpretation of *ikuji* is the conclusion he drew: "In *iki* lives a vivid *bushidō* ideal. The sentiment expressed in the aphorism 'Though a samurai goes without a meal, still a toothpick dangles from his lips' ultimately became the pride of an *Edokko* who would 'spend all his money before the night is out.'" With these words, Kuki located the source of the prodigal spending habits of the *Edokko* in a samurai ethic of spartan endurance. *Iki*, he argued, was inseparable from the moral idealism of *bushidō*.[76] True, the *Edokko* was reputed to

73. Kuki, "*Iki*" no kōzō, *KSZ*, 1:23.

74. Ibid., 1:18, 1:19. These are the lyrics of the *nagauta* (long song) "Tsui no amigasa" (A pair of reed hats). In "'Iki' no honshitsu," Kuki cited a Taishō collection of *nagauta* (*Kōtei nagautashū*) as the source of his many *nagauta* quotations. In "*Iki*" no kōzō, Kuki no longer credited his source.

75. In Japanese, this verse exploits the dual meanings of *musubi* in En-musubi-no-kami to mean both "tying a knot" and "the god of love."

76. Kuki, "*Iki*" no kōzō, *KSZ*, 1:19, 1:81.

have disdain for money, but this was a disdain premised on wealth, a sign of abundance rather than privation. "Success or failure in the quarter depends on how one spends his money. Unless one spends a great deal of money, he will not be able to enter the realm of happiness," explains Kyōden in his *Yoshiwara yōji*.[77] Though money was not the point of "play," it was clearly the precondition. The wealthier of the *Edokko*, those reputed to have mastered the secrets of style, might spend unthinkable amounts of money for an evening of lavish entertainment. Flaunting their power to spend, Edo commoners cast ridicule on the impoverished samurai unable to buy himself a meal, not to mention a night of pleasure in the quarters. The aphorism Kuki quotes — "Though a samurai goes without a meal, still a toothpick dangles from his lips" — may have begun as a celebration of the pride and moral fortitude of the samurai; pronounced by an increasingly affluent merchant class, the same words became a sneer at his straitened circumstances.[78]

It has been suggested that Kuki discovered the link between *bushidō* and the ethos of Edo commoners in his Taishō sourcebooks on Edo customs.[79] Other students of Edo culture followed suit, in particular Asō Isoji, who rendered Edo popular culture as a synthesis of merchant realism and samurai idealism.[80] The assumption behind such historical interpretations was that only through the assimilation of the values of the ruling class could the popular classes produce a culture worthy of attention. No doubt this was an interpretation that fell into step with more practical attempts on the part of Meiji modernizers to construct a productive and orderly state by advocating samurai values as a national ethos.

Iki did in fact have aristocratic aspirations, but this was a plebeian aristocracy that defined itself against the ruling class. Even some of Kuki's most sympathetic readers have felt compelled to take issue on the question of *bushidō*.[81] The contempt among Edo commoners for their

77. Quoted in Martin, "Santō Kyōden and His Sharebon," 107.
78. It should be noted that the Tokugawa concept of *bushidō* memorialized a form of life that had largely disappeared from Tokugawa society, in which administrative arrangements had transformed warriors into bureaucrats.
79. Minami, "'*Iki*' no kōzō o megutte," 8–19. Minami quotes from Saitō Ryūzo's *Kinsei Nihon sesōshi* (1923) to the effect that popular ideals had their source in the ethos of the ruling class, in particular, *bushidō*. Perhaps the best-known of modern *bushidō* apologists, Nitobe Inazo, in response to accusations by Western critics that Japan was without chivalry or any comparable ethical institution, argued that Japan possessed an indigenous moral system, *bushidō*, one that rivaled Christianity in the West. Nitobe, *Bushidō*.
80. Asō, "Tsū — iki," 103–16.
81. Minami Hiroshi, for example, in "'*Iki*' no kōzō o megutte," despite his admiration for Kuki, expresses serious doubts concerning the connection between *ikuji* and *bushidō*.

samurai rulers was legendary. Kuki himself quotes one of the many insults that Agemaki, Sukeroku's favorite, hurls at Ikyu, her samurai suitor: "Pardon me, but this is Agemaki you're dealing with! Do you think I could take you for Sukeroku, even in the dark?"[82]

If Kuki overlooked the social implications of Edo cultural style, other students of Japanese aesthetics have been especially attentive to those nuances. Nakai Masakazu, Kuki's student and later colleague at Kyoto Imperial University, traced *iki* back to its source in Matsuo Bashō's concept of *karumi*, literally "lightness," but suggesting the notion of catching an ever-changing reality on the wing.[83] According to Nakai, this new Edo spirit that found its expression in the aesthetic of *iki* stood in direct opposition to the cumbersome and ponderous disposition of the samurai. The urban commoners responded to the self-preserving caution of a deteriorating ruling class with *chōnin konjō* (townsfolk guts), creating within the dominant system bold new social and cultural forms.

In a more recent study of the *Edokko*, Nishiyama sketches out a local history for this class-based spirit of resistance. In a city with nearly equal populations of the samurai aristocracy and commoners, townspeople were especially susceptible to abuses of power on the part of their samurai rulers. Under Tokugawa law, they had virtually no legal recourse. Fueled by a sense of home-grown justice, self-styled *machi yakko* (neighborhood toughs) took it upon themselves to limit blatant misuses of power. During the Genroku period, says Nishiyama, this Edo type was symbolized on the Kabuki stage by Edo *aragoto* (rough style) fashioned by the first Ichikawa Danjurō. This local history of popular resistance appeared in its most popular *aragoto* guise as Sukeroku, that dandy of rare *Edokko* style.[84] In the play *Sukeroku: Yukari no Edo zakura* (Sukeroku: Flower of Edo), the image of the Edo *ikina date sugata* (a dandy with *iki*) is superimposed on a much older local legend hailing from the Kantō region surrounding Edo, *Soga monogatari* (The Tale of the Soga Brothers). Based on a historical incident in the twelfth century, this medieval tale recounts how two young sons revenge the death of their father by killing his murderer, now in the service of Minamoto no Yoritomo, at a hunt near Mount Fuji. The older brother is killed in the fray, while the younger, Gorō, survives, only to be executed at the behest of the son of his father's murderer.[85] This local tale of opposition to official

82. Kuki, *"Iki" no kōzō, KSZ*, 1:18.

83 Nakai, "Nihon no bi," in *Nakai Masakazu zenshū*, 2:245–46.

84. Nishiyama, *Edokko*, 129–31, 131–36.

85. This account of "Soga monogatari" follows D. E. Mills's entry s.v. *Soga monogatari* in *Kodansha Japanese Encyclopedia*.

power became a favorite among the inhabitants of Edo. In an updated Kabuki version, Sukeroku transgresses historical time to reveal his true identity as the legendary warrior, Gorō. Gorō, it seems, has disguised himself as an Edo dandy to search for the sword of his enemy in order to exact his revenge. *Sukeroku* appeared with great regularity in Edo theaters, its historical double exposure lending heroic stature to the defiance of the Edo townspeople. The aesthetic style with which the *chōnin* held their own, concludes Nishiyama, was referred to as *iki*.[86]

Others have suggested that popular defiance of the status quo grew directly out of the material conditions of life in the plebian districts of Edo. In his essay on the moods of Fukagawa, Nishimura Shinji argues that the economic acumen and self-sufficiency of the fishermen, artisans, merchants, and geisha who inhabited the water-bound districts of Edo encouraged the development of "a will to resist oppression" and "a desire to destroy conventional forms."[87] It is of particular interest that the Fukagawa geisha who appears so frequently in the pages of *"Iki" no kōzō* enjoyed a degree of autonomy unheard of in Yoshiwara's oppressive world of licensed prostitution. She was given the name *haori* geisha, a reference to the masculine halfcoat she wore and a sign of her new status as an independent contractor. With his usual candor in matters of finance, Tamenaga Shunsui describes the working conditions of his heroine Yonehachi in a manner that casts doubt on Kuki's idealized vision of the Edo ethos. Her former patron, Tō-san, having just redeemed her contract in Yoshiwara, demands a show of gratitude: "Thanks to me, you can come and go as you please with no boss to stand over you, and all the money you make goes straight into your own pocket."[88] For the geisha in the unlicensed quarters, this measure of economic independence encouraged independence of spirit as well, enough at least for Yonehachi to keep Tō-san in his place and withhold the "gratitude" he craved.

In *"Iki" no kōzō*, the link between popular cultural forms and the material transformations of Tokugawa society has effectively disappeared. In Kuki's view, the spirit of resistance inherent in *iki* was not an expression of the newly acquired productive power of urban commoners but rather a manifestation of an essential, aristocratic disposition in the possession of all Japanese. Though some claim that Kuki was a champion of Edo popular culture, I would argue rather that he obscured the social

86. Nishiyama, *Edokko*, 135–37.
87. Nishimura, "Edo Fukagawa jōchō no kenkyū," 127–33.
88. Tamenaga, *Shunshoku umegoyomi*, 82.

character of *iki* by severing the ties between culture and its conditions of production. In the last analysis, the "dematerialized" interpretation of Edo aesthetic style in *"Iki" no kōzō* betrayed Kuki's deep distrust for the mass culture of his own era.

Finally, Kuki turned to the last of the three attributes of *iki, akirame* or resignation: "[*Akirame*] is an attitude of disinterestedness toward fate, free from all attachments, an attitude that has its source in an awareness of fate. Refined down to the last detail, *iki* requires a frame of mind that is fresh, simple, and elegant." Kuki explained that resignation was the consequence of long experience in the pleasure quarters, or *ukiyo* (the floating world), where impermanence had become an irrefutable fact of everyday life. Here the text is rich with the lore of love from the quarters. One verse from a *nagauta* expresses the wisdom of the women who made their living in the *ukiyo*: "A man's heart changes like the Asuka River; that's what you learn the hard way in this line of work." Another verse records their laments: "Unable to keep my head above water, this sorrowful life of mine, left to be washed away with the current (*Ukami mo yaranu, nagare no ukimi*)."[89] The homophonic play on the verb *uku* (to float) calls up both the transient pleasures of the quarters and Buddhist conceptions of life as suffering. Kuki suggested that the notion of *iki* had its source in *kugai,* an expression with multiple semantic resonances. Of Buddhist origins, *kugai* meant the "world of grief," or, as it was first written, "sea of grief." During the Tokugawa era, *kugai* came to be identified with the pleasure quarters, where the expression "to labor in the world of grief" referred to the career of a prostitute from her first customer to her last.[90] No doubt Kuki had read the opening chapters of Tamenaga Shunsui's *Shunshoku umegoyomi,* where Buddhist practice and worldly pleasures flirt irreverently with one another: "Not nine, but ten years, decked out in flowery robes they do their time in a world of grief; once you reach enlightenment, how delightful, this transient world of pleasure, where all the beauties are gathered together in a single district, in this long-flourishing town of Yoshiwara."[91]

89. Kuki, *"Iki" no kōzō, KSZ,* 1:19, 1:26.

90. Kuki did not mention one further semantic resonance of *kugai,* despite its association with the pleasure quarters. Written with a different first character, *kugai* also meant "public world." Once a reference to the free cities in the late medieval period, *kugai,* perhaps because of its connotations of nonconnectedness and freedom from outside interference, became identified with the districts specially designated for sexual pleasure and play.

91. Tamenaga, *Shunshoku umegoyomi,* 62.

Through a series of allusions, this passage evokes the life of Daruma, who reached enlightenment after nine years of seated meditation facing a wall. The popular wisdom of the time compared the ten-year period of indentured prostitution to Buddhist practice, each a different path to enlightenment. But the parodic overtones of Shunsui's language also suggest that Yoshiwara, the world of *iro* (a word signifying both deceptive appearances and pleasures of the flesh) was a more than adequate substitute for Buddhist enlightenment.

Shunsui's impiety would not have suited Kuki's earnest interpretation of the Buddhist moment in *iki*. The life of the Edo prostitute, Kuki explained, was burnished to a deep luster through trial and tribulation: "A true and devoted heart, cruelly betrayed time and time again, a heart tempered by sorrow piled upon sorrow, becomes in the end indifferent to the goal so apt to deceive. The heart that has lost its innocent trust in the opposite sex and become completely resigned is acquired at a high price." Without attachments or regrets, disinterested and freed from all of life's shackles, the owner of such a heart attains a wisdom that is Buddhist in nature: "A Buddhist worldview in which life's vicissitudes and impermanence are seen as a form of discrimination, while emptiness and nirvana constitute the principle of nondiscrimination; a religious view of life that teaches both a serene acceptance of destiny and resignation in the face of evil fate—with this worldview as its foundation, the moment of resignation in *iki* is both strengthened and purified."[92] Finally what accounted for the irresistible charm of the women of the quarters were the traces of an experience that led them from love to disappointment, and from disappointment to spiritual detachment worthy of a Buddhist sage.

A Rare Trinity: The Paradoxes of Particularity

At the conclusion of this exposition of the meaning of *iki*, Kuki asked, rhetorically to be sure, whether the three attributes—allure, pride, and resignation—are not in fact mutually incompatible. Reminding his readers that the essential condition for erotic allure is the *"possibility* of union," he explained that pride serves to sharpen one's resolve to maintain possibility indefinitely, and that resignation enables

92. Kuki, *"Iki" no kōzō, KSZ*, 1:19–20, 1:21.

one to forgo fulfillment. In this manner, the two attributes that accounted for the national character of *iki* also guaranteed that its prospects for perpetuating possibility as possibility became absolute. Sounding the ideographic resonance of *sui* (often read as *iki*), Kuki wrote, "*Iki* is the 'quintessence' of erotic allure (*bitai no 'sui' de aru*)."[93] In this unlikely alliance of opposites, Kuki discerned a logic unheard of in the West, a defiance of the fundamental precepts of Western thought: "Affirmation through negation. . . . A commitment to freedom forced by fate."[94] The aesthetic of *iki* evaded the rule of noncontradiction, escaped the logic of identity, exceeded the limits of the syllogism. Emptied of instrumentality, *iki* offered the prospect of seductiveness for its own sake, with no thought of the prize. Freed from the chain of cause and effect, *iki* replaced a belabored love with "disinterested free play."

Kuki claimed that *iki* expressed Japan's essential difference from the West not only because it subverted a rationality of ends but for one other crucial reason as well: "For Western culture, formed under the influence of a Christianity that categorically cursed all flesh, sexual relations outside of sanctioned union, along with materialism, were relegated to hell at an early date."[95] Kuki located the value of *iki* in its capacity to integrate body and spirit. In contrast, the West was severely limited by its condemnation of the flesh:

For Christianity and for those who submit to its influence unconsciously, heaven and hell can only be alternatives. . . . To prohibit often means to give up. To deny is easy, to act is difficult. An idealism that excludes realism is a pseudo-idealism that makes an easy peace with dualism. On the other hand, voluptuousness of flesh animated by nobility of spirit bears witness to a highly developed civilization rich in idealism. This is the reason why Baudelaire, for example, has so many admirers in Japan.

Whereas the Western worldview was held captive by a facile logic of either/or, Japan had long since realized that "the principle of contradic-

---

93. Ibid., 1:22.

94. Though the phrases Kuki uses to illustrate the moment of resignation in *iki* no doubt have Buddhist connotations, they raise other specters as well. In fact, this logic was not unheard of in the West but appeared with a vengeance at the end of the Weimar period in Germany. In his 1929–30 lectures, Heidegger argued that the German people must "take on the burden of opening a historical world in which entities could manifest themselves anew. Only in self-abandonment to the disclosive power at work through them could Germans become truly free: *freedom is affirmation of necessity.*" To accomplish that task, Heidegger called for a "manager" (*Verwalter*) who would command the "inner greatness of Dasein and its necessities." Zimmerman, *Heidegger's Confrontation with Modernity*, 33.

95. Kuki, *"Iki" no kōzō, KSZ*, 1:80.

tion holds only in the domain of formal logic."[96] Transcending both the philosophical logic and the ethical limits of the West, *iki* became a sign of exceptional difference at the level of national culture.

Yet despite these claims of difference, Kuki has been charged with expropriating the very structure of *iki* itself from European sources. The harshest of such accusations comes from Peter Dale, author of *The Myth of Japanese Uniqueness:* "Kuki's work is essentially one of disguised transposition, of discovering a Japanese counterpart to the occidental coxcomb, with his 'physionomie distincte,' and then erasing all comparison with his original. We see this clearly in his failure to cite Barbey d'Aurevilly, though his analysis of *bitai, ikuji,* and *akirame* derives directly from the latter."[97] In the course of a rambling tribute to dandyism, Barbey d'Aureville did indeed identify the qualities of the dandy in a language that prefigures *"Iki" no kōzō: coquetterie d'esprit* (seductiveness of the spirit), *orgueil* (pride), *insolence du désintéressement* (insolence of disinterestedness).[98] Though Kuki did not cite—and may not have even read— Barbey d'Aureville, in the endnotes of *"Iki" no kōzō* he did acknowledge the resurgence of a discourse on dandyism in Europe of the 1910's and 1920's.[99] It is perhaps fitting that a Europe undergoing the equalizing transfigurations of a mass-produced mass culture should revive a discourse that eulogized an aristocracy of spirit and advocated the distinction of "rare goods" in the developing stages of a commodity culture. Kuki, as we have seen, felt a kinship with Baudelaire, the most lyrical champion of the dandy. In successive drafts of *"Iki" no kōzō,* he was at great pains to both defer to and differ from the French poet. The mood of resignation, the discriminating tastes of a *décadent,* the autumnal tints, the nostalgia for the past—such were the qualities of *Les fleurs du mal* that inspired Kuki to quote entire stanzas in the earlier *Shisō* version of *"Iki" no kōzō* published at the beginning of 1930. As if to defend against too great an identification, stanzas dwindled to fragments in the final version: "Spring, the Beloved, has lost its scent," and "Lament the incandescent Summer day / Savour the golden sweetness of decline."[100] To distinguish *iki* from these depictions of decadent melancholy, Kuki

96. Kuki, "Geisha," *KSZ,* 1:241–42.
97. Dale, *The Myth of Japanese Uniqueness,* 72.
98. Barbey d'Aurevilly, "Du dandysme," 221–78.
99. Kuki, *"Iki" no kōzō, KSZ,* 1:82, n. 25.
100. From "Le goût du néant" and "Chant d'automne" respectively, as translated by Marthiel and Jackson Mathews in Baudelaire, *The Flowers of Evil.* In the *Shisō* draft, Kuki quoted full stanzas of "Recueillement," a poem that evokes a profound sense of nostalgia. *"Iki" no kōzō, KSZ,* supplementary volume, 100–101.

put forward a number of arguments, none particularly persuasive: the dandy, he claimed, was lacking the requisite *ikuji* (pride); his gender was wrong (the heroism of *iki* belonged to the weak and defenseless women of the quarter); the poet Baudelaire spoke only for himself, and not for an entire people. Nevertheless, Kuki included this line from Baudelaire's *Le peintre de la vie moderne:* "Dandyism is the last spark of heroism in a decadent era. . . . Without heat, filled with sadness, it has the elegance of a setting sun."[101] At some level, these words were perfectly tailored to the vision Kuki projected in *"Iki" no kōzō*, a vision that revealed more about an early Shōwa modernist *"arrière-garde"* than it did about Edo style.

Finally, *"Iki" no kōzō* deferred to its cultural other not only in the substance of its message but also in its form. At the conclusion of his exposition of its meaning, Kuki offered his readers an overview of *iki:* "In sum, *iki* is the perfect self-realization of the material cause of erotic allure by means of the formal cause of moral idealism [*bushidō*] and the religious belief in the unreality of the world [Buddhism], both distinctive signs of the culture of our country."[102] In the course of *"Iki" no kōzō*, Kuki had transformed *iki* into a vision of a synthetic whole, one that combined sensual, moral, and spiritual attributes. This encompassing triad was more than vaguely reminiscent of the cosmopolitan repertoire of humanist values tendered by neo-Kantian idealism: the true (*shin*), the good (*zen*), and the beautiful (*bi*). In a gesture that simultaneously reproduced and resisted the imagination of the other, Kuki envisioned Japan as a more than adequate match for the West. Thus, Kuki's project, one that began as a search for difference, ended by replicating the image of a universalizing West that pictured itself as both replete and complete.

In the second chapter of *"Iki" no kōzō*, Kuki argued that the spirit of *iki* was far removed from the "intoxication that Stendhal had called *amour-passion*": "She who wears her kimono in the style of *iki*,[103] having attained by necessity a state of Buddhist deliverance, gathers uncommon grasses in a rarefied atmosphere redolent of *amour-goût*." Kuki, however, recruited once again the very passion that *iki* had abandoned, this time in the service of national culture: "There is nothing for us but to perse-

101. Kuki, *"Iki" no kōzō, KSZ*, 1:79.
102. Ibid., 1:23.
103. Kuki uses the expression *hidarizuma* here, an allusion to the unusual manner in which a geisha wrapped her kimono, with the left side over the right, a custom that no doubt facilitated the practice of one of her principal arts: the shamisen.

vere in our passionate eros for our culture of *bushidō* idealism and the Buddhist belief in the unreality of the world. *Iki* stands in inseparable and internal relation to *bushidō* idealism and Buddhist nonrealism. *Iki* is an *allure* that, once having attained *resignation* toward its fate, lives in the freedom of *fearless* pride."[104] As Hosoi and Pigeot astutely point out in their critique of *"Iki" no kōzō, iki,* in the company of other local particularities of Edo, was destined to disappear under the relentless nationalizing pressures to standardize custom. Such was the case with the local idiom, the Edo dialect.[105] Ironically, *"Iki" no kōzō* made its own discursive contribution to the inexorable "spread of civilization" by substituting a logic of cultural nationalism for the historical distinctiveness of Edo cultural style. To make that substitution, Kuki deployed the strategies he had learned from European *Kulturwissenschaften* and hermeneutics.

104. Kuki, *"Iki" no kōzō, KSZ,* 1:23, 1:81.
105. Hosoi and Pigeot, "La structure d'iki," 51.

CHAPTER 4

Hermeneutics; Or, Culture Repossessed

The encounter with art belongs within the process of integration given to human life which stands within traditions. Indeed, it is even a question whether the special contemporaneity of the work of art does not consist precisely in this: that it stands open in a limitless way for ever new integrations. . . . The real being of a work is what it is able to say, and that stretches fundamentally out beyond every historical imitation.

Hans-Georg Gadamer, Truth and Method

If the history of thought could remain the locus of uninterrupted continuities, if it could undo without abstraction, if it could weave around everything that men say and do obscure syntheses that anticipate for him, prepare him, and lead him endlessly towards his future, it would provide a privileged shelter for the sovereignty of consciousness.

Michel Foucault, The Archaeology of Knowledge

There is no document of culture which is not at the same time a document of barbarism. And just as such a document is not free of barbarism, barbarism taints also the manner in which it was transmitted from one owner to another.

Walter Benjamin, "Theses on the Philosophy
of History"

In his essay "On Collecting Art and Culture," James Clifford describes the collector as one who deploys a system of objects to create a world of value. The collector substitutes the symbolic temporality of an imposed system for the "real time" of historical and productive processes, an illusory relation for a social relation.[1] Practitioners of hermeneutics are not unlike the collector: the objects they gather are primarily verbal, their selection and disposition hardly random. They insert those objects into the symbolic constellation of value — the journey of Spirit, for instance, the meaning of Being, or the genius of a people. By means of the objects they appropriate, they lay hold of a past (of their own making) and forge its continuity with their own present. A subscriber to the hermeneutic method, Kuki also played the role of collector in the archives, constructing a world of value in the name of culture. In *"Iki" no kōzō*, he submitted a diverse assemblage of verbal artifacts to the dictates of an imperious symbolic system, one estranged from the "real time" both of the objects at hand and of his own social present. Ultimately, Kuki discovered his theoretical coordinates for a timeless world of value in a Heideggerian hermeneutics of Being.

Kuki's philosophical generation, well schooled in German neo-idealist thought, was early disposed toward the philological methods and humanist values of nineteenth-century hermeneutics. For many, however, the advent of Heidegger's existential hermeneutics, sometimes referred to as "Dasein analysis," served as a common point of departure for new directions in philosophical discourse. Japanese students and scholars, whether firsthand in German universities or indirectly through transmission in Japan, followed the textual labor of *Being and Time* (1927) with rapt attention. In that monumental undertaking, Heidegger transformed hermeneutics from a historiographical methodology to an existential inquiry into the (presumably) everyday dimensions of being.[2] As Naoki Sakai observes in an essay on Watsuji, not only was Heidegger widely read during the 1920's and 1930's by Japanese intellectuals but the particular tenor of that reading indicated an intellectual's position in an increasingly ideologically valanced discursive field.[3] Even before the publication of *Being and Time,* Tanabe Hajime had already introduced the fundamentals of Dasein analysis to Japanese readers (1924), and Miki Kiyoshi had submitted Pascal to the illumination of Heideggerian hermeneutics (1926). Within the next several years, Kuki and Watsuji

---

1. Clifford, "On Collecting Art and Culture," 221–22. In this section, Clifford bases his discussion on the views of Jean Baudrillard and Susan Stewart.

2. The present chapter will demonstrate that Heidegger's existential analysis in fact operated at the expense of everyday social relations and contemporary material forms.

3. Sakai, "Return to the West / Return to the East," 158. According to Graham Parkes's introduction to *Heidegger and Asian Thought,* Japan's reception of Heidegger was the most enthusiastic of any country, including Germany (9).

each revised Heidegger's method to produce the dehistoricized contours of a distinctively Japanese mode of being. From an entirely different angle, Marxist critic Tosaka Jun indicted Heidegger for furnishing a Japanese intellectual bourgeoisie with the ideological apparatus for Japanese fascism. Following discursive itineraries from Germany to Japan, this chapter explores the formation and orientation of the hermeneutic enterprise with particular attention to its operation in *"Iki" no kōzō*.

Advocates have consistently claimed hermeneutics to be a rigorously and radically historicizing enterprise. Hermeneutics, it is said, offers a historical vision in which the past — itself "ultimately no more determined and no more finished than either the present or future" — actively informs the present by virtue of both its continuities and its discontinuities with that present.[4] Hans-Georg Gadamer has called this notion "effective history" and has traced its development through Hegel, Marx, Nietzsche, Dilthey, and Heidegger. In practice, however, hermeneutics has lent itself to conservative, even reactionary, perspectives on history. If there was an initially productive perception of the groundlessness of history, it was expeditiously displaced by newly fabricated myths of foundation. In the course of the hermeneutic enterprise, the search for national origin, identity, and continuity regularly has overshadowed its founding recognition of historical discontinuity and indeterminacy. Moreover, a reading of the major practitioners of hermeneutics reveals that this humanist discipline has consistently denied the historical condition that produced it and against which it has reacted — a radical rupture with the past. In Japan, as in Europe, the hermeneutic project in philosophy is intimately linked to massive and unprecedented transformations in social structure and material culture: the emergence of urban masses, the mechanization of everyday life, the progressive rationalization and control of social life, and the increasing dissemination and standardization of culture. These new social and cultural forms threatened not only to destroy cultural difference and annihilate remaining vestiges of traditional forms of culture but also to place cultural and social power in the hands of new mass constituencies. Pitted against the onslaught of change wrought by an expansive modernity, hermeneutics staked its claim to the past and to a privileged understanding of its "legacy." In this light, hermeneutics appears as a peculiarly modern ideological inter-

---

4. Schmidt, *The Ubiquity of the Finite*, 190. The following explanation of "effective history" also relies heavily on Schmidt's lucid introduction in his sixth chapter, "History, Heraclitus, and the 'Not Yet,'" 190–94.

vention against the conditions of the modern itself. In Japan, this intervention was embraced with extraordinary passion, though not, it must be added, without reservation. While hermeneutics provided its Japanese practitioners with compelling answers to the predicament of culture, these same practitioners often found it necessary to take a revisionist stance toward a methodology bearing the impress of its European provenance.

Perhaps the most striking aspect of *"Iki" no kōzō* is the urgency with which the issue of methodology is posed. Kuki begins with these questions: "What kind of structure does the phenomenon called *iki* possess? First of all, with what method can we elucidate the structure of *iki* and grasp its being?" Inspired, no doubt, by the phenomenological injunction to "return to the things themselves," Kuki called for a method that would enable the inquirer to "grasp the living form as it is." The content of the inquiry, suggested Kuki, must determine its form. In the first lines of the text, he poses the question he believed to be the most crucial one concerning the content of *iki*: "Does the word *iki* possess the kind of universality that would allow us to find it in any national language?" As if leaving the question open might allow doubt to slip in, Kuki follows immediately with a denial, thinly disguised in the rhetoric of hypothesis: "If it were true that the word *iki* existed only in our national language, then its meaning could not but be endowed with distinctive ethnicity. And when we address ourselves to a meaning endowed with distinctive ethnicity, that is to say, with distinctive cultural being, what kind of methodological attitude should we assume?"[5] Faced with an inexorable process of cultural assimilation to a modernized West, Kuki was persuaded that the hermeneutic method would enable him to defend and preserve cultural difference. Yet this recourse to a theory of European derivation posed problems for a theorist of Japanese cultural exceptionality.

Displacing the Hermeneutic Horizon: An Equivocal Undertaking

Hermeneutics takes credit for the fundamental insight that all theoretical reflection is rooted in history. That is to say, people understand themselves only in relation to the conditions of their exis-

5. Kuki, *"Iki" no kōzō, KSZ,* 1:11, 1:12, 1:7.

tence, whether those conditions are understood in historiographical terms (Dilthey) or in existential terms (Heidegger). In Dilthey's view, the practice of the cultural sciences grew directly out of the investigator's experience of his own historicity: "The language in which I think and my concepts originated in the course of time. Thus, to impenetrable depths within myself, I am a historical being. The fact that the investigator of history is the same as the one who makes it is the first condition which makes scientific history possible."[6] Not only are the cultural sciences deeply rooted in "a historical and understood world" but they also react back upon that world. This two-way relationship between theory and experience is intimately bound by a common language.

Yet despite this recognition of the historicity of reflection, practitioners of hermeneutics routinely neglected the founding insight of their own discipline. In Dilthey's hermeneutic project, as a prime example, Habermas discerns a conflict between the two tendencies of life and contemplation, between the practical interests of existence and an ideal scientific objectivity. Not surprisingly, Dilthey gave less than full consideration to the historical context that had given rise to his own undertaking and to the practical interests that had given hermeneutics its lease on life. Nor did he account for the ideological effects that the contemporary inquirer might wreak on the past. Dilthey's hermeneutic was a fundamentally conservative response, one that, in the words of Habermas, "determined the direction in which a cultural tradition [was] appropriated and developed in the practical consciousness of the educated bourgeois strata."[7] This historical blind angle in the European practice of the cultural sciences might account for historical oversights on the part of Japanese practitioners. Kuki, for one, never directly posed the question of whether a method derived from one "historical and understood world" — particularly a method presupposing its own cultural-historical boundedness — could be transplanted to a different setting without consequences. Conversely, Kuki's confidence in the efficacy of German cultural theory might have been a sign that the "life worlds" of the Japanese and European intelligentsia had come to resemble one another to a surprising degree, that Japan and Germany, in particular, shared common concerns endemic to a belated modernity. Ironically, the theoretical idiom of *"Iki" no kōzō*, designed to demonstrate a Japanese cultural authenticity rooted in an indigenous past, simultaneously

6. Dilthey, *Pattern and Meaning in History,* 66–67.
7. Habermas, *Knowledge and Human Interests,* 178, 177.

bore witness to the interval of a heterogeneous modernity that irrevocably separated contemporary Japan from its premodernity.

In a 1931 lecture on Heideggerian philosophy, Kuki described the hermeneutic endeavor in mythic terms: "At the time when Theseus was about to enter the labyrinth, he was given a spool of string by Ariadne. He attached one end of the string to the entrance of the cave and was thus able to find his way out again. In the same manner, we fasten one end of the string that guides all philosophical questioning to our point of departure."[8] Kuki invoked the mythic metaphor to demonstrate Heidegger's conviction that philosophical inquiry must take human existence both as its point of departure and as its destination. But there is an additional, if unacknowledged, signification for the mythic labyrinth. For a moment, imagine Kuki in the role of Theseus, lured into the winding passages of European discourse by the promise of knowledge/ power. Once inside the now familiar (but not wholly hospitable) passages of the labyrinth, did he perhaps suffer the anxiety that return might no longer be possible? Was it the unspoken apprehension of an impossible return that engendered the fantasy of deliverance from the labyrinth? Kuki did in fact believe that he had returned to his "origin" — a self-possessed Japan untainted by its cultural other. But we might entertain the metaphoric possibility that Kuki never found his way out of the labyrinth; rather, he constructed an imaginary site called "Japan" within the more insular passageways of modern theoretical discourse.

The hermeneutic enterprise presented still another quandry for its Japanese advocates. From its inception as a cultural science in the late nineteenth century, hermeneutics claimed access to a truth that was broadly and fundamentally human. The practical interests of hermeneutics, however, were often much more narrowly circumscribed. Dilthey extended the promise of an expansive universalism with his appeals to world history, to mankind, and to a global *Geist:* "Throughout history, a living, active, creative, and responsive *Geist* is present at all times and places. Every first-class document is an expression of such a *Geist.*"[9] Clearly, there is a principle of cultural selectivity operating in the reference to "first-class" documents. The range of Dilthey's practical interests, as they were reflected in the projects he undertook, extended not to all times and places but only to the boundaries of Western civilization. The universal pretensions of hermeneutics very often

---

8. Kuki, "Kōgi: 'Heidegger' no genshōgakuteki sonzairon," *KSZ,* 10:10.
9. Dilthey, *Pattern and Meaning in History,* 67.

masked a European ethos; cosmopolitan appearances concealed a local reality.

The potential for something less than a universal science can be read even in the intricacies of hermeneutic theory. What, asked Dilthey, is the motivating impulse for the cultural sciences? First, he explained, we will understand something only if our interest is deeply engaged; further, it will engage our interest only if it is ultimately assimilable to our own experience. In other words, the ideal object of the cultural sciences offers a limited degree of resistance to the understanding, but only with the assurance that it will soon turn tractable: "Interpretation would be impossible if the expressions of life were totally alien. It would be unnecessary if there was nothing alien in them. Hermeneutics thus lies between these two extreme opposites. It is required wherever there is something alien that the art of understanding has to assimilate." [10] Here, Dilthey suggested the inherent limits of the hermeneutic enterprise, limits that might be mapped onto a geographical or even social space. Hermeneutics had been devised to reclaim a selected past from which the present had become increasingly estranged — not to confront stark differences between past and present, between an educated bourgeoisie and workers, or between Europe and its others. [11]

The universal ambitions of Dilthey's rhetoric, however, served not only as a disguise for interests particular to caste and locale. Those ambitions also reflected, however faintly, a continuing imperialist project on the part of the West to extend its control, whether material or ideological, to the far reaches of the globe. [12] "Across the limits of his own time," wrote Dilthey, modern man "peers into vanished cultures, appropriating their energies and taking pleasure in their charm." [13] Cast in the form of voyeuristic (one might even say cannibalistic) pleasure, the European cultural hermeneutic followed on five centuries of Western ventures of conquest and domination. Some of the vanished cultures to which Dilthey alluded were located on the site of existing cultures — cultures that

10. Quoted in Habermas, *Knowledge and Human Interests*, 164, from Dilthey, "The Construction of the Historical World in the Cultural Sciences."

11. Habermas points out that Gadamer's hermeneutics promotes an attitude of passive receptivity toward tradition. Gadamer, like Dilthey before him, fails to recognize the power of reflection to modify or reject tradition. Habermas, *Knowledge and Human Interests*, 356–59.

12. In their introduction to *Postmodernism and Japan*, Miyoshi and Harootunian remark that by the end of the nineteenth century, the West ruled or dominated 80 percent of the globe (388).

13. Dilthey, "The Rise of Hermeneutics," 231.

Europe had coerced into its colonial domains. The colonized had become captive subjects of European customs, administrative systems, and ethical injunctions, while their ancestors had become the objects of European literary, historical, and anthropological investigation. The universalist claims of European theory, on first glance so benignly and humanistically neutral, were in fact shot through with relations of power imposed by Europe's aggressive expansion across the globe.

This contrast between expansive universalist claims and culturally or nationally circumscribed interests was perhaps even more striking in the writings of Heidegger. *Being and Time,* with its virtual absence of concrete referents of time and place, readily lent itself to universal application. The "protagonist" of this massive philosophical narrative, Dasein, is defined as "an entity whose Being has the determinate character of existence," an entity who has "an understanding of the Being of all entities of a character other than its own." In an age of accelerated translation, Dasein might stand in for any human existent.[14] Heidegger's Japanese advocates may have differed with particular aspects of his philosophy, but they rarely questioned its general applicability to the Japanese case. In his lectures on the history of Western philosophy, Kuki classified Heidegger as a fellow humanist and participant in *seishin tetsugaku* (philosophy of *Geist*/Spirit) — neither of which categories Heidegger would have accepted as descriptive of his undertakings.[15]

Heidegger himself pointed out that his philosophical project had clearly defined ethnolinguistic boundaries. He insisted that any attempt to translate his writings would be futile. Such, he felt, "was the total inherence of his meaning in German and its linguistic past."[16] In Heidegger's view, the problematic of Dasein enjoyed an exclusive relation with the German language. Time and again, he traced the German linguistic past back to pre-Socratic Greece, a moment that he identified as

---

14. Heidegger, *Being and Time,* 34. "Dasein" previously had entered the Japanese philosophical vocabulary with Tanabe's 1924 article "Genshōgaku ni okeru atarashiki tenkō." Based on Heidegger's explanation of *faktisches Leben* ("factical" life), Tanabe rendered "Dasein" as "Genjitsu sonzai, sunawachi genjitsu no sei" (actual being, i.e. actual life). Kuki later abridged that unwieldy phrase to *gensonzai.*

15. In fact, this "misclassification" may have been less an erroneous reading of Heidegger's intentions than a strong reading of the German Romanticist line of filiation running through Heidegger's thought. For reflections on Heidegger's Romanticist inclinations, see Lacoue-Labarthe, *Heidegger, Art, and Politics,* 56–57, and Zimmerman, *Heidegger's Confrontation with Modernity,* 20–21.

16. Steiner, *Martin Heidegger,* 11. It is notable that Steiner questions neither the validity nor the ideological implications of Heidegger's linguistic bias.

the utopian origin of thought and philosophy: "The word philosophy," he claimed, "still speaks Greek."[17] Indeed, the reader of Heidegger is given the impression that the world of the ancient Greeks is separated from Germany's modernity by little more than a metaphysical detour. This familial relation between the two languages and the ensuing privilege accorded to the German language as the inheritor of true philosophy could not but serve an exclusionary function. In his reminiscences of conversations with Kuki recorded in "A Dialogue on Language," Heidegger reiterates his view that Asia lay beyond the pale of philosophy. When his Japanese interlocutor notes how compelling European aesthetics had been for Kuki's generation, Heidegger responds as follows: "Here you are touching on a controversial question which I often discussed with Count [sic] Kuki—the question whether it is necessary and rightful for Eastasians to chase after the European conceptual systems."[18] Heidegger did not think to include Kuki's response in the "Dialogue."

This conflict between universal pretensions and European interests, deeply entrenched in the hermeneutic enterprise, generated a number of ironies and contradictions when that enterprise was expatriated to a non-Western society. The expansive claims of hermeneutics authorized its use in a different cultural context, and yet those same expansive claims had their beginnings in the fact of Western hegemony. Kuki's faith in the hermeneutic method was directly connected to its promise of unmediated access to cultural reality "without doing harm to its concrete reality." Nevertheless, he cultivated a certain distrust for all theory, including hermeneutics. No doubt at some level he detected the hegemonic thrust of "universalism" in European theory. Contesting just such universalist claims, Kuki intervened on behalf of Japan's cultural particularity, and he did so by transforming the often covert particularism of European hermeneutics into an explicit program. Summarizing his inquiry into Japanese aesthetics, Kuki wrote: "In a word, the study of *iki* can be successfully undertaken only as a *hermeneutic of national being*."[19] But we should not forget that it was under the sway of the German cultural sciences that Japan began to imagine its own "national being," and it did so in the terms set forth by that other tradition.

17. Ibid., 23.

18. Heidegger, "A Dialogue on Language," 3. Heidegger mistakenly referred to Kuki as "Count"; Kuki had inherited the title of baron from his father Ryūichi.

19. Kuki, *"Iki" no kōzō, KSZ*, 1:12, 1:78.

As will become clear in the ensuing discussion, the Japanese practitioners of hermeneutics viewed culture through the eyes of their European counterparts—as an organic unity dwelling in the embrace of its past, an immovable stage for the appearance of Spirit, the manifestation of Being, and the sovereignty of consciousness.

The fact that Japanese theorists of culture found this model so conducive to their own interests suggests the possibility of one more convergence between Japan and the West. While Japanese thinkers hoped to resist the hegemonic drive of Western imperialism, they nevertheless reproduced its shape in theoretical terms. This pattern of resistance through replication was already familiar in the more practical negotiations of geopolitics. Beginning with the Meiji *ishin,* Japan's bulwark against Western empire had taken the form of emulation: the end of three decades of quasi-colonialism in the unequal treaty system coincided with Japan's own emergence as a colonial power in the 1890's. Building on victories over China and Russia in late Meiji, Japan renewed its expansionist efforts during Taishō, despite short-lived pretensions toward liberalization of colonial policy. Though the "formal empire" was complete by 1922, the 1920's saw Japan pressing further into Asia, particularly into China, where the Versailles settlement endorsed Japan's claim to special interests and privileges. While certain anomalies have been noted in the Japanese practice of empire, in its broadest outlines, Japanese imperialism resembled the new imperialism of an industrialized West. Both versions instituted rule by a minority who assumed their own superiority over indigenous majorities, and in both cases, the ruling minority represented itself as a machine-oriented civilization with a "mission" to bring development and progress to its colonies.[20] If, as Germaine Hoston argues, a tacit consensus over maintaining a Japanese sphere of military and economic influence on the Asian mainland reigned even during the more liberal Taishō years, we must consider the possibility that the relatively "free intellectual inquiry" of the 1920's reflected that consensus in some form. One might speculate that a philosophically articulated "horizon of being"—superimposed on the space of an "organic, self-conscious state that brooks no contradictions"—was itself implicated in the cultural foundations of the imperialist project.[21]

---

20. For a comparison of Japanese and European imperialism, see Peattie's introduction in *The Japanese Colonial Empire,* particularly 5–15. Included in Japan's formal empire were Taiwan, Korea, Karafuto, the Kwantung Leased Territory, and Micronesia.

21. This conjecture was suggested by my reading of Neil Larsen's discussion of Latin American liberation philosophy in *Modernism and Hegemony,* xxxix–xl. He argues, how-

The Logic of Organicism and the Abiding Subject of Culture

Hermeneutics permitted its practitioners to reimagine the collective entity instituted earlier by a centralized state in terms that differed from and yet ultimately coalesced with state ideology. Situating itself at a remove from the state, hermeneutics encouraged cultural contemplation instead of production goals, belonging instead of loyalty, the freedom of aesthetic distance instead of the proximity of coercive social control. Nevertheless, the terms favored by hermeneutics suggest that its real though implicit opponent was not the state but rather a Marxist perception of history as fueled by class conflict and of the present as rent by economic inequity, social discord, and alienation. To mask those duly noted conflictual divisions, hermeneutics fashioned a veil of organic unity and harmonious commonality. To supplant a history of traumatic discontinuity and dispossession, hermeneutics cultivated the continuity of a self-possessed spiritual tradition.

In a tactical move to unseat a new Marxist class subject, Kuki installed a national subject, to which he gave the name *minzoku* — a new collective agent in a conserving and conservative accord. Relying on a logic reminiscent of Descartes, Kuki took his point of departure from what he deemed a fundamental and therefore incontrovertible truth: "What is given to us directly is 'ourselves' and what is thought to be the synthesis of ourselves, the *minzoku*." [22] Like the Cartesian cogito, this subject, in its pure self-evidence, serves as the unquestioned guarantor of all further thought. For Kuki, however, the subject in question was collective and, as will soon become clear, predicated on experience rather than rationality. Japanese scholars note that Kuki was among the first in Japan to elaborate the notion of *minzoku*. (References to *minzoku* were soon to gain ascendancy in the wake of the Manchurian Incident in 1931.) [23] With this new signifier of collectivity, Kuki recast Japan in a shape distinctly different from both statist conceptions of a collective imperial subject and the participatory citizenry of a civil society. Without provision for

ever, that this philosophical critique of the metropolitan center often ends, ironically, by reifying alterity, lending it both geographical locus and spatial being. Kuki made a similar move when he identified the philosophical notion of contingence with the origin and essence of Japan.

22. Kuki, *"Iki" no kōzō, KSZ,* 1:7–8.
23. Tada and Yasuda, *"'Iki' no kōzō" o yomu,* 35–36.

class, gender, or regional locale, *minzoku* represented a new kind of national subjectivity—a subjectivity transformed by technologies of the self, interiorized and withdrawn from all social and political specificity. *Minzoku* became a signifier of a cultural community, timeless in its capacity to preserve the past in the present, joined together by a shared consciousness. In its insistence on homogeneous unity, the notion of *minzoku* raised the specter of internal dissension. In its obsession with continuity, this same notion suggested the powerful effects of its historical antithesis. Kuki, it must be remembered, was among a generation born into a post-Meiji society that had cut itself loose from the past in an attempt to invent itself anew. As a student of philosophy in the first decades of the twentieth century, he participated in an intellectual enterprise engendered by the modern sciences, an enterprise committed to "permanent revolution" in the domain of knowledge. Yet his preoccupation with *minzoku* betrayed the apprehensions of the more conservative of the early Shōwa intelligentsia, who suspected that they had been dispossessed of an indigenous past and who mistrusted a present that threatened to slip from their grasp. Learning from the example of European cultural hermeneutics, Kuki attempted to allay those apprehensions by renaturalizing the conception of society.

To accomplish this task, Kuki relied on the logic of organicism. In his study of the poetics of nineteenth-century European historiography, Hayden White explains that organicist strategies require "a metaphysical commitment to the paradigm of the microcosmic-macrocosmic relationship." White attributes the organicist argument to the midcentury nationalistic historians—most notably Leopold von Ranke—who aspired to draw a vast dispersion of events into an integrated totality. The organicist "desires to see individual entities as components of processes which aggregate into wholes that are greater than, or qualitatively different from, the sum of their parts."[24] As a rule, the whole or macrocosm posited by the organicist lies beyond the reach of inquiry and can be known only through its parts. True to this organicist logic, Kuki's *minzoku*, a recessive category of being, was fundamentally inaccessible.

For the task of representing what remained invisible and elusive, Kuki called upon the expressive power of language: "When a mode of being of the *minzoku* is central to that *minzoku*, it shows itself as a determinate 'meaning.' This determinate meaning then clears a path through 'language.' Consequently, this single meaning and its linguistic render-

24. White, *Metahistory*, 15.

ing serve as the self-expression of the national mode of being in past and present, the self-revelation of a unique culture endowed with its own history." The collective subject not only expresses itself through language, it also recognizes itself in language. Moreover, the word *iki* will ultimately be made to bear witness to essential cultural difference: "It is only when we have grasped the fact that the structure of this crucially important meaning of *iki* is equivalent to the self-revelation of our *minzoku* that we have reached a full understanding." A single word, albeit a privileged one, stands in for the whole. *Iki* reveals ontological truth, and as such, it is "by necessity deeply dyed in the distinctive experience of the *minzoku.*"[25] Here, clearly, a single word is assigned to represent the *minzoku* as the inviolable subject of experience. As will become clear, this representative function operates at the expense of language, depriving it of a productive role in relation to being. Language in *"Iki" no kōzō* is fated to express an eternal repetition of the same.

Since language was to bear the burden of proof, it is not surprising that Kuki turned immediately to the evidence of ethnolinguistics. The languages surveyed for cultural equivalents are, however, exclusively European, Asia being virtually excluded from this inquiry. At the conclusion of his survey of European languages, Kuki writes: "I can only conclude that *iki* is the distinctive self-expression of a special mode of being of Asian culture; or rather, to be more precise, of the Yamato *minzoku*. If Asia exists at all in this discourse, it is only as a shadowy extension of Japan."[26] Shaped (or misshaped) by this exclusive opposition between Japan and the West, Kuki's ethnolinguistic investigations were guided by the conviction that the constellations of meanings in different languages are semantically incommensurable with one another. His preliminary examples are telling ones, *esprit* in French, *Sehnsucht* in German — words for which he claimed a privileged relation with a people or *minzoku: esprit*, for example, reflects "in its entirety the history and disposition of the French people."[27] In the final analysis, *"Iki" no kōzō* demonstrated the incommensurability not only of words or particular cultural moments but of national cultures as a whole.

Perhaps Kuki's insistence on difference might not have been so unre-

---

25. Kuki, *"Iki" no kōzō, KSZ*, 1:8, 1:81, 1:8.

26. Ibid., 1:12. Interestingly, a Korean folklorist, in a recent critique of *"Iki" no kōzō*, draws close parallels between the *yūjo*, or Edo prostitute, who displayed the sensibility and style referred to as *iki*, and the Korean *kisang*, or courtesan, who possessed *motsu* — both, he claims, modes of resistance to their oppressive conditions and outcast social status. See Kim, "Iki, iki, motsu," 63–77.

27. Kuki, *"Iki" no kōzō, KSZ*, 1:10.

lenting had the risk of sameness not been so great. Despite the fact that his readings of Baudelaire and other French writers had in fact suggested a language for his interpretation of *iki,* it was the French contenders for equivalence that Kuki felt most compelled to disqualify. *Coquet, raffiné, chic*—each, he admitted, bears some resemblance to the notion of *iki,* but none, he insisted, has quite the same nuance. Yet even as Kuki expounded on the etymologies of these words for which he claimed an inalienable relation with the *minzoku,* he himself gave unwitting evidence for the malleability of meaning and the migration of language across national boundaries. Choosing the word *chic* as a prime example, Kuki speculates that "the original form of *chic* was *schick,* from the German *schicken*" or *geschickt,* meaning "skillful ingenuity." This word, he continues, "was then imported by France, where it gradually altered meaning and came to be used to express something close to 'elegant' in matters of taste." Finally, in this new French form "it was reimported back into Germany."[28] It is revealing that Kuki never attempted a historical etymology for the word *iki;* nor did he examine the multitude of ideographic variants that figure so prolifically in the popular literature of Edo. Either endeavor might have run the risk of suggesting the transferability and mutability not only of language but of culture as well. Kuki chose to write *iki* in *hiragana,* the phonetic syllabary. He enclosed his word in quotes as if to mark it off as separate (and sacred) space, rendering it a clear channel for national being.

Kuki's argument by way of language proves to be tautological. While language must testify to being, being must account for language: "Though a special mode of being central to one *minzoku* may be expressed in the form of meaning and language, when the same kind of experience (*taiken*) is not central for another *minzoku,* that particular meaning and language is clearly lacking." The circularity of this relation between part (a word and its meaning) and whole (the *minzoku*) relies once again on the logic of organicism: "The relation between meaning and language on the one hand and the conscious being of the *minzoku* on the other is not one in which the former aggregates to construct the latter; rather, it is the living being of the *minzoku* that creates meaning and language. The relation between the two terms is not a mechanical one in which the parts precede the whole but an organic one in which the whole determines the parts."[29] Kuki's organicist vision of a language born from the womb of the *minzoku* calls to mind, by contrast, a history

28. Ibid., 1:11.
29. Ibid., 1:9, 1:8.

of language reform during the not so distant Meiji era — a history marked by invention, artifice, and compulsion. The project to recreate Japan in the image of a "civilized" West required not only the construction of new vocabularies, both technical and cultural, but also an entire restructuring of language. Individual philosophers invented specialized terms to allow for the dissemination of new intellectual systems; writers transformed the notion of narrativity and literary voice under the banner of *genbunitchi,* a movement to unify the spoken and written languages; new educational and media apparatuses undertook the construction and inculcation of a national language through massive standardization and rationalization. In response to this history of rupture — which had generated the possibility of Kuki's own discourse — Kuki reenvisaged Japan as a natural and self-contained collectivity in full possession of all its parts. The only sure fact about the organic society, suggests Raymond Williams, is that it has always already passed.[30] In the midst of Japan's historical modernity, Kuki's organicist undertaking could not but be informed by reactionary longings.

More than a few observers of Japan's modern predicament have argued that the massive changes undertaken during the Meiji era outpaced Japan's capacity for assimilation. Such was the view of Meiji novelist Natsume Sōseki, who remarked unhappily that Japanese civilization had not developed internally but rather had been imposed from without. The strain of "catching up" with the West, predicted Sōseki, would inevitably lead to collective nervous exhaustion, (a condition the author frequently inflicted on his male protagonists).[31] With these comments, Sōseki not only confirmed the fact that a preponderance of power/ knowledge would remain on the side of the West for the foreseeable future but also provided, if only in a privitive mode, the touchstone for an "internally" developed and hence self-possessed society. The recent history that Sōseki found so disruptive was by no means exclusive to Japan, not in its most general outlines. Marshall Berman, in the book he titles *All That Is Solid Melts into Air* after Marx's assessment of the bourgeois epoch, suggests that the experience of shock, dislocation, and dispossession lies at the heart of modernity.[32] It was because Kuki shared this experience with his European colleagues that he found the organicist logic of the hermeneutic so compelling.

30. Williams, *The Country and the City,* 9–12.
31. Natsume Sōseki, "Gendai Nihon no kaika," 70–71.
32. Berman, *All That Is Solid Melts into Air,* 21.

That logic first entered the stream of the German cultural sciences with Dilthey, who transformed older forms of textual interpretation into a methodology for the *Geisteswissenshaften*. With painstaking rigor, he elaborated a theory of understanding cultural-historical artifacts based on organicist assumptions. Hoping to move beyond the closed sense of unity and identity that had characterized the organicist visions of his more Romantic predecessors, Dilthey sought a historiographical middle road between the theoretical naiveté of positivism on the one hand and the imaginative flights of a Romantic idealism on the other. Kuki, as we shall see, neglected the subtleties of these epistemological gains; instead, he mined the rich vein of idealism that still ran through Dilthey's logic. Dilthey conceptualized the part-whole relationship both as a methodological premise of the *Geisteswissenshaften* and as a description of the fundamental structure of life: "The connectedness of history is that of life itself integrated under the conditions of its natural environment. A part has meaning for the whole to which it belongs only if it is linked to it by a relationship found in life. . . . We must construct the whole from its parts and, yet, the whole must contain the reason for the meaning given to the part and for the place assigned to it."[33] The equation of history with "life," conceptualized in organicist terms, guaranteed that any fragment left from the past would find a meaningful place in larger, interconnected unities extending from past to present.

This guarantee of cultural-historical coherence was first offered by the hermeneutic sciences "in reaction to a decline in the binding character of traditions."[34] Those traditions had acted as guardian of distinctions not only between cultures but also between social classes. Invented under the impending disappearance of these distinctions, cultural hermeneutics aimed toward their recuperation in new forms of ethnic and national identities. The hermeneutic method made it possible to replace oneself in a continuing and often single current of tradition and to understand the present life-world in terms of that continuous tradition. Needless to say, such "understanding" operated in the interest of a privileged minority.

In Japan, during the years that spanned the end of Taishō and the beginning of Shōwa, new forms of social and cultural modernity had begun to take hold, threatening to shake society loose from the already enfeebled grasp of indigenous customs. By the end of World War I,

33. Dilthey, *Pattern and Meaning in History*, 73–74.
34. Habermas, "A Review of Gadamer's *Truth and Method*," 356.

industry had bypassed agriculture as the major contributor to the national product. In the decade that followed, people were drawn in increasing numbers to Japan's metropolitan centers, which were being rapidly transformed by the key technologies of a second industrial revolution (radio, cinema, telephone, automobile, etc.). Along with urbanization and new lifestyles came changes in family structure, particularly in the social status of women.[35] These same years also saw the crystallization of movements aiming at democratizing or revolutionizing Japanese society. Like their European colleagues, conservative Japanese theorists of culture had recourse to hermeneutics as an antimodern, even counterrevolutionary, strategy. Japan, however, had acceded late to a modernity already marked by the cultural hegemony of the West. And though the greater part of the philosophical discussions during Japan's interwar years was firmly grounded in modern theoretical discourse, for increasing numbers of intellectuals, modernity began to appear in the guise of the other, "the enemy from without."[36]

Watsuji communicated something of the paradoxical nature of this perception in *Fūdo* (An Existential Climate; 1935). He tells the story of how he returned to Japan in 1927 from a year-long visit to Europe with the impression that nothing in that supposedly foreign place had seemed strange or unusual: "To one who had understood the normal appearance of European architecture from examples seen in Japan, European cities, where buildings were as they should be, had nothing strange to offer." The defamiliarizing moment occurs after his return to Japan, which he now apprehends as strange: "In other words, the normal conditions in which I had lived and which I had grown used to seeing through the years remained identical; but there was exposed a much more fundamental condition lying underneath the surface which I had failed to perceive hitherto and which was now interpreted as rare or abnormal in contrast to what I had come to understand previously as normal." What Watsuji believed he had uncovered was a fundamental incongruity between material modernization and an essentially Japanese way of being that revealed itself to him as unusual or exceptional. To describe a scene of trams and cars moving through the city streets of his native land, he uses the metaphor of "a wild boar rampaging through fields." The houses that line the tracks seem to "crouch and bow spirit-

35. See Miriam Silverberg's discussion of working women and reform of the civil code in "Modern Girl as Militant," 255–60.

36. Kunō, "Bunkateki nashonarizumu no mondai," 64.

lessly just as the commoner would grovel in the face of a feudal lord's procession."[37]

Ironically, Watsuji's description demonstrates the degree to which the "enemy from without" already had entrenched itself deep within the structures of contemporary Japanese life. The recovery of the "rarity" of Japan could only be symbolic and nostalgically retrospective, a recovery of something invisible, hidden beneath the surface of modernity. Not surprisingly, Watsuji found the ready-made ineffability of *Geist* extremely expedient. In Watsuji's case, as in Kuki's, the salvaging of the ineffable was carried out in the name of a resistance to the West. In the hands of these Japanese philosophers, the European-derived hermeneutic became a powerful tool for fashioning cultural exceptionalism.

Culture as Truth

The Japanese critical reflection on culture and modernity borrowed heavily from nineteenth-century idealist notions of culture embedded in hermeneutics. But the question of difference, which dominated the Japanese reflection, invested that idealization with intense nationalist passion and anti-Western resonance. A crucial premise of the *Kulterwissenschaften,* and one that found ready converts among Japanese theorists of culture, held that the object of the cultural sciences differs from that of the natural sciences by virtue of its individuality and particularity. According to Dilthey, the entire task of philology and history is to develop a mode of objectively valid knowledge capable of appropriating the artifactual singularities left behind by the human spirit. Hoping to salvage the spiritual dimensions of a past that threatened to submit to the reductions of positivist explanation, Dilthey proposed a method he called *Verstehen* (understanding), a mode of experiential indwelling central to the hermeneutic enterprise. "*Verstehen,*" he explained, "is the process by which an inside is conferred on a complex of external sensory signs."[38] Habermas explains the process in these terms: "In understanding, I transpose my own self into something external in such a way that a past or foreign experience again becomes present in my own."[39] The

37. Watsuji, *A Climate,* 156–58.
38. Dilthey, "The Rise of Hermeneutics," 230–32.
39. Habermas, *Knowledge and Human Interests,* 146.

relations between an experience in the past, its expression in fixed form, and one's understanding of it in the present were assumed to be unimpeded and unproblematic. Thus, Dilthey believed that it is possible for the observer to "transpose" himself, attaining simultaneity with his object, that is, an ideal intersubjectivity between his own historical time and another.

Dilthey was convinced that this nearly perfect transposition was possible because of the special nature of the cultural object:

We can always make mistakes about the motivation of the principal actors in history; they themselves can indeed spread misconceptions about their own motives. But the work of a great poet or innovator, or a religious genius or a genuine philosopher can never be anything but the true expression of his spiritual life; in that human community delivered from all falsehood, such a work is ever true and unlike every other type of expression registered in signs; it is susceptible of complete and objective interpretation.[40]

Unlike politics, culture (narrowly construed as aesthetic and ethical attainment) was presumed to produce works immune to false consciousness, exempt from ideological distortion. In this "human community delivered of all falsehood," there were to be no gaps or contradictions, whether in the relation between a creator of culture and his own time or in the relation between a contemporary observer and the cultural past. This exclusive relation between culture and truth deeply impressed a subsequent generation of cultural theorists, particularly in Japan. On these grounds, for example, Watsuji, in his study of the thirteenth-century founder of the Sōtō Zen sect, was able to represent Dōgen — a master who advised devotees to simply throw away body and mind in pursuit of Buddha *darma* — as a cultural treasure in whose "extraordinary personality" a "world of truth" crystallizes.[41]

In his critique of the *Geisteswissenschaften*, Habermas points out that the model for Dilthey's notion of *Verstehen* is to be found in the life history of an individual, held together by an ego identity, in Dilthey's words, "a self-identical being characterized by the noteworthy matter of fact that every part of it is related in consciousness with the other parts by an experience somehow characterized by the continuity, connectedness, and sameness of the process."[42] This wholeness of experience guar-

40. Dilthey, "The Rise of Hermeneutics," 233.
41. Watsuji, *Nihon seishinshi kenkyū*, 156–66, 169–70.
42. Quoted in Habermas, *Knowledge and Human Interests*, 153, from Dilthey's *Gesammelte Schriften* (Göttingen: Vandenhoeck Ruprecht, 1913–1967), 7:73–74.

anteed that any particular fragment would be significant by virtue of an immanent relation of similitude with the whole.[43] Raised to a collective level, this model authorized a belief in the fundamental identity of humanity, or of particular cultures, over the course of time.[44] The "particularist" possibilities of this mode were ingeniously exploited by Dilthey's successors.

Dilthey imagined world history as an individual life history multiplied to the highest power, the sum total of all human experience. What assured the unity and connectedness of this total history was "an omnipresent stream of life . . . the basic fact which must form the starting point for philosophy. It is known from within. It is that behind which we cannot go. Life cannot be brought before the bar of reason."[45] Dilthey's critics have argued that, in the last instance, his theory of understanding rests on the vitalist and biological assumptions of a *Lebensphilosophie*.[46] But it was precisely that appeal to a prerational, fundamental, and totalizing sense of life that appealed so strongly to Japanese theorists of culture in the 1920's and 1930's. More often than not, "life" came to be circumscribed to the life forms unique to Japan. Kuki, for one, mobilized the homophonic resonances of the term *iki* to designate "life" as "a way of life" that was not only unique to the Japanese *minzoku* but that also transcended the vicissitudes of reason and history.

Though Kuki drew heavily on the cultural theory that informed Dilthey's historical method, his use of hermeneutics was tempered by a resistance to historical time. In his later lectures at Kyoto Imperial University, Kuki elucidated with great clarity the intimate correspondence linking experience, expression, and understanding—the triad that Dilthey had identified as both the structural character of life and the methodological core of his hermeneutic.[47] In fact, the argument of *"Iki" no*

43. Half a century later, after this notion of hermeneutic understanding had become entrenched in forms of insular culturalism, Miki Kiyoshi argued that it is the immanentism of hermeneutics that makes it unworkable in a world requiring complex mediations between radically different experiences. Miki, "Kaishakugaku to shujigaku," in *Miki Kiyoshi zenshū*, 5:149–52. I am indebted to William Haver for bringing this article to my attention.

44. Makkreel, *Dilthey*, 346–56. Dilthey's *Weltanschauungslehre* (theory of worldviews), though not correlated in any precise way with particular cultural sites, suggested possibilities for notions of a more insulated cultural horizon.

45. Ibid., 120.

46. Arendt, *The Human Condition*, 313 n. 76; Habermas, *Knowledge and Human Interests*, 182.

47. Kuki, "Kōgi: Gendai tetsugaku no dōkō," *KSZ*, 9:372.

kōzō rests squarely on the conviction that artworks "express" subjective "experience," and further, that experience can be "understood" because of a fundamental unity between the one who understands and the one who gives expression. In other words, Kuki shared Dilthey's faith in the possibility of an ideal intersubjectivity across historical time. But in Dilthey's methodological system, the verbal artifact from the past does not make itself immediately accessible to the investigator. Historical time interposes a moment of alienation, temporary though it might be, between expression and understanding. Accordingly, the act of interpretation requires a series of complex mediations between "a diffusely pre-understood whole" and the data or the parts encompassed by the whole. Kuki, on the other hand, hoped to eliminate even that initial moment of alienation from the past; for him, there was (or should be) no separation between contemporary Japanese subjects and the cultural artifacts of the past. In *"Iki" no kōzō* a disappearing cultural form is re-presented as if it had never been stricken by the alienation of historical time. Hence, the methodological relation between part and whole no longer required the mediation of reflective activity, as it had for Dilthey.

In Kuki's methodological rendering of the cultural hermeneutic, the concern for scientific validity (so central for Dilthey, not to mention the *Kulturwissenschaften* philosopher Rickert) virtually disappeared, and the efforts of the German historical philosophers to bring the particular into relation with general or universal concepts gave way to an overriding concern for the particular. For Kuki, part and whole alike, withdrawn from the movement of history and lodged in abiding national being, were suffused with the same particularity. The concept of universality, rejected as an empty abstraction, was summarily dismissed from the epistemological domain of culture. Kuki had pushed the circularity of the cultural hermeneutic to its logical limit in cultural closure. In the eyes of the theorist of Japanese culture, the very concept of the universal, oriented as it was toward Western interests, simultaneously excluded and diminished the cultures beyond its horizon. But his reactive insistence on particularity also implied submission to a system in which Europe posed as universal in relation to which all other cultures must appear as particular.[48] As Japan moved into the 1930's, the equation between *fuhen* (the universal) and *seiyō* (the West) would be drawn with increasing frequency.

---

48. For an extended discussion of the interdependence between the concepts of "universal" and "particular," see Sakai's "Modernity and Its Critique," 475–78.

Hermeneutics and the Erasure of Historical Time

Despite Kuki's efforts to erase all traces of the historical alienation that provided the inaugural occasion for Dilthey's hermeneutics, there is a brief moment in *"Iki" no kōzō* when he anxiously gauges the gap separating contemporary Japan from the indigenous forms of culture he so devotedly catalogues. In the concluding lines of the text, Kuki entreats his readers to resist the temptation toward a universalization of culture and to "recall . . . rather what the spirit sees." His ardent appeal to Platonic *anamnēsis, (sōki,* recollection) already suggests a certain lapse of memory: "How is it that we can reclaim the possibility of recollection in this sense? The answer is simple: Despite our forgetfulness, our spiritual culture has not been obliterated."[49] In his comments on the era in which *"Iki" no kōzō* was written, Yasuda observes that the transition years from Taishō to Shōwa witnessed the fading of Edo culture from memory; a familiarity with the aesthetic style of *iki* nearly had vanished, along with the last remnants of the Edo pleasure quarters, long since gone to seed.[50] The town geisha — those purveyors of pleasure who served Kuki as exemplars of *iki* — were themselves not exempt from the modernizing pressures of state and capital. By the second half of Meiji, their affairs had become largely codified and centralized, their wages fixed, their clientele controlled. But it was during the 1920's that the appearance of the geisha districts in urban centers underwent drastic change. Failing teahouses gave way to dance halls and cafés, traditional dance lost out to French-style Folies Bergère pieces, and geisha eager to maintain their role as leaders of fashion bobbed their hair and shed kimono for the latest Parisian styles.[51]

It was during his stay in Paris that Kuki first committed his image of the geisha to writing. No doubt his geographical distance from the cultural site he described made it easier to envisage a Japan resistant to the leveling effects of recent history. In theory, however, it was the hermeneutic that allowed Kuki to reclaim the past as real presence. Despite the different methodological orientations of a historiographically inclined German *Geisteswissenschaft* and a dehistoricized Japanese hermeneutic,

---

49. Kuki, *"Iki" no kōzō, KSZ,* 1:95.
50. Tada and Yasuda, *"'Iki' no kōzō" o yomu,* 122.
51. Dalby, *Geisha,* 77–83.

the gap between the two may not have been nearly as wide as one might expect. The possibility for denying differences and discontinuities in the archives already had presented itself in Dilthey's synthesis of hermeneutics and history. By means of that synthesis, the historian might "hold the entire past of humanity present within himself."[52] As Miki Kiyoshi later pointed out in his critique of hermeneutics, the three terms in Dilthey's triad—experience, expression, and understanding—were related to one another "in a continuative and confluent mode."[53] That confluence rendered historical time transparent and assimilable. Interpretation thus became a way by which to stave off the ravages of time, change, and discontinuity endemic to modern times.

The poet and critic Octavio Paz invoked precisely those qualities hermeneutics sought to suppress in his description of modernity, an epoch that was "cut off from the past and continuously hurtling forward at such a dizzy pace that it cannot take root, that it merely survives from one day to the next: it is unable to return to its beginnings and thus recover its powers of renewal."[54] The hermeneutic method sought to restore the rootedness that modern history had annihilated. In the most general sense, then, hermeneutics might be thought of as an imaginary antidote for the condition of modernity. In Japan, a society that had undergone massive transformations in an exceedingly brief span of time, the sense of uprootedness was registered with particular intensity; the imaginary solution presented by hermeneutics was especially seductive.

The Hermeneutic Shift: From History to Presence

In *"Iki" no kōzō*, the hermeneutic effectively shifts its focus from history to a philosophical analysis of existence. From the outset, the orientation of the text is systematic and architectonic; the operative axis is synchronic rather than diachronic. Kuki believed the nature of his object dictated such an orientation. Culture, he explained, is a "living form," a mode of being, that is to say, a fitting object for philosophical

52. Dilthey, "The Rise of Hermeneutics," 231.
53. Miki, "Kaishakugaku to shujigaku," in *Miki Kiyoshi zenshū*, 5:151.
54. Paz, *Alternating Current*, translated by Helen R. Lane (New York: Seaver Books, 1983), 162–62, cited in Berman, *All That Is Solid Melts into Air*, 35.

analysis rather than historical investigation. In prefatory remarks, Kuki outlines the task of a philosophical reflection on culture: "Living philosophy must attain an understanding of reality. We know that the phenomenon referred to as *iki* exists. But what kind of structure does it have? . . . The task at hand is to grasp the phenomenon as it is in reality and to give theoretical expression to an experience meant to be savored."[55] In other words, it is the task of theory—an impossible one, as Kuki claims in his concluding remarks—to go in hot pursuit of real being and to capture its living presence in the snare of structure. The fixed frame of structure, while it risked reducing the real to an abstraction, also lent distinctness and durability to a precarious cultural formation, one that was rapidly losing its solidity in everyday life.

Kuki used the word "structure" to indicate an analysis of lived experience into its constituent conceptual moments, ever at a remove from the experience it models. In addition, he employed "structure" in a more literal sense to refer to the graphic schematicizations of formal systems he invariably included in his text. In a chapter entitled "'Iki' no gaienteki kōzō" (The Extensive Structure of *Iki*), Kuki offers his readers the final version (rehearsed variously in preparatory drafts of *"Iki" no kōzō*) of a system of aesthetic taste in the shape of a rectangular solid or hexahedron (see Figure 1). At opposing right angles he situates binary pairs of aesthetic terms: *iki/yabo; shibumi* (astringent, sober, severe) / *amami* (sweet); *jōhin* (elegant, high-class) / *gehin* (vulgar, low-class); *hade* (flashy) / *jimi* (somber). Some of these pairs imply a value judgment, as in *jōhin/gehin*; others are value-neutral, as in *hade/jimi*. Some apply to life in general, others specifically to relations between the sexes. One of the virtues of this schema was that it allowed Kuki to derive the subtleties of *iki* from a complex negotiation of opposite pairings. Poised at the midpoint between high-class and low-class, sweet and astringent, somber and flashy, *iki* embraced elements seemingly at odds with one another—elegance with a hint of a crude come-on, self-promotion tempered by passivity, a flash of crimson underskirt from beneath a kimono of muted tones.

In *"Iki" no kōzō*, Kuki produced a phenomenology of taste, a systematic analysis of a language of everyday discernment. But while the majority of his chosen terms had become generic markers of taste or status, *iki* and *yabo* were intimately linked to Edo life, now largely replaced by more modern social formations. Kuki's geometrical structure worked to

55. Kuki, *"Iki" no kōzō, KSZ,* 1:12, 1:3.

obliterate that time differential by spatializing terms embedded in diverse historical temporalities. In this manner, the "structure" of *iki* produced an illusion of simultaneity. Some readers have discerned in this geometrical schematicization a prescience for the abstract play of binary oppositions which would later characterize structuralism proper.[56] To the extent that such a reading is justified, we should pay heed to Derrida's insight into the motives of structuralism. The structuralist passion, with its "frenzy of experimentation and proliferation of schematizations," develops during "epochs of historical dislocation, when we are expelled from the *site* [of being]."[57] Derrida recognizes in the structuralist triumph the pathos of having arrived at a scene of ruins when the object of desire already has been lost to history. That same pathos of the latecomer lurks between the lines of *"Iki" no kōzō*.

From the perspective of Tosaka Jun, this structuralist turn in hermeneutics had more ominous implications than simply pathos. In *Nihon ideorogīron* (1935), Tosaka critically assessed the hermeneutic enterprise, tracing its genealogy from classical beginnings to contemporary applications. He demonstrated that hermeneutics, presumably an art of deciphering ancient texts, even in its inception exceeded the limits of the written document per se. In fact, long before the interventions of Dilthey and Heidegger, hermeneutic ambitions extended beyond strictly linguistic tasks to a broader notion of cultural understanding. However, with the appearance of Dilthey, hermeneutics expanded its aspirations beyond deciphering classical texts and philology proper to a much more broadly construed notion of historical understanding. As a central tenet of his *Geisteswissenschaften,* Dilthey proclaimed that the understanding of historically situated classics is the essence of human knowledge; the interpretation of expression in the past became the condition for an understanding of life in the present. For Tosaka, however, it was Heidegger who made the most fateful revision of the hermeneutic project. By bringing hermeneutics to bear on phenomenological analysis, Heidegger decisively alienated the ancient art of interpretation not only from linguistics but from historiography as well. With Heidegger's intervention, hermeneutics reached the stage of pure philosophy — a systematic

56. See, for example, Sugimoto, "Tetsugakuteki zuan," 56. According to J. G. Merquior, however, "high structuralism" is based not on architectural or organic modeling of a singular phenomenon (as is the case in *"Iki" no kōzō*) but rather on the universalist assumptions of a mathematical model in which kaleidoscopic bits of generic data vary and combine according to laws. *From Prague to Paris,* 189–90.

57. Derrida, "Force and Signification," 6.

and structural method for the interpretation of existence in the here and now.[58]

Why did Tosaka find this recent turn of events so suspicious? The danger, he argued, lay in the persistent metaphysical aspirations of a discipline wedded to the past. Hermeneutics, particularly as it had been elaborated in the context of a Protestant humanism, retained vestiges of its inaugural theological desires — a nostalgia for an idealized past and a yearning for the infinite: "It is in this retrospective longing for all the worlds that have passed away," observed Tosaka, "that the German Romantic finds his dwelling place."[59] In a similar vein, Miki Kiyoshi likened hermeneutics to the owl of Minerva, a creature that appears only at dusk, when the day's events are done: "Hermeneutics attends to what has already been done, to the completed work. In the words of the eminent philologist Böckh its object is 'knowledge of the known.'"[60] Addressing itself to written records, hermeneutics is most at home in the archives.

With the lineage and orientation of hermeneutics established, Tosaka proceeds to assess the effects of its alliance with contemporary philosophy. He argues that Heidegger's synthesis of a historical hermeneutics (Dilthey) and phenomenology (Husserl) raises a serious problem. Phenomenology, a fundamentally nonhistorical method, focuses on the visible surface of things in the present; hermeneutics, on the other hand, inevitably searches out a meaning hidden deep within or behind things — another stage, where metaphysical depth is supposed to become manifest. This other stage was commonly designated as "life," "consciousness," or "Being." The nonhistorical orientation of phenomenology, suggested Tosaka, had altered the aims of hermeneutics. Originally a technique for deciphering cherished biblical and classical texts, hermeneutics retained a retrospective and aesthetic orientation even when it retrained its gaze on the present. The primary tool of hermeneutics, philology, severed from its historical function, became a mere caricature of itself in its new alliance with philosophy. "The contemporary actuality of the world," declares Tosaka, "is clearly not an object of philology."[61] In words reminiscent of Marx's "Theses on Feuerbach," Tosaka concluded that hermeneutics is a form of idealism, a pacified phi-

58. Tosaka, "'Bunkengaku'-teki tetsugaku no hihan," in *Nihon ideologīron,* 2:235–43.
59. Ibid., 2:239.
60. Miki, "Kaishakugaku to shujigaku," 380.
61. Tosaka, "'Bunkengaku'-teki tetsugaku no hihan," in *Nihon ideologīron,* 242.

losophy that has "contented itself with merely interpreting the world."

Approaching the problem from a different perspective, Miki Kiyoshi deemed hermeneutics inadequate not only as a philosophical logic for the understanding of Being but also as a historical logic for a history enacted in the present. Hermeneutics, he argued, brings to its objects the perspective of understanding, an essentially contemplative stance unsuited to the social action that generates history in the present. In place of hermeneutics, Miki proposed rhetoric as the model for a new concrete philosophical logic. Fundamentally instrumental, rhetoric concerns itself with effects in the domain of social practice.[62] By the late 1930's, when he constructed this argument, Miki had in fact chosen to work from within, in collaboration with the state—a form of social practice that Tosaka might not have condoned. Nevertheless, the two were in agreement that hermeneutics had outlived its usefulness in a historical present that, increasingly and urgently, demanded some form of engagement from intellectuals.

"Iki" no kōzō presents an exemplary case of the unseemly coupling of hermeneutics and phenomenology that Tosaka found so disturbing. The text pleads passionately for the recollection of a meaning fully present— a meaning concealed behind the often deceptive surface of things. Faced with "universal appearances" that would deny cultural difference, Kuki counseled his readers to entrust themselves to memory: "When we encounter such illusions, we must recall, rather, 'what the spirit sees' in its concrete and true form. This recollection is nothing other than the horizon for the hermeneutic recognition that iki belongs to us ("iki" ga wareware no mono)."[63] Under the impact of Heidegger's existential phenomenology, the hermeneutic project of reconstructing the experiential fullness hidden behind historical traces had shifted its focus to the present, but with its nostalgia for the past still intact. While Dilthey had deployed hermeneutic strategies in a project to recover human particularity concealed in the archives of the past, Kuki invoked the hermeneutic to recover an ethnically determined particularity no longer subject to historical time. The spirit of iki is, in his view, enduringly present.

In defense of this ahistorical appeal to particularity, Kuki marshaled an eclectically cosmopolitan array of argumentation, from medieval theology to contemporary phenomenology. Invoking an eleventh-century Christian debate over the nature of the Trinity, he sided decisively with

62. Miki, "Kaishakugaku to shujigaku," 382–83.
63. Kuki, "Iki" no kōzō, KSZ, 1:95.

the nominalist heretic Rocelinus, who had opposed the conflation of Father, Son, and Holy Ghost into a single universal essence: "When it comes to understanding '*iki*,'" Kuki claimed, "we also need the determination of a heretic to resolve the problem of *universalia* on the side of nominalism" — a resolution that, in *"Iki" no kōzō,* translated as an appreciation of the absolute particularity of culture.[64] The key to culture, Kuki claimed, lies not in generic concepts or universal essences but rather in the particularity and concreteness of national experience. In addition to Heidegger's existential hermeneutic, a method that inadvertently lent itself to the production of ontological diversity, Kuki found a ready ally in Bergson's radical subjectivism. In the following passage, he paraphrases a well-known anecdote from Bergson's *Essai sur les données immédiates de la conscience:*

When Bergson smells the rose and remembers the past, it is not that these recollections have been called up by the fragrance of the rose. Rather, he breathes them in with the very scent of the rose. A fixed, unchanging thing called the scent of a rose, a generic idea accessible to everyone, does not exist as a reality. The only thing that does exist is each particular fragrance, with its own content. Therefore, says Bergson, to explain the experience as an association between something general called the smell of a rose and something particular called recollection is like setting side by side certain letters of an alphabet common to a number of known languages in order to imitate the unique sounds of a new language.[65]

As with the scent of the rose, the aesthetic style of *iki* could be understood only in relation to subjective experience and meaning, without recourse to generic and objectifying codes. Any outward sign necessarily would compromise the authenticity of experience. There was, however, one crucial difference between the French philosopher and his Japanese admirer: Bergson affirmed the particularity of inner experience in order to defend the creative autonomy of an individual subject. Kuki, on the other hand, addressed himself to the autonomy of a collective subject and the authenticity of culture, that is to say, the lived experience of a people.

In the final pages of *"Iki" no kōzō,* Kuki warned that this collective authenticity was under siege. A universal sameness, indifferent to cultural distinctiveness, threatened to evict culture from its ethnic address: "'*Iki*' as experiential meaning has been realized in accordance with the

64. Ibid., 1:18.
65. Ibid., 1:17–18.

distinctiveness of national determinations of being in our country. Yet all too often we come across illusory copies of *iki* that have lapsed into a voidlike world of abstraction and *eidos* (form)." *"Iki" no kōzō* issued a clarion call to defend cultural form from being stripped of its essential Japaneseness. Yet that very Japaneseness, as conceptualized in *"Iki" no kōzō*, was itself the effect of the hermeneutic strategies Kuki had gleaned from modern philosophical discourse. It was there that he found the name for that "other stage" concealed behind the illusory appearances of a contemporary material reality: *Geist*, or what had become its local equivalent, *Yamato-damashi* (the Japanese spirit). There he discovered the logic of organicism that enabled him to posit a Japanese spirit cease- lessly expressing itself in culture.

Phenomenology and the Self-Evidence of Being

No doubt it was Kuki's overriding concern for cultural particularity that led him to choose sides in a philosophical dispute be- tween neo-Kantians and phenomenologists over the status of the real. Neo-Kantians, as we saw earlier, argued for the primacy of practical rea- son in the construction of reality. For them, reality owes its status to the synthetic activity of the human mind. Thus, the primary task of knowledge consists in determining the validity of the categories by which the mind predicates the real. Phenomenologists, accusing their rivals of an ill-begotten idealism, claimed that a more originary reality, the being of a thing, is given before any kind of predication. Positioning himself on the phenomenological side of the debate, Kuki argued that "the question of validity does not render the question of being extrane- ous; rather, it is often the question of being that is fundamental."[66] In a later reflection on Husserl and the phenomenological project, Maurice Merleau-Ponty sheds a revealing light on the priority given to being, things as they are, rather than validity, things as they should be: "To return to things themselves is to return to that world which precedes knowledge, of which knowledge always *speaks*, and in relation to which every scientific schematization is an abstract and derivative sign- language, as is geography in relation to the countryside in which we

66. Ibid., 1:12.

have learned beforehand what a forest, a prairie, or a river is."[67] It is worth attending to Merleau-Ponty's metaphoric appeal to nature—a sign, perhaps, of the nostalgic impulse of phenomenology in an era so deeply imprinted by artifice that nature no longer existed as a viable opposition to culture.[68] The world imagined by phenomenology is "given" in all its primitive immediacy. Urbane sophisticate that he was, Kuki demonstrated little philosophical concern for nature as such; he was, however, deeply committed to the possibility of a primitive and unmediated connection between a subject and a cultural world.

When Kuki affirmed the phenomenological priority of being as a reality preexisting reflection, he envisioned a local application not likely to have been foreseen by his European colleagues. The methodological affirmation itself served to call attention to a mode of being unique to a particular *minzoku* and cultural locus: What exists in Japan does not exist in the West. Moreover, it exists equally and absolutely for all Japanese. What lent such reified and reductive concepts of culture and *minzoku* their legitimacy was the methodological attitude of phenomenology, a philosophy that insisted that the real gives itself directly to intuition or contemplation: "The real has to be described, not constructed or formed."[69] This methodological choice had serious ideological implications for philosophical discourse. The apparent ingenuousness of the phenomenon, defined as what shows itself in itself, and of a world that gives itself directly to consciousness, renders the fundamental assumptions of philosophy exempt from critical reflection. As Herbert Marcuse so aptly observed in his critique of the German phenomenologists, the questions of what is to be known and by whom are decided beforehand in accordance with an unacknowledged hierarchy of value.[70]

In just such a phenomenological maneuver, Kuki positioned the category of "Japanese culture" beyond the reach of critical reflection. What counts as culture, who produces culture, who participates in it, and who interprets it were questions foreclosed by a theory that granted itself immediate access to "the things themselves." Like the European phe-

---

67. Merleau-Ponty, *Phenomenology of Perception*, ix.

68. In a provocative reversal, Roland Barthes described modernity as an era in which "nature has changed, has become social: everything that is given to man is *already* human, down to the forest and river which we cross when we travel." "The Structuralist Activity," 153.

69. Merleau-Ponty, *Phenomenology of Perception*, ix.

70. Marcuse, "The Concept of Essence," 65–66.

nomenologists, Kuki smuggled validity back into theory through the back door, disguising it with a naturalized vocabulary of life (being, *sonzai*), race (*minzoku*), and sensation (experience, *taiken*). Validity no longer was the concern of critical reason but rather a natural imperative of racialized being.

Heidegger's Hermeneutic of Being

If Kuki can be called a phenomenologist, it is in the style of the existentialist Heidegger rather than the rationalist Husserl. Following Heidegger, Kuki conducted a form of "Dasein analysis," an inquiry into how "Being-in-the-world" reveals itself to itself. But before we explore the limits of the common ground between German and Japanese philosophers, a few observations on the significance of Heidegger's most important work during the 1920's, *Being and Time,* are in order. In his attempt to bring philosophy to bear directly on the practical conduct of life, Heidegger had taken the phenomenological method of his teacher, Husserl, in the direction of an existential hermeneutic, an inquiry into the ways in which the "Being" of Dasein manifests itself. (This application of phenomenology to a hermeneutics of being was precisely the move that Tosaka Jun had cited as an ideologically dangerous contradiction in terms.) In the opening pages of *Being and Time,* Heidegger begins to redefine the phenomenological vocabulary:

Our investigation will show the meaning of phenomenological description as a method lies in *interpretation.* The *logos* of the phenomenology of Dasein has the character of a *hermeneuien,* through which the authentic meaning of Being, and also those basic structures of Being which Dasein itself possesses, are *made known* to Dasein's understanding of Being. The phenomenology of Dasein is a *hermeneutic* in the primordial signification of this word, where it designates this business of interpreting.[71]

Hermeneutics, then, is not one method among others but rather a fundamental orientation inherent in the structure of the kind of Being "we" are. Phenomenology normally concerns itself with the appearance or manifestation of things. But for Heidegger, the way things appear — that is, show themselves or conceal themselves — conforms to the con-

71. Heidegger, *Being and Time,* 61–62.

crete situation of human existence and the structure of human under-standing. Heidegger claimed that he had delivered Husserl's promise of a concrete philosophy: he had situated both the motive and the method of philosophy in the existential conditions of the being he called Dasein.

In a style that mirrors the circularity of hermeneutic understanding, Heidegger proceeded to describe the distinctiveness of human exis-tence: "Dasein is an entity which does not just occur among other enti-ties. Rather it is ontically distinguished by the fact that, in its very Being, that Being is an *issue* for it."[72] Dasein does not subsist as an object but rather ex-ists (outside itself) as a possibility. Thus, the very structure of existence draws Dasein into a continually renewed project of under-standing its own possibilities of Being. With this form of Dasein analysis in *Being and Time,* Heidegger claimed to have radically historicized phenomenology. It should be noted, however, that he aspired not to his-torical understanding in any kind of local sense but rather to an un-derstanding of existence in relation to temporality.[73] Perhaps not so par-adoxically, Kuki and others were able to draw on Heidegger's ontologi-cal vocabulary in a manner that definitively severed it from history.

Kuki's Hermeneutic of National Being

Kuki followed closely in the tracks of his Marburg mentor in his efforts to turn philosophical inquiry toward the real stuff of hu-

---

72. Ibid., 32.

73. Critics, particularly those of a Marxist orientation, have questioned whether tem-porality in *Being and Time* actually has anything to do with concrete history. See in partic-ular Terry Eagleton's discussion in *Literary Theory,* 65. In a recent contribution to a long-standing Heidegger controversy reignited by Victor Farias's indictment in *Heidegger and Nazism,* Luc Ferry and Alain Renaut argue that Heidegger's analysis of Being is riven by a fundamental ambiguity between timeless ontology and a historical specificity belonging to his own era of urban, industrial capitalism. The historicist option allows the critic to locate theoretical possibilities for a conservative activism in a text like *Being and Time,* written some years before Heidegger's induction into the National Socialist party. See Ferry and Renaut, *Heidegger and Modernity,* 34–39. Others indict Heidegger less for his omission of history than for a surreptitious historical intentionality—a political aspira-tion, veiled in the language of ontology, to curtail the possibility of mass empowerment and entrust the direction of the folk to an existential elite. See, for example, Bourdieu, *The Political Ontology of Martin Heidegger,* 52–53, 95–96, and especially 63–69. In an unpub-lished paper, Geoffrey Waite offers a brilliant theoretical elaboration of this "political on-tology," investing Heidegger with the dubious credentials of a modern political philoso-pher committed to reactionary ends. Waite, "Political Ontology."

man existence. Nevertheless, Kuki went much further than Heidegger in explicitly particularizing the question of being. A more fundamental difference, however, concerns the status assigned to theory. Heidegger was convinced, as was Dilthey before him, of the continuity between theoretical reflection and the practical interests of living in the world, a continuity that accounts for the reflexive character of understanding. This was perhaps the most significant contribution of hermeneutics. Kuki, despite his passionate pronouncements in favor of the hermeneutic method, largely abandoned the efforts of his European cohorts to articulate the relation between theory and practical activity. For Kuki, the hermeneutic method signaled rather an "unbridgeable chasm" between experience and theoretical reflection. However strongly hermeneutics might appeal to the reality of experience, he believed it is ultimately denied access to the real, along with all other conceptual methods. In this sense, Kuki was perhaps a better phenomenologist than Heidegger: the phenomenologist can describe only what is already given. Irrevocably severed from the real, philosophy is deprived of its powers of critical intervention.

Why did Kuki insist so strongly on the definitive alienation of theory from the real stuff of experience? No doubt he shared the distrust of concepts and abstractions that emerged so prominently in early-twentieth-century European philosophical practices pitted against their own discipline. But Kuki's suspicions signal another ambiguity as well, one that has its source in the complexities of his cultural predicament, which made him an outsider within his own discipline. Kuki chose to defend the propriety of his engagement with Western philosophy by arguing that philosophy and its requisite rationality are universal. Nevertheless, the European provenance of specific discourses and of the claim to universality itself was difficult to deny. Kuki suspected that there was a different reality to be accounted for, a reality that risked obliteration if submitted to conceptual systems inscribed with the hegemony of the West.

Those suspicions notwithstanding, the language deployed in *"Iki" no kōzō* is more than reminiscent of *Being and Time*. As if echoing Heidegger's opening remarks on the question of Being, Kuki appealed to a shared understanding, however vague, of a phenomenon fundamental to the being of the Japanese: "We know that the phenomenon of *iki* exists," he wrote; "but what kind of structure does it possess?" Furthermore, Kuki claimed that understanding of this crucial phenomenon had become distorted through the objectifying habits of modern thought. In what might have been a translation from Heidegger's German, he warned against "noisy chatter and empty words that pass off illusions as if they were truth." "We must not be led astray," he cautioned, "by ready-made generic concepts." Heidegger believed that his reverence for the real and his respect for the earliest Greek origins of philosophy qualified him to decipher the true meaning of Being, a meaning consistently misrecognized by a long line of venerable predecessors. Kuki also turned to the past, though a much less distant one, to bear witness to his interpretation of culturally determined being. He, too, promised to reveal the meaning of *iki* in a manner both fundamental and concrete, "as it is in reality."[74]

It might be argued that the comparison between *Being and Time* and *"Iki" no kōzō* flounders on the striking disparity in the scope of these two projects. Heidegger spoke to fundamental philosophical issues, while Kuki merely addressed a single term in a local repertoire of taste. But it was precisely the historical and material particularity of *iki* that provided Kuki with an exemption from the expansive universalist pretensions of Heideggerian philosophy and of European theoretical discourse in general.[75] Moreover, Kuki endeavored to persuade his readers that the supposedly marginal phenomenon of *iki* was in fact central to their common existence as Japanese. In *"Iki" no kōzō, iki* signifies not "style," in the limited sense of the word, but rather "lifestyle" in the broadest sense — a fundamental way of existing in a world. Kuki's interpretation of *iki* ultimately implies an existential structure rivaling Heidegger's "Being-in-the-world."

Kuki added existential weight to the notion of *iki*, first by exploiting homophonic equivalents: "Is it not the case," he begins, "that *iki* is an *iki-kata* (a way of life) unique to our *minzoku?*"[76] On the evidence of phonics alone, Kuki commits *iki* to a microcosmic representation of the national existent. Perhaps the closest approximation to an etymology comes in a final endnote; it is an idiosyncratic etymology, which relies on the suggestiveness of poetic resonance rather than philological research. (Philological research might have suggested that *iki* had its etymological origins in China.) Note that all the terms placed in quotes in the passage below are homophones for *iki,* that is, different characters with the same pronunciation:

Etymological research on *iki* must go hand in hand with an ontological clarification of the relation between "life," "breath," "going," and "spirit."

74. Kuki, *"Iki" no kōzō, KSZ*, 1:3, 1:80–81, 1:92.

75. Kuki was not alone in his appeal to the concrete. Watsuji also had made historical relics the touchstone of cultural difference. To insure the continuing significance of those relics, he theorized a Hegelian dialectic that would preserve the past rather than negate it.

76. Kuki, *"Iki" no kōzō, KSZ*, 1:7.

Clearly, "life" is the fundamental horizon. The verb "to live" has two meanings: the first, "to live" *biologically,* forms the foundation for the special domain of sexuality. The material cause of erotic allure is rooted in this meaning of "to live." "Breath" is the biological condition for life. . . . The verb
"to go" stands in an inseparable relation with the verb "to live." It was
Descartes who argued that *ambulo* should be considered the epistemological
foundation for *sum.*[77]

The note continues with poetic and colloquial evidence to demonstrate
the resonance of "moving toward" and thus a disposition toward the
other. This resonance accounts for the second meaning of *iki* — to live
spiritually, in the specific sense already given to the word *iki,* with resignation and fearless pride. Calling on etymology as witness, a tactic borrowed from Heidegger, Kuki substantially altered the terms of Heideggerian ontology. He situated desire in the center of philosophical
inquiry and affirmed the priority of intersubjectivity in the question of
being.

The poetic persuasiveness of Kuki's "etymology" is not without
effect. Nevertheless, he is vulnerable to the same charges leveled against
Heidegger for equating his own etymological speculations — whimsical
if not deceptive — with philosophical truth. In the note quoted above,
Kuki retraced the structure of *iki* in the rhetoric of etymology; like Heidegger, however, Kuki had abandoned the concrete ground of history for the rarefied and timeless realm of ontology. As the 1930's drew
to a close, Kuki would push etymology to absurd but ideologically
potent extremes. Responding no doubt to the proliferation of such
discursive strategies, Tosaka Jun argued in his *Nihon ideorogīron* that philology had no place in a theory that addressed itself to contemporary
issues: "The reality of the contemporary world cannot be treated as an
object of philology." The attempt to explain things in the present by
dredging up the origins of words ends in the destruction of theory, if
theory means, as Tosaka believed, a "relation of correspondence with
the real."[78]

Reconstructing a Different Subject

While Kuki may have aimed for an ontology in the style
of Heidegger, he neglected certain critical implications present in *Being*

77. Ibid., 97 n. 29.
78. Tosaka, "'Bunkengaku'-teki tetsugaku no hihan," in *Nihon ideorogīron,* 245.

and Time. Heidegger had introduced the working concept of "Being-in-the-world" in hopes of overcoming the fateful dualities of Western metaphysics — dualities that had mired philosophy in theories of transcendental consciousness on the one hand and visions of objective truth on the other. The world, Heidegger explained, never presents itself as a neutral object to a detached beholder. Between subject and object, consciousness and world, there are no clear lines of demarcation. Rather, Dasein always already is bound up with the world in any number of practical relationships.[79] Dasein's relationship with the world unfolds within a symbolic nexus that, Heidegger tells us, is both public and inauthentic. As we saw in chapter 2, these last two terms were crucial ones for *Being and Time,* suggestive of the estrangement of the individual in the "averageness" of the "they," or mass society. But this "inauthenticity" inheres in Being-in-the-world, and so Dasein always begins by misrecognizing the conditions and possibilities of its own being. In the course of an elaborate analysis that I can only allude to here, Heidegger submits the aspiring transcendental subject to a series of decentering moments intended to reveal the extent to which that subject is subjected to a world. Yet it is the anxiety provoked by this inauthentic mode of Being-in-the-world that provides the occasion for a realization of Dasein's authentic potentiality-for-Being. In this act of self-possession, Dasein recognizes the groundlessness and finitude of existence and becomes answerable to and for its own Being. This analysis of Being-in-the-world has encouraged more than a few readers to hail Heidegger as a proponent of existential freedom and responsibility in a world stripped of absolutes. This decentering operation did not, however, prevent Heidegger from finally reinstalling an authentic subject. Nor did it save him from the charge of substituting the heroic pathos of Being toward death for the common, everyday life of the masses.

Unlike Heidegger, who felt it necessary to deconstruct (however selectively) the metaphysical foundations of his own tradition, Kuki was more concerned with (re)constructing the pillars of a Japanese tradition. The notion of Being-in-the-world, along with all its various permutations from inauthenticity to authenticity, is conspicuously absent from *"Iki" no kōzō.* For Kuki, the problem was not nearly so complex: to recover the authenticity and integrity of the collectivity, the Japanese needed only remember a world that they themselves had created. Inau-

---

79. The use of the term *Dasein* was itself a tactical maneuver meant to disarm the notion of an essentialized and self-identical human subject. Heidegger argued that the subject exists not as a centered essence but as excentric process.

thenticity, estrangement in the "they," was neither an existential condition nor a historical necessity but rather a contingent predicament imposed by Japan's exposure to the West. Kuki collapsed Heidegger's meticulous ontological distinctions into a single term, *sonzai,* which in *"Iki" no kōzō* always refers back to a particular kind of being that is rooted in a unique national subjectivity. His aim was not to deconstruct the subject but rather to restore it in all its cultural authenticity. Yet despite these disparities, the contrast between Heidegger and Kuki was not as great as many of Heidegger's Japanese readers believed, especially when it came to the *minzoku,* the folk.

In the final section of *Being and Time,* Heidegger already had begun to announce his hopes for the restoration of an authentic cultural community. In the space of several pages, the hard-won authenticity of Dasein—attained at the expense of a public world overrun by the nondescript "they"—is abruptly and somewhat mysteriously collectivized in the form of an "authentic folk." Whether by contiguity or by semantics, the salvation of an individual Dasein becomes closely linked to the destiny of a not yet specified community, and what was dehypostatized in individual Dasein becomes rehypostatized in collective Dasein. In this final section, Heidegger grants all of the authentic modes of being a pluralized form: the historicizing of Dasein becomes the cohistoricizing of Being-with-others; assuming the burden of the past becomes a "handing down" of "the heritage"; the resoluteness in which Dasein discloses authentic possibilities for the future becomes the *destiny* of the people. Along with the collective dimensions of Heidegger's Dasein analysis, its radically conservative outlines also emerge in high relief: "When, however, one's existence is inauthentically historical, it is loaded down with the legacy of a 'past' which has become unrecognizable, and it seeks the modern. But when historicality is authentic, it understands history as recurrence of the possible, and knows that a possibility will recur only if existence is open for it fatefully in a moment of vision, in resolute repetition."[80] In the early 1930's, Heidegger added further resolution to both the collective and the conservative dimensions of Dasein in his theoretical writings and in his more practical association with National Socialism.

In what I would call a calculated oversight, Kuki, Watsuji, and Miki—all conscientious students of Heidegger—neglected the implications of this last section of *Being and Time.* As if with one voice, they

80. Heidegger, *Being and Time,* 429–44.

criticized the German philosopher for his preoccupation with the individual at the expense of sociality and the community, a preoccupation that they identified as the essential difference between Japan and the West. In his 1930 essay "Heidegger's Ontology," Miki faulted Heidegger (not without reason) for his fixation on individual subjectivity and the marked absence of a social context.[81] Similarly, in the introduction to *Fūdo,* Watsuji recalled how a reading of *Being and Time* in 1927 Berlin provoked his own interest in the question of climate. In contrast to the Heideggerian focus on temporality, Watsuji proposed that Dasein discovers itself in a qualitative space determined by climate, a space in which Dasein finds itself "always already" with others. Watsuji's "climate," determined less by natural environment than by history and social custom, referred to a space of human intentionality. Since climate exists equally and identically for all within its purview, the fundamental existential unit is homogeneously collective. *Fūdo,* addressing itself to "the distinctiveness of distinctive being," was Watsuji's response to the cultural particularism he detected in Heidegger's project. But Watsuji's selective reading of *Being and Time* yielded stark and total differences between Japan and the West—space versus time, individual versus community. These oppositions, which both presupposed and produced a homogeneous Japan in contrast to a diametrically opposed West, acquired the power of dogma in the years to follow.

In similar fashion, Kuki was determined to reconstruct a subject of a different magnitude from Heidegger's Dasein. And like Miki and Watsuji, Kuki was persuaded that Heidegger had missed something essential when he gave ontological priority to time over space in what concerns authentic existence. In Heidegger's view, Dasein bears a structure that is fundamentally temporal—a being stretched, as it were, between two voids: a rootless origin and a self-negating end. Only through a realization of temporality in this sense, in other words, of the nonbeing or nullity upon which its being depends could Dasein come into its own. Such a realization, maintained Heidegger, might be attained in a moment of vision when Dasein succeeds in extricating itself from the nexus of meanings and relationships that ordinarily characterize Being-in-the-world. On the other hand, as long as Dasein remains entangled in a world interpreted as spatial, a world filled with undistinguished others, Dasein exists in a state of dispossession from what is most essentially its own—its own finitude and its own possibility.

81. Miki, "Haidegga no sonzairon," in *Miki Kiyoshi zenshū,* 10:89–90.

In Kuki's view, this debasement of spatiality on Heidegger's part translated into a disregard for the communal dimensions of existence. In a 1933 essay titled "Haidegga no tetsugaku" (Heidegger's Philosophy), Kuki disclosed his doubts: "It is also questionable whether Heidegger has completely realized his intention to reduce space to temporality. For Heidegger, the foundation of existential spatiality is a mode of temporality that 'empresents' an inauthentic present, and existential spatiality is the ground for the discovery of spatiality in the world. However, in the final analysis, is this set of mutual relations as unequivocally clear and evident as Heidegger claims?"[82] Heidegger had apprehended existential space primarily as a set of instrumental and calculated relations determining the intentions Dasein brings to bear on things in the world. It is this spatial relation with the world that keeps Dasein from its ultimate possibility, a solitary and nonrelational being toward death. On this issue, Kuki differed with his German colleague. The privilege Heidegger apparently accorded to an isolated individual bore witness, Kuki claimed, to an enduring obsession in Western philosophy with the monad.

In what he believed to be a sharp contrast with Heidegger, Kuki located Dasein's ultimate possibility not in the severance of relations with the world but rather in a purification of relationality itself.[83] Dasein exists most authentically in infinite pursuit of another, a pursuit untainted by utilitarian aims or a rationality of ends. This intersubjective relation — untouched by political issues of power and conflict — became the foundation for a more comprehensive notion of sociality and community. Clearly, Kuki's critical response to Heidegger was informed by a desire to locate Japan in a cultural space apart from and different from the West. Yet at the same time, the conspicuous absence of politics from Kuki's conception of community defined a particular kind of political horizon for Japan.

National Consciousness and Cultural Closure

One might well locate the founding moment for Kuki's conceptual schema in a Romantic impulse that pitted the human soul

82. Kuki, "Haidegga no tetsugaku," *KSZ*, 3:268.
83. Similarly, Watsuji suggests that transcendence is not to be found in the temporal structure of individual Dasein but in the relations between individuals, the community,

against an external world conceived as machinelike and alien.[84] No doubt the radical subjectivism of Bergson provided a powerful model for Kuki. But Kuki might also have looked to Dilthey and the *Kulturwis-senschaften* philosophers who had drawn on the scientific conventions of their day to buttress this Romantic impulse with systematicity and disciplinary status. As if to erase the anguished conflict between the soul and a hostile universe, they constructed a domain of human activity within which the subject was granted primacy and autonomy. They called this domain "culture," and within its boundaries, the subject might play out with impunity its leading role as arbiter of ethical and aesthetic value.

This tradition, rather than the radically reinterpreted ontology of *Being and Time,* offered Kuki a philosophical language for the hierarchical opposition between subjective consciousness and objective expression. Dilthey had defended his key concepts of *Erlebnis* (lived experience) and *Leben* (life) from charges of subjectivism by arguing that these concepts implied a relation between inner and outer realities. But for Dilthey, the ultimate reference of life and lived experience was the subject, to whom he granted a fullness and perfection lacking in any objective act or expression:

The act proceeds from the fullness of life into finite one-sidedness. No matter how it may have been arrived at, it still expresses only a part of our essence. Potentialities that are contained in this essence are annihilated through the act. Thus the act separates itself from the background of a life context. And without explanation of how circumstances, end, means, and life context are connected in it, it allows no comprehensive determination of the inner realm in which it originated.[85]

It was, of course, this asymmetry itself that authorized Dilthey's hermeneutic project. One restored full meaning to relics from the past by reexperiencing and reconstructing the meaning of the life that had created them.

Kuki was similarly convinced of the priority of consciousness and the "inner realm" over any kind of objectification: "It is virtually never the

which constantly reaches out into the future. As Watsuji's *Rinrigaku* (Ethics) makes clear, the state ultimately provides the space and the motive for transcendence. See Naoki Sakai's discussion of *Rinrigaku* in "Return to the West / Return to the East," 168–70, 188–89; see also the "Introduction" to Watsuji's *A Climate.*

84. Wilson, *Axel's Castle,* 3–5.

85. Quoted in Habermas, *Knowledge and Human Interests,* 165, from Dilthey's *Gesammelte Schriften,* 7:206.

case that an objective expression of *iki* discloses all of its nuances. Because any objectification is bound by various limitations, the objectification of *iki* rarely if ever embodies the breadth and profundity of the
entirety of *iki* as a phenomenon of consciousness. Objective expressions
are merely symbols of *iki*." This view of subjective consciousness as the
initiatory site of meaning accounts for the passion with which Kuki insisted on methodological priorities: "First we must understand (*etoku*)
the mode of Being of *iki* that is constituted as a *phenomenon of consciousness*. Only then can we proceed to an understanding (*rikai*) of the mode
of being of *iki* that has become an objective expression." Even the quality of understanding Kuki brings to bear on consciousness is different;
etoku suggests an existential process of encounter and appropriation,
whereas *rikai* signals a more abstractly rational operation. Kuki continues with the following caution: "If one were to proceed inversely, the
attempt to grasp *iki* would be nothing more than empty intentions, and
the explanation of consciousness would end in abstractions and vague
concepts." The risk incurred by such a misguided procedure would be
the failure to grasp the national particularity of *iki*. What Kuki's argument implies is that abstractions, far too accessible, lend themselves to
a kind of cultural promiscuity: "If *iki* is defined in such a nebulous and
obscure fashion, then we are certain to discover many examples in Western art as well."[86] Ultimately, Kuki's logic drew him into a paradoxical
state of affairs in which tangible objects become the purveyors of illusions, while intangible, interiorized subjectivity become the site of
truth. Such a logic, however, was well suited to his defense of cultural
authenticity. At a time when Japan was becoming disturbingly similar
to Europe and America in its material forms of culture, Kuki turned
instead to spiritual forms of culture in search of difference.

The claim that material forms of culture are "mere symbols" of national consciousness had a number of consequences that were not without ideological impact. First, such a claim presupposed a unique and
inimitable source of culture largely inaccessible to another whose experience was presumably rooted in a different, but equally inaccessible, "national being." If one argued, as Kuki did, that culture is essentially self-
contained and self-referential, cultural transactions across national borders could appear only in the guise of an "artificial and forced infusion."
In other words, cultural borrowing became equivalent to cultural contamination. Second, the notion of a collective national subject allowed

86. Kuki, *"Iki" no kōzō, KSZ*, 1:88–89, 1:14, 78–79.

Kuki to conceal a heterogeneous social space of plural and conflicting interests behind a veil of cultural homogeneity. Magnifying the differences between so-called national cultures, Kuki obscured the differences within one culture, and here I use the word "culture" in its broadest, anthropological sense. In his *Imagined Communities,* Benedict Anderson depicts the nation, or what he calls "nation-ness," in similar terms: "[The nation] is a cultural artifact of a particular kind. It is . . . imagined as a *community,* because, regardless of the actual inequality and exploitation that may prevail in each, the nation is always conceived as a deep, horizontal comradeship."[87] Despite the very rare references to nation or state in *"Iki" no kōzō,* the cultural community that the text presupposes may in fact represent the preferred idiom for the expression of nationalism. By fixing a national consciousness at the origin of culture, Kuki implied that culture is created without the mediation of the social and political conditions of contemporary life. In so doing, not only did he fatefully widen the gap between culture and politics, he also placed consciousness as a spiritual and subjective point of origin beyond the reach of history.

87. Anderson, *Imagined Communities,* 13–14.

CHAPTER 5

An Aristocracy of Taste in an Age of Mass Culture

Pendant que des mortels la multitude vile,
Sous le fouet du Plaisir, ce bourreau sans merci,
Va cuillir des remords dans la fête servile,
Ma Douleur, donne-moi la main, viens par ici,

Loins d'eux. Vois se pencher les défuntes Années,
Sur les balcons du ciel, en robes surannées;
Surgir du fond des eaux le Regret souriant.

While the vile multitude of common men,
Whipped on by unrelenting festivals,
Lay up regrets, like servile citizens,
Come you, Affliction, far from carnivals,

Give me your hand. See the dead Years lean down,
In dated dress, from balconies in heaven;
Behold Regret rise from the deep, unbowed.

From Charles Baudelaire, "Recueillement"

Following his own methodological priorities, Kuki turned to artifacts and other visible manifestations of *iki* only after he had thoroughly interpreted *iki*'s subjective meaning. Yet despite the prerogative he accorded to consciousness, a good part of *"Iki" no kōzō* is devoted to the material texture of objects and to the sensual cast of bodies and gestures. In his inventory of the natural and artistic expressions of *iki*, Kuki included everything from the tenor of the voice to teahouse architecture.[1] The sheer exhaustiveness of his catalogue suggests, once

---

1. Nature, it should be noted, is largely restricted to the female body. This feminization of *iki* poses the possibility, as suggested earlier, of a reverse self-exoticization, while

again, the dedication of a collector laboring against time in a project to preserve artifacts threatened with oblivion. That urgent act of collection — "gathering up possessions in arbitrary systems of value and meaning" — served to flesh out the body of an imaginary collective subject.[2] As self-appointed connoisseur/collector, Kuki assembled a set of culturally marked objects, endowing them with the status of cherished "national" possessions. By means of this linguistically rendered collection — a collection defined by its exclusions as well as by its inclusions — Kuki constructed an ideal cultural self-representation.

The Tyranny of Meaning

The objects Kuki depicted are specific to the narrowly circumscribed world of the Edo pleasure quarters: the enticing gestures of geisha, the colors and patterns of their clothing, interiors suggestive of short-lived liaisons, the *shamisen* music that drifted out of teahouses and Kabuki theaters. What allows Kuki to assimilate these quite specific depictions to a much broader and comprehensive notion of culture is the power of interpretation. *"Iki" no kōzō* puts things in their place, at the beck and call of national subjectivity. Still, however skillful the assimilation, a certain unresolvable tension remains. How, one is tempted to ask, can the bare foot of a geisha signify the essence of Japanese culture?

A formidable necessity operates in this text, a necessity that comes of the tyranny of meaning over things. It begins in earnest when Kuki first introduces his lengthy inventory of objects: "What form does the objectification of *iki* take? First, it must express the duality of *bitai* (erotic allure). Second, the expression of that duality must be accompanied by a determinate objectification of *ikuji* (fearless pride) and *akirame* (resignation)." This interpretive necessity yields a catalogue of redundant bodies and artifacts, all reduced to the same signification. To cite a few provocative examples, first, the motif of *usumono* (a thin silk

---

the imposition of an erotic etiquette on the female body suggests Kuki's resistence to the "modern girl" who subverted and altered traditional gender distinctions and sexual norms.

2. Clifford, "On Collecting Art and Culture," 217. Clifford is paraphrasing Richard Handler's article "On Having a Culture: Nationalism and the Preservation of Quebec's *Patrimoine*," in *History of Anthropology,* edited by George Stocking, vol. 3, *Objects and Others* (Madison: University of Wisconsin Press, 1985), 192–217.

garment): "The relation between material and formal causes of *iki* is expressed in the dual role of a semitransparent, thin silk garment that, on the one hand, frees the way to the other sex, and on the other, acts as a veil, thus interposing an impediment in the path of desire." The material and formal causes, it may be recalled, have already been equated with the three attributes of *iki: bitai, ikuji, akirame.* Kuki turns next to the line of the body: "An almost imperceptible relaxation of the posture is another expression of *iki*. . . . To destroy the self-contained equilibrium of the body expresses a receptivity that invites the other sex with a promise of possibility. But the nonrealism and idealism of *iki* adds a note of restraint and control to the destruction of equilibrium and imposes a check on unbriddled dualism."

At his best, Kuki evokes eroticism as an evasive promise that awakens and perpetuates desire. That eroticism, however, bears the mark of a culturally exclusive meaning. Every description, whether the nape of a woman's neck or the design of an alcove, carries the burden, word for word, of Kuki's interpretation of collective cultural consciousness, a mandate carried out by means of a phenomenological reduction: "In this manner, we have reduced objective expressions of *iki* to the phenomenon of consciousness, and in elucidating the relation between these two modes of being [subjective and objective], we also hope to have made the structure of *iki* clear."[3] Ultimately, Kuki's reduction has transformed beings (objects and women's bodies) into pale copies of Platonic being—an essential form of Japaneseness.

The Freedom of Creation

As Kuki practiced it, the art of interpretation imprinted a single stamp of meaning on artifacts received from the past. In contrast to that interpretive necessity, Kuki claimed that present acts of artistic creation express subjective experience under conditions of absolute freedom: "Though the artistic impulse often works unconsciously," he explained, "unconscious creation is nonetheless an objectification of experience. In other words, an individual or communal experience *unconsciously, but freely,* chooses its formal principles and attains self-expression

3. Kuki, *"Iki" no kōzō, KSZ*, 1:53, 1:43, 1:42, 1:71.

as art."[4] To support his Romantically inclined aesthetic claims, Kuki turned to modern European reflections on art, in particular to the prose of Paul Valéry. At great length, he quoted from *Eupaulinos ou l'architecte,* Valéry's lyrical variation on a dialogue between Socrates and Phaedrus. In the following lines, Phaedrus paraphrases the words of the architect Eupaulinos, who attests to the subjective origins of the work of art:

The little temple that I built for Hermes, just a few steps from here, if you only knew what it means to me! Where a passerby sees nothing but an elegant chapel—such a small thing: four columns, the most unadorned of styles—I have put into that temple the memory of one single radiant day in my life. Oh sweet metamorphosis! No one knows, but that delicate temple is the mathematical image of a girl from Corinth whom I loved blissfully. It reproduces her unique proportions.[5]

The aesthetic pronouncements in Valéry's *Eupaulinos,* though not lacking in passion, are tempered by an irony implicit in their dialogic structure. The title itself, *Eupaulinos ou l'architecte,* suggests the rivalry in art between the desire of the subject (Eupaulinos the man) and the requirements of form (the architect). Kuki, however, read the passage as a license for unmediated cultural expressivity. Just as Eupaulinos transforms his love for the Corinthian girl into architectural form, so, too, the collective cultural subject transforms its own collective experience into art.

In his defense of creative freedom, Kuki also suggested that the artistic impulse works most often in an unconscious register. Though he offered no explanation for this claim, perhaps he believed, like another of his favorite French writers, that the past lay "somewhere beyond the reach of the intellect."[6] For Marcel Proust, conscious memory served the intellect all too obediently, retaining only information, but no trace of the real texture of lived experience. Proust posited a *mémoire involuntaire* that would respond to a chance encounter with some material object, the *madeleine* for the narrator of *À la recherche du temps perdu,* to resurrect in full a personal past. For Proust, the *mémoire involuntaire* served both as the subjective repository for an experienced past and as a limitless resource for artistic creation—this at a time when both appeared to be at risk. To borrow the words of Benjamin, this unconscious

4. Ibid., 1:76.
5. Valéry, *Eupaulinos ou l'architecte,* 33–34.
6. Benjamin, *Charles Baudelaire,* 112. Benjamin was quoting from Marcel Proust, *À la recherche du temps perdu,* vol. 1, *Du côté de chez Swann* (Paris, 1979), 69.

memory provided an interiorized refuge from the atomization of experience and disintegration of identity in "the inhospitable, blinding age of
big-scale industrialism."[7] Unconscious memory guaranteed a truth that
differed from the data obtained in a conscious encounter with the
present.

Similarly, Kuki sought safe harbor from contemporary conditions in
art and the aesthetic function. Working from such distinctively modern
aesthetic premises, Kuki deemed *iki* to be the unconscious expression of
national experience. As an aesthetic form, it had emerged directly from
the core of the national subject without submitting to the mediation of
consciousness, to say nothing of material conditions. The artifacts that
bore its imprint provided Kuki with privileged access to the truth of
collective cultural being. Here again, we can hear echoes of Dilthey's
definition of culture as a human community "delivered of all falsehood."
In Dilthey's view, a work of art represents nothing less than the genuine
expression of the spirit of its maker.

The Edo Pleasure Quarters: Materiality and Metaphor

From Kuki's post-Romantic perspective, the aesthetic
style of *iki* had been created in the unconscious interiority of the collective cultural subject. Nevertheless, the writers of *gesaku* fiction, those
whom Kuki called on to provide *"Iki" no kōzō* with its material texture,
held very different views concerning the provenance of style. *Sharebon*
writers of the late eighteenth century demonstrated their connoisseurship as they meticulously inscribed the rules of style and etiquette that
regulated life in the pleasure quarters. *Iki* was an acquired knowledge
demanding a long apprenticeship among the denizens of the quarters.
In the *ninjōbon* of the early nineteenth century, *iki* became a privileged
predicate in theatrical narratives about the romantic embroilments of
geisha and their clients.

Consider for a moment the parvenu geisha Yonehachi, heroine of
Tamenaga Shunsui's *Shunshoku umegoyomi* (The Colors of Spring: A
Plum Calendar). She has just moved from a licensed house in Yoshiwara

7. Ibid., 110–12.

to self-employment as a *haori* geisha in Fukagawa.[8] Tō-san, Yonehachi's patron and aspiring lover, already piqued at her persistent evasion of his affections, takes her to task for her still unfashionable accent: "Well, it's clear to me that you haven't dipped deeply enough into the waters of Fukagawa. You haven't even learned to speak right yet!"[9] Tō-san's injured pride aside, *gesaku* representations of the subtleties of style suggest not the freedom of an internal, creative process but rather a very immediate engagement with the material specificities of everyday life. Kuki's retrospective meditation on *iki* selectively excluded these concrete conditions of Edo style. Between the *gesaku* of the early nineteenth century and *"Iki" no kōzō* of the early twentieth century, *iki* had migrated inward to the recesses of subjective freedom, beyond the reach of the material conditions of life.

Though Kuki's encounter with Edo culture may have been less than historically attentive, it was nevertheless metaphorically potent. While Kuki never specified the nature of the metaphor, the text itself suggests symbolic resemblances between the Edo pleasure quarters and the Kantian conception of aesthetics to which Kuki subscribed. Whether literally or figuratively, both represented sites of nonconnectedness. In his study of Tokugawa art and society, Abe Jirō described the quarters as both *ikoku* (a strange or exotic land) and *hikoshiki no ana no sekai* (an unofficial world situated in a gap or hole), thereby calling attention to the real as well as the symbolic boundaries that separated the quarters from the world of ordinary concerns and official control.[10] An extraordinary environment, the pleasure quarters were devoted not to "wholesome production" but to highly charged human relations and elaborate forms of cultural display.[11] Once a customer passed through the gates that enclosed the quarters, he was delivered from the common nexus of social and economic necessity (providing, of course, he had sufficient wealth). Inside the gates, he devoted himself to play in a world radically stylized, down to its finest details.

Over this material site in the urban topography of Edo, Kuki mapped what he imagined to be the spiritual contours of Japanese culture.

---

8. *Haori* was a half coat worn by men until the Bunka Bunsei era, when it became the fashion among Fukagawa geisha, who affected masculine ways. These geisha were also referred to as *ni mai kanban* (two shingles over the door), since they were reputed to sell art in the open and sex on the sly.

9. Tamenaga, *Shunshoku umegoyomi*, 82.

10. Abe, *Tokugawa jidai no geijutsu to shakai*, 41–43.

11. Nishiyama, *Edogaku nyūmon*, 204.

Though he hoped to guarantee the "Japaneseness" of *iki,* his rendering of Edo style suggests, in fact, other affinities. Kuki described the aesthetic and moral disposition of *iki* in a manner worthy of Kant's third *Critique,* replicating nearly all of the significant moments of aesthetic judgment: disinterestedness, purposiveness without purpose, and the free play and autonomy of the aesthetic function.[12] "*Iki* ignores the prospect of reality at a low price and boldly brackets out practical, everyday life. Breathing in the neutralized air of a transcendental atmosphere, *iki* engages in autonomous play (*jiritsuteki yūgi*) without purpose (*mumokuteki*) or interest (*mukanshin*)."[13] The aesthetic function, as it was conceived in the third *Critique* and in much of subsequent European reflection on art and culture, points to a realm of "pure pleasure, pleasure totally purified of all sensuous or sensible interest."[14] Distinct from (and superior to) the gratification of natural desires on the one hand and utilitarian motives on the other, the aesthetic function exists for its own sake. The Kantian aesthetic finds its echo in the "allure for its own sake"[15] of *"Iki" no kōzō.*

Just as *iki* signified purification of erotic allure, Japan represented a spiritual and moral transcendence over the necessities and interests that regulated ordinary life. In the short essay "Time is Money," Kuki invoked the samurai tradition of contempt for mercantile activity to attest to an enduring Japanese aspiration for the ideal. "We have been nourished and raised," he wrote, "in an atmosphere far from counting houses, far from shops."[16]

With this remarkable (but unacknowledged) recontextualization of Kantian aesthetics, Kuki intimated that Japan was the privileged site of an aesthetic mode of existence. In the same manner that Kant's view of aesthetic judgment invoked the superior ethos of a cultured elite,[17] the aesthetics of *iki* called attention to the moral excellence of the Japanese

12. Had Kuki included Kant's provision for the universality of aesthetic judgment, the resemblance might have been complete.

13. Kuki, *"Iki" no kōzō, KSZ,* 1:22. It is also interesting to note that this description closely resembles the phenomenological reduction as Husserl described it (and as Kuki translated it). Here, Kuki has transformed methodological considerations into content: like the phenomenological method, *iki* requires impassive detachment from practical interests.

14. Bourdieu, *Distinction,* 493.

15. Kuki, *"Iki" no kōzō, KSZ,* 1:22.

16. Kuki, "Time is Money," *KSZ,* 1:249. The original is in French, with its aphoristic title in English.

17. Bourdieu, *Distinction,* 491–92.

minzoku (and, as I will propose below, of its representative elite). In the concluding lines of *"Iki" no kōzō,* Kuki wrote: "Were we not a people that stared at human fate with unclouded eyes and turned toward the freedom of the soul with anguished longing, erotic allure would never have taken the form of *iki*." [18] Japan itself had become the privileged site of the ethical and spiritual qualities of culture over and against the material and mechanical qualities of civilization.

Symbolic Correspondences

Within the borders of this imaginary cultural site — severed by definition from the material specificity of contemporary life — Kuki sought to mend the rupture between subject and object in a system of symbolic correspondences between external things and inner life. *"Iki" no kōzō* pictures a world awash with meaning, a world in which bodies, gestures, and artifacts are transmuted into signs of lived experience and abiding value. A gesture, a glance, a color, or a line all "express a personality and narrate the experience of a past." The life most emblematic of *iki* was the life of the Edo geisha viewed through a veil of sentimentality: "It is only after catching a glimpse of the faint traces of sincere tears behind a seductive and nonchalant half smile that one first understands the true visage of *iki*." The connoisseur of *iki* reads in its seductive signs the layers of past experience that constitute a life: "An amorous glance in itself is not yet *iki*. It only becomes *iki* when her eyes shine with a luster that evokes the misty outlines of her past." Kuki describes the allure of *iki* as a muted glow, the "negative afterimage of a colorful experience." In that allure, he discerns the traces of a "rich past," rich both in love and in disillusionment: "A devoted heart, cruelly betrayed time and time again, draining the cup of sorrow to the very dregs — that heart, hardened like tempered steel, finally loses interest in the faithless prize." [19] This history of betrayal was supposed to leave in its wake a cultivated and refined disposition, a disposition capable of disinterestedness and renunciation. Ultimately, the special charm of *iki* represented the ethical and spiritual redemption of the losses suffered to love.

18. Kuki, *"Iki" no kōzō, KSZ,* 1:81.
19. Ibid., 1:48, 1:20, 1:45, 1:20.

Kuki read in the signs of *iki* the redemption not only of a personal past but also of a cultural past. To appreciate the collective implications of his narrative, we need only recall that it was *bushidō* and Buddhism that enabled the bearer of *iki* to transcend the ordinary: "*Iki* makes it possible for erotic allure to realize its own being by virtue of the moral idealism and religious belief in the nonreality of the world that characterize our national culture. That is why *iki* commands an unrivaled authority and an irresistible appeal." Kuki attempted to convey the meaning of *iki* with this quotation from an Edo source: "All the while knowing it to be a lie, the one whose heart bears the signs of *iki* takes it as if it were true."[20] No doubt he had in mind the image of a geisha who entertained prospects of a love in which she had lost faith. But perhaps Kuki also hoped to suggest the existential credentials of a culture capable of philosophical irony. Watsuji had earlier set the tone for such claims. In his *Gūzō Saikō* (The Restoration of Idols), Watsuji claimed that the iconoclastic insight of Nietzsche was old hat for a Japan nurtured on a Buddhist worldview: "It is only a personal cowardice in the face of the facts that keeps people today still believing in things like a god or in a life-after-death. But to those for whom these things have for a long time already flown in the face of common sense, a declaration now such as that 'God is dead!' says nothing new at all. For them God had already been non-existent all along."[21] Here, Watsuji played a game of existentialist one-upmanship in the arena of national cultures. Similarly, in an essay extolling the virtues of *bushidō*, Kuki intimated that Japan was a more than worthy inheritor of a heroicized legacy of Sisyphus and the moral philosophy of Kant: "The infinite good will, which can never be realized in full, and which is destined always to be 'deceived,' must forever renew its efforts. . . . Let us pursue perfection with a clear awareness of its 'deception.'"[22] Such was the philosophical value that Kuki assigned to Japan's cultural experience, the same value that he read in the formal attributes of *iki*.

Kuki's theory of a world of symbolic correspondences between the *minkozu* and expressive form recalls the much more lyrical version of that theory articulated by Charles Baudelaire, a poet he greatly admired: "L'homme y passe à travers des forêts de symboles / Qui l'observent avec des regards familiers."[23] Benjamin described Baudelaire's theory of cor-

---

20. Ibid., 1:23.
21. Translated by William R. LaFleur in "A Turning in Taishō," 240.
22. Kuki, "La Notion du temps," *KSZ*, 1:286.
23. Baudelaire, "Correspondances," in *Selected Poems*, 42. The English translation reads: "Man wends his way through forests of symbols / Which look at him with their

respondences as "an experience which seeks to establish itself in crisis-proof form," a utopian ideal designed to counterbalance the spleen of *Les fleurs du mal*: "The *idéal* supplies the power of remembrance; the *spleen* musters the multitude of the seconds against it." The power of remembrance called forth by "Correspondances," argued Benjamin, attested to the real disintegration of experience witnessed by Baudelaire in the Paris of the Second Empire.[24] When Kuki imagined an aestheticized world replete with meaning, he, too, called attention, however inadvertently, to a contemporary reality that was far from satisfactory — to the ravages of capitalism and the dehumanization endemic in urban industrial society. But while Baudelaire transcribed and transfigured the alienating effects of modernization in poetic images, Kuki buried them beneath a philosophical ontology of Japaneseness.

The Claims of Contemporary Culture

In *"Iki" no kōzō,* Kuki admitted only one cultural adversary — the West. The text constructs a mirror-image symmetry that opposes a homogeneous same (Japan) against a monolithic other (the West). The homogeneity of Japanese culture, however, was clearly not a referent of the text but rather its effect. In actuality, the Japan Kuki addressed was heterogeneous, long since invaded by otherness and rent by the tensions and contradictions of its own modernity. Much of what Kuki labeled "Western" had already become deeply entrenched in Japanese life. The most salient aspects of culture during the early Shōwa years — increasing specialization in arts and letters, the commodification of culture on a large scale, the proliferation of mass culture, and the appearance of a proletarian art movement and an avant-garde — slip into concealment between the lines of *"Iki" no kōzō.* A student of Japanese modernism, Taki Kōji, wrote that the 1920's saw the birth of collage, the abstract, and kitsch, a brief observation, but one that suggests the emergence of new stratifications in the cultural consumption of that era.[25]

Behind the cover of Kuki's aesthetics of cultural opposition, the out-

---

familiar glances." Multiple copies of *Les fleurs du mal* (The Flowers of Evil) in Kuki's personal library, all with meticulous marginalia, confirm the deep affinity he felt for the French poet.

24. Benjamin, *Charles Baudelaire,* 142, 139–40.
25. Taki, *Modanizumu no shinwa,* 157–60.

lines of a response to the radically altered configuration of culture in a modernizing and modernist Japan are dimly visible. In my own attempt to draw *"Iki" no kōzō* into more explicit dialogue with other contemporary voices, I have turned to cultural critics of a more progressive cast than Kuki, critics who addressed themselves in a different fashion to the most pressing concerns of contemporary culture in Japan. While Kuki used all the theoretical resources available to him in his effort to sever culture from contemporary social conditions, Nakai Masakazu, his colleague at Kyoto Imperial University, sought to repoliticize culture within a context of new relations of production. In his essay "Shisōteki kiki ni okeru geijutsu narabi ni sono dōkō" (Art and Its Trends in a Time of Intellectual Crisis), Nakai set his critical sights on those intellectuals who saw themselves as the last defenders of art and philosophy against the threat of a vulgarized and mechanized anticulture. These defenders of culture, Nakai argued, were themselves already victims of the dehumanization they deplored. The most ominous trend in contemporary culture was neither "massification" nor material mechanization (though he readily acknowledged both) but rather a phenomenon he called the "mechanization of mind." "Thought has merely become another profession," Nakai proclaimed, "its function has become commodified."[26] He pointed out how the disciplines — science, philosophy, literature — had become increasingly autonomous and isolated from one another.[27] The division of labor, arguably modernity's most questionable contribution, had infiltrated even the most privileged sites of culture — academe and "pure art." Nakai's analysis of the specialization and professionalization of culture supplies us with the outlines of a contemporary context for *"Iki" no kōzō*. Within this timely context, Kuki's vision of a cultural abode saturated with collectively shared memory and meaning appears as a protest, in a reactionary mode, against the progressive rationalization and atomization of contemporary intellectual and aesthetic practices — a reaction to the prominent participation of the masses in culture and a protest against the invasion of profitability and instrumentality into the domain of art and philosophy.

Kuki overlooked not only the historical conditions of his own intellectual practice but also the extent to which modern culture had taken

26. Nakai, "Shisōteki kiki ni okeru geijutsu narabi ni sono dōkō," in *Nakai Masakazu zenshū*, 2:46–48. French theorist Michel de Certeau has expressed the same idea in his sly observation that philosophers are experts in the universal. See *The Practice of Everyday Life*, 6–7.

27. Nakai, "Shisōteki kiki," in *Nakai Masakazu zenshū*, 2:46–48.

hold in Japan. Observers of the contemporary scene differed in their appraisal of modern culture, but most agreed on its revolutionary implications. Ōya Sōichi, a Marxist critic, defined the underlying disposition of *modan raifu* (modern life) as "a diseased and insane quest for the new . . . a preference for heightened stimulation over truth or depth."[28] Modern life, he claimed, is the expression of bourgeois decadence in an era of high capitalism. In a pictorial essay that captures the dominant mood of the era from a less unflattering angle, Maeda Ai specifies the relation between modern life and a new mass constituency: "The 1920's was a decade given over to popular custom and fashion, an era that concentrated on the outermost surface of things. The masses, who had never doubted the virtue of knowing their place during Meiji, rose up to the social surface on a wave of popular custom."[29] This rise to cultural visibility of the masses was reflected in new, widely accessible and mechanized forms of culture. The decade of the 1920's witnessed the first broadcasts on Tokyo's earliest radio station, JOAK, the sudden and overwhelming success of cinema, and a revolution in the publishing industry that flooded the market with inexpensive books for a vastly expanded readership. Publishers described their new strategy as *masu puro, masu ado, masu sēru*" (mass production, mass advertising, mass sales)—a description that might have been applied to other areas of a burgeoning culture industry as well.

In *"Iki" no kōzō*, these new claims of Japanese culture are displaced beyond Japan's cultural horizon. Accordingly, the full weight of Kuki's cultural criticism falls on the West. Though Kuki refused to recognize fundamental changes in Japanese cultural practices, in writings other than *"Iki" no kōzō*, he grudgingly acknowledged that the West had, in fact, made major inroads into Japanese life: "every aspect of our life is tainted by the West," he lamented without further comment. Had there been no cause for worry, Kuki would not have felt it necessary to call for a "moratorium on spiritual imports" (*seishinteki sakoku*) in order to "return to Japan." But *"Iki" no kōzō*'s condemnation of the brash, exhibitionist, and unrefined aspects of Western culture bespeaks a profound dissatisfaction with things much closer to home. The burlesque review, the flapper, and jazz—pervasive signs of a new, modern age that Kuki confined to the West as emblems of cultural difference—were no less common on the Ginza than on the boulevards of Paris.

28. Ōya, "Modan sō to modan sō," in *Ōya Sōichi zenshū*, 2:5.
29. Maeda, "Tōkyō 1925," 72.

The Aesthetic Defense

In *"Iki" no kōzō*, Kuki strove to conceal contemporary conditions of cultural production, including his own condition as producer of academically specialized texts. His recourse to aesthetic forms that predated Japan's modernity was guided, however, not only by an escapist impulse but by a utopian vision as well. In its utopian dimension, the aesthetics of *iki* represent Kuki's desire to recover, or imagine anew, forms of experience sacrificed to the imperatives of modernization. Kuki's contemporary, Nakai, explained how newly mechanized technologies had permeated every aspect of life, revolutionizing the foundations of perception. Individual time and private memory, he claimed, had given way to collective history and documentation; body and mind had yielded to the machine.[30] Nakai found reason to celebrate this expansion of rational, mechanical, and collective subsystems into the domain of art. From his perspective, this transformation signaled the end of an overindulgent Romantic aesthetic, an aesthetic that represented the interests of a newly entrenched and reactionary elite. In contrast, Kuki saw in that same expansion nothing less than an impending threat to the integrity of culture and all that is genuinely human. He chose to address that threat in the language of modern aesthetics, a language that claimed absolute autonomy for art and the aesthetic function. And it was precisely this claim to autonomy that allowed Kuki to exempt culture from the irreversible effects of historical modernity.

In the rarefied realm of aesthetics, Kuki invested human experience with the depth, complexity, and fullness of meaning that modern social life had both promised and denied. In the words of Benjamin, he designated art as the region of things "on which man has bestowed the imprint of his soul."[31] *"Iki" no kōzō* represents Kuki's attempt to imagine a symbolic system that would reclaim what had been lost to the rational and instrumental demands of modernization.

In place of a univocal and utilitarian sign, Kuki proposed an ambiguous and disinterested one. The increasingly dubious guarantees of enlightened modernization—that what you see is what you get, that the end justifies the means—were not, he implied, necessarily desirable. In *iki,* Kuki wrote, "we see an affirmation by way of negation." Whether a refusal disguised as an offer or an offer disguised as a refusal, *iki* appealed

30. Nakai, "Shisōteki kiki," in *Nakai Masakazu zenshū,* 54–55.
31. Benjamin, *Charles Baudelaire,* 146.

by virtue of its undecidability: "Even while *iki* entices, it demonstrates at the same time a strength that resists the other." Kuki traced and re-traced this double movement of solicitation and refusal in his chosen objects. Such was the meaning he attributed to the vertical stripes fa-vored among the geisha of Kaseiki Edo. "Parallel lines," he wrote, "eter-nally moving, but never meeting, are the purest visual expression of *iki*." Refusing closure and central focus, parallel lines conveyed the "cool in-difference" so crucial to the aesthetics of *iki*. Their "ceaseless pursuit of dualism" signified a perpetually renewed promise of a union never real-ized. Faced with the pragmatic principle of satisfaction of needs, Kuki celebrated the virtues of inexhaustible desire. In a manner prescient of the post-structuralist posture, Kuki excluded figural and mimetic realism from the aesthetic repetoire of *iki* for its "persistent symbolization" of a message. Whether in art or in romance, *iki* required a disinterested disposition able to transcend the temptations of both sincere love and unequivocal meaning.[32]

Iki was also an aesthetic of decline, one that favored "autumnal tints" and "a minor mode." As a sign, *iki* suggested its own disappearance, as in the waning beauty of an older geisha or in the hints of physical decline in the delicately slender figures of Utamaro. "Elongated forms," wrote Kuki, "suggest both the degeneration of the flesh and the power of the spirit."[33] Again, we might locate here another site of aesthetic protest against attempts on the part of state and capital to impose a standard of functional beauty, one that would serve the cause of increased produc-tivity. The *eisei bijin* (a hygienic beauty), an expression that dated from the Meiji years, represented official aspirations to replace the decadent image of the geisha in the public imagination with a more wholesome ideal of femininity. One might even argue, with some reservation, that the Shōwa heir of the *eisei bijin* was the *moga,* or modern girl, a woman who mobilized, voluntarily, to labor for national productivity. Kuki's *iki na onna* (a woman with style) evoked a world of unlimited leisure, de-sire, and decadence — in other words, a world that transgressed the man-date to produce in a rapidly expanding national economy. Kuki's insis-tence on the intimacy between death and desire stands in sharp contrast to myopic optimism entertained by an ethos of enlightened progress.

If Kuki called on older cultural codes as a means of protest against

---

32. Kuki, *"Iki" no kōzō, KSZ,* 1:22, 1:18, 1: 53, 1:57. It must, however, be added that if the aesthetics of *iki* refused essential meanings and stable identities at the level of form, it reinstated both at the level of collective culture. In the equivocal appeal of *iki*, Kuki discov-ered the unequivocal meaning of a transhistorical Japan.

33. Ibid., 1:44.

the norms of enlightened rationalism and progress, his aesthetic of decline also shared in a more contemporary mood that prevailed at the
end of the 1920's. Tada and Yasuda agree that one need not look as far
as the Buddhist worldview for an explanation of the nihilist flavor in
"Iki" no kōzō. The early years of Shōwa, they suggest, were prey to a
sense of desperation and pessimism, which made itself manifest in contemporary popular culture. The lyrics to one song that circulated in the
late 1920's used a botanical metaphor to express the prevailing mood:
"I'm a withered reed on the riverbank, you too, a withered reed." [34] During the same years, social critics began to use the expression "people
who are like grass with no roots" for the masses of *déraciné* salaried
workers who had so recently made their way to the city. The "resignation" that Kuki read into the aesthetic style of *iki* resonated with a contemporary mood of social resignation in the face of narrowing of opportunity. The hopes raised by Taishō democracy and the faith in the
unconditional benefits of modernization had come up against a wall of
economic despair and political frustration. *"Iki" no kōzō* both reflects that
despair and seeks distance from its mass character in an aristocracy of
taste.

In the *gesaku* fiction of late Edo, one of the many characters used to
write *iki* was *hodo*, a word that signifies a limit or an appropriate degree.
The eroticism of *iki*, Kuki maintained, must be tempered by a certain
reserve. A slight lilt in the voice, a wisp of hair out of place, a mere trace
of makeup—only the most delicate hints of seductiveness or wanton
disarray were permissible. The aesthetics of *iki* called for deviation from
the norm, but deviation of the subtlest order. The Edo *tsū* distinguished
himself by his knowledge of just how far to go and where to stop.
Though Kuki accounted for that reserve with a transhistorical narrative
of moral and spiritual heroism, once again, his exclusions suggest a
more timely context for his preferences. In his catalogue of natural expressions of *iki*, Kuki insisted that "the facial expressions characteristic
of *iki* have no relation at all to Western vulgarities, including winking
an eye or puckering up the lips to play jazz." [35]

While Kuki expressed his distaste for jazz solely on the basis of appearances, he might well have rejected jazz for its musical qualities as
well. This new breed of music clearly overstepped the limits of subtle
deviation into unreserved dissonance. In the words of Ōya Sōichi, jazz

34. Tada and Yasuda, *"Iki' no kōzō o yomu*, 75.
35. Kuki, *"Iki" no kōzō, KSZ*, 1:46.

had ushered in "the tyrannical rule of cacophony."[36] Furthermore, jazz had insinuated itself much further into Japanese urban life than Kuki was willing to admit. The reconstructed capital to which Kuki returned in 1929 already had fallen under the sway of new rhythms, and the significance of that fact was not confined solely to the aesthetic domain: "On the pavement of the modern city whose pride is its modern vanguard, jazz captures the souls of the ones who make their appearance on the night streets along with an array of artificial lights."[37] Ōya saw Tokyo's taste for jazz as the sign of a barbaric impulse breaking through the extreme limit of a decadent modernism, an impulse that had brought new cultural constituencies into urban visibility. For Ōya, this new sensibility represented raw and revolutionary prospects, a desire to break free from the proprieties of bourgeois culture. In contrast, Kuki's plea for resistence to the excesses of jazz sounds suspiciously like the voice of bourgeois reaction. And indeed, Kuki did cast himself in the role of guardian of older forms of culture.

If the aesthetics of *iki* appealed to moderation in the face of crude extremities, they also favored subtlety over a contemporary taste for total exposure. In the final pages of *"Iki" no kōzō*, Kuki quoted Verlaine's poetic imperative: "Pas la couleur, rien que la nuance!" (Not the color, nothing but the nuance).[38] Similarly, the aesthetics of *iki* endorsed subtle nuances and suggestive hints. In the logic of symbolist poetics, to name an object was to take away the possibility of imagining it. No doubt Kuki hoped to preserve a place in contemporary life for the free play of imagination, a human faculty that risked paralysis under a mechanical barrage of information and stimulation. But once again, his predilection for nuance had other and more timely implications. Like the symbolists, Kuki was persuaded that human experience is fundamentally ineffable, its richness and complexity far exceeding the powers of conventional language and referential signification. Consequently, experience could be intimated only through subtle and indirect means. Here, Kuki took a tacit stand against the prevailing trends of contemporary culture. In the cultural vanguard of the 1920's, Ōya observed a surprising affinity for barbarism—a barbarism that he believed to be the dialectical outcome of the excesses of bourgeois culture. As examples of this "primitive" and "artless" culture, Ōya cited the vogue for "the wild

---

36. Ōya, "Kindai bi to yaban bi," in *Ōya Sōichi zenshū*, 2:27.
37. Ibid., 2:27–28.
38. Kuki, *"Iki" no kōzō, KSZ*, 1:86.

frenzy of the jazz music created by the Negroes . . . the loud, brash colors worn by dancers and waitresses . . . the mascara and lipstick that resembled the tattoos of savages." This vanguard, he concluded, relying on a language stocked with racialized imagery, favored stimulation over refinement, primary colors over complex nuances.[39]

The aesthetic of *iki* resisted an era that discovered beauty in scenery viewed from the window of a speeding train. An appreciation of the nuance, Kuki suggested, required a time and space conducive to contemplation. Within this contemplative atmosphere, the subtlest of sensations could call up desire out of the depths of remembrance: "For the light that floats through the space evocative of *iki*, we must have the pale glow of a *tasoya andon* (hanging lantern); in the dim light, one can breath in the faint traces of perfumed sleeves that penetrate to the depths of the soul."[40] The space appropriate to the proportions of *iki*, Kuki explained, must be large enough to include two, but small enough to exclude the crowd: "A small room of four-and-a-half mats; outside the paper doors, a veranda; inside, a lover's tryst."[41] We need only compare Kuki's ideal aesthetic space, the secluded teahouse, with evocations of the contemporary urban scene to realize that he was attempting to reclaim a quality of space and time that had largely yielded to newly organized patterns of work and leisure. The following impressionistic description of the urban landscape comes from Ōya's "Modan sō to modan sō" (Modern Stratum, Modern Mores): "Every morning, hundreds of thousands of [people, their nerves sharp and receptive like] antennas, rush in to the cluster of buildings that overlooks the center of the metropolis, the heart of the nation. When evening comes, once again they rush out en masse. From that moment on, their *modan raifu* progressively unfolds." In this essay, Ōya goes on to evoke the excesses of a new consumer life (*shōhi seikatsu*). From the aerial perspective Ōya employs in the passage above, the individual is annihilated in the crowd, and time, reduced to a uniform present, is endlessly repeated. If a *Shinkankakuha* (New Sensationist) writer were to describe the scene, Ōya added, he might say that the human crowds swarming at the exits of tall buildings at closing time resemble piles of ruble notes scattered over the ground.[42] Solitary yet uniform among the urban working masses, the

---

39. Ōya, "Kindai bi to yaban bi," in *Ōya Sōichi zenshū*, 2:24–28.

40. Kuki, *"Iki" no kōzō, KSZ*, 1:67.

41. Ibid., 1:75. Quoted from an unreferenced Edo source. The *en* of *en no shōji*, a *kakekotoba* (pivot word), plays on double meanings: first, the veranda that surrounds the structure, and second, the romantic liaison between those inside the sliding doors.

42. Ōya, "Modan sō to modan sō," in *Ōya Sōichi zenshū*, 2:5, 2:6.

human personality was reduced to exchangeable monetary value, precisely what Kuki hoped to forestall with his theory of experience.

In his aesthetic profile of the modern vanguard, Ōya also noted a trend toward unabashed exposure, "an aesthetic without modesty."[43] Kuki may well have been responding to this new taste for exposure when he praised the aesthetic (and erotic) powers of concealment. The erotic appeal of *iki* required that much be kept in reserve.[44] In defiance of an empirical demand for total visibility, Kuki attempted to recover the secret of eroticism and its relation to aesthetic form. In one passage, he described the way a geisha wore her kimono, the collar pulled back to reveal the nape of the neck, "faintly suggesting to the other sex a pathway to the skin still concealed." He contrasted this image with the décolletté, a style that "exposed completely the back and everything from shoulder to breast." This latter, he claimed, was an unmistakable sign of Western boorishness (*yabo*). Another passage opposed the *yuagari no sugata*, the image of a woman fresh from her bath, a *yukata* carelessly wrapped around her body, to the European nude. And still another illustration compared a fleeting glimpse of a geisha's leg as the hem of her kimono flashed open with the high-heeled, but nearly nude, dancer on the Paris burlesque stage.[45]

After nearly a decade in Europe, what greeted Kuki upon his homecoming was a cultural modernity he might have hoped to leave behind in the West. In his article entitled "Tōkyō 1925," Maeda Ai shows us a *Kurabu keshōhin* (Club cosmetics) advertisement from the mid-1920's featuring a full-length figure of a woman. The lines of her long muslin gown are reminiscent of a sculpted Greek goddess; the décolletage exposes the flesh of her shoulders and neck. In the accompanying caption, Maeda describes the norm that dominated the feminine body during those years: "The woman of the twenties was completely engrossed in becoming beautiful, in polishing her bare skin to a brilliant luster: Club powder, Shiseido coldcream, and the beauty secrets revealed in women's magazines. . . . The women painted by Takehisa Yumeji, with their sloping shoulders and small breasts, conquered a generation. They symbol-

---

43. Ōya, "Kindai bi to yaban bi," in *Ōya Sōichi zenshū*, 2:28.

44. In a later wave of critical reflection on modernity, Roland Barthes identified the erotic as the place where the garment gapes: "It is intermittence which is erotic, the intermittence of skin flashing between two articles of clothing, between two edges; it is this flash itself which seduces, or rather: the staging of an appearance-as-disappearance." Playing between registers of body and text, Barthes suggested that the unveiling of the truth in narrative realism, like a corporeal striptease, reflects the empiricist demand for complete knowledge and total exposure. Barthes, *The Pleasure of the Text,* 9–10.

45. Kuki, *"Iki" no kōzō, KSZ,* 1:47, 1:43–44, 1:56.

ized a skin without depth, the upper torso an extension of the feminine face."[46] If, as Kuki's biographers claim, the figure of Kuki's mother Hatsu does indeed cast her shadow over the pages of *"Iki" no kōzō*, might this less welcome image of the "woman of the twenties" also lurk somewhere nearby? Because the modern woman displayed more of herself to full view, she deprived Kuki of the opportunity to imagine what she concealed — whether her flesh or her soul.

The Emblematic Value of "Woman" in the Debate on Culture

Kuki was not the only one to inscribe his critique of culture on the feminine body. Women were often at the center of contemporary debates on modern culture. Sympathetic observers of this modernity counted the liberation of women from tradition as one of its most significant contributions. Hirabayashi Hatsunosuke located the *moga* at the vanguard of a free sexual life, a life no longer condemned to "furtive acts in dark, secret rooms." Chiba Ryūtaro claimed that the changes wrought by large-scale mechanization of everyday life had brought liberation for women.[47] Ōya, a less optimistic observer of the modern, noted, nonetheless, that women enjoyed great prominence in the modernist vanguard, both as the principal subject under discussion and themselves as producers of culture.

The advent of the "modern girl" inspired a mixed array of responses, from admiration and awe to disapproval and anxiety.[48] In his fiction from the late 1920's and early 1930's, Tanizaki Junichirō documented the more extreme of those responses. First, there was Naomi, the *moga* femme fatale of *Chijin no ai* (Naomi) (1924), who hopelessly attracts and ultimately emasculates her patron when he becomes her husband. Next came O-hisa, the contrived Kyoto beauty of *Tade kuu mushi* (Some Prefer Nettles). O-hisa is designated the doll-like prize for the hero Kaname's defection from the modern and his return to a newly exoticized (and eroticized) tradition. The wife he disowns, along with his erstwhile

46. Maeda, "Tōkyō 1925," 74.

47. Hamil, "Nihonteki modanizumu no shisō," 106, 107.

48. It is interesting to note that the response called forth by her cross-gender counterpart, the *mobo*, or modern boy, was limited largely to contempt and ridicule.

modern tastes, is, in his own analysis, a half-hearted "modern girl" over-come by apprehensions and consumed by regrets for her abandonment of traditional Japanese womanhood. Tanizaki's catalogue of question-able heroines highlights the emblematic function of women in contem-porary discussions on modernity and culture.

As the lure of tradition grew more potent in the 1930's, reactionaries identified the geisha as a symbolic condensation of the value of Japanese culture. One advocate referred to the geisha as "the navel of society," explaining that she represented the center of strength and the route of nourishment for Japan.[49] Here, the geisha served as metaphoric link to the comfort of the maternal womb, an imagined cultural origin that would shelter Japan from the dislocating effects of its own modernity. It comes as no surprise, then, that Kuki transacted his cultural critique largely on the terrain of the female body, or that he argued for a return to cultural authenticity in the name of the Edo geisha.

Taste as the Organ of Culture

How, then, was Kuki to recover this authenticity and reclaim a cultural world impervious to the fragmentation and the alienation endemic to modern social life and contemporary cultural practices? Clearly, not with a neo-Kantian epistemology. Kuki had deter-mined early on that neo-Kantianism yielded nothing but concepts es-tranged from experience, indifferent to the distinctions he believed to be most crucial. Though he took recourse to conceptual language for its clarity of exposition, Kuki regarded that clarity with some misgiving:

The abstract conceptual moments into which I have dissected *iki* merely indicate several aspects of the concrete entity of *iki*. Although it is possible to dissect *iki* into discrete conceptual moments, conversely, it is impossible to realize the being of *iki* on the basis of these discrete moments. *Bitai, ikuji, akirame* — these concepts do not count as real parts of *iki*, but simply as moments. Between *iki* as a synthesis of conceptual moments and *iki* as an experience of meaning, there stretches an unbridgeable chasm.[50]

49. Dalby, *Geisha*, 81. The advocate was journalist Tanaka Iwao, cited originally in *Geigi tokuhon*, edited by Miyake Koken (Tokyo: Zenkoko Dōmei Ryōriya Shinbunsha-han, 1935).

50. Kuki, *"Iki" no kōzō, KSZ,* 1:74.

At the outset, Kuki had invested the hermeneutic with great promise—a "living philosophy" he had called it. Yet in the final analysis, the hermeneutic method—its appeal to unmediated experience notwithstanding—yielded nothing more than the "conceptual moments" he depreciated. In Kuki's view, the hermeneutic was at its best when it acknowledged the "relation of estrangement" between theoretical reflection and experience.

In search of a counterepistemology, Kuki turned finally, in the last chapter of *"Iki" no kōzō,* to the notion of direct experience in the tradition of Nishida, Bergson, and James. He identified experience as a mode of apprehending meaning that stands in stark contrast to that of conceptual knowledge: "A meaning rich in the concrete, strictly speaking, is experientially appropriated in the form of a direct realization (*gotoku no katachi de mikai*)."[51] The two character compounds, *gotoku* and *mikai,* suggest respectively Buddhist enlightenment and the sense of taste, a conjunction that links truth directly to the body. (Note, however, that what Kuki ultimately intended was less an individual body than the body of the nation.) Taste was, in fact, conceived of as the principal and primordial "organ" of experience. In Kuki's explanation, the boundaries between the taste of the senses (*aji*) and the taste of reflection (*shumi*) gradually disappear:

"Taste" (*shumi*), as in preference, begins with the experience of "taste" (*ajiwau*), as in the sense of taste. We literally "acquire a taste" (*aji o oboeru*), and based on that acquisition, we make value judgments. But it is rare that taste is composed purely of the sense of taste proper. The expression "something with taste" (*aji na mono*) evokes not only the sense of taste but also an aroma to be discerned by the sense of smell. It suggests to us the faint traces of a subtle and elusive fragrance. Moreover, the sense of touch often plays a part as well; the feel on one's palate is part of what makes up a taste. The "feel" of something touches the depths of one's soul in a movement that is altogether ineffable. Together, the sense of taste, smell, and touch make up what we call "experience" in its most fundamental sense.[52]

In this manner, the sensate body could guarantee a relation of absolute intimacy between subject and world, a relation denied to the intellect as well as to the "higher senses," presumably the senses of sight and hearing. In the conventional wisdom of European aesthetics, the higher senses were more advanced human faculties enabling the individual to

51. Ibid., 1:72.
52. Ibid., 1:72–73.

make clear discriminations between stimuli, but they also were the faculties that "place things in objective opposition to the self," thus estrang-
ing the subject from its surroundings.[53] Kuki suggested that only a more
primitive faculty could bring the body into unmediated contact with
the rich detail of the sensory world: "To appropriate as experience the
delicate nuances of shades and tones that slip between the clear visual
and aural discriminations of colors and sounds—this is what we call
taste from the viewpoint of sensation (*kankakujō no shumi*). In the same
manner as the taste of the senses, what is generally called taste (*shumi*)
also concerns the 'nuances' of things. In other words, taste is the personal or collective cultural nuance that becomes visible at the time of an
aesthetic or moral judgment." As the passage progresses, the focus sub-
tly shifts from the nuances of the object to the nuances of the subject.
The ground is now prepared for the return to the subject that lies at the
heart of *"Iki" no kōzō:* "In short, *iki* is a taste that has been determined
by the *minzoku*. As such, it must be appropriated experientially by the
sens intime in the most profound sense of the term."[54] Kuki borrowed
the expression *sens intime,* or intimate sense, from Maine de Birain, an
important predecessor of Bergson and the French *Spiritualiste* tradition,
to invoke an inner world of experience through which reality is to be
interpreted and judged.[55] Though he left the precise nature of the relation between the taste of the senses and the taste of reflection undefined,
Kuki would have us believe that the taste of reflection is as natural and
unmediated as sense perception. As the "natural body" is the repository
of sensate experience, the "national body" is the repository of culture.
Not only does taste represent a counterepistemology, an alternative
mode of knowing the world, it also serves as a biologically rooted faculty of collective cultural identity.[56] Kuki's theory of taste had the virtue

53. Though Kuki never refers explicitly to "lower sensation," he seems to have intended it as the more desirable opposite of "higher sensation." A Japanese philosophical
encyclopedia defines *katō kankaku* as the senses that arise when a stimulus touches more
directly on the body. Touch, smell, and taste are considered to be the lower sensations
(a judgment with which feminist criticism has taken serious issue). *Tetsugaku jiten,* s.v.
katō kankaku.

54. Kuki, *"Iki" no kōzō, KSZ,* 1:73, 1: 87.

55. Maine de Birain had used the term to posit an active and independent self based
on volition over and against a passive self subjected to external sensory experience. Mandelbaum, *History, Man, and Reason,* 283–84. Kuki, however, had in mind a much less an-
tagonistic relationship between *sens intime* and sensory experience.

56. Watsuji's *Fūdo* also invoked nature—though less through the mediation of the
human body than geography and seasonal variation—to authorize a theory of cultural exceptionalism.

of fulfilling two missions simultaneously, one overt, the other covert. Read at its overt level, the theory of taste invoked the shared experience of the *minzoku* as a whole, a set of cultural credentials distinctively Japanese as opposed to Western. Read at a covert level, taste became a means to make distinctions of value within the social whole.

Taste as the Agency of Distinction

In *"Iki" no kōzō,* Kuki appealed to taste as the arbiter of cultural identity and difference. A more recent and less reverent theorist of taste, Pierre Bourdieu, confirms Kuki's insight. The function of taste, he explains, is precisely to unite and separate.[57] For Bourdieu, however, the most important distinctions instituted by taste are not between national cultures but within them. At first glance, Bourdieu seems to share at least one premise with Kuki. He, too, begins with a move to reintegrate the taste of the senses with the taste of reflection. But the respective projects of the French sociologist and the Japanese aesthete could hardly be more dissimilar. Kuki aspired to forge a link between aesthetic taste and a sensate body—a body that, when raised to a higher power, became a national body equipped to incorporate cultural meaning with the immediacy and directness of sensory appropriation. In this manner, Kuki suggested that the assimilation of culture is in fact natural. Viewed as such, culture assumed a quality that was at once both material and mystical: material, because it shared the immutable substantiality of body and terra firma; mystical, because its transmission was seen as ineffable.[58]

Bourdieu also abolishes what he calls "the sacred frontier" between aesthetic taste and ordinary taste, but Bourdieu does so in order to dismantle the myth of natural taste. By reintegrating aesthetic taste into a broader "logic of consumption," he brings into view the ideological premises of the aesthetic disposition:

The ideology of natural taste owes its plausibility and its efficacy to the fact that, like all the ideological strategies generated in the everyday class struggle, it *naturalizes* real differences, converting differences in the mode of acquisition of culture into differences of nature; it only recognizes as

57. Bourdieu, *Distinction,* 56.
58. I am indebted to Norma Field for this observation on culture.

legitimate the relation to culture (or language) which least bears the visible marks of its genesis . . . but manifests by its ease and naturalness that true culture is nature—a new mystery of immaculate conception.[59]

In Bourdieu's analysis, natural taste provides an alibi for the social function of culture, namely, to reproduce and legitimate disparities between social classes. The acquisition of culture, he argues, is neither spontaneous nor intuitive but rather a cognitive act of deciphering and decoding that "presupposes practical or explicit mastery of a cipher or code."[60] As testimony to Bourdieu's analysis, we need only recall Kuki's endeavor to cover the tracks of his scholarly efforts in mastering the Tokugawa repertoire of popular culture. *Iki*, he had suggested, could be reclaimed through *anamnēsis*, a natural act of recollecting what is essentially and fundamentally one's own. *Iki* could be recognized in objects by means of an intuitive act of empathy. But as Bourdieu explains, empathy both presupposes and conceals a cognitive process of decoding.

Kuki presumed to speak for an entire cultural community, undifferentiated by social strata, gender, or region. On the surface of his text, there are no signs of social fissure. Ostensibly, all Japanese were to be included in his aristocracy of taste. One might argue that *iki*, in fact, signified the expansion of an aristocratic ethos to the popular classes, and therefore the ennoblement of the masses. But Bourdieu's insights into the social uses of taste suggest that the distinction drawn by *"Iki" no kōzō* between Japan and the West might well conceal other distinctions within the boundaries of Kuki's imagined community.

Kuki chose for his theme an elusive notion of style dating from the Bunka-Bunsei era, a style once claimed by a self-made elite to distinguish themselves from all that was ordinary. Kuki's preference for a style cresting during the early-nineteenth-century Kaseiki was perhaps not mere coincidence. As a historical era, Kaseiki bears significant resemblances to Kuki's own 1920's. Both Kaseiki and the years following World War I witnessed a dramatic migration of provincials to the economic and cultural center, once Edo, now Tokyo. In the course of both eras, forms of popular culture expanded and diversified with precipitous speed. During the 1920's, as we have seen, technologies of mass production thoroughly penetrated the domain of culture. Kaseiki a century earlier ushered in the beginnings of professionalization of cultural production, the proliferation of literary genres, and a vastly expanded

59. Bourdieu, *Distinction*, 68.
60. Ibid., 2.

readership. To a large degree, the cultural character of late Edo emerged as a reaction to radical demographic transformation. The recognition accorded to *Edokko*, the *tsū*, and *iki* was the cultural currency of the born and bred Edoite in the face of a sudden and drastic influx of people from the provinces who lacked comparable economic and cultural credentials. In a move to distinguish themselves from the throngs of newcomers, long-time Edo residents cultivated aristocratic forms of refinement and exclusive aesthetic tastes.

To the cosmopolitan aesthete Kuki, the social and cultural transformations of his own time were likely to have appeared in the guise of a threat. In the words of Andreas Huyssen, "mass culture depends on technologies of mass production and mass reproduction and thus on the homogenization of difference."[61] Though Kuki presented his argument as a polemic against the leveling of differences between national cultures — that is, against the assimilation of Western cultural forms — the implicit object of his criticism was the leveling of social difference within Japan.

Taste served Kuki, just as it did Baudelaire's dandy, as a means of "reaffirming hierarchy in the face of equality."[62] The ability to manifest and to discern a rare sense of style conferred upon its subjects the social blessings that accrue to connoisseurship. Bourdieu explains that connoisseurship attests to the superiority of the "personality," in other words, to "the quality of the person which is affirmed in the capacity to appropriate an object of quality."[63] Kuki shared in the connoisseurship of his Edo precursors, though at a distance once removed. As he rendered his collection in the technical and esoteric languages of contemporary philosophical discourse and Tokugawa colloquialism, he showed himself worthy of symbolically appropriating artifacts all the more rare because of their dated flavor.

Kuki deployed the language of modern European aesthetics (a language with its own aristocratic ambitions) to rearticulate *iki* as a distinctive expression of a privileged position. As had been the protocol in European aesthetic theory since the Symbolists, Kuki preferred the formal moment in art over the figurative. Art, he believed, should be divided into two groups: objective or imitative art, and subjective or free art. In the first group, "the content of art is determined by a concrete representation," while in the second, "the formative principle of art cre-

61. Huyssen, *Across the Great Divide*, 9.
62. Baudelaire, *The Painter of Victorian Life*, 30.
63. Bourdieu, *Distinction*, 281.

ates freely in an abstract manner." Kuki explained his preference for "free art" as follows: "The fact that objective art has the potential to treat *iki* as its content acts as an obstacle to the full realization of *iki* as pure artistic form."[64] Abstract form, on the other hand, allows the creative subject to attain absolute autonomy from the constraints of the external world. What is then embodied in art serves as a nearly perfect sign of the value that the subject claims for itself.

With his predilection for nonrepresentational form, Kuki introduced an aesthetic distance from the immediate world into the practice of art, a distance that is simultaneously a social distance from the masses. The objectless representation signifies, at least indirectly, "the refusal of any sort of involvement, any 'vulgar' surrender to easy seduction and collective enthusiasm," as Bourdieu puts it.[65] The aesthetics of *iki* underlined this "distance distinction" not only by displacing interest from content to form but also by requiring an attitude of detachment and disinterestedness, an indifference toward a prize too easily attained. This disinterested disposition, at the heart of the aesthetic function since Kant, suggests a break from the ordinary and a freedom from necessity—a necessity that is, in the last analysis, economic necessity.

Kuki's interpretive rendering of *iki* faithfully follows the logic of the "double negative," an unmistakable sign, suggests Bourdieu, of dominant aesthetics. The logic of the double negative mandates a return to sobriety, simplicity, and an economy of means. This return differs, however, from true privation by virtue of its quality of voluntary denial: "A soul that has gorged itself on the passion of warm colors sips at the tranquility of a cool-colored afterimage."[66] Kuki maintained that the "double negative" of the aesthetics of *iki* chronicled a sentimental history of unrequited love. Many times over a victim of her own passion, the experienced geisha contented herself with the play of desire and relinquished her claim to earnest passion. Alternatively or simultaneously, this poverty once removed presupposes "both the (inherited) capital needed to make renunciation materially possible and the—highly aristocratic—disposition to renounce."[67] As such, it marks the distinction between high culture and low.

In the end, Kuki extended the aesthetics of *iki* to his own task as a

---

64. Kuki, *"Iki" no kōzō, KSZ,* 1:51, 1:52.
65. Bourdieu, *Distinction,* 35.
66. Kuki, *"Iki" no kōzō, KSZ,* 1:63.
67. Bourdieu, *Distinction,* 295.

philosopher. On the first pages of *"Iki" no kōzō,* he had defined his task as "giving logical expression to an experience meant to be savored experientially."[68] In the conclusion, Kuki elaborated further on this initial reflection in a manner that suggested the philosopher himself might share in the ethical and spiritual qualities that lent *iki* its irresistible allure:

Does the value of conceptual analysis lie simply in its practical value? Should the conceptual effort to transform the potentiality of a logical representation of experienced meaning into actuality be evaluated from a utilitarian perspective? In other words, should it be judged on the basis of whether or not it has practical value, or how much practical value it has? No! The entire significance of intellectual activity lies rather in *the process* leading from the experience of meaning to its conceptual realization. The existence or degree of practical value is not the issue here at all. To "eternally" pursue one's "task" of actualizing logical expression even as one maintains a clear awareness of the boundless incommensurability between experienced meaning and conceptual cognition—herein lies the entire significance of scholarship.[69]

Like the Edo geisha of *"Iki" no kōzō,* the Shōwa philosopher successfully brackets out the ordinary world, displaying "a durable inclination and aptitude for practice without practical functions."[70] And like her, he is capable of an infinite repetition of will, even while resigning himself to the ultimate impossibility of his goal. In sum, the philosopher might serve as an exemplary representative of what Kuki would later call *bunka minzoku,* an ethnically distinctive national community in exclusive possession of inimitable cultural credentials.

68. Kuki, *"Iki" no kōzō, KSZ,* 1:1.
69. Ibid., 1:88.
70. Bourdieu, *Distinction,* 54–55.

Epilogue: How the Cultural Landscape Became the Property of the State

> *In the face of logical contradiction, Heidegger has undertaken the construction of a hermeneutical phenomenology. That is to say, he has eliminated the historical function from hermeneutics and philology. In place of historical knowledge, he has instituted a philosophical structure of a different order from historical knowledge, one that is systematic and, as such, metaphysical. Philology and hermeneutics, once deprived of their historical function, are readily enlisted in phenomenological tasks. No doubt the time was ripe to break the deadlock of a German idealist worldview with just this kind of ahistorical philosophical system. And it is precisely this philosophical "system" that is responsible for the fact that the Nazi agenda seduced not only the petit bourgeoisie but also a "cultivated" intelligentsia.*
>
> Tosaka Jun, *Nihon ideorogīron*

> *Ideologies as a necessary superstructure of a particular structure . . . have a validity which is "psychological"; they "organize" human masses, they form the terrain on which men move, acquire consciousness of their position, struggle, etc.*
>
> Antonio Gramsci, *Selections from Prison Notebooks*

In a lecture delivered at the Third Higher School in 1937, Kuki entreated his youthful audience to cultivate a devotion for *jun Nihonteki na mono*, literally, "a pure Japanese thing." Whether the tea ceremony, a *waka* verse, or a bowl of noodles, "no matter how trifling a thing," he insisted, "as long as it is purely Japanese, it shelters within itself the form of the Japanese cultural totality."[1] By the late 1930's when Kuki issued this appeal, the logic of cultural organicism already had become a primary instance of common sense, both in scholarly and official discourse. As such, it sanctioned not merely an efflorescence of things Japanese but also a total mobilization of the Japanese spirit in the service of a repressive and militarist regime. According to the dictates of this organicist logic, the nation-state became subject to representation as a natural community that authenticated itself both in and as an aesthetic object. In his critical reading of Heidegger, Philippe Lacoue-Labarthe has given a name to this recruitment of cultural organicism for political ends: "national aestheticism."[2]

Kuki had long since laid the groundwork for a Japanese version of national aestheticism in his 1930 inquiry into Edo aesthetic style. Clearly, the ambitions of *"Iki" no kōzō* extended beyond its Edo setting and beyond aesthetics per se. In that text, Kuki deployed the organicist strategies implicit in hermeneutics to transmute his collection of Edo artifacts into topographical markers of a distinctive cultural landscape. By means of this discursive operation, he was able to redefine the geopolitical space of modern Japan as an enclave of the spirit—timeless, authentic, and essentially different from the West. And by joining hermeneutics with connoisseurship, Kuki tacitly designated himself custodian of this newly appraised cultural property.

In preceding chapters, a largely retrospective focus allowed me to construct a prehistory for *"Iki" no kōzō* in a number of conjunctures between theoretical discourse and the social specificity that provided its often suppressed occasion. Tracing genealogies for Kuki's text between Europe and Japan, from nineteenth-century cultural sciences to twentieth-century hermeneutics, from late Edo cultural practice to early Shōwa cultural history, I attempted to excavate the ideological conditions for the production of this particular text within Japan's modernity. In a final shift of focus from the conditions of ideology to its effects, this epilogue will broach the posthistory of *"Iki" no kōzō*, and in the process test the boundary between cultural text and historical context. It is in the crossing of this boundary that the more potent and disturbing historical implications of this discourse on Japanese culture come into view.

Let us start then with a brief sketch of the historical developments

1. Kuki, "Nihonteki seikaku ni tsuite," *KSZ,* 3:397.
2. Lacoue-Labarthe, *Heidegger, Art, and Politics,* 58.

subsequent to Kuki's return to Japan and the publication of *"Iki" no kōzō*. As the decade of the 1930's deepened, the sense of national urgency and historical crisis intensified sharply. Internationally, Japan was becoming deeply embroiled in an imperialist war on the Asian mainland and was increasingly isolated diplomatically. On the domestic front, right-wing activism and official policies of repression incrementally but unrelentingly had dismantled the last remaining props of civil society. In intellectual circles, the suppression of all liberal and progressive scholarship—punctuated by the expulsion of legal scholars Takigawa Yukitori of Kyoto Imperial University (1933) and Minobe Tatsukichi of Tokyo Imperial University (1935) from institutional and public life—signaled defeat for even the most modest academic freedoms. In the years that followed, varying degrees of compliance and complicity with official policy closed the ranks of intellectuals across what had once been a wide ideological spectrum. The intellectual archives of the 1930's and early 1940's are filled with documents of "Japanism," sanctions for authoritarian rule, and endorsements for expansionist policies in the name of the "Japanese spirit," the emperor, and the *kokutai*.[3]

Some fundamental questions concerning this complicity still remain unanswered, however. How extensive was the intellectual participation in the interests of the state? What forms did it take? Was it voluntary or coerced? The notion of ideological apostasy on the part of individual intellectuals during the 1930's—typically sudden and invariably from left to right—that has dominated the Japanese reflection on the question of intellectual collaboration has, despite its explanatory power, obscured certain aspects of the issue. In my own attempt to dispel some of that obscurity, I have shifted the center of attention from intellectual biography to broader formations, both discursive and social, that placed intellectual production in close ideological proximity to the state.

In 1937, even before explicit endorsements of official policy became a critical necessity, Kuki produced a number of essays that might give pause even to those who would absolve the man and his works of the slightest hint of reaction.[4] Yet Kuki's complicity in the reactionary turn in cultural discourse has gone largely undocumented. Concentration on biography at the expense of history has yielded a portrait of Kuki Shūzō

3. The term *kokutai* has been variously translated as "national entity" (Robert King Hall) and "national polity" (Ivan Morris). A literal reading of the multivalent ideographs might yield something between "the body of the nation" and "the substance of the state."
4. For a brief discussion of Kuki's preemptive appropriation of imperial iconography, see Terada Tōru's reminiscences of the era in "Kuki tetsugaku no shūhen," 2–7.

as a lone figure on the margins of reigning academic orthodoxies and scholarly propriety. This particular representation has shielded Kuki from or rendered him unworthy of the kind of sustained intellectual-historical scrutiny that might situate his work within a larger discursive formation. To complicate matters, Kuki's war record is an ambiguous one, cut short by his untimely death in 1941.[5] To his credit, Kuki took the initiative in 1933 to assist the Jewish philosopher Karl Löwith in finding refuge in Japan from the newly installed Nazi regime. An exception among many of his colleagues who lent their talents to the production of state propaganda, Kuki did not sit on the advisory committee appointed by the Ministry of Education to draft *Kokutai no hongi* (Cardinal Principles of the National Essence of Japan) (1937).[6] Unlike other Kyoto-school philosophers, Kuki refrained from practical engagement in public affairs, preferring a stance of intellectual detachment. In 1941, he prefaced an anthology of essays on aesthetics titled *Bungeiron* (A Discussion of the Literary Arts) with a self-portrait reminiscent of Baudelaire's dandy. "I wish only," he began, "to seek the serene eternity of Truth and Beauty and, together with my small circle of readers, to think, to feel, and to yearn as we meander down the small path between philosophy and literature."[7] This pose of aesthetic withdrawal, taken at face value, has precluded any discussion of connections between art and politics in his work. In 1939, Kuki — whose chair at Kyoto Imperial University conferred upon him the status of an academic imperial servant — made the obligatory tour of China and Manchuria to demonstrate his ratification of Japan's expanded boundaries. A committed cosmopolitan, he lamented the German invasion of Paris, though, admittedly, his regret had more to do with cultural preference than political conviction. In short, for the empirically inclined investigator hoping to pass judgment on the ideological credentials of a single intellectual, the historical record offers nothing but mixed messages.

Some point to Kuki's cosmopolitan credentials to clear him of the charge of ultranationalism.[8] Others take recourse in the Oedipal tactics of psychobiography to exempt him from accountability in the produc-

5. Kuki was hospitalized at Kyoto Prefectural University Hospital on April 10, 1941, when he was diagnosed as suffering from peritonitis. He died there on May 6, 1941.

6. This text has been translated by John Owen Gauntlett as *Kokutai no Hongi: Cardinal Principles of the National Essence of Japan.*

7. Kuki, *Bungeiron, KSZ,* 4:4.

8. Washida, *Shōwa shisōshi 60 nen,* 128–29. Taishō cosmopolitanism was not necessarily incompatible with or unrelated to the return to an exceptional site of cultural creation.

tion or endorsement of family-state ideology. The most common gesture, however, is simply to exclude Kuki's more explicitly ideological writings from discussion. Dismissing the later essays as inferior or as a momentary aberration, apologists isolate *"Iki" no kōzō* as a masterpiece of Japanese aesthetics, choosing to canonize rather than historicize the cultural document. Even when Kuki's later sympathies do come under suspicion, the sanctity of *"Iki" no kōzō* goes unquestioned as in this exchange from *"'Iki' no kōzō" o yomu:*

Yasuda: Even though he initiated the concept of *minzoku,* there's not the slightest suspicion of fascism. It's got nothing to do with the kind of fanaticism of people who invoked *minzoku* at every turn after 1931.

Tada: That's true, but then, even Kuki himself changed a bit in the late 1930's. . . .

Yasuda: Yes, he does change. It's a little disturbing, but he never became as possessed as some people. . . .

Tada: Anyway, at the stage of *"Iki" no kōzō,* there's none of that in Kuki.[9]

Here Tada and Yasuda attempt to distinguish a culturally productive use of the term *minzoku* in *"Iki" no kōzō* from its shrill ubiquity following the Manchurian Incident in 1931.

The divide, however, that separates *"Iki" no kōzō* from later discursive developments is not nearly as great as these scholars would have it. To the contrary, the theoretical framework elaborated in *"Iki" no kōzō* served as a firm foundation for the more militant pronouncements of the later texts. Moreover, the theoretical consistency that links these two discursive moments—the first coming at the culmination of what is often described as a liberal Taishō era and the second coinciding with a marked acceleration of militarism and national mobilization—signals in turn continuities of a more practical nature. In the latter half of the 1930's, the boundaries of the cultural landscape first drafted in *"Iki" no kōzō* became increasingly and coercively inclusive of the domestic populace (and colonial subjects) on the one hand, increasingly and aggressively exclusive of the West on the other. Yet the question of why this "culturescape" so readily assimilated the distended territory of a "Greater Japan" has hardly been asked, much less resolved.

The omission, it seems to me, is rooted in a failure to imagine any but the most literal of linkages between philosophical or aesthetic proj-

9. Tada and Yasuda, "'Iki' *no kōzō* " *o yomu,* 39–40.

ects and their social formation. This failure of imagination has its source in the most common postures of a liberal academe — an aspiration toward academic neutrality, a defense of disciplinary boundaries, and a desire to enshrine venerable figures in a national canon. In an attempt to cross these established disciplinary and canonical boundaries, I would pose the following questions: Does *"Iki" no kōzō*, a study in aesthetics dating from the end of what is commonly called an era of cosmopolitanism and liberalism, offer insight into the subsequent complicity of cultural discourse with the designs of an imperialist and authoritarian state? Conversely, what does a retrospective view from the late 1930's disclose about the ideological affinities of *"Iki" no kōzō* and the cultural project of which it was a part? The task of this epilogue is to impose one last layer on the dense intertextual network summoned up in the pages of *"Iki" no kōzō*.

Among Kuki's essays of the late 1930's, two in particular demonstrate the increasing coerciveness of the culturescape — one, a meditation on the Japanese character, the other, a brief commentary on the outbreak of war with China. In these essays, Kuki enlisted the discursive tactics and objects first deployed in *"Iki" no kōzō* in a widening movement to suppress pluralism at home and mobilize the Japanese populace for an expansionist war in Asia. By the end of the decade, the discourse on culture — in a blunt rapprochement with a repressive and militarist state apparatus — had placed itself at the disposal of what has been called, with much exception, Japanese fascism.[10]

I use the term "fascism" with some hesitation, not only because its applicability to Japan in the 1930's and early 1940's has been debated but also because a basic definition of fascism continues to be the subject of heated controversy. While Marxist historians have routinely defined fascism as a profound structural crisis of late capitalism, others of a more psychoanalytic bent have focused on monolithic leadership cults and authoritarian personalities. Western scholars committed to liberal political philosophy are more likely to view fascism as an aberrant and localized solution to a unique set of sociopolitical problems, if they consent

---

10. The question of whether it was in fact fascism that made its appearance in 1930's Japan has been hotly contested from the moment when it was first sighted on the Japanese horizon to our own present. Whether within Marxist, liberal, or right-wing debate, the ground of this continuing controversy has been carefully surveyed in Japanese- and English-language scholarship. For an early overview and insightful discussion, see Halliday, "The Question of Japanese Fascism," in *A Political History of Japanese Capitalism*, 133–40, and McCormack, "Nineteen-Thirties Japan: Fascism?" 20–34.

to use the term at all.[11] In contrast, "fascism" is a term accepted by many postwar Japanese historians, Marxists as well as progressive historians like Maruyama Masao, though not without provisos meant to distinguish the Japanese version from its European model.[12]

Perhaps the most compelling argument against the fascist label for Japan has been made by British Marxist historian Jon Halliday in *A Political History of Japanese Capitalism*. With no coup d'état, no radical change to mark either the beginning or the end of the regime, and no mass fascist party, the Japanese political landscape differed markedly from that of Germany and Italy. While Halliday acknowledges the existence of fascist movements and forces, he argues that Japan experienced a level of continuity unknown in Europe, undergoing change through an already established system. "Posing the question 'what was the nature of the Japanese regime' exclusively in terms of 'fascism,'" suggests Halliday, "may be a Eurocentric approach which obscures the specific features of the Japanese regime."[13] Unlike the cultural particularism of the prewar culturalists or postwar *Nihonjinron* proponents, the specificity Halliday claims for Japanese fascism is based on a set of historically determined political differences. Nevertheless, others have suggested that the specificities of Japan's interwar history fit well within the framework of recent theorization of fascism as a "force which worked within the existing economic and social hierarchies."[14]

11. Following an analysis of the class dynamics of German fascism by Wolfgang Wipperman, Gavan McCormack suggests that "bourgeois scholars are inclined to want to set aside the theoretical problems of definition, partly because they see further research as necessary to elucidate substantive problems, but also because of a more fundamental ideological reason; too many of the paths of theoretical inquiry lead to various formulas for the association of fascism with 'liberalism, middle-class society and capitalism,' a trinity to whose defense bourgeois scholars are quick to rally." "Nineteen-Thirties Japan: Fascism?" 25. The attempt on the part of modernization historiography to separate Japan's fascist interlude from the positive norms of democratic capitalism is reflected in epigraphs such as "What went wrong?" and "pathology of growth" in Morely, ed., *Dilemmas of Growth in Prewar Japan*.

12. For Marxist debates on fascism both before and after the Pacific War, see Germaine Hoston's discussion in *Marxism and the Crisis of Development in Prewar Japan*, 257–64. Maruyama sets out his definition of fascism and its Japanese version in "The Ideology and Dynamics of Japanese Fascism," in *Thought and Behavior in Modern Japanese Politics*, 25–83. For an overview of the principal theories of Japanese fascism in Japanese, see Igarashi, "Fashizumu bunken annai" (An Introduction to the Literature on Fascism), in Igarashi, ed., *Kita Ikki ronshū*, 347–58.

13. Halliday, *A Political History of Japanese Capitalism*, 134.

14. Waite, "Political Ontology." A similar argument is made by Bix in "Rethinking 'Emperor-System Fascism,'" 2–19, and McCormack in "Nineteen-Thirties Japan: Fascism?" 2–19, 20–33.

While the fascist credentials of the political regime may be in doubt, the cultural landscape of Japan's interwar years bears an unmistakable resemblence to its European fascist counterparts. In an instructive overview of European fascism, George Mosse explains that fascism, in fact, represented itself primarily as a cultural movement — (all the while harboring a deep-seated mistrust of art and intellect) — promising its audience an end to alienation through a defense of the spirit. With an eye to the interclass dynamics of fascism, Mosse explains that cultural elements were deployed by the bourgeois proponents of fascism to tame the revolutionary impulses of fascist movements from below. The most typical of these elements included the organic and religious nature of fascist cults, the quest for authenticity, the retreat into the "community of the nation," and the construction of "the folk" from archival remainders.[15] While Mosse describes these elements as "cultural," at least temporarily, I would prefer to use the term "ideological" to distinguish my own analytic language from the preferred idiom of those who constructed the culturescape, a highly aestheticized representation of the nation-state, just as it was becoming an instrument of nearly naked domination. Here, I use the term "ideology" as Althusser defined it — the "representation of the imaginary relationship of individuals to their real conditions of existence."[16] It is in this ideological elaboration of fascism that students of Japan's interwar years will discover common ground with European fascism. To keep this common ground in view, I will refer to a fascist turn in the discourse of Japan's interwar years. But however one chooses to describe Japan in the 1930's and early 1940's — fascist, militarist, or ultranationalist — it is imperative to account for the aggressive itinerary of the discourse on culture, just as it is important to explore the relation between cultural production and more pragmatic political projects.

In Japanese scholarship, the question of culture and politics traditionally has been posed in voluntarist terms: What stance did artists and intellectuals assume in response to a reactionary or fascist regime? In a political or official sphere that was not their own, did they support or resist fascist developments? One of the most influential explanations has been offered by Tsurumi Shunsuke and his colleagues in their explora-

---

15. Mosse, "Introduction," 168–69, 6–7, 9–11. Mosse argues that the question of culture should be at the center of any comparative study that hopes to account for the mass consensus commanded by fascist movements.

16. Althusser, "Ideology and Ideological State Apparatuses," 162.

tion of *tenkō,* the notion of ideological apostasy mentioned earlier. The term *tenkō* was first appropriated by the Ministry of Justice in 1933 to refer to the process of redirecting an individual's thought into what the state judged to be the proper channels, but Tsurumi reappropriated the term, revising its meaning to allow for a complex appreciation of the dual aspects of "coercion" and "spontaneity" in the ideological apostasies of leftist and liberal intellectuals.[17] Nevertheless, the theory of *tenkō,* simply by virtue of citing sudden conversions, installed a radical ideological shift between the liberal and progressive mood of "Taishō democracy" and the more oppressive realities of the 1930's. However unwittingly, the notion of *tenkō* served to confirm the claims of modernization historians that the 1930's represented a deplorable deviation from what was otherwise the positive growth of a democratic, capitalist society. In a more theoretical vein, *tenkō* theory offered sanction for a common-sense view of historical causality that assigns "thought" a subordinate status in relation to "event"—a hierarchical pairing that should be requestioned in its entirety.

In critical response to these assumptions, others have underscored the continuities in intellectual development during the interwar years, as well as the active role of intellectuals in Japan's fascist turn. In *The Search for a New Order: Intellectuals and Fascism in Prewar Japan,* Miles Fletcher identifies an unchanging set of positions and social perspectives on the part of intellectuals who ultimately lent their talents to the Shōwa Kenkyūkai, Konoe Fumimaro's brain trust, in the latter part of the thirties. In a revision of both *tenkō* theory and conventional views of fascism, Fletcher argues that the rational and progressive coloring of the ideas of individuals like Miki Kiyoshi, Royama Masamichi, and Ryū Shintarō was by no means incompatible with fascist sympathies and visions of "a new totalitarianism." Far from resisting a fascist movement, concludes Fletcher, Japanese intellectuals stood at its forefront.[18]

Andrew Barshay, in *State and Intellectual in Imperial Japan: The Public Man in Crisis,* argues that the explanation for intellectual compliance is to be found primarily in the preponderance of state authority in the structures of social life. The system of ideological mobilization insti-

17. Tsurumi, *Tenkō kenkyū,* 4, 10–12.

18. Fletcher, *The Search for a New Order,* 156–57. Fletcher suggests that their "apostasy" consisted of little more than a transfer of allegiance from the proletarian movement to an ethical state as the agent of reform. Despite his argument for the fascist credentials of particular intellectuals, Fletcher argues, ultimately, that fascism failed to take hold as a system in Japan.

tuted in the 1930's functioned as effectively as it did because the "public sphere" and its "intellectual specialists" were so thoroughly hegemonized by the state, whether through the definition of their professional status or through a state monopoly on questions of cultural identity. Following Maruyama's analysis, Barshay distinguishes between two kinds of "public men": insiders close to the center of power in imperial Japan who were ideologically "'on call' all of the time," and outsiders typically engaged in smaller, less socially legitimate organizations whose distance from the privileged locus of authority allowed for a certain amount of autonomy and freedom of expression. While Barshay largely reserves the prerogative of withdrawal into private aesthetic concerns for the outsider, he surrounds the word "withdrawal" with quotation marks, perhaps to mark his own skepticism regarding the marginal significance Maruyama assigned to the widespread tendency toward an aestheticized "culturalism" in the 1930's.[19]

Maruyama argued that the essentially European culture of prewar Japanese intellectuals left them stranded ineffectually between untenable choices. Too sophisticated to respond to the "low tone of the fascist movment," intellectuals nevertheless lacked the moral integrity to mount a resolute defense against fascism. In the end, the vast majority of intellectuals, already in a position of intellectual detachment and isolation, were driven to retreat into "a hesitant and impotent existence" during the war years — impotent, perhaps even acquiescent, but also, according to Maruyama, well-intentioned: "The fashion for 'culturalism' during the war," he maintained, "may be considered an expression of passive resistance to fascism by the intelligentsia."[20]

Maruyama's argument rests on two critical assumptions: first, that the "European culture" of the Japanese intelligentsia, however superficial, served as a buffer against fascism, and second, that the recourse to aesthetic projects and cultural criticism represented a radical disengagement with politics. If, however, "culture" is given the weight of an effective force in restructuring real social relations, then the ubiquity of "culturalism" in interwar Japan, rather than a retreat into isolation, might be seen to signify a highly mediated but potent form of political practice. Furthermore, the lineage of culturalism may well have been

19. Barshay, *State and Intellectual in Imperial Japan*, 12–15. See 23–31 for an overview of the debate over the concept of *tenkō* and Barshay's own reservations about its usefulness.

20. Maruyama, "The Ideology and Dynamics of Japanese Fascism," in *Thought and Behavior in Modern Japanese Politics*, 57–61.

longer and more deeply entrenched than Maruyama's analysis suggests, extending back to early stages of the dialogue of Japanese intellectuals with European thought from Hegel and neo-idealism to *Lebensphiloso-phie* and Heidegger. Rather than protecting a Japanese intelligentsia from radical reaction, this European dialogue supplied at least some of the theoretical resources for a fascist turn in discourse.

Perhaps the most incisive critic of this ill-fated engagement with the more reactionary elements in European philosophical discourse was To-saka Jun. In his *Nihon ideorogīron,* Tosaka argued that, in fact, there was no breach between the liberal humanist mapping of Japanese culture in 1920's and the reactionary Japanism of the 1930's. With the weight of his analysis on questions of methodology, he revealed how a liberal her-meneutic, well-equipped with the methods of philology, first staked out the new ideological territory of *Nihonshugi* or Japanism. In essence, To-saka's inquiry demonstrated the affinities between an aestheticizing phil-osophical practice deeply rooted in German Romanticism and rising forms of ultranationalist reaction in Japan. In chapter 4, I followed To-saka's lead to explore the ideological implications of the methodology central to *"Iki" no kōzō.* In these concluding remarks, I venture further into speculative territory in search of a more comprehensive and com-pelling explanation for the eventual destination of the discourse on cul-ture and the logic of its fascist turn.

We saw earlier that the strategies of cultural organicism enabled Kuki to transform the artifactual remainders of a specific historical site into signifiers of a disembodied and "dislocated" metaphysical space. Through discursive means, he constructed a purified cultural landscape that revealed the subjectivity of a naturally determined community. By situating this imaginary representation of the culturescape in its own historical moment, I suggested that it was linked to more practical inter-ests of social power. As will become clear in the ensuing discussion, the construction of this culturescape represented an attempt to produce and secure the space of an embattled hegemony within Japan. This drive for hegemony accounts for the aggressive itinerary of cultural theory; it placed the culturescape squarely within the purview of a state from which it provisionally (and only apparently) kept its distance.

In his study of Latin American fiction and film, *Modernism and He-gemony,* Neil Larsen presents a suggestive etiology for this discursively articulated cultural landscape in a non-Western context. Fundamentally contradictory in its formation, the culturescape appears as a space puri-fied of "the taint of the West," suffused with the expressive power of a decidedly non-modern (and, most likely, nonrational or prerational) ethnic subject. For example, Larsen identifies this prerational subjectivity in the case of one Latin American modernist writer, Juan Rulfo, as *mexicanidad,* or, in more abstract terms, as "oral culture." Contrary to expectations, the culturescape is itself a modernist projection, but one conditioned by its distance from the European metropolitan centers of aesthetic and philosophical modernism. Larsen calls this paradoxical formation "peripheral modernism." On the modernist periphery—or semiperiphery, as the case may be in Japan—the resources of modernism, particularly its penchant for antirationalism, are mobilized in a "countermediation" against the West, from which they were culled. Metropolitan versions of antirationalism might encompass anything from Bergsonian vitalism and Heideggerian authenticity to primitivism in the visual arts. Constructed from these modernist elements, the rarefied culturescape does not, however, exhaust its usefulness in a negation of the West. Rather, it is turned to domestic account as a strategy for containing mass aspirations and consolidating an internal hegemony.[21] Larsen's concept of peripheral modernism has proven to be a useful tool for deciphering the logic of progression from *"Iki" no kōzō* to Kuki's later essays, and more generally, for understanding the continuities between the differing discursive moments of Taishō and early Shōwa.

However, before elaborating further on this alliance between modernist strategies and indigenous images of the nonmodern, I would like to turn first to those of Kuki's later essays in which affinities with fascist cultural discourse stand out in clear relief. These essays are part of a larger discourse in the 1930's that served to veil but also to validate brutal forms of aggression within Japan and on the Asian continent. They share both language and sentiment with *Kokutai no hongi* and other state-sponsored tracts that became ideological staples during the late thirties and early forties. A montage of textual fragments from a selected classical repertoire, Kuki's later essays presented Japanese readers with a cultural fait accompli, hailing them as involuntary members of an imaginary community rendered largely in ethical and spiritual terms. Brooking no deviation, this imaginary community served in turn to eliminate dissent and mobilize the populace for "total war." This is a far cry, it would seem, from the delicately eroticized aestheticism of *"Iki" no kōzō,* a text that ventured into the unorthodox margins of modern Japanese historical consciousness, yet it was within the less coercive boundaries

21. Larsen, *Modernism and Hegemony,* xxxv–xxxvii.

of *"Iki" no kōzō* that Kuki first refined the strategies of, and created a space for, national aestheticism. Once created, this imaginary space, increasingly absorbed by the interests of the state, might be filled with any of the aesthetic, ethical, or spiritual values implied by the term "culture."

By the late 1930's, Kuki had clearly moved toward the mainstream, both in tone and content—concessions, perhaps, to a broader audience and to a heightened mood of "national emergency." Unlike *"Iki" no kōzō,* these 1937 essays are woven through with allusions reflecting the rule rather than the exception of an officially sanctioned canon. The concern for the national subject and its expressibility, largely implicit and complexly mediated in *"Iki" no kōzō,* has, in these later essays, become disquietingly explicit. As a form of methodological intervention, philosophy has yielded wholesale to philology, while modernist strategies for engaging the ephemeral and the accidental have given way to claims of immutability and necessity. Liberal, humanist rhetoric has been pressed into the service of an authoritarian emperor-state, and a discursive commerce that once ranged across national boundaries has reached its limit in an ultranationalist monopoly discourse, cultural cosmopolitanism having produced its own obsolescence. Yet despite these departures from Kuki's earlier essay on Edo style, the structural foundations laid down in *"Iki" no kōzō* remain firmly in place. And while the complexities of modern philosophical discourse and the subtleties of aesthetic modernism have largely disappeared, the now compulsory boundaries of the culturescape were first discovered and charted in *"Iki" no kōzō* through distinctively modern strategies. These essays demonstrate how the reduction of geopolitical space to the coordinates of a purely aestheticized culture first enacted in *"Iki" no kōzō* cleared the ground for the installation of a militant Japanese spirit.

The first of the essays in question, "Nihonteki seikaku ni tsuite" (Concerning the Japanese Character), was published as an article in the February 1937 issue of *Shisō* and then delivered as a lecture at the Third Higher School in May of the same year.[22] Even the most cursory reading confirms that *"Iki" no kōzō* provided the blueprint for the construction of a "Japanese character." Precisely analogous to the structure of *iki,* the

22. Two slightly different versions of this essay are included in volume 3 of *KSZ.* The first, entitled "Nihonteki seikaku," appeared as an article in the February 1937 issue of *Shisō.* The second, slightly expanded version, "Nihonteki seikaku ni tsuite," appears to have been presented as a lecture at the Third Higher School to the entire student body in May of the same year. Based on Kuki's margin notes, the *KSZ* editors speculate that this expanded version was in turn based on a similar lecture delivered at Osaka Higher School.

Japanese character is presented as a synthetic unity of three attributes —
a unity presuming to represent the totality of Japanese culture. As was
the case in *"Iki" no kōzō*, the heightened cultural particularism of this
representation defines itself in terms of "universal" values.

The moderate tone of the opening rhetoric is belied by a vocabulary
turned militantly nationalist, "Japan" having conspicuously yielded to
"Japanism." Kuki no longer draws his references from the literature of
plebeian Edo but from the archives of *kokugaku* (nativism) and *bushidō*.
He is addressing not the heirs of "low-city" style but rather the contemporary subjects of an aggressively expansionist empire. His illustrative
examples have grown noticeably martial: "Though our military may be
organized and trained according to standards borrowed from the West,"
he intones, "the power that moves it is *Yamato-damashi* (the Japanese
Spirit)." [23] The motif of the West as other has become increasingly insis-
tent, while Asia has become a visible, rather than hidden, handmaid
of Japan.

In the opening remarks of "Nihonteki seikaku ni tsuite," the binary
opposition of particular/universal exposes itself in the less mediated
form of Japanism/cosmopolitanism. This latter pair, claims Kuki, is in
no way mutually incompatible. The world, he explains, resembles a city
that offers different views and moods relative to the position of the
viewer. In this analogy, the position of that viewing subject is occupied
by none other than the nation: "If we compare the entire world to a
city, each nation in its cultural particularity, has its own way of perceiv-
ing that city. In truth, the city possesses no view or mood in itself apart
from the varying views and moods viewed from each particular perspective. The city itself is given only as a synthesis." [24] Kuki already had prepared the ground for this nationalist version of subjective idealism in
"Iki" no kōzō, where the "real" became an exclusive attribute of a nationally inscribed culture. Tosaka Jun, in his critique of a 1934 issue of *Shisō*
devoted to "the Japanese spirit," had exposed the logic of this position,
so often invoked with references to *Nihonteki na mono* or "things Japanese": "In fact, this so-called discovery of *Nihonteki na mono* and the
concentration on Japan's particular circumstances can be approached
from two diametrically opposed perspectives, each with its own motivation and interest. . . . Either one can take *Nihonteki na mono* as the prin-

---

23. Kuki, "Nihonteki seikaku ni tsuite," *KSZ*, 3:376.
24. Ibid., 3:368. Needless to say, Kuki denied this same autonomy of perspective and
cultural particularity to the countries included within Japan's formal and informal empire,
in particular, to China.

ciple of explanation for everything else, or one can undertake the concrete task of submitting *Nihonteki na mono* itself to an explanation based on other principles." The first approach, explains Tosaka, seeks to sever a Japanese reality completely from international conditions. It is the preferred strategy of what he calls *kokusui fashizumu* (national-essence fascism). The second approach treats Japanese exceptionalism as one particular case of a more general reaction to a crisis of capital of international proportions.[25] While Kuki makes rhetorical gestures toward internationalism, those gestures hardly sustain Tosaka's hopes for a materialist critique of Japanism. Kuki's claim that Japanism is compatible with internationalism holds true only to the extent that the international is deprived of substance and reduced to a mental synthesis. (The precise nature of this synthesis, it might be added, presumably could be mandated by the national culture that attains global hegemony.) The balance between universal norms and their manifestation in particular cultures, a legacy of Taishō cosmopolitanism, long since had shifted in favor of the particular, as *"Iki" no kōzō* so persuasively demonstrates. In "Nihonteki seikaku ni tsuite," however, the universal has been reduced to a mirage, or as Kuki mentions in an offhand remark, to a notion of "division of labor among nations." The implications of such a remark could only be sinister in light of Japan's selective exploitation of its expanding Asian empire, an exploitation soon to be sanctioned and further promoted by the Konoe cabinet formulation of a Greater East Asia Coprosperity Sphere.

The introduction to "Nihonteki seikaku ni tsuite" makes another liberal gesture, this one in the direction of individualism. Kuki might have been attempting to distinguish himself from his more reactionary colleagues who chose to frame *Kokutai no hongi* in terms of safeguarding the national community from the "deadlock of individualism."[26] His example, however, demonstrates that the distinction is less real than apparent. The relationship between individual human being, (national) culture, and world, he explains, resembles three circles, each enclosed by the next. Kuki proceeds to supply the nationalist logic of this schema with an example from the 1936 Berlin Olympics. Why, he asks, did a Japanese gold medalist weep when the Japanese flag was raised and the anthem, "Kimi ga yo" (The Reign of Our Lord), played? The journal of the German Olympics committee supplies his answer: "Because this athlete fought for Japan, his own victory is Japan's victory. He wept

25. Tosaka, *Nihon ideorogīron*, 279–81.
26. *Kokutai no Hongi: Cardinal Principles,* 54.

from the profoundly moral and religious emotion of having fulfilled his responsibility to Japan."[27] Despite the thoroughly generic quality of this response, Kuki finds it eloquently expressive not only of the distinctiveness of Japan's national character but also of the distinctiveness of the individual: another athlete, it seems, might not have wept in precisely the same way as this Japanese champion. Finally, the fact that a German might offer such an explanation and that readers of various nationalities might understand it bore witness, in his view, to the international character common to all countries. Kuki's exegesis grants the individual significance only as an impassioned standard-bearer for the state, while it reduces international common ground to the shared passion of patriotic duty. In terms of his three-circle schema, it appears that the middle circle — national culture — has expanded out of proportion and drawn both individual and world wholly into its orbit. Kuki's timely example serves only to expose the impoverishment of a discourse that has surrendered all its resources to the state.

In the "Japanese character," the tripartite structure first developed in *"Iki" no kōzō* has been both preserved and further essentialized. The first attribute, *bitai* (erotic allure), has been replaced by a less provocative *shizen* (nature), rendered in a now reactionary idiom of nativist Shintō. In a departure, however, from his nativist predecessors, Kuki has reserved the place of the other for the West rather than China. In marked contrast to nativist strategies for enlisting a renaturalized community against officially sanctioned knowledge expressed in terms of Confucian ethics, Kuki places the nation firmly at the disposal of a selectively Confucianized family state: "The reason why our national morality places loyalty and filial piety at its foundation is simply because that is the Way that comes most naturally. It is perfectly natural that worshiping the gods (*matsurigoto*) and ruling the people (*seiji/matsurigoto*) are united in the *emperor;* and that in the *parent,* the subject who receives the service of the family and the subject who officiates over the family are one and the same." This same ideologically potent mixture of nativist appeals to feeling and natural spontaneity with a hierarchical organization sanctioned by a patriarchal Confucian code was advocated even more aggressively in *Kokutai no hongi.* The subjugation of individuals to absolute power, whether household patriarch or "family-state" patriarch, was identified as "the Way that comes most naturally."[28]

27. Kuki, "Nihonteki seikaku ni tsuite," *KSZ,* 3:372–73.
28. Ibid., 3:383.

The second attribute of the "Japanese character" is a near equivalent of the "fearless pride" of *"Iki" no kōzō*. A homophone for *iki*, this attribute, written with the first two of the three characters used to write *ikuji*, reinvokes the pluck and pride of the Edo townfolk in that earlier text. But if the first attribute signals the merging of the "Japanese character" into national morality, the second indicates its thorough aristocratization. Rather than eliciting *iki* from the fishmongers, firemen, and prostitutes of Edo, Kuki turns instead to Yamaga Sokō, a belated apologist of *bushidō*, and Yoshida Shōin, a powerful advocate of warrior virtue and loyalty to the emperor at the end of the Tokugawa period. "Flowing in our veins as the spirit of *bushidō*," writes Kuki, *iki* signifies the will to "set one's ideals high and stake one's life on their realization." The nuances of resistance and arrogance (however politically tamed) still adhering to the notion of *ikuji* in *"Iki" no kōzō* have yielded to the "fortitude" of the Japanese character — a fortitude manifested in "the spirit of self-sacrifice born of a pure heart."[29] *Iki* has taken a full turn toward a heroic ethos of sacrificial death, an ethos that Kuki traces from the *gunki monogatari* (military tales) of the medieval period through the *jōruri* libretto of the Tokugawa puppet theater to the Asian battlefields of Japan's modern wars. Though he may have implied as much in earlier essays, here Kuki explicitly and definitively extends "the benefits of noble standards to all classes." This tactic, which Hannah Arendt locates at the source of "race-thinking," simultaneously denies the reality of internal (class) divisions and nourishes the aspirations of bourgeois intellectuals, liberal and conservative, to replace old governing classes with a new "elite" through nonpolitical means.[30] If there is a populist thrust to this discourse, it might be distilled as a democracy of death, a democracy in which all Japanese are equal as willing subjects of sacrifice. The modern, if absolutist, political structure within which that equality of sacrifice prevailed was more bluntly articulated in *Kokutai no hongi:* "The Emperor's deeds that remain with us are so many as to defy enumeration when we cite such things as how he enshrines as deities in Yasukuni Shrine those loyal subjects that have sacrificed their lives for the nation since about the time of the Restoration, lauding their meritorious deeds without regard to standing or position."[31] For Kuki, this "egalitarian" imperative was deeply rooted in the "Japanese character" and its enduring

29. Ibid., 3:383, 3:384.
30. Arendt, *The Origins of Totalitarianism*, 180, 173–75.
31. *Kokutai no hongi: Cardinal Principles*, 77.

inclination for idealism; but it had a more timely and practical derivation in the demands of a national mobilization for a war that would soon extend deep into the Asian mainland and beyond.

The third attribute of the "Japanese character," *teinen,* is intimately related by the first of its two ideographs to *akirame,* the spirit of resignation that the author of *"Iki" no kōzō* deciphered in the speech of Edo prostitutes. But prostitutes and geisha, along with their bittersweet experience of unrequited love, have disappeared without a trace from the pages of "Nihonteki seikaku ni tsuite." In their stead are the Japanese, a generic category no longer requiring mediating representation by local historical figures (or even by history in the guise of collective experience). Japanese culture, Kuki claimed, is based on "a spirit of resignation, with its gaze trained on nothingness."[32] In a more practical vein, Kuki argued that the Japanese character, "divorced from money," is ill-suited to commercial endeavor. He attributed this renunciation of tangible assets to a purely Japanese Buddhism identified with the medieval religious figures Hōnen and Shinran. Both are associated with Buddhist doctrines that stressed the futility of salvation by one's own power and advocated entrusting oneself to the saving grace of Amida Buddha. Kuki concluded that the Japanese spirit of resignation deriving from this Japanized Buddhist sentiment reflects a recognition of one's own powerlessness and an attitude of detachment toward the things of this world.

Following the protocol of *"Iki" no kōzō,* Kuki demonstrated that the three attributes — *shizen, iki, teinen,* now explicitly identified with the three teachings of Shintō, Confucianism, and Buddhism — transcended their apparent contradictions in a higher synthesis. First, however, he had to ward off accusations that Confucianism and Buddhism represented foreign intrusions into a purely Japanese cultural ken. This was apparently a point of some contention among the Monbushō-appointed editorial advisory committee for *Kokutai no hongi,* one that allegedly provoked Kyoto-school members to walk out on the more xenophobic *kokusuishugisha* (advocates of the "national essence") majority. In defense of his catholicity, Kuki invoked nativist Kitabatake Chikafusa and syncretist rural reformer Ninomiya Sontoku — figures of indisputable pedigree in a nationalist canon — to demonstrate that idealism (*iki*) and detachment (*teinen*) were inherent in Shintō naturalism.[33] As incontrovertible evidence that heroic idealism possessed an indigenous lin-

---

32. Kuki, "Nihonteki seikaku ni tsuite," *KSZ,* 3:386–87.
33. Ibid., 3:388–89.

eage, he cited the reading of a tenth-century *Manyōshū* poem composed by Ōtomo no Yakamochi in the text of another renowned nativist, Kamo no Mabuchi:

> In the ocean, bodies sodden with water
> In the mountains, bodies molder on grass,
> If I but die by my Lord,
> I will have no regrets.[34]

Significantly, the lyrics of this ancient poem would also sound the concluding note of the imperial rescript declaring war with the United States read by Prime Minister Tōjō over the radio in December of 1941. And the same heavily freighted words provided the preface to *Kore dake yomeba ware ga kateru* (Read This, and the War Is Won), a pamphlet regularly recovered from the corpses of Japanese soldiers littering the battlefields of Southeast Asia.[35] Ultimately, Kuki's synthesis of seemingly irreconcilable elements found its perfected form in a Heideggerian "Being toward death" now in the service of a renaturalized state. Kuki's concluding characterization of the Japanese personality as a "dialectical synthesis" between powerlessness and superordinate power seems strangely apropos, in historical hindsight, to a populace persuaded to pay the exorbitant price for a Japanese bid for hegemony in Asia.

In the final section of "Nihonteki seikaku ni tsuite," Kuki submits the attributes of the Japanese character to two noteworthy discursive exchanges. In the first exchange, the payback is the "universal" currency of the Kantian trilogy: knowledge, feeling, and will. That currency serves as a reminder of the cosmopolitan derivations of even the most ultranationalist of discourses. As in *"Iki" no kōzō*, the particularist terms in which Kuki defined Japan lead back ineluctably to European representations of the universal. In Naoki Sakai's words, the "insistence [within the discourse on culture] on Japan's particularity and difference from the West embodies a nagging urge to see the self from the viewpoint of the Other."[36] Nevertheless, while such currency may have lent a coveted universal value to the Japanese character, it could hardly be left as the final pronouncement in this discourse on Japaneseness. As if to finally foreclose on all exchangeability, Kuki equates the three moments of the Japanese character with the "Three Divine Regalia" (jewel,

---

34. Cited in *KSZ*, 3:388. The original can be found in *Manyōshū*, vol. 5, ed. Aoki Takako, et al., in *Shinchō Nihon koten shūsei* (Tokyo: Shinchōsha, 1984), 143. My translation.

35. Dower, *War Without Mercy*, 25–26.

36. Sakai, "Modernity and Its Critique," 104–5.

mirror, and sword), objects whose fetishistic quality had the advantage of permanently lodging meaning in the unique existence of a material thing. In this case, the attributes of the Japanese character now add up, if only metaphorically, to the unique national essence:

> We have thus far observed the fusion of nature, fortitude, and resignation — the three moments that make up Japanese culture embodied in the Japanese character. Might we not envision the symbolization of this fusion in the "Three Divine Regalia"? Particularly when we consider that the jewel is said to represent compassion, the mirror, wisdom, and the sword, valor, or that the jewel is seen as a symbol of refinement, the mirror, of civilization, and the sword, of sovereignty over the world. Thus, it is far from implausible to see the jewel as symbolizing nature, the sword, fortitude, and the mirror, resignation.[37]

With only the faintest gesture of rhetorical hesitancy, Kuki has moved squarely into the mystified territory of the *kokutai*. As early as 1929, the *kokutai* had been sanctified by the Supreme Court as "the condition whereby a line of emperors unbroken for ages eternal deigns to reign over our empire and to combine in itself the supreme right to rule."[38] With the advent of the 1930's, *kokutai* became "an incantatory symbol to the nationalists, and 'failure to appreciate the national polity' was almost the gravest charge that could be levelled against an opponent."[39] In other words, the word signified a potent fusion of the "sacred and inviolate" body of the emperor with a mythic national past — a fusion that served as a coercive guarantee of submission to an increasingly non-pluralist and repressive present. Kuki first suggests the semiotic immanence within the emperor — identified here with the classical Japanese reading *sumeramikoto*: "august, manifest deity" — of "life," "unity in one rule," and "serenity." With only a small leap of linguistic faith, he is able to claim an equivalence with the three attributes of the Japanese character: nature, fortitude, and resignation. Leaning heavily on the interpretive power of classical philology, Kuki has managed a symbolic merger of the Japanese character with the divinized figure of the emperor.[40] In this final concurrence with the now compulsory concept of *kokutai*, he has demonstrated that cultural theory and the state have become inseparable.

37. Kuki, "Nihonteki seikaku ni tsuite," *KSZ*, 3:394.
38. Maruyama, *Thought and Behavior in Modern Japanese Politics*, 316–17.
39. Ibid.
40. Ibid., 395–96.

This inseparability already had become a distinct possibility in *"Iki" no kōzō*, the discursive culmination of Kuki's Taishō itinerary nearly a decade earlier. With the formal strategies of that earlier text, he had mapped out the coordinates for an untoward intimacy between state and culture. Here we must recall that what Kuki discovered deeply embedded in the German Romantic and hermeneutic traditions—and widely circulating in Europe's interwar philosophical discourse—was a logic of organicism applied to a culturally (or racially) determined collectivity, a logic that typically placed itself at the disposal of the state. That logic received its clearest articulation in the opening lines of *"Iki" no kōzō*, which I will quote here once again for clarity: "The relation between meaning and language on the one hand and the conscious being of the *minzoku* on the other is not one in which the former aggregates to construct the latter; rather, it is the living being of the *minzoku* that creates meaning and language. The relation between the two terms is not a mechanical one in which the parts precede the whole but an organic one in which the whole determines the parts."[41] Following this logic, any cultural phenomenon (the part) that finds expression in language—*iki* in this case—fulfills a single mission: the self-revelation of the *minzoku* (the whole) to itself. In identifying this kind of discursive formation as "national aestheticism," Lacoue-Labarthe, a cautious critic of fascist strains in Heidegger, explains that the essential organicity in this formation is "infra-political, even infra-social."[42] That is to say, it bypasses modern forms of political and social practice in a return to earlier (and largely imaginary) notions of a prepolitical, precapitalist community—in German, the *Volkstum;* in Japanese, *bunka minzoku,* literally, the "culture folk." This is a naturally determined community that can be accomplished and revealed to itself only through its works—specifically, art, philosophy, and language (the language of the community). It is in this aesthetic surplus that the community "deciphers," presents, and recognizes itself.[43] In Lacoue-Labarthe's words, "the political itself is instituted and constituted (and regularly re-grounds itself)

41. Kuki, *"Iki" no kōzō, KSZ,* 1:8.
42. Lacoue-Labarthe, *Heidegger, Art, and Politics,* 68–70.
43. Philosopher Jean-Luc Nancy calls this strategy "immanentism" and demonstrates the opacity of its intransitive logic when he describes it as a condition in which it is "the aim of the community of beings in essence to produce their own essence as their work (*oeuvre*), and moreover to produce precisely this essence *as community.*" From Lacoue-Labarthe's discussion of Nancy's *La communauté désoeuvre* in *Heidegger, Art, and Politics,* 70.

in and as work of art."[44] Ultimately, Kuki's cultural organicism also required that social agency yield its place to the tautological demands of national aestheticism—the immediate display of the "communal essence" through its "works."

By the late 1930's, Kuki's brand of cultural organicism no longer required even the pretext of mediation between part and whole. Whereas the aesthetic style of *iki* had once offered the interpreter a suggestive path to a still-elusive national being, the author of "Nihonteki seikaku ni tsuite," a compendium of the ideological requirements of the state at hand, dissected the character of the Japanese subject into its constituent parts. With the need for interpretation largely superseded, the elaborate philosophical structure of hermeneutics vanished, leaving as its only vestige a method of argument rooted in philology. This elimination of formal mediation in "Nihonteki seikaku ni tsuite" corresponds to the collapse of any separation between state and culture by the late 1930's, a collapse that critical observers had anticipated early on in the Taishō era.

Whether presented as a veiled totality in *"Iki" no kōzō* or as its exposed immediacy in "Nihonteki seikaku ni tsuite," the logical requirements of organicism remained the same. The *minzoku*, newly incarnated as a collective imperial subject—equal to nothing other than itself (or the incalculable sum of its parts)—appears as unique and autonomous. With no relation to anything other than itself, an empty, hypostatized category, how can this totality recognize itself but through its own self-expression, its "works"? Nakano Shigeharu suggested as much in his 1936 poem "Kawase sōba" (Rate of Exchange), Nakano's indictment, in Miriam Silverberg's words, of "ideologues who served to reproduce the ruling ideas of the era—ideas about nationhood and the Japanese nation in particular":[45]

> If Japan is
> That different from all of the countries of the world
> Even if Nihonjin
> Is read as NIPPONJIN   The sound sounds good
> If we're that different from all the foreigners in the world
> Tell me how you tell yourself apart[46]

In the stanza following this, Nakano invites an analogy between claims of cultural exceptionality and the mystified existence of a national cur-

---

44. Ibid., 64.
45. Silverberg, *Changing Song*, 204.
46. Ibid., 204–5. I am indebted to Miriam Silverberg for her translation and insightful discussion of this poem.

rency whose thorough integration in an international money exchange has been concealed, as has its arbitrary origins. Since Nakano's
imagined ideologues would sever Japan from any relationship to other
cultures — a relationship from which any notion of difference must be
derived — how, then, were they to recognize themselves? From this
paradox arises a demand for self-recognition that is both infinite and in-
satiable.

Toward the end of 1937, after an exchange of hostilities at Marco Polo
Bridge provided Japan with the final pretext for a full-scale war of invasion against China, Kuki published his reflections on the "incident" in
the journal *Bungei shunjū* under the title "Jikyoku no kansō" (Thoughts
on the Current State of Affairs). Acknowledging that the "Marco Polo
Bridge Incident" did indeed amount to war, he asserted that a victory
over China would bear witness to the philosophical and aesthetic credentials of the Japanese army: "By vanquishing China, we Japanese
must teach them in a decisive manner the spirit of Japanese philosophy.
It is our cultural-historical mission to lend spiritual succor to the renewal of their motherland by imprinting *bushidō,* our idealistic philosophy, in the innermost recesses of their bodies."[47] Ultimately, Japan's cultural exceptionality ("culture," in the narrowest sense of ethical norms)
was to find its immediate effectuation not in the work of art but on the
battlefields of Asia, inscribed — here, in the most violently literal sense
of the word — on the bodies of non-Japanese soldiers and civilians.[48]
Several years later, in the *Kindai no chōkoku* (Overcoming the modern)
debates, Kōsaka Masaaki echoed the same widely shared sentiments
when he claimed that the outcome of the Sino-Japanese war would bear
witness to the moral superiority of Japan.[49]

In the final analysis, the logic of organicism — a logic that Kuki first
articulated in *"Iki" no kōzō* and simply presumed in the later essays —
underwrote the Japanese invasion of China in particular, and the excesses of national aestheticism in general. Those excesses were to expand
on a monstrous scale: just weeks after the publication of "Jikyoku no

47. Kuki, "Jikyoku no kansō," *KSZ,* 5:38.

48. For the outlines of this discussion, I owe much to Lacoue-Labarthe's treatment
of the aestheticization of politics in the context of National Socialism. See *Heidegger, Art,
and Politics,* 67–70.

49. Sakai, "Modernity and Its Critique," 493. In the *Kindai no chōkoku* debates that
followed the outbreak of the Pacific War in 1941, many of the participants imagined the
war as a cleansing or purifying process, purging the authentic Japanese subject of a modernity — a term about which there was little agreement — imposed from without. For an
overview and critical analysis of the debates, see Hiromatsu, *"Kindai no chōkoku" ron,* especially 3–7, 230–54, and Takeuchi, *Kindai no chōkoku,* 53–113.

kansō" came the Nanking massacre. At precisely the same historical moment, Walter Benjamin invoked the notion of "aestheticization of the
political" to describe the operation of fascism in Europe. "Fascism," he
explained, "attempts to organize the newly created proletarian masses
without affecting the property structure which the masses strive to eliminate." The aim is to give "these masses not their right, but instead a
chance to express themselves."[50] Ultimately, the outlet for that mass expression, Benjamin believed, could only be war. The exemplary case was
Filippo Marinetti and the Italian Futurists, who expected war to provide
new forms of aesthetic expression and gratification, but this same tactic
of expressive aestheticization operated less flagrantly as well. Unlike the
Futurists, Kuki never reveled in the radiance of mechanized warfare; he
did, however, praise the beauty of the Japanese spirit, whether it found
expression in kimono patterns or suicidal bomber missions. The Japanese spirit, he suggested in "Jikyoku no kansō," could not but prevail
on the battlefield, and the significance of that triumph was to be construed not in geopolitical but in cultural-historical terms.[51]

New directions in critical theory suggest that this enduring inclination to aestheticize the state and the violence it sponsored was itself
predicated by the aesthetic modernism Kuki and others supposedly disavowed. In *Modernism and Hegemony*, Neil Larsen reopens the question
of aesthetics and politics, paying particular attention to how that question is resolved in non-Western societies. He begins with the general
observation that one of the fundamental tactics of modernism is the
displacement of historical agency by aesthetics. He traces the beginnings
of this displacement to a "'crisis in representation' affecting the construction of what are initially political and social identities."[52] That crisis, in Larsen's view, was first precipitated by the modernization of capital during the nineteenth century, specifically by the ascendancy of
monopoly/state capitalism and imperialism.[53] With the transformation
of capital into what appears to be "a superordinate agency with no fixed
political or cultural subjectivity," the conviction that "social and historical agency is exercised by subjects linked to society as a whole by repre-

---

50. Benjamin, "The Work of Art in an Age of Mechanical Reproduction," in *Illuminations*, 241–42.
51. Kuki, "Jikyoku no kansō," *KSZ*, 5:37–39.
52. Larsen, *Modernism and Hegemony*, xxiv.
53. In Japan, a latecomer to the global market, this ascendancy came abruptly and
intensely, due in large part to the central role of the state in the early development of capitalism.

sentational bonds of identity" begins to falter.[54] Kuki's colleague, Nakai Masakazu, sounded the epistemological dimensions of this transformation in his 1936 *Iinkai no ronri* (The Logic of Committee). Under the conditions of advanced monopoly capitalism, he wrote, "a general and comprehensive concept of existence is absorbed into an immense mechanism no longer accessible to representational synthesis in the mind of a single individual."[55] When the place of traditional actors is usurped by this "immense mechanism," in other words, by anonymous forces, historical narratives begin to decompose and historical agency disintegrates.

Modernist aesthetics, explains Larsen, stems from this crisis of agency—and then proceeds to invert it. Aesthetic works and practices become "the conceptual inversions of historical aporias, conceptual forms of anticapital." In answer to the question of why aesthetics alone appears to offer the promise of oppositional synthesis, Larsen looks back to Kant's designation of aesthetics as an autonomous domain of pure representational activity marked off from the "fallen world of objects and practices." Given this grant of autonomy, aesthetics is well prepared for its subsequent mission to substitute its own subjective fullness and perfection for a social world drained of subjective meaning and agency. For Larsen, the unifying thread in modernist ideology is this aesthetic aptitude for "occupying the lost terrain of social representation."[56] Although modernist discourse is shrouded in an aesthetic idiom, it bears the burden of signifying something other than, something more than, aesthetics per se. Outside the fray, aesthetics is free to signify historical agency on its own terms—an observation with considerable relevance to the cultural production of interwar Japan. Whether in the cultural histories of Kuki and Watsuji, the aesthetics of Tanizaki, or the fiction of Kawabata Yasunari, the cultural discourse so prevalent in interwar Japan aspired to reclaim diminished possibilities at the level of social and political practice in an aestheticized reflection on culture. The aim of these theorists and writers was not simply to rescue art from its debasement (whether to mere reflection by Marxist economism or to a commodity under the conditions of capitalism) but to restore a space, however imaginary, for authentic subjectivity and utopian practice. In their inclination to substitute an immaculate aesthetics for a tainted so-

54. Larsen, *Modernism and Hegemony*, xxiv.
55. Nakai, "Iinkai no ronri," in *Nakai Masakazu zenshū*, 1:56–57.
56. Larsen, *Modernism and Hegemony*, xxiv–xxv.

cial practice, Japanese theorists and writers did not differ appreciably
from their European modernist counterparts. The issue, however, does
not end with this recognition of similarity.

Aesthetic modernism, in its capacity as "traveling theory," necessarily
encountered new conditions and new applications when it left its point
of origin and migrated outward.[57] In an endeavor to address these com-
plicating circumstances, Larsen examines what happens when the modernist aesthetic inversion travels away from the metropolitan centers of
Anglo-Europe and toward what he calls the "modernist periphery."
Most strikingly, the subject represented on aesthetic terrain is overwhelmingly a national — or ethnic — subject. At the periphery, the tensions in modernist movements between internationalism and nationalism, between a newly compressed global time and vanishing local
realities, are typically resolved on the side of the national community
and the native place. The reasons for this resolution, Larsen suggests,
can be traced to a set of contradictory impulses toward complex hegemonic processes. The peripheral modernist text, in an endeavor to resist
mediation by a dominant "civilization," begins by engaging the notion
of alterity or otherness as a "formal means serving an aesthetics of
countermediation." This notion of alterity, however, often ends as a spatial locus of "absolute, irreducible content."[58]

Kuki's continuing philosophical reflection on contingence arrived at
a similar conclusion. He began with a critical attempt to demonstrate
the limits of rationality, particularly as it was articulated through various
phases of European philosophy; he ended with Japan, identified by its
ancient epithet Onokorojima, as the exemplary site of *Urzufall*, or ab-
original contingence.[59] In other words, a critical and transcultural discursive itinerary terminated in a nationally bound space of indigenous
culture represented as authentic, essential, and other. Larsen contends
that this short-circuiting of a critical countermediation occurs when an
antihegemonic practice simultaneously conspires in a project to construct an internally hegemonic space. In textual terms, this conspiracy
produces a geographically specific and substantialized space of culture
rewritten as alterity.[60] This complex space is the equivalent of the cul-

57. See Edward Said's seminal essay for elaboration of the concept: "Traveling Theory," in *The World, the Text, and the Critic*, 226–47.

58. Larsen, *Modernism and Hegemony*, xxxix.

59. Kuki, "Ningen to wa nani ka," *KSZ*, 3:46–47.

60. Larsen points out the reactionary tendencies associated with this subversion of an
initially critical practice — tendencies he observes in metropolitan postmodernist practices

turescape drafted in *"Iki" no kōzō* and kindred texts. Historically, the formal features of this culturescape persisted from the liberalism of Taishō democracy to the repressive politics of early Shōwa, from the cultural criticism of the 1920's to the propaganda of the late 1930's.

The culturescape in *"Iki" no kōzō*—created and inhabited by a collectivity defined in ethnocultural rather than political terms, pure "Japaneseness," so to speak—appears to take its distance from the state in its guise as a rational, bureaucratic agent of modernization. Nor did it resemble, at this stage, the *kazoku kokka*, the "family-state" ideology systematically promulgated in national textbooks and public documents in the years immediately following the Russo-Japanese War (1904–1905).[61] One need only recall Kuki's portrait of the Japanese people on the final page of *"Iki" no kōzō*: "*Iki* is an erotic allure that has attained 'resignation' and lives (*ikiru*) in the freedom of 'fearless pride.' Erotic allure never could have assumed the form of *iki* if we were not a people (*minzoku*) who gazed at fate with unclouded eyes and nurtured a melancholy longing for freedom of the spirit."[62] Not surprisingly, readers of the Taishō discourse on culture have been tempted to fill this distance from the state with aspirations toward a civil society. I have suggested, to the contrary, that the culturescape served to conceal and contain new mass forms of cultural and social practice emerging conspicuously during the Taishō era. In other words, what first appeared as an aestheticized representation of an incipient civil society in late Edo operated as a strategy for the containment of popular aspirations in early Shōwa. Most significant, however, is the fact that this socially reactionary proj-

---

as well: "The turn from alterity as a formal means serving an aesthetics of countermediation to alterity as a kind of absolute, irreducible content . . . shows a peculiar tendency to contradict its (arguably) radical political impulse with a distinctly right-wing epistemology." *Modernism and Hegemony*, xxxix.

61. See Irokawa Daikichi's useful discussion of the Japanese family-state ideology in *The Culture of the Meiji Period*, 280–87. Irokawa explains that the "family-state" linking household to nation was made up of four ideological intermediaries: the imperial myth, the religious tradition of ancestor worship, the social structure of the family system, and customary folk morality (282–83). Interestingly, he argues that "family-state" ideology took hold only when the state was able to successfully link family rites for the huge numbers of sons and fathers sacrificed in the Russo-Japanese War with national deification at Yasukuni shrine (287). See also Carol Gluck's brief but illuminating discussion of historical changes in both representations and realities of the family system during the Meiji era. Gluck points out that the metaphoric links between family and nation were being strengthened during the same era in which the traditional rural household was becoming victim to defection to the cities and large landlords. *Japan's Modern Myths*, 187–88.

62. Kuki, *"Iki" no kōzō, KSZ*, 1:81.

ect was conducted, in the last analysis, in the interest of the state—a state whose interest the producers of the culturescape made their own.

Despite the marked absence of the state on the surface of the text, *"Iki" no kōzō* in fact represented the state in another form. I use the word "represent" here in its complex sense, as both a political and a textual act, to suggest not only common interests with a state for which its author spoke but also the refiguration of state in the medium of discourse. The culturescape drawn in the text accomplished two tasks simultaneously: first, it resolved a problem of representation for a late-developing state beset by intimations of its own negativity as an autonomous power, and second, it reserved for its author a position of power and authority within and by means of this newly represented state. In its capacity to command authority through a refiguration of the collective contours of self-knowledge, the culturescape calls to mind Antonio Gramsci's concept of hegemony—the production of knowledge and value in the interest of class power. This concept of hegemony is a crucial one because it has the theoretical power to illuminate the concealed connections between highly aestheticized discursive practices and real political and social effects. But before reconsidering *"Iki" no kōzō* in this light, we might do well to take a brief excursus through Gramsci's theory of hegemony and its recent reconsideration in postcolonial contexts.

In his *Prison Notebooks,* the Italian Marxist described the operation of "hegemony" as follows: "The realization of a hegemonic apparatus, in so far as it creates new ideological terrain, determines a reform of consciousness and of methods of knowledge: it is a fact of knowledge, a philosophical fact."[63] These facts, in turn, are instruments of persuasion (if not domination). According to Gramsci, an aspiring dominant class—the bourgeoisie in this case—typically wages a "war of position" on the terrain of culture. If the stake in this war is "the historical unity of the ruling classes," then hegemony is the master strategy for forging that unity. In a departure from received Marxist theory, Gramsci linked the unity of the ruling classes closely to a state that is not merely a political apparatus but rather an "integral state," at once political and civil,

63. Gramsci, "Hegemony, Relations of Force, Historical Block," in *A Gramsci Reader,* 189–217. See especially 189–99. "The Art and Science of Politics," 222–45. See especially 222–37, 192. Gramsci envisaged ideology not as an abstract set of ideas but (in the words of Raymond Williams) as something so total as to correspond with the "substance and the limit of common sense" and "the reality of social experience." *Problems in Materialism and Culture,* 37.

coercive and consensual.[64] This redefinition is significant because it draws not simply the political activity but also the cultural and social practices of the ruling classes into the purview of the state. In fact, Gramsci argued that the unity of the dominant classes is first realized outside the juridical political sphere, preeminently in the domain of culture. It is this prior integration of the supposedly autonomous zones of civil society into "the locus of an essentially transpolitical power" — in other words, hegemony — that allows for the subsequent conquest and consolidation of state power in the strict sense.[65]

In the 1920's, when Gramsci theorized this prior consolidation of hegemony, his attention was fixed on the entrenched power of civil society in the capitalist countries of Europe, countries where Marxist revolutionary movements had encountered insurmountable obstacles. Beyond the boundaries of Europe, however, in societies with relatively belated capitalist development, where the power of a national bourgeoisie was not nearly so firmly rooted, the sequence of events did not necessarily follow Gramsci's model. It is with these societies in mind that Larsen proposes a substantial revision of the Gramscian notion of hegemony — a revision that, as we shall see, speaks compellingly to the cultural politics of interwar Japan as well. In the Latin American postcolonial societies Larsen surveys, the historical sequence in which hegemony is implicated is often played out in reverse. There, a bourgeois revolution — inaugurated first by a political-juridical separation from the colonialist state — begins without an effective, integrated base in civil society and without a unified class subject: "What [the state] lacks," explains Larsen, "is precisely what the modern European nation-state, as understood by Gramsci, presupposes: hegemony." Accordingly, the most pressing objective of an incipient but disunified bourgeoisie

---

64. Classical Marxism exclusively stresses the coercive role of the state: "The state is essentially the institution whereby a dominant and exploiting class imposes and defends its power and privileges against the class or classes which it dominates and exploits." Gramsci maintained that the state is also engaged in organizing consent through superstructural means. See Bottomore, ed., *A Dictionary of Marxist Thought,* 467. Though neither classical Marxism nor Gramsci's revision hold that the state is merely an instrument of external forces, the question of the "relative autonomy" of the state and its complex relation to society is the subject of ongoing controversy, one that I cannot hope to resolve here. My aim is rather to illuminate just one aspect of those complexities under particular historical conditions.

65. Larsen, *Modernism and Hegemony,* 72. Gramsci's revisionist concepts of state and hegemony allow one to imagine integral strategies of power that override conventional boundaries between official and private activity, between economic base and ethico-political superstructure, and between violence and persuasion.

on the periphery is "not the conquest of state power in the political-juridical sense but the *conquest of civil society*."[66]

To add to its travail, the postcolonial state is beset by the issue of its own legitimacy, an issue made more urgent by a persistent lack of parity in global politics and markets. Modeled after the modern European nation-state as disseminator of civilization and locus of bureaucratic and technical rationality, the postcolonial state is distinctly derivative of its former colonizer; in practical terms, it is often economically subject as well. The new state has to "continually face external threats to its existence and may, within the global relations of power, represent little more than a semiautonomous commercial agency."[67]

The postcolonial state must resort to both synthesizing the subject it is supposed to represent and fabricating the autonomy it is supposed to possess. Modernism, explains Larsen, provides the resources to accomplish both tasks. Modernist discourse already has marked off the aesthetic as a utopian space for the resolution of real historical contradictions. The peripheral modernist superimposes the antirationalism of metropolitan modernism on images of prerationalized native culture to produce an indigenous culturescape from which all trace of the central "civilizing" and rationalizing authority of the state has been effaced. It is by means of this discursive production that the state resolves its "extraterritoriality through its 'spontaneous' derivation in the organic, spatial coordinates of 'culture.'" The inhabitants of this essentialized space are represented in naturalized images of "*barbarie*" — an organic society sheltering an ethnically unique collective subject. At the same time, this representation of an organically unified (and counterhegemonic) culture reserves first right on the question of the nation, thus suppressing other, less totalizing, antihegemonic representations.[68]

Clearly, Larsen's postcolonial model differs appreciably from the historical circumstances of Japan's mid-nineteenth-century entry into a world market and subsequent state building. Japan was neither totally lacking in a collective consciousness of unity at the time of the Meiji

---

66. Ibid., 73. See also Horace B. Davis's discussion of different (European) versions of nationalism, in which he adds this proviso: "This idea of the nation as preceding the state and eventually leading to its formation is very distinctly European; it has no relevance to the problems of newly formed nations such as most of those in Africa, where the state preceded the nation and conditioned its whole existence." *Toward a Marxist Theory of Nationalism*, 18.

67. Larsen, *Modernism and Hegemony*, 73.

68. Ibid., 74–75.

ishin nor colonized by Western powers. Yet despite these historical factors, the discursive strategies Larsen describes — strategies for producing the space of a missing hegemony as if it were a preexisting authentic cultural substance — have powerful resonances in Japan's interwar discourse on culture. Larsen's schema of an "inverted hegemony" does, in fact, have relevance, if only in modified form, for a society that was late developing and non-European, though not postcolonial. In these last few pages, I can merely sketch out the beginnings of an argument that calls for major reconsideration of Japan's interwar cultural production in light of postcolonial studies.

Like Larsen's postcolonial model, the modern Japanese nation-state, from its inception, suffered the effects of a disadvantageous assimilation into a highly stratified world system. From the mid-nineteenth century through the interwar period, the problems besetting Japanese state and society bore more than a passing resemblance to the predicament of the postcolonial societies described by Larsen, Partha Chatterjee, and others. In Japan, the European model of a centralized nation-state embodying historical rationality was chosen from within rather than imposed from without; nevertheless, the choice to become a "civilized" nation in the image of the West was exercised under threat, imagined or real, of colonization. As Halliday explains it, "Japan was not jarred right off track by external pressures as were most countries subjected to classical colonialism. It continued structurally along its own course, but the pace and timing of its economic development were fundamentally altered by the irruption of the West. International bourgeois terror, as Mao calls it, forced the Japanese ruling coalition to press the country into a mould as similar to imperialist Western societies as possible, as fast as possible."[69] In the interest of survival in an era of rapacious imperialism, the new Meiji state modeled itself on its Western predators with a rare and exacting passion. Yet despite — or more precisely, because of — the attainment of Meiji ambitions of *fukoku kyōhei,* a rich country and strong military, the specter of derivative beginnings haunted the Japanese state.[70] Moreover, the process of state building continued to register the residual effects of European and American imperialism. Unequal treaties maintained by Western powers throughout the second

---

69. Halliday, *A Political History of Japanese Capitalism,* 22.

70. An official revival of Confucian moral rhetoric, the production of an imperial myth, and the Japanist movement in the Ministry of Education all testify to an anxious effort to domesticate the new nation-state.

half of the nineteenth century, an elusive diplomatic parity with the West, and exclusionary immigration laws in the United States and elsewhere in the early twentieth century all worked to impugn the dignity and autonomy of the Japanese state. Halliday theorizes the complex conditions for Japan's entry into the global economy as an "internal-external dialectic," a concept that John Dower, in his introduction to Halliday's book, explicates as follows: "From its very inception, the nature of the modern state has been influenced not only by the direct impact of the West . . . but also by the nature of the global imperialist system in which Japan was forced to operate." Despite the fact that Japan was able to "separate and control three crucial levers commonly associated with imperialist encroachment: technology, imports, and capital," continues Dower, external factors nonetheless "strongly influenced the structure of capitalist development in Japan and the specific nature of Japanese imperialism."[71] In light of this internal-external dialectic, one might view Japan as an attenuated version of Larsen's model, modified by the fact that the crisis that precipitated and shaped the modern state was not colonialism per se but its narrow escape.

If the Japanese state was unable to dispel the specter of its Western other, whether as model or as threat, it was also confronted with the task of establishing the class subject that would represent its rule. Following an accelerated transformation from semicentralized feudalism to capitalism, the newly installed Meiji state endeavored to create a bourgeois class capable of manning positions of power in public bureaucracy and private enterprise. Under the slogan of *bunmei kaika*, ideologues already or soon to be absorbed by state business sought to unleash knowledge in the service of national progress. Frequently under the tutelage of the state, former samurai—inspired by the quasi-Confucianized precepts of Victorian "self-help"—were encouraged to become entrepreneurial capitalists. By the end of the 1880's, a carefully plotted two-track educational system began to produce masses of loyal subjects and an elite core of technical experts. While the state attempted to fashion a social class in its own interest, it also stole the initiative historically taken by that class in the development of capitalism. In economic terms, the new Meiji state opted for policies of active intervention rather than the laissez-faire policies of a liberal state.[72]

71. John W. Dower, "Introduction," in Halliday, *A Political History of Japanese Capitalism,* xxiii–xxiv.

72. As Germaine Hoston explains, the state "encouraged industrialization both indirectly, by providing essential preconditions of capitalism—a stable currency, a unified national banking system, efficient transportation and communication facilities, a mobile la-

The question of whether Japan underwent a "bourgeois revolution" has been posed and reposed in various ways; the response also has varied dramatically. A debate on the nature of Japanese capitalism and the class character of the state divided Marxist thinkers from the late 1920's through the postwar era. The orthodox Kōzaha, the "Lecture" school, which remained loyal to the Japanese Communist Party and to the Comintern line, and the more revisionist Rōnōha, the "Labor and Farmers" faction, which saw the bourgeois revolution as already accomplished during the Meiji era, differed principally in whether they gave more weight to "feudal remnants" or to the advanced capitalistic development of the urban sector. Despite their differences, both factions shared the view that the "combined and uneven development" of a traditional sector and an industrial capitalist sector had generated severe contradictions in Japanese society.[73] This recognition of the nonsynchronicity of development in Japan also shaped later modernization theories of a dual-structure economy in which traditional and modern sectors existed side by side. In Marxist arguments, the specific conditions attending the development of Japanese capitalism account for the weakness and disunity of a Japanese bourgeoisie. Its entrepreneurial role assumed largely by the Meiji state, the Japanese bourgeoisie never fully consolidated its own class power, nor was it able to bring large segments of the population under its control. Ultimately, as Halliday argues, the Japanese bourgeoisie did not "stake out a new political position for itself" but instead resorted to a "historical compromise-cum-imbrication" with other groups, in particular the older Meiji ruling class.[74]

Immediately after World War I, a bourgeois class — strengthened economically though it was by the benefits of a war fought and funded by others — found itself caught between an overbearing state not securely its own and rising mass aspirations for political representation and social power. In Gramscian terms, one might say that the bourgeois conquest of civil society remained incomplete. Not surprisingly, culture became the focus of intense struggle during the 1920's and 1930's. As if in belated compensation for the unfinished project of hegemony, an elite corps of writers and theorists — representatives of a compromised but dominant class — attempted to produce a missing unity in discursive terms. Their aggressive aestheticization of the nation in the form of a

bor force — and directly, by participating in the economy itself." *Marxism and the Crisis of Development*, 6.

73. Ibid., 16, 60–65.
74. Halliday, *A Political History of Japanese Capitalism*, 120.

culturescape provided an effective representation of the prevailing presence of the West as a violation of Japanese authenticity; at the same time, it offered an imaginary but politically potent solution to division and dissent within Japan.

Another of Kuki's contemporaries, Hasegawa Nyozekan (1875–1969), charted the aesthetic dimensions of hegemonic processes under conditions of uneven development. In his 1932 "Nihon fashizumu hihan" (Critique of Japanese Fascism), Nyozekan identified the cultural means by which the dominant classes in Japan endeavored to link the interests of subordinate classes to their own.[75] According to his account, a cultural elite thoroughly immersed in bourgeois forms of social and cultural life — a life with no real connection to the feudal structures that still persisted in other segments of society — had begun to seek expressive forms in the cultural resources of a vanished past. "Even while they succumb to the seduction of neon signs in their art," he wrote, "the Japanese bourgeoisie dreams of hanging lanterns from a bygone feudal era." For the bourgeois artist, explained Nyozekan, this sterile repetition of superseded forms amounted to a reactionary nostalgia, but for a petit bourgeoisie who sought refuge from the material and mental realities of an increasingly bankrupt everyday life and whose lives still came under the sway of older social forms, this "reactionary art" spoke with a persuasive pathos. In this convergence of elite reaction and mass reality, the commodity value of "fascist art" multiplied.[76]

Nyozekan believed that particular conditions of economic and political development made Japan susceptible to fascist inroads — its relatively late development as a capitalist state, a bourgeoisie lacking in social power, and an increasingly beleaguered parliamentary system. With extraordinary prescience, he predicted that fascism as a revolutionary movement from below would be absorbed by what he called a "cool" or legal fascism from above, controlled by entrenched elites.[77] Cultural producers played a crucial role in that process of absorption, shrewdly exploiting the nonsynchronicity of cultural forms circulating among different social strata in interwar Japan. "Fascism built its nest," claimed

75. Hasegawa Nyozekan, "Nihon fashizumu hihan," 366–408. See also Barshay's discussion of this text in *State and Intellectual in Imperial Japan*, 191–202.

76. Hasegawa Nyozekan, "Nihon fashizumu hihan," 367, 407.

77. Barshay, *State and Intellectual in Imperial Japan*, 193, 195–96. Clearly, Nyozekan's two-stage theory of fascism made a strong impression on Maruyama Masao in his own attempts to define the dynamics of Japanese fascism. See Maruyama, "The Ideology and Dynamics of Japanese Fascism," *Thought and Behavior in Modern Japanese Politics*, 25–83.

Nyozekan, in the "feudal remnants" still embedded in the social lives of the lower and middle social strata — feudal remnants irrevocably transformed, he added, by their incorporation in a prevailing capitalist system.[78]

In what was otherwise a highly abstract argument, Nyozekan provided one concrete example of a commodified fascist art form: *chanbara eiga*, the ubiquitous sword-fight film that dominated Japan's movie industry during the interwar years.[79] While the mass appeal and obvious commodification of a popular film genre would appear to be far removed from the discourse on culture produced by academic philosophers, Nyozekan suggested that a common configuration linked mass and elite cultural productions. That configuration might be called, somewhat paradoxically, an "elitist populism" — one of the more conspicuous signs of an intensifying hegemonic struggle. Just as commercial filmmakers drew expediently on traditional cultural forms to suppress mass political aspirations and safeguard their own class privilege, the cultural discourse of scholars who presumed to speak of and for the entire Japanese populace ultimately served the interests of an elite — Kuki's select followers of the "small path" or Watsuji's "community of truth." To return to the cartographic metaphor, there were the few who were empowered to map the culturescape and the many who were bound to inhabit it.

Even while Nyozekan strove to unmask the myth of aesthetic autonomy and reveal the hegemonic function of art, he demonstrated a certain susceptibility to its modernist overvaluation. Despite an initial confirmation of Marxist logic, Nyozekan argued that art, at its most "artistic," reaches a perfect and unmediated accord with historical reason, fulfilling its chief function of embodying life and "reproducing the real."[80] Perhaps it was this inclination to equate art with historical agency — along with a certain susceptibility to the idea of an organic community — that made Nyozekan prey to the temptation to resolve the contradictions of the state through its aestheticization. With what seemed to be an almost ineluctable tragic irony, not long after Nyozekan

78. Hasegawa Nyozekan, "Nihon fashizumu hihan," 401–2.

79. This was perhaps too summary a judgment of a complex genre that included within its repertoire strains of resistance as well as reaction. See the discussion of the "period film" in Anderson and Richie, *The Japanese Film*, 64–66. The authors argue that the period film, particularly during its "golden age" in the first years of Shōwa, offered an opportunity for social criticism.

80. Hasegawa Nyozekan, "Nihon fashizumu hihan," 386–90.

completed his survey of the territory of fascist aesthetics, he, too, through some incalculable proportion of consent and coercion, strayed inside its boundaries.[81] As an exemplary demonstration of national aestheticism and its demand for immediate collective self-revelation, he proclaimed that life (presumably national life) must be crafted like a work of art, that, in Barshay's paraphrase, "with this spirit . . . Japan had embarked, unwillingly, but now with total dedication, on an effort to display its character."[82]

By the late 1930's, the discourse on culture had moved precipitously into the embrace of a state bent on suppressing all autonomous mass organization and mobilizing the entire population for Japan's militarist mission. Signs of intimacy, however, between cultural criticism and state ideology had appeared much earlier, in the hegemonic outlines of the culturescape produced in *"Iki" no kōzō* and similar texts. From the beginning of the decade, critics on the Left recorded their apprehensions about this complicity of cultural production with the state. Miriam Silverberg notes that in 1930, Nakano Shigeharu already had called attention to "the mobilization of cultural forces by a bourgeoisie working to solidify the philosophy, science, and art that directly and indirectly protected the relation of production, the state, and the law."[83] In the middle of the decade, Tosaka Jun, in his *Nihon ideorogīron,* suggested that the Japanese intelligentsia, far from resisting an intensifying policy of cultural control, was actually receptive to, even supportive of, repressive state policies toward culture. He traced the source of this complicity to a bourgeois liberalism espousing freedom from political practice. As in Germany, Japanese liberalism found both its refuge and its defense in a hermeneutically elaborated realm of cultural freedom and expression, a realm that elicited a devotion almost religious in nature. It was this culturally distended form of liberalism, argued Tosaka, that so easily allied itself with the emerging idiom of Japanism.[84]

81. As Barshay suggests, by the mid-1930's, the rhetoric of class struggle in Nyozekan's writing yielded to one of national integration and communitarian harmony; critical dissent gave way to cultural description. In the last years of the decade, Nyozekan joined the Bunka Mondai Kenkyūkai (Research Committee for Cultural Issues), a subgroup within the Shōwa Kenkyūkai, where he worked with Miki Kiyoshi and others to conceptualize a "New Asian Order" and rationalize Japan's increasingly aggressive posture in China. See Barshay, *State and Intellectual in Imperial Japan,* 202–3, 211, 214, and Crowley, "Intellectuals as Visionaries of the New Asian Order," 366–67.

82. Barshay, *State and Intellectual in Imperial Japan,* 219.

83. Nakano's essay "Handōki no sakusha seikatsu" is cited in Silverberg's *Changing Song,* 184.

84. Tosaka, *Nihon ideorogīron,* 227–34.

While intellectuals decreased their distance from the center of official power, the center in turn endeavored to take command of a discourse that served its own interests. Ultimately, the state made the culturescape its own both by borrowing its rhetoric and by enlisting its producers in an official capacity. Following the China Incident in 1937, the continuing struggle on the part of the state to conceal its resemblances to the West acquired special urgency, as did the need to mobilize the population — both in the *naichi* (inner land / Japanese home islands) and *gaichi* (outer land / Japanese empire). In the midst of an intensifying imperialist project in which force had become predominant, the state had to mask a military enterprise in Asia at least as opportunistic, as racist, and as brutal as Western forms of imperialism.[85] Not only were Japanese policies in Asia represented as belonging to a different order from those of Europe and America, but Japan was seen as uniquely appointed to act as the defender of Asia against European imperialism. As Kuki put it in "Jikyoku no kansō," Japan had no choice but to accept a mission mandated by a natural affinity with Asia (an irrevocable "blood connection") to establish a "cooperative community of Asian culture." "In the international arena," he wrote, "we need to offer ongoing protection from the Westerners to our Asian brothers, the Chinese. Should they attempt to estrange themselves from us, we must first reflect upon ourselves to divine the cause, and then devote ourselves wholeheartedly to establishing a true foundation for Japanese-Chinese cooperation."[86] The collective self-reflection Kuki advocated tended, however, to further sharpen the boundaries of a specially sequestered culturescape — as in the Japanist discourse of "Nihonteki seikaku ni tsuite." And as Kuki's later essays make disturbingly clear, the formation of the culturescape required that its boundaries be relentlessly expanded in aestheticized acts expressing the essence of an indwelling collective spirit.

Tosaka argued that what distinguished this Japanist discourse from an international trend toward political reaction and fascism was the canon of *kokushi*, the select documents of a nationalist history on which it drew. But the historical sensibility that informed much of this discourse on culture was decidedly modern, even modernist — from the critical cultural impulse that contributed to its beginnings in Taishō to

85. Mark Peattie identifies an emerging "anti-colonial" perspective toward the end of the decade. An intensifying assault on Western colonial regimes went hand in hand with a newly revised "non-colonialist" rhetoric of the Japanese Coprosperity Sphere. This ideological process culminated in 1942 with the replacement of the Colonial Ministry by the Greater East Asia Ministry. See Peattie, "Japanese Attitudes Toward Colonialism," 123–24.

86. Kuki, "Jikyoku no kansō," *KSZ*, 5:37–38.

the hegemonic thrust that lent it a coercive authority in Shōwa. Kuki's evocation of late Edo as an unchanging landscape of the spirit in *"Iki" no kōzō* is animated by the same images that informed a modernist vision of history: tragedy, loss, and redemption. For the modernist, writes Habermas, "historical memory is replaced by the heroic affinity of the present with the extremes of history." The desire for an "undefiled, immaculate, and stable present" explains the often "abstract language in which the modernist temper has spoken of the 'past.'" At its most reactionary, the modernist disposition was adamantly ahistorical; at its most radically progressive, subversive of the "false normativity of history." [87] An exemplar on the progressive end of the continuum, Walter Benjamin spoke eloquently for this posthistoricist engagement with the past: "To articulate the past historically does not mean to recognize it 'the way it really was' (Ranke). It means to seize hold of a memory as it flashes up at a moment of danger." For the critical historian, the task was to charge a moment in the past with *Jetztzeit*, the time of the now, and "blast it out of the continuity of history." [88] Benjamin aimed his assault on the homogeneous and continuous time of history against a hegemonic narrative that accounts only for the victors of history. For Benjamin, the victors were the ruling classes in European societies progressing inexorably toward fascism.

Was Kuki, then, doing Benjamin's bidding when he salvaged a historical "memory" at risk in Japan's modernity? In a distinctively modernist intervention, Kuki liberated Edo from normative historical narratives seeking to transfigure a defiled present and redeem the losses suffered to modernity. In *"Iki" no kōzō*, he transmuted the "memory" of Edo into an "eternal now," the pristine present of authentic experience. But who was the victor from whom he seized that memory? In all likelihood, Kuki would have claimed that the victor was Western civilization, or its invasive and unnatural replication in Japan's Enlightenment.

Nevertheless, Kuki's venture into critical alterity was compromised from the outset by a compulsion to reproduce the expansive identity that it opposed — a compulsion enacted in the interests of a domestic hegemony and on the side of ruling interests within his own society. Enlisting the reactionary possibilities of modernism, sifting from the archival resources of a local past, Kuki intervened against normative historical time only to produce a rarefied space of "Japanese culture," purged of the social conflicts and cultural differences that had risen to the surface of society during the years of his own philosophical educa-

---

87. Habermas, "Modernity," 5.
88. Benjamin, "Theses on the Philosophy of History," in *Illuminations*, 255, 261.

tion. On this increasingly pluralistic and indeterminate social formation — a formation extending beyond the borders of the Japanese archipelago — Kuki imprinted the stamp of a unitary "Japanese character," subject to the mandates of a repressive and imperialist state. This state — rhetorically enhanced by its representation in the cultural discourse generated by Kuki, Watsuji, the Kyoto-school philosophers, and, at last, Nyozekan — presumed to have drawn the entirety of historical time into a spatialized, eternalized, and flawless present: "That our Imperial Throne is coeval with heaven and earth means indeed that the past and the future are united in one in the 'now,' that our nation possesses everlasting life, and that it flourishes endlessly. Our history is an evolution of the eternal 'now,' and at the root of our history there always runs a stream of eternal 'now.'"[89] This passage from *Kokutai no hongi* was the ideological offspring of an intellectual lineage to which Kuki belonged, the lineage of what I have chosen to call the fascist turn in Japanese cultural discourse.

In the half century since the Pacific War, *"Iki" no kōzō* and kindred texts have been reenlisted in new celebrations of the Edo past, of postmodern aesthetics, and of Japaneseness, without critical deliberation on the history in which those texts are implicated. Clearly, Japan is not the only society to hesitate before the task of confronting the excesses, the offenses, and the injuries committed in the name of the modern nation. Yet in a postwar society that has relied upon economic power to regain the preeminence in Asia and the world that it once sought through military means, and where the instruments of information and education are more closely controlled by centralized authority than is usually the case in democratic societies, the mainstream of Japanese society has been particularly resistant to public dialogue and scholarly reflection on issues of historical guilt and responsibility. Predisposed by its very form to deflect this kind of reflection, the cultural discourse that prevailed during the years leading into war has been an unlikely object of critical scrutiny, veiled as it is in a rhetoric of beauty, spirit, and value. Yet as Adorno pointed out in the case of Germany, the "insistence on the autonomy of the spirit and the absolute idea of idealism participated in a motion" that led ultimately to "absolute horror."[90] It is this discursive itinerary, from culture as ideal to culture as terror, that I have endeavored to trace in this study of *"Iki" no kōzō*.

89. *Kokutai no Hongi: Cardinal Principles*, 64.

90. Theodor W. Adorno, "Auf die Frage: Was ist Deutsch," *Gesammelte Schriften* 10 vols., ed. Rolf Tiedemann (Frankfurt: Suhrkamp, 1977), 2:695, quoted and paraphrased in Berman, "Foreword: The Wandering Z."

Works Cited

Japanese-Language Sources

Abe Jirō. *Santarō no nikki.* In *Abe Jirō zenshū.* Vol. 1. Tokyo: Kadokawa Shoten, 1960.

————. *Tokugawa jidai no geijutsu to shakai.* Tokyo: Kadokawa Shoten, 1931.

Asaō Naojiro, ed. *Sekaishi no naka no "kinsei."* In *Nihon no kinsei.* Vol. 1. Tokyo: Chūō Kōronsha, 1991.

Asō Isoji. "Tsū — iki." In *Nihon bungaku kōza.* Vol. 7. Tokyo: Kawade Shobō, 1951.

Fujita Shōzō. *Seishinshiteki kōsatsu: Ikutsuka no danmen ni sokushite.* Tokyo: Heibonsha, 1982.

Hamil, Barbara. "Nihonteki modanizumu no shisō." In *Nihon modanizumu no kenkyū.* Edited by Minami Hiroshi. Tokyo: Brenn Shuppan, 1982.

Hasegawa Nyozekan. "Nihon fashizumu hihan." In *Hasegawa Nyōzekan zenshū.* Vol. 2. Tokyo: Kurita Shuppankai, 1969.

Hayashiya Tatsusaburō, ed. *Kasei bunka no kenkyū.* Tokyo: Iwanami Shoten, 1978.

Hiromatsu Wataru. *"Kindai no chōkoku" ron.* Tokyo: Kōdansha, 1989.

Igarashi Akio, ed. *Kita Ikki ronshū.* Tokyo: Sanichi Shobō, 1979.

Ishimatsu Keizō. "Haiderubāgu no Kuki Shūzō." In *Kuki Shūzō zenshū geppō.* Vol. 2. Tokyo: Iwanami Shoten, 1980.

Kanō Masanaō. "Nihon bunkaron no rekishi." *Shigaku zasshi* 87, no. 3 (March 1978): 1–35.

Karatani Kōjin. "Edo no seishin." *Gendai shisō* 14, no. 10 (September 1986): 8–27.

————. "Fūkei no hakken." In *Nihon kindai bungaku no kigen,* 5–43. Tokyo: Kōdansha, 1980.

Kim Hakuhyon. "Iki, iki, motsu: Nihon no 'iki' to Chōsen no 'motsu.'" *Bungaku* (May 1986): 63–77.

Kitamura Tōkoku. "Tokugawa shi jidai no heiminteki risō." *Happyō: Jogaku*

zasshi (June 1892). Reprinted in *Kitamura Tōkoku senshū*. Edited by Katsu-
moto Seiichirō. Tokyo: Iwanami Shoten, 1970.

Kobayashi Hideo. "Kokyō o ushinatta bungaku." In *Kobayashi Hideo zenshū*.
Vol. 2. Tokyo: Shinchōsha, 1956.

————. "Rekishi to bungaku." In *Hankindai no shisō*. Vol. 32 of *Gendai Nihon
shisō taikei*. Tokyo: Chikuma Shobō, 1965.

Kuki Shūzō. *Kuki Shūzō zenshū*. Edited by Amanō Teiyū, Omodaka Hisayuki,
and Satō Akio. 12 vols. Tokyo: Iwanami Shoten, 1981.

Kunō Osamu. "Bunkateki nashonarizumu no mondai." *Tenbō* 9 (1973). Reprinted in *Fashizumu no naka no 1930 nendai*. Tokyo: Libro, 1986.

Maeda Ai. "Tōkyō 1925." *Gendai shisō: Sōtokushū—1920 nendai no hikari to kage*
7, no. 8 (June 1979): 72–80.

Maruyama Masao. *Nihon no shisō*. Tokyo: Iwanami Shoten, 1961.

Matsuo Takayoshi. *Taishō demokurashī no gunzō*. Tokyo: Iwanami Shoten, 1990.

Miki Kiyoshi. *Miki Kiyoshi zenshū*. Edited by Ouchi Hyōe et al. Tokyo: Iwanami Shoten, 1967.

————. *Pasukaru ni okeru ningen no kenkyū*. Tokyo: Iwanami Shoten, 1926.

Minami Hiroshi. *"Iki' no kōzō o megutte."* *Gendai esupuri*. "Gendai ni ikiru
Nihonjin no biishiki: iki—inase." 144 (1979): 32–45.

————, ed. *Nihon modanizumu no kenkyū*. Tokyo: Brenn Shuppan, 1982.

Nagai Kafū. *Edo geijutsuron* (1920). In *Nagai Kafū zenshū*. Vol. 11. Tokyo:
Chūō Kōronsha, 1948.

Nakai Masakazu. *Nakai Masakazu zenshū*. Edited by Kunō Osamu. 4 vols.
Tokyo: Bijutsu Shuppansha, 1965.

Nakano Hajime. "Kuki Shūzō." In *Genron wa Nihon o ugokasu*. Vol. 2. Tokyo:
Kōdansha, 1985–86.

Nakaō Tatsurō. *Sui—tsū—iki: Edo no biishiki kō*. Tokyo: Sanmi Shoten, 1984.

Natsume Sōseki. "Gendai Nihon no kaika." In *Hankindai no shisō*. Edited by
Fukuda Tsuneari. *Gendai Nihon shisō taikei*. Vol. 32. Tokyo: Chikuma
Shobō, 1965.

————. *Natsume Sōseki zenshū*. Tokyo: Iwanami Shoten, 1965–67.

Nishimura Shinji. "Edo Fukagawa jōchō no kenkyū." *Gendai espuri*. "Gendai
ni ikiru Nihonjin no biishiki: iki—inase." 144 (1979): 127–33.

Nishiyama Matsunosuke. *Edogaku nyūmon*. Tokyo: Chikuma Shobō, 1981.

————. *Edokko*. Tokyo: Yoshikawa Kōbunkan, 1980.

————. *Edo seikatsu bunka*. Vol. 3 of *Nishiyama Matsunosuke chosakushū*. Tokyo:
Yoshikawa Kōbunkan, 1983.

————. "Iki no biishiki to sono haikei." *Gendai espuri*. "Gendai ni ikiru Nihonjin no biishiki: iki—inase." 144 (1979): 8–19.

———— et al., eds. *Edogaku jiten*. Tokyo: Kobunkō, 1984.

Omodaka Hisayuki. *kuki-shūzō bunkō mokuroku*. Kobe: Kōnan Daigaku Tetsugaku kenkyū-shitsu, 1976.

Ōka Nobu. "Hatsuko, Tenshin, Shūzō." *Iwanami Shoten Zusho* 12 (1980): 8–15.

Ōya Sōichi. *Ōya Sōichi zenshū*. Edited by Aochi Shin and Inoue Yasushi. 26
vols. Tokyo: Soyosha, 1981.

Sakabe Megumi. "Kuki Shūzō no sekai." A series of seven articles that appeared in *Kikan asuteion*: (1) "Tenshin no kage," 8 (spring 1988): 190–207;

(2) "Pari shinkei," 10 (fall 1988): 198–207; (3) *"Iki' no kōzō,"* 11 (winter 1989): 108–22; (4) "Pontinī kōen," 12 (spring 1989): 104–20; (5) "Gūzensei no mondai," 13 (summer 1989): 176–86; (6) "Bungaku gairon," 14 (fall 1989): 148–56; (final installment) *"Nihonshi no ōin,"* 15 (winter 1990): 112–19. Collected as *Fuzai no uta: Kuki Shūzō no sekai.* Tokyo: TBS Buritanika, 1990.

Shimonaka Kunio, ed. *Tetsugaku jiten.* Tokyo: Heibonsha, 1971.

Shisō-Bunka Kenkyū Iinkai and Nihon Kagakusha Kaigi, eds. *"Bunka" o yosō kiken shisō: "Nihon bunkaron" hihan.* Tokyo: Suiyōsha, 1991.

Sugimoto Hidetarō. "Tetsugakuteki zuan." In *Nishi mado no hikari.* Tokyo: Chikuma Shobō, 1983.

Sugiura Hinako. "Edo tsū kagami." *Gendai shisō: Edogaku no susume* 14, no. 10 (September 1986): 143–46.

Tada Michitarō and Yasuda Takeshi. *"Iki' no kōzō" o yomu.* Tokyo: Asahi Shinbunsha, 1979.

Takazawa Shūji. *Shōwa seishin no pāsupekutibu: Taishū no keisei kara posuto-modan made.* Tokyo: Gendai Shokan, 1991.

Takeuchi Yoshimi. *Kindai no chōkoku.* Tokyo: Chikuma Shobō, 1983.

Taki Kōji. *Modanizumu no shinwa.* Tokyo: Seidōsha, 1985.

Tamai Tetsuo. *Edo: Ushinawareta toshi kūkan o yomu.* Tokyo: Heibonsha, 1986.

Tamenaga Shunsui. *Shunshoku umegoyomi.* In *Nihon koten bungaku taikei.* Vol. 64. Edited by Nakamura Yukihiko. Tokyo: Iwanami Shoten, 1962.

Tanabe Hajime. "Genshōgaku ni okeru atarashiki tenkō — Haideggā no sei no genshōgaku." *Shisō* (October 1924): 1–23.

Terada Toru. "Kuki tetsugaku no shūhen." *Zusho* 12. Tokyo: Iwanami Shoten, 1980.

Tosaka Jun. *Nihon ideorogīron.* In *Tosaka Jun zenshū.* Vol. 2. Tokyo: Keiso Shobō, 1966.

Tsuda Sōkichi. *Bungaku ni arawaretaru kokumin shisō no kenkyū: Heimin bungaku no jidai.* Vol. 4. Tokyo: Iwanami Shoten, 1955.

Tsurumi Shunsuke. *Tenko kenkyū.* In *Tsurumi Shunsuke shū.* Vol. 4. Tokyo: Chikuma Shobō, 1991.

Washida Koyata. *Shōwa shisōshi 60 nen.* Tokyo: Sanichi Shobō, 1986.

Watsuji Tetsurō. *Genshi bukkyō no jissen tetsugaku.* Tokyo: Iwanami Shoten, 1927.

———. *Nihon kodai bunka.* Tokyo: Iwanami Shoten, 1920.

———. *Nihon seishinshi kenkyū.* Tokyo: Iwanami Shoten, 1926.

———. *Zoku Nihon seishinshi kenkyū.* Tokyo: Iwanami Shoten, 1935.

English and European-Language Sources

Adams, Robert. "The Feasibility of the Philosophical in Early Taishō Japan: Nishida Kitarō and Tanabe Hajime." Ph.D. diss., University of Chicago, 1991.

Adorno, Theodor W. *The Jargon of Authenticity.* Translated by Knut Tarnowski and Frederic Will. Evanston: Northwestern University Press, 1973.

———. *Prisms.* Translated by Samuel Weber and Shierry Weber. Cambridge, Mass.: MIT Press, 1988.

Althusser, Louis. "Ideology and Ideological State Apparatuses." In *Lenin and Philosophy and Other Essays.* Translated by Ben Brewster. New York: Monthly Review Press, 1971.

Anderson, Benedict. *Imagined Communities.* London: Verso, 1983.

Anderson, Joseph, and Donald Richie. *The Japanese Film: Art and Industry.* Princeton: Princeton University Press, 1982.

Arendt, Hannah. *The Human Condition.* Chicago: University of Chicago Press, 1958.

———. *The Origins of Totalitarianism.* San Diego: Harcourt Brace Jovanovich, 1948.

Bakhtin, Mikhail M. *The Dialogic Imagination.* Translated by Caryl Emerson and Michael Holquist. Austin: University of Texas Press, 1981.

Barbey d'Aurevilly, Jules. "Du dandysme et de George Brummell." In *Les Oeuvres complètes de Jules Barbey d'Aurevilly.* Paris: François Bernouard, 1927.

Barshay, Andrew. *State and Intellectual in Imperial Japan: The Public Man in Crisis.* Berkeley: University of California Press, 1988.

Barthes, Roland. *Empire of Signs.* Translated by Richard Howard. New York: Hill and Wang, 1982.

———. *The Pleasure of the Text.* Translated by Richard Miller. New York: Hill and Wang, 1975.

———. "The Structuralist Activity." In *The Structuralists from Marx to Lévi-Strauss.* Edited by Richard DeGeorge and Fernande DeGeorge. New York: Doubleday, 1972.

Baudelaire, Charles. *The Flowers of Evil.* Translated by Marthiel Mathews and Jackson Mathews. New York: New Directions, 1955.

———. *The Painter of Victorian Life: A Study of Constantin Guys.* Edited by C. Geoffrey Holme. Translated by P. G. Konody. New York: William Edwin Rudge, 1930.

———. *Selected Poems.* Translated by Joanna Richardson. New York: Viking Penguin, 1975.

Bellah, Robert. "Japan's Cultural Identity: Some Reflections on the Work of Watsuji Tetsurō." *Journal of Asian Studies* 24, no. 4 (August 1965): 573–94.

Benjamin, Walter. *Charles Baudelaire: A Lyric Poet in the Age of High Capitalism.* Translated by Harry Zohn. London: NLB, 1973.

———. *Illuminations.* Translated by Harry Zohn. New York: Schoken, 1969.

Bergson, Henri. "Introduction à la métaphysique." *Revue de métaphysique et de morale* (1903). Reprinted in *La Pensée et le mouvant.* Paris: Librairie Félix Alcan, 1934.

———. *Time and Free Will: An Essay on the Immediate Data of Consciousness.* Translated by F. L. Pogson. London: Macmillan, 1910.

Berman, Marshall. *All That Is Solid Melts into Air: The Experience of Modernity.* New York: Penguin, 1982.

Berman, Russell. "Foreword: The Wandering Z: Reflections on Kaplan's Reproductions of Banality." In Alice Yaeger Kaplan, *Reproductions of Banality:*

Fascism, Literature, and French Intellectual Life. Minneapolis: University of Minnesota Press, 1986.

Bix, Herbert. "Rethinking 'Emperor-System Fascism': Ruptures and Continuities in Modern Japanese History." *Bulletin of Concerned Asian Scholars* 14, no. 2 (April–June 1982): 2–19.

Bottomore, Tom, ed. *A Dictionary of Marxist Thought*. Cambridge, Mass: Harvard University Press, 1983.

Bourdieu, Pierre. *Distinction: A Social Critique of the Judgement of Taste*. Translated by Richard Nice. Cambridge, Mass.: Harvard University Press, 1984.

———. *The Political Ontology of Martin Heidegger*. Translated by Peter Collier. Stanford, Calif.: Stanford University Press, 1991.

Braudel, Fernand. *On History*. Translated by Sarah Matthews. Chicago: University of Chicago Press, 1980.

Bubner, Rüdiger. *Modern German Philosophy*. Cambridge: Cambridge University Press, 1981.

Clifford, James. "On Collecting Art and Culture." In *The Predicament of Culture*. Cambridge, Mass.: Harvard University Press, 1988.

Crowley, James B. "Intellectuals as Visionaries of the New Asian Order." In *Dilemmas of Growth in Prewar Japan*. Edited by James W. Morley. Princeton: Princeton University Press, 1971.

Dalby, Liza. *Geisha*. New York: Random House, 1983.

Dale, Peter. *The Myth of Japanese Uniqueness*. New York: St. Martins Press, 1986.

Davis, Horace B. *Toward a Marxist Theory of Nationalism*. New York: Monthly Review Press, 1978.

de Certeau, Michel. *The Practice of Everyday Life*. Translated by Steven F. Rendall. Berkeley: University of California Press, 1984.

Derrida, Jacques. "Force and Signification." In *Writing and Difference*. Translated by Alan Bass. Chicago: University of Chicago Press, 1978.

Descombes, Vincent. *Modern French Philosophy*. Translated by L. Scott-Fox and J. M. Harding. Cambridge: Cambridge University Press, 1980.

Dilthey, Wilhelm. *Pattern and Meaning in History*. Edited and translated by H. P. Rickman. New York: Harper and Row, 1962.

———. "The Rise of Hermeneutics." Translated by Fredric Jameson. *New Literary History* 2 (winter 1972): 229–44.

Doak, Kevin Michael. *Dreams of Difference: The Japanese Romantic School and the Crisis of Modernity*. Berkeley: University of California Press, 1994.

Dower, John W. "E. H. Norman, Japan, and the Uses of History." In *Origins of the Modern Japanese State: Selected Writings by E. H. Norman*. Edited by John W. Dower. New York: Random House, 1975.

———. *War Without Mercy*. New York: Pantheon, 1986.

Duus, Peter, and Irwin Scheiner. "Socialism, Liberalism, and Marxism, 1901–1931." In *The Cambridge History of Japan*. Vol. 6, *The Twentieth Century*. Edited by John W. Hall et al. Cambridge: Cambridge University Press, 1988.

Eagleton, Terry. *Literary Theory: An Introduction*. Minneapolis: University of Minnesota Press, 1983.

Feenberg, Andrew, and Yoko Arisaka. "Experiential Ontology: The Origins of the Nishida Philosophy in the Doctrine of Pure Experience." *International Philosophical Quarterly* 30, no. 2 (June 1990): 173–204.

Ferry, Luc, and Alain Renaut. *Heidegger and Modernity.* Chicago: University of Chicago Press, 1990.

Fletcher, Miles. *The Search for a New Order: Intellectuals and Fascism in Prewar Japan.* Chapel Hill: University of North Carolina Press, 1982.

Foucault, Michel. *The Archaeology of Knowledge and the Discourse on Language.* Translated by A. M. Sheridan Smith. New York: Pantheon, 1972.

Gluck, Carol. *Japan's Modern Myths: Ideology in the Late Meiji Period.* Princeton: Princeton University Press, 1985.

Gramsci, Antonio. *A Gramsci Reader: Selected Writings, 1916–1935.* Edited by David Forgacs. London: Lawrence and Wishart, 1988.

Guénon, René. *East and West.* Translated by William Massey. London: Luzac, 1941.

Habermas, Jürgen. *Knowledge and Human Interests.* Translated by Jeremy J. Shapiro. Boston: Beacon Press, 1971.

———. "Modernity — An Incomplete Project." In *The Anti-Aesthetic: Essays on Postmodern Culture.* Edited by Hal Foster. Port Townsend, N.Y.: Bay Press, 1983.

———. "A Review of Gadamer's *Truth and Method.*" In *Understanding and Social Inquiry.* Edited by Fred R. Dallmayr and Thomas A. McCarthey. Notre Dame, Ind.: University of Notre Dame Press, 1977.

Halliday, Jon. *A Political History of Japanese Capitalism.* Introduction by John W. Dower. New York: Pantheon, 1975.

Harootunian, Harry D. "Between Politics and Culture: Authority and the Ambiguities of Intellectual Choice in Imperial Japan." In *Japan in Crisis: Essays in Taishō Democracy.* Edited by Harry D. Harootunian and Bernard Silberman. Princeton: Princeton University Press, 1974.

———. "Introduction: A Sense of an Ending and the Problem of Taishō." In *Japan in Crisis: Essays in Taishō Democracy.* Edited by Harry D. Harootunian and Bernard Silberman. Princeton: Princeton University Press, 1974.

———. "Late Tokugawa Culture and Thought." In *The Cambridge History of Japan.* Vol. 5, *The Nineteenth Century.* Edited by Marcus B. Jansen. New York: Cambridge University Press, 1989.

———. *Things Seen and Unseen.* Chicago: University of Chicago Press, 1989.

Harvey, David. *The Condition of Postmodernity.* Cambridge: Basil Blackwell, 1989.

Havens, Thomas R. H. "Comte, Mill, and the Thought of Nishi Amane in Meiji Japan." *Journal of Asian Studies* 27, no. 2 (February 1968): 217–28.

Heidegger, Martin. *Being and Time.* Translated by John Macquarrie and Edward Robinson. New York: Harper and Row, 1962.

———. "A Dialogue on Language." In *On the Way to Language.* Translated by Peter D. Hertz. New York: Harper and Row, 1971.

Hosoi, Atsuko, and Jacqueline Pigeot. "La structure d'iki." *Critique* 29, no. 308 (January 1973): 40–52.

Hoston, Germaine. *Marxism and the Crisis of Development in Prewar Japan.* Princeton: Princeton University Press, 1986.

Huyssen, Andreas. *Across the Great Divide*. Bloomington: Indiana University Press, 1986.

Irokawa, Daikichi. *The Culture of the Meiji Period*. Translated by Marius B. Jansen. Princeton: Princeton University Press, 1985.

Ivy, Marilyn. "Critical Texts, Mass Artifacts: The Consumption of Knowledge in Postmodern Japan." *South Atlantic Quarterly* 87, no. 3 (summer 1988): 419–43.

Jameson, Fredric. "Postmodernism and Consumer Society." In *The Anti-Aesthetic*. Edited by Hal Foster. Port Townsend, N.Y.: Bay Press, 1983.

Jansen, Marius B. "Japanese Imperialism: Late Meiji Perspectives." In *The Japanese Colonial Empire, 1895–1945*. Edited by Ramon H. Myers and Mark R. Peattie. Princeton: Princeton University Press, 1984.

Karatani Kōjin. "One Spirit, Two Nineteenth Centuries." *South Atlantic Quarterly* 87, no. 3 (summer 1988): 615–28.

———. "The Discovery of Landscape." In *The Origins of Modern Japanese Literature*. Translated by Brett de Bary. Durham, N.C.: Duke University Press, 1993.

Keene, Donald, ed. *Anthology of Japanese Literature*. New York: Grove Press, 1955.

———. *Dawn to the West*. New York: Henry Holt, 1984.

Kokutai no Hongi: Cardinal Principles of the National Essence of Japan. Translated by John Owen Gauntlett. Introduction by Robert King Hall. Newton, Mass.: Crofton, 1974.

Kōsaka, Masaaki. *Japanese Thought in the Meiji Era*. Translated by David Abosch. Tokyo: Pan-Pacific Press, 1958.

Kuno, Osamu. "The Meiji State, Minponshugi, and Ultranationalism." In *Authority and the Individual in Japan: Citizen Protest in Historical Perspective*. Edited by Victor Koschmann. Tokyo: University of Tokyo Press, 1978.

Lacoue-Labarthe, Philippe. *Heidegger, Art, and Politics*. Translated by Chris Turner. Oxford: Basil Blackwell, 1990.

LaFleur, William R. "A Turning in Taishō: Asia and Europe in Early Writings of Watsuji Tetsurō." In *Culture and Identity in Taishō Japan*. Edited by J. Thomas Rimer. Princeton: Princeton University Press, 1990.

Larsen, Neil. *Modernism and Hegemony: A Materialist Critique of Aesthetic Agencies*. Minneapolis: University of Minnesota Press, 1990.

Light, Stephen. *Shūzō Kuki and Jean-Paul Sartre: Influence and Counter-Influence in the Early History of Existential Phenomenology*. Carbondale: Southern Illinois University Press, 1987.

Lyotard, Jean-François. *The Postmodern Condition: A Report on Knowledge*. Translated by Geoff Bennington and Brian Massumi. Minneapolis: University of Minnesota Press, 1984.

Makkreel, Rudolf A. *Dilthey: Philosopher of the Human Studies*. Princeton: Princeton University Press, 1975.

Mandelbaum, Maurice. *History, Man, and Reason*. Baltimore: Johns Hopkins University Press, 1971.

Marcuse, Herbert. "The Concept of Essence." In *Negations: Essays in Critical Theory*. Translated by Jeremy J. Shapiro. Boston: Beacon Press, 1968.

————. *Hegel's Ontology and the Theory of Historicity*. Translated by Seyla Benhabib. Cambridge, Mass.: MIT Press, 1987.

Martin, Jo Nobuko. "Santō Kyōden and His Sharebon." Ph.D. diss., University of Chicago, 1979.

Maruyama, Masao. *Studies in the Intellectual History of Tokugawa Japan*. Translated by Mikiso Hane. Tokyo and Princeton: Tokyo and Princeton University Presses, 1974.

————. *Thought and Behavior in Modern Japanese Politics*. Edited by Ivan Morris. London: Oxford University Press, 1963.

Massis, Henri. *Defense of the West*. Translated by F. S. Flint. New York: Harcourt Brace, 1928.

Matsumoto, Sannosuke. "The Roots of Political Disillusionment: 'Public' and 'Private' in Japan." In *Authority and the Individual in Japan: Citizen Protest in Historical Perspective*. Edited by J. Victor Koschmann. Tokyo: University of Tokyo Press, 1978.

McCormack, Gavan. "Nineteen-Thirties Japan: Fascism?" *Bulletin of Concerned Asian Scholars* 14, no. 2 (April–June 1982): 20–34.

Merleau-Ponty, Maurice. *Phenomenology of Perception*. Translated by Colin Smith. London: Routledge and Kegan Paul, 1962.

Merquior, J. G. *From Prague to Paris: A Critique of Structuralist and Post-Structuralist Thought*. London: Verso, 1986.

Michener, James A. *Floating World*. Honolulu: University of Hawaii Press, 1954.

Miyoshi, Masao. *Accomplices of Silence*. Berkeley: University of California Press, 1974.

————. "Beyond the End of the Open Road: Jippensha Ikku's *Hizakurige*." Unpublished manuscript.

———— and Harry D. Harootunian. "Introduction." *South Atlantic Quarterly* 87, no. 3 (summer 1988): 387–97.

Mori, Ogai. "The Dancing Girl." Translated by Richard Bowring. *Monumenta Nipponica* 30, no. 2 (summer 1975): 151–66.

Morley, James W., ed. *Dilemmas of Growth in Prewar Japan*. Princeton: Princeton University Press, 1971.

Mosse, George. "Introduction: Towards a General Theory of Fascism." In *International Fascism: New Thoughts and New Approaches*. London: Sage Publications, 1979.

Najita, Tetsuo. "Idealism in Yoshino's Political Thought." In *Japan in Crisis*. Edited by Bernard S. Silberman and Harry D. Harootunian. Princeton: Princeton University Press, 1974.

Nancy, Jean-Luc. *La communauté désoeuvré*. Paris: Christian Bourgois Editeur, 1986.

Natsume, Sōseki. *And Then*. Translated by Norma Field. New York: G. P. Putnam's Sons, 1978.

Nietzsche, Friedrich. "On the Uses and Disadvantages of History for Life." In *Untimely Meditations*. Translated by R. J. Hollingdale. Cambridge: Cambridge University Press, 1983.

Nishida, Kitarō. *An Inquiry into the Good*. Translated by Abe Masao and Christopher Ives. New Haven: Yale University Press, 1990.

Nitobe, Inazo. *Bushidō: The Soul of Japan*. 1905. Rutland and Tokyo: Charles E. Tuttle, 1969.

Okakura, Kakuzō. *The Ideals of the East with Special Reference to the Art of Japan*. London: John Murray, 1903.

———. "Modern Problems in Painting." In *Collected English Writings*. Vol. 1. Tokyo: Heibonsha, 1984.

Parkes, Graham, ed. *Heidegger and Asian Thought*. Honolulu: University of Hawaii Press, 1987.

Peattie, Mark R. "Introduction." In *The Japanese Colonial Empire, 1895–1945*. Edited by Ramon H. Myers and Mark R. Peattie. Princeton: Princeton University Press, 1984.

———. "Japanese Attitudes Toward Colonialism, 1895–1945." In *The Japanese Colonial Empire, 1895–1945*. Edited by Ramon H. Meyers and Mark R. Peattie. Princeton: Princeton University Press, 1984.

Pyle, Kenneth. *The New Generation in Meiji Japan: Problems of Cultural Identity, 1885–1895*. Stanford, Calif.: Stanford University Press, 1969.

Roden, Donald. *Schooldays in Imperial Japan*. Berkeley: University of California Press, 1988.

Said, Edward. *The World, the Text, and the Critic*. Cambridge, Mass.: Harvard University Press, 1983.

Sakai, Naoki. "Modernity and Its Critique: The Problem of Universalism and Particularism." *South Atlantic Quarterly* 87, no. 3 (summer 1988): 475–504.

———. "Return to the West / Return to the East." In *boundary 2* 18, no. 3 (fall 1991): 157–90.

Schmidt, Dennis J. *The Ubiquity of the Finite: Hegel, Heidegger, and the Entitlements of Philosophy*. Cambridge, Mass.: MIT Press, 1988.

Seidensticker, Edward. *Kafū the Scribbler*. Stanford, Calif.: Stanford University Press, 1965.

Silverberg, Miriam. *Changing Song: The Marxist Manifestos of Nakano Shigeharu*. Princeton: Princeton University Press, 1990.

———. "Modern Girl as Militant." In *Recreating Japanese Women, 1600–1945*. Edited by Gail Lee Bernstein. Berkeley: University of California Press, 1991.

Steiner, George. *Martin Heidegger*. Chicago: University of Chicago Press, 1978.

Tanaka, Stefan. "Beauty: Contesting Universals for a Japanese Space." Unpublished paper presented at UCLA under the auspices of the Center for Japanese Studies, fall 1993.

Tanizaki, Junichirō. *In Praise of Shadows*. Translated by T. J. Harper and Edward G. Seidensticker. New Haven: Leete's Island Books, 1977.

———. *Some Prefer Nettles*. Translated by Edward G. Seidensticker. New York: Perigee Books, 1981.

Tsuda, Sōkichi. *An Inquiry into the Japanese Mind as Mirrored in Literature: The Flowering Period of Common People Literature*. Translated by Fukumatsu Matsuda. Tokyo: Japan Society for the Promotion of Science, 1979.

Valéry, Paul. *Eupaulinos ou l'architecte*. Paris: NRF Gallimard, 1944.

Waite, Geoffrey. "Political Ontology." Paper delivered at the Institute of Philosophy, Soviet Academy of Sciences, Moscow, October 19, 1989.

Watsuji, Tetsurō. *A Climate*. Translated by Geoffrey Bownas. Tokyo: Japanese Government Printing Bureau, c. 1961.

White, Hayden. *Metahistory: The Historical Imagination in Nineteenth-Century Europe*. Baltimore: Johns Hopkins University Press, 1973.

Willey, Thomas E. *Back to Kant: The Revival of Kantianism in German Social and Historical Thought, 1860–1914*. Detroit: Wayne State University Press, 1978.

Williams, Raymond. *The Country and the City*. New York: Oxford University Press, 1973.

———. *Keywords*. New York: Oxford University Press, 1976.

———. *The Politics of Modernism: Against the New Conformists*. London: Verso, 1989.

———. *Problems in Materialism and Culture*. London: Verso, 1980.

Wilson, Edmond. *Axel's Castle*. New York: Charles Scribner's Sons, 1931.

Zimmerman, Michael. *Heidegger's Confrontation with Modernity: Technology, Politics, Art*. Bloomington: Indiana University Press, 1990.

Index

Abe Jirō, 39, 57, 113, 115–18, 187
"Achilles paradox," 127
Adams, Robert, 62n, 67
Adorno, Theodor, 24, 93, 98, 247
Aeba Jun, 7n
Aesthetics: and abstract form, 206–7; and
    ambiguity, 194–95; and collectivity,
    186; and decline, 195–96; and experi-
    ence, 73, 194–95; and hermeneutics,
    49; and Japanese uniqueness dis-
    course, 12, 188–89; and Kyoto school,
    11; and neo-Kantianism, 65–66,
    187–89; and nonconnectedness, 187;
    and nuance, 197–99; Okakura on, 112;
    and Seikyōsha, 12; and social pro-
    cesses, 24; and subjectivism, 184–86,
    206–7; and taste, 204–8. See also Cul-
    ture; National aestheticism
Akai Tatsurō, 129
Akirame, 126, 134–35, 183, 196, 226
"À la manière d'Hérodote" (Kuki), 51–52
All That Is Solid Melts into Air (Berman),
    154
Althusser, Louis, 216
Amano Teiyū, 57, 59
Ambiguity, 194–95
"L'Âme japonaise" (Kuki), 79–80, 81
Anamnēsis, 161, 205
Anderson, Benedict, 181
Anderson, Joseph, 243n
Anpo, 4
Anya kōro (Tōson), 72n

Archaeology of Knowledge (Foucault), 23
Arendt, Hannah, 225
Aristotle, 58, 126n
Aron, Raymond, 59
Asaō Naojiro, 103, 111n
Asiaticism, 94–97
Asthetik und allgemeine Kunstwissenschaft
    (Aesthetics and a Comprehensive
    Study of Art) (Dessoire), 65–66

Bakhtin, Mikhail, 22
Barbey d'Aureville, Jules, 137
Barshay, Andrew, 217–18, 244
Barthes, Roland, 8, 10, 199n
Bashō, 49
Baudelaire, Charles, 182, 206; elitism of,
    18–19; and experience, 76; Kuki's
    affinity with, 44, 153; and resignation,
    137–38; symbolic correspondence the-
    ory, 190–91
Becker, Oscar, 57
Being and Time (Heidegger), 77n, 84, 141,
    170–71, 174; decentering in, 175; experi-
    ence in, 71n, 74, 75; language in,
    172–73; universal application of, 147.
    See also Heidegger, Martin
Benjamin, Walter, 73n, 76–77, 90, 98, 140,
    185–86, 190–91, 194, 232, 246
Berdyaev, Nikolai, 59
Bergson, Henri, 55, 57, 67–68, 179; and ex-
    perience, 73, 167, 202; and taste, 203
"Bergson au Japon" (Kuki), 67–68, 69, 86

Idealism (*continued*)
racy, 37–38. *See also* European philosophy; Neo-Kantianism
Ideals of the East (Okakura), 32, 90, 96, 112
Ideology, 216, 236
Iki: and ambiguity, 194–95; and analytic
classification, 64–65; and concealment,
199–200; conceptualizations of, 107–8,
126–7, 186–87; and cultural transplantation, 97; and decline, 195–96; and detachment, 207; and eroticism, 126,
127–29, 224; etymology of, 173–74; and
experience, 167; and "fearless pride,"
126, 130–34, 225; and mass culture/poli-
tics, 19; and nuance, 197–99; and organicism, 152; and play, 15, 41; and redemption, 189–90; and resignation,
126, 134–35, 137, 196, 226; structure of,
126–37, 163–64, 172, 183, 221–22,
224–28; as synthesis, 15, 126–27, 135–37,
138, 226; and Western metaphysics, 93.
See also *"Iki" no kōzō*
"Iki' ni tsuite" (Concerning "Iki") (Kuki),
45–46, 49–51, 60; and Bergson, 68–69;
neo-Kantianism in, 62–65; and phenomenology, 70. *See also "Iki" no kōzō*
"Iki' no honshitsu" (The Essence of
"Iki") (Kuki), 57, 60, 70, 77–78, 85–86,
89
"Iki" no kōzō (The Structure of Edo Aesthetic Style) (Kuki), 2–3; and Abe,
117–18; and *Being and Time*, 172–3,
174–5, 176; class in, 108–9, 126; collecting in, 141, 182–83; collectivity in, 176;
critical assessments of, 3–4, 6, 7, 19–20,
108–9, 131–32, 213; and cultural transplantation, 97; denial of class in,
133–34; denial of history in, 16, 17, 166,
246; as example of *Nihonjinron*, 5; and
exoticization, 97; experience in, 78–79;
and fascism, 220–21, 229, 235–36; feminine image in, 93; importance of, 7–8;
intertextual network in, 99; language
in, 119–20, 152, 172–73; meaning in,
183–84, 189–91; methodology in, 20,
21, 143, 180, 219; national aestheticism
in, 229, 230, 234–36, 244; 1960s–70s
interest in, 3, 4–5, 7; particularity in,
120–26, 223, 227; play in, 15, 41; postmodern interpretation of, 8–9; publication of, 2, 3, 7n, 60; on rationalism,
64; significance of, 23–24; state in,

236; utopian vision in, 194; and Wat-
suji, 120–21; Western-Japanese synthe-
sis in, 19–22. See also *Iki; "Iki' ni
tsuite"; "Iki' no honshitsu"; Kuki
Shūzō; specific topics*
"Iki' no kōzō o megutte" (Minami), 131n
Ikuji, 126, 130–34, 183, 225
Imagined Communities (Anderson), 181
Immanentism, 159, 229n
Imperialism. *See* Japanese imperialism;
Western imperialism
Inase, 120
Individualism, 30, 223–24
Inei raisan (In Praise of Shadows) (Tani-
zaki), 81, 101, 111
Inoue Tetsujirō, 112
Intentionality, 84–85
Interiority. *See* Subjectivism
Interpretation, 56, 230. *See also* Herme-
neutics
Irokawa Daikichi, 95n, 235n
Isami, 120
Italian Futurists, 232
Iwamoto Tei, 33–34
Iwanami Shoten, 7n
Iwasaki Akira, 3

James, William, 55, 71, 202
Jameson, Fredric, 14
Japanese Film, The (Anderson and Richie),
243n
Japanese imperialism, 211; and European
racism, 12n; and hermeneutics, 21, 149;
and history, 100; intellectual complicity with, 244n; and Japanese uniqueness discourse, 15–16, 81–82; Kuki's
complicity with, 2, 212, 222–23; and
particularity, 222–23, 227; state mask-
ing of, 245; and war, 231–32. *See also*
Fascism
Japanese uniqueness discourse, 3, 4–7;
and aesthetics, 12, 188–89; contradictions in, 4–5; and cultural transplantation, 97; and elitism, 19, 188–89; and
European exoticization, 91–92, 97; and
experience, 79; and fascism, 6, 209–10,
230–31; and *harakiri,* 79–81; and hermeneutics, 143, 157, 167–68; and history,
86–87, 104; and interest in *"Iki" no
kōzō,* 4–5; and Japanese imperialism,
15–16, 81–82; and *kokugaku,* 5n; Kyoto
school, 11; and language, 19n, 152–54;

"Modan sō to modan sō" (Modern Stratum, Modern Mores) (Ōya), 198
Modernism, 191, 221; and culturescape, 220; and denial of history, 22, 119, 246; and fascism, 16, 22; and hegemony theory, 238, 245–46; Kuki's affinity for, 22, 43–45, 98–99; and national aestheticism, 232–34; peripheral, 220, 234; and rejection of neo-Kantianism, 69. *See also* Modernization
Modernism and Hegemony (Larsen), 219–20, 232–33
Modernization: and *bunmei kaika,* 10, 27–28, 31, 40, 110–12, 240; and cosmopolitanism, 40; and Edo culture, 161; and European-Japanese convergences, 35–36, 61–62; and experience, 55, 76, 90–91; and fascism, 215, 217; and history, 13, 86, 100–101, 232–33; and language reform, 154; Meiji *ishin,* 10, 18, 100, 110, 149, 238–39; postmodern critique of, 8–9; and private sphere, 86; and return, 100–101; and Western imperialism, 239–40. *See also* Modernism; Modernization anxiety; Western values, resistance to
Modernization anxiety: and ambiguity, 194–95; and concealment, 199–200; contradictions of, 10–11, 14, 157, 191–93; and dandy figure, 44–45; and decline, 196; and denial of history, 142; and elitism, 18–19, 82–83, 194, 196–97; and European-Japanese convergences, 144, 154; and feminine image, 52, 195, 199–201; and hermeneutics, 17, 142–43, 154, 156, 162; and Japanese uniqueness discourse, 7, 10–11, 12, 79; and meaning, 191; and neo-Kantianism, 40; and nuance, 197–99; and resistance to Western values, 18–19, 32, 191, 193; and social dislocations, 35–36, 155–56; and war, 231n
Mori Ōgai, 35, 46
Morris, Ivan, 211n
Mosse, George, 216
Motoori Norinaga, 79, 80
Myth of Japanese Uniqueness (Dale), 5–6, 137

Nagai Kafū, 52–53, 113–14
Nagauta, 49, 119n, 130
Najita Tetsuo, 37–38
Nakai Masakazu, 3, 132, 192, 194

Nakano Shigeharu, 230–31, 244
Nakazato Kaizan, 99
Nancy, Jean-Luc, 229n
Nanking massacre, 232
Naoki Sakai, 141, 227
Naruto Hicho (Yoshikawa), 99–100
National aestheticism, 229–30; and culturescape, 219–21, 234–36, 241–42, 244, 245; and denial of history, 232–33; and hegemony theory, 236; and ideology, 216; Japanese intellectual complicity in, 216–19, 244–45; and Japanese uniqueness discourse, 230–31; Kuki's contribution to, 210, 229, 230, 234–36; and modernism, 232–34; and war, 231–32. *See also* Fascism
National essentialism. See *Kokusuishugi*
Nationalism. See Fascism; National aestheticism
Nativism, 5n, 79, 224. *See also* Japanese uniqueness discourse; *Kokugaku*
Natorp, Paul, 56n
Natsume Sōseki, 33n, 46–47, 69, 72, 80–81, 154
Naturalism, 55
Nature, 169, 182n, 203n, 224
Naturwissenschaften, 60–61
Neo-Kantianism, 60–61; and aesthetics, 65–66, 187–89; and analytic classification, 63–64; and cosmopolitanism, 38, 40, 63, 138; culture as privileged domain in, 65–66; elitism of, 61, 62; in "'Iki' ni tsuite," 62–65; and *iki* as synthesis, 138; and intentionality, 84n; Japanese interest in, 62; Kuki's abandonment of, 66–69, 201; and modernization anxiety, 40; vs. phenomenology, 70–71, 168; and science, 67; and Tokugawa era historiography, 117; and universalism, 62–63. *See also* European philosophy
Nietzsche, Friedrich von, 11, 85, 99, 142, 190
"Nihon fuashizumu hihan" (Critique of Japanese Fascism) (Nyōzekan), 242–44
Nihon ideorogīron (Tosaka), 164–66, 174, 219, 244
Nihonjinron. See Japanese uniqueness discourse
"Nihon no bunka" (Japanese Culture) (Kuki), 48

Tak

Taishō era (*continued*)
102, 196, 217; and European philosophy, 35–41; Japanese imperialism during, 149; *kyōyōshugi*, 34
Takaō, 25
Takehisa Yumeji, 199–200
Takigawa Yukitori, 211
Taki Kōji, 191
Tamenaga Shunsui, 122, 123, 124–25, 128, 133, 134–35, 186–87
Tanabe Hajime, 11n, 67, 141; on Dasein, 147n; and Heidegger, 58n; on history, 83–85; on phenomenology, 70–71, 72, 83–85
Tanaka, Stefan, 11n
Tanizaki Junichirō: and feminine image, 48–49, 200–201; and history, 100, 101, 111, 233; and Japanese uniqueness discourse, 11, 82
Taoism, 96
Taste, 202–8; and aesthetics, 204–8; and experience, 202–4
Teinen, 226
Tenkō, 217
"Tetsugaku no shiken" (My Own View of Philosophy) (Kuki), 64
Tezuka Tomio, 21, 93
"Theses on Feuerbach" (Marx), 165
"Things Japanese" (Chamberlain), 52n
"Time is Money" (Kuki), 82–3, 188
Tōjō Hideki, 227
Tokugawa era, 2, 16, 117, 118; and *harakiri*, 80, 81; social organization during, 104–8, 132. *See also* Edo culture; *"Iki" no kōzō*; Tokugawa era historiography; *specific topics*
Tokugawa era historiography, 102–4, 108, 110–19; Abe, 113, 115–18; and class resistance, 108; and modernization, 14, 110–12; Okakura, 112–13; Tsuda, 114–15
Tokugawa Ieyasu, 104
Tokugawa jidai no geijutsu to shakai (Art and Society in the Tokugawa Era) (Abe), 115–18
Tokyo, 18, 100, 104, 193, 197, 205
"Tōkyō 1925" (Maeda), 199–200
Torii Kiyonaga, 118
Tosaka Jun, 17, 164–66, 170; on etymology, 174; on fascism, 142, 209, 219, 222–23, 245; on Japanese uniqueness discourse, 82; on national aestheticism, 244

Treatise on the Essence of Human Freedom (Schelling), 58
Tsū, 2, 42, 123, 129, 206. *See also* Dandy figure
Tsuda Sokichi, 114–15
Tsurumi Shunsuke, 216–17
Two Women at a Mirror Stand (Utamaro), 115–16

Uchida Ginzo, 111n–12n
Ukiyoe, 49, 108, 118, 128
Ukiyo zōshi, 106
United States–Japan Security Treaty (1951), 4
Universalism, 91, 143; and Eurocentrism, 15, 43, 147–48, 160; and hermeneutics, 145–49, 160; and neo-Kantianism, 62–63; vs. particularity, 161, 173, 222–23; and Western imperialism, 146–47. *See also* Cosmopolitanism
Utagawa Kunisada, 129
Utamaro, 115–16, 118, 124, 195

Valéry, Paul, 69, 185
Verlaine, Paul, 197
Verstehen, 157–58
Volk, 21, 55, 85
Volkstum, 229

Waite, Geoffrey, 171n
War, 82, 231–32. *See also* Japanese imperialism
Watsuji Tetsurō, 32, 109n, 158, 173n, 178–79n, 203n; on collectivity, 31, 77n, 177; cultural layeredness theory, 120–21; on culture as truth, 158; elitism of, 243; and Heidegger, 141–42, 176–77; and history, 100, 101, 233; and Japanese uniqueness discourse, 11, 81; and Köber, 34–35; modernization anxiety, 156–57; and redemption, 190
Weimar republic, 82n, 87, 136n
Weltanschauungslehre, 159n
Western imperialism, 43; and Asiaticism, 95n; and European-Japanese convergences, 149; and European philosophy, 15; and exoticization, 91–92; and hermeneutics, 146–47; and interpretation, 56n; Japanese emulation of, 15, 149; and Japanese modernization, 239–40; and Japanese uniqueness discourse, 11–12; and Tokugawa era his-

toriography, 117; and universalism, 146–47. *See also* Western values, resistance to
Western values. *See* European philosophy; European racism; European views of Japan; Western imperialism
Western values, resistance to, 90; and aesthetics of concealment, 199–200; and denial of history, 246; and elitism, 18–19, 102, 196–97; and fascism, 6; and hermeneutics, 143, 156, 157; and Japanese uniqueness discourse, 10–11, 15, 79, 81–83; materialism, 82–83; vs. modernization anxiety, 191, 193; and Oedipus complex, 30; and Seikyōsha, 12. *See also* Japanese uniqueness discourse; Kuki's cultural borrowing contradiction
White, Hayden, 151
Wilde, Oscar, 68–69
Willey, Thomas E., 40, 57n, 61
Williams, Raymond, 22, 43, 78, 236n
Windelband, Wilhelm, 61

Wipperman, Wolfgang, 215n
"World of Kuki Shūzō" (Sakabe), 29–31
World War I, 94
The Wretched of the Earth (Fanon), 25

Yamaga Sokō, 225
Yamato-damashi, 168, 222
Yanagita Kunio, 32, 100
Yasuda Takeshi, 3, 108–9, 161, 196, 213
"Yellow peril," 95n
Yoake mae (Before the Dawn) (Shimazaki), 100
Yoshida Shōin, 225
Yoshikawa Eiji, 99–100
Yoshino Sakuzō, 37–38
Yoshiwara yōji (Kyōden), 131

Zen no kenkyū (A Study of Good) (Nishida), 71
Zeno's paradox, 127
Zoku Nihon seishinshi kenkyū (Watsuji), 109n

Designer:	Barbara Jellow
Compositor:	Graphic Composition, Inc.
Text:	10/13 Galliard
Display:	Galliard
Printer:	BookCrafters, Inc.
Binder:	BookCrafters, Inc.